DATE DUE

DEMCO 128-5046

SOMETHING ABOUT THE AUTHOR®

Something about
the Author *was named
an "Outstanding
Reference Source,"
the highest honor given
by the American
Library Association
Reference and Adult
Services Division.*

ISSN 0276-816X

R

SOMETHING ABOUT THE AUTHOR®

**Facts and Pictures about Authors
and Illustrators of Books for Young People**

**EDITED BY
ALAN HEDBLAD**

VOLUME 104

The Gale Group

DETROIT • SAN FRANCISCO • LONDON • BOSTON • WOODBRIDGE, CT

STAFF

Editor: Alan Hedblad
...phy Features Coordinator: Motoko Fujishiro Huthwaite
Associate Editor: Melissa Hill

Contributing Editors: Sheryl Ciccarelli, Sara L. Constantakis, Catherine Goldstein, Maria Job,
Arlene M. Johnson, Thomas F. McMahon

Editorial Technical Specialist: Karen Uchic

Managing Editor: Joyce Nakamura
Publisher: Hal May

Research Manager: Victoria B. Cariappa
Project Coordinator: Cheryl L. Warnock
Research Associates: Tracie A. Richardson, Robert Whaley
Research Assistants: Patricia Tsune Ballard, Phyllis Blackman,
Wendy K. Festerling, Corrine A. Stocker

Permissions Manager: Maria L. Franklin
Permissions Associates: Sarah Chesney, Edna Hedblad, Michele Lonoconus

Production Director: Mary Beth Trimper
Production Assistant: Cindy Range

Graphic Artist: Gary Leach
Image Database Supervisor: Randy Bassett
Imaging Specialists: Robert Duncan, Michael Logusz
Imaging Coordinator: Pamela A. Reed

Library of Congress Catalog Card Number 72-27107

ISBN 0-7876-2125-0
ISSN 0276-816X

Printed in the United States of America

10 9 8 7 6 5 4 3 2 1

Contents

Authors in Forthcoming Volumes vii
Introduction ix
Acknowledgments xi

A-B

Alarcon, Francisco X(avier) 1954- 1

Baca, Maria 1951- 4

Berg, Elizabeth 1948- 6

Betteridge, Anne
  See Potter, Margaret (Newman) 140

Borden, Louise (Walker) 1949- 7

Bowie, C. W.
  See Wirths, Claudine (Turner) G(ibson) 205

Buehner, Caralyn M. 1963- 11

Buehner, Mark 1959- 13

C

Canyon, Christopher 1966- 17

Chapman, Jean 18

Clements, Andrew 1949- 21

Cooper, Ann (Catharine) 1939- 26

Cooper, Susan (Mary) 1935- 28

D-E

Doney, Todd L. W. 1959- 39

Doyle, Brian 1935- 41

Edmund, Sean
  See Pringle, Laurence (Patrick) 141

Elborn, Andrew
  See Clements, Andrew 21

Elisha, Ron 1951- 47

G

Gallo, Donald R. 1938-
  Autobiography Feature 49

Gerber, Perren 1933- 60

Gibbons, Gail (Gretchen) 1944- 61

Gilman, Phoebe 1940- 68

Gleason, Katherine (A.) 1960- 72

Gold, Alison Leslie 1945- 73

Gray, Nigel 1941- 74

Guile, Melanie 1949- 78

H

Hansen, Brooks 1965- 79

Hoban, Lillian 1925-1998 80

Hoban, Tana 81

J

Johnson, Meredith Merrell 1952- 87

Johnson, Sylvia A. 89

Jones, Volcano
  See Mitchell, Adrian 114

K

Keegan, Marcia 1943- 94

Kent, Deborah Ann 1948- 95

Klemm, Barry 1945- 98

Krasno, Rena 1923- 98

L

Langley, Andrew 1949- 101

Lewis, J. Patrick 1942- 104

Lewis, Shari 1934-1998 108

Lucado, Max (Lee) 1955- 109

Lucashenko, Melissa 1967- 111

M

Mangione, Gerlando
  See Mangione, Jerre 113

Mangione, Jerre 1909-1998 113

Mcmorrow, Annalisa 1969- 113

Melville, Anne
  See Potter, Margaret (Newman) 140

Mitchell, Adrian 1932- 114

Mitchelson, Mitch

  See Mitchelson, Peter Richard 118

Mitchelson, Peter Richard 1950- 118

Mitton, Tony 1951- 119

Morgan, Stacy T(owle) 1959- 121

Morris, Gilbert (Leslie) 1929- 122

Moss, Marissa 1959- 126

Mudgeon, Apeman

  See Mitchell, Adrian 114

N

Nathan, Amy 130

Novak, Matt 1962- 131

O-P

Oughton, (William) Taylor 1925- 135

Pausewang, Gudrun 1928- 137

Pearce, Margaret 139

Potter, Margaret (Newman) 1926-1998 140

Pringle, Laurence (Patrick) 1935- 141

Pringle, Laurence P.

  See Pringle, Laurence (Patrick) 141

R

Reim, Melanie (K.) 1956- 151

Robinet, Harriette Gillem 1931- 152

Roy, Gabrielle 1909-1983 154

S-T

Sachar, Louis 1954- 157

Sharratt, Nick 1962- 161

Shine, Andrea 1955- 164

Sierra, Judy 1945- 166

Silverberg, Robert 1935-

  Autobiography Feature 169

Singer, Muff 1942- 190

Speck, Nancy 1959- 192

Stevenson, Sucie 1956- 193

Stillerman, Marci 196

Stimpson, Gerald

  See Mitchell, Adrian 114

Stutson, Caroline 1940- 197

Sully, Tom 1959- 199

Taback, Simms 1932- 201

W

Webb, Jacquelyn

  See Pearce, Margaret 139

Wirths, Claudine (Turner) G(ibson) 1926- 205

Wojciechowska, Maia 1927-

  Autobiography Feature 208

Wolfer, Dianne 1961- 226

Woodruff, Joan Leslie 1953- 227

Woolf, Paula 1950- 228

Authors in Forthcoming Volumes

Below are some of the authors and illustrators that will be featured in upcoming volumes of *SATA*. These include new entries on the swiftly rising stars of the field, as well as completely revised and updated entries (indicated with *) on some of the most notable and best-loved creators of books for children.

*Greg Bear: The recipient of several prestigious science-fiction awards, Bear is best known for his critically acclaimed "Eon" series. His most recent works include *Dinosaur Summer* and *Foundation and Chaos.*

Errol Broome: In books such as *Rockhopper, Nightwatch,* and *Tangles,* Australian author Broome tackles difficult topics faced by young people, such as losing a parent and dealing with disabilities and moral dilemmas.

Ruth Brown: The author and illustrator of numerous books published in both her native England and the United States, Brown provided the illustrations for *Baba Yaga and the Wise Doll,* Hiawyn Oram's well-received adaptation of the traditional Russian folktale.

*Anthony Browne: Two-time Greenaway Medal-winner Browne, a British author and illustrator, is praised for the spare text and surrealistic illustrative details of his works, which have helped to define the modern picture book.

Roch Carrier: Considered one of French Canada's most important novelists, Carrier is among the most widely read Quebecois writers in North America and England. His translated works for children include *The Hockey Sweater* and *The Basketball Player.*

*Eloise Greenfield: Celebrated African-American writer Greenfield, whose diverse body of work includes fiction, nonfiction, poetry, and picture books, affirms the positive attributes of the black experience in a manner considered both specific and universal. She has received three Coretta Scott King Awards, as well as several other noteworthy honors, for her work.

Adele Griffin: Griffin has garnered critical acclaim for *The Other Shepards*, one of her several novels for young adults.

*James S. Haskins: An award-winning, prolific writer of nonfiction, Haskins is best known for his biographies of Rosa Parks, Langston Hughes, Diana Ross, Magic Johnson, and other notable African Americans from all walks of life.

*Lisa Kopper: Prolific illustrator Kopper, whose drawings grace the volumes of Hugh Lewin's "Jafta" series on life in South Africa, has written and illustrated a series of picture books starring Daisy, an endearingly drawn bull terrier who is treated like one of the family by her owners.

A. LaFaye: LaFaye has been praised for her characterization of the complex, believable young protagonists of her four novels for young adults, which include the well-received *Year of the Sawdust Man.*

Jerdine Nolen: Nolen's popular picture books include *Harvey Potter's Balloon Farm,* an American Library Association Notable Book for Children that has been adapted for film by Disney.

*Chris Van Allsburg: Author and illustrator Van Allsburg, a two-time Caldecott Medal-winner for *Jumanji* and *Polar Express,* has continued to create imaginative and groundbreaking works of fiction for children with such books as *The Sweetest Fig* and *Bad Day at Riverbend.*

Nance Van Laan: Van Laan is acclaimed for her adaptations of folk tales and legends from around the world, including *Rainbow Crow: A Lenape Tale* and *Shingebiss: An Ojibwe Legend.*

Introduction

Something about the Author (*SATA*) is an ongoing reference series that examines the lives and works of authors and illustrators of books for children. *SATA* includes not only well-known writers and artists but also less prominent individuals whose works are just coming to be recognized. This series is often the only readily available information source on emerging authors and illustrators. You'll find *SATA* informative and entertaining, whether you are a student, a librarian, an English teacher, a parent, or simply an adult who enjoys children's literature.

What's Inside SATA

SATA provides detailed information about authors and illustrators who span the full time range of children's literature, from early figures like John Newbery and L. Frank Baum to contemporary figures like Judy Blume and Richard Peck. Authors in the series represent primarily English-speaking countries, particularly the United States, Canada, and the United Kingdom. Also included, however, are authors from around the world whose works are available in English translation. The writings represented in *SATA* include those created intentionally for children and young adults as well as those written for a general audience and known to interest younger readers. These writings cover the entire spectrum of children's literature, including picture books, humor, folk and fairy tales, animal stories, mystery and adventure, science fiction and fantasy, historical fiction, poetry and nonsense verse, drama, biography, and nonfiction.

Obituaries are also included in *SATA* and are intended not only as death notices but also as concise overviews of people's lives and work. Additionally, each edition features newly revised and updated entries for a selection of *SATA* listees who remain of interest to today's readers and who have been active enough to require extensive revisions of their earlier biographies.

New Autobiography Feature

Beginning with the current issue, *Something about the Author* will feature three or more specially commissioned autobiographical essays in each volume. These unique essays, averaging about ten thousand words in length and illustrated with an abundance of personal photos, present an entertaining and informative first-person perspective on the lives and careers of prominent authors and illustrators profiled in *SATA*.

Two Convenient Indexes

In response to suggestions from librarians, *SATA* indexes no longer appear in every volume but are included in alternate (odd-numbered) volumes of the series, beginning with Volume 57.

SATA continues to include two indexes that cumulate with each alternate volume: the Illustrations Index, arranged by the name of the illustrator, gives the number of the volume and page where the illustrator's work appears in the current volume as well as all preceding volumes in the series; the Author Index gives the number of the volume in which a person's biographical sketch, autobiographical essay, or obituary appears in the current volume as well as all preceding volumes in the series.

These indexes also include references to authors and illustrators who appear in Gale's *Yesterday's Authors of Books for Children, Children's Literature Review,* and *Something about the Author Autobiography Series.*

Easy-to-Use Entry Format

Whether you're already familiar with the *SATA* series or just getting acquainted, you will want to be aware of the kind of information that an entry provides. In every *SATA* entry the editors attempt to give as complete a picture of the person's life and work as possible. A typical entry in *SATA* includes the following clearly labeled information sections:

- *PERSONAL:* date and place of birth and death, parents' names and occupations, name of spouse, date of marriage, names of children, educational institutions attended, degrees received, religious and political affiliations, hobbies and other interests.

- *ADDRESSES:* complete home, office, electronic mail, and agent addresses, whenever available.

- *CAREER:* name of employer, position, and dates for each career post; art exhibitions; military service; memberships and offices held in professional and civic organizations.

- *AWARDS, HONORS:* literary and professional awards received.

- *WRITINGS:* title-by-title chronological bibliography of books written and/or illustrated, listed by genre when known; lists of other notable publications, such as plays, screenplays, and periodical contributions.

- *ADAPTATIONS:* a list of films, television programs, plays, CD-ROMs, recordings, and other media presentations that have been adapted from the author's work.

- *WORK IN PROGRESS:* description of projects in progress.

- *SIDELIGHTS:* a biographical portrait of the author or illustrator's development, either directly from the biographee—and often written specifically for the *SATA* entry—or gathered from diaries, letters, interviews, or other published sources.

- *FOR MORE INFORMATION SEE:* references for further reading.

- *EXTENSIVE ILLUSTRATIONS:* photographs, movie stills, book illustrations, and other interesting visual materials supplement the text.

How a SATA Entry Is Compiled

A *SATA* entry progresses through a series of steps. If the biographee is living, the *SATA* editors try to secure information directly from him or her through a questionnaire. From the information that the biographee supplies, the editors prepare an entry, filling in any essential missing details with research and/or telephone interviews. If possible, the author or illustrator is sent a copy of the entry to check for accuracy and completeness.

If the biographee is deceased or cannot be reached by questionnaire, the *SATA* editors examine a wide variety of published sources to gather information for an entry. Biographical and bibliographic sources are consulted, as are book reviews, feature articles, published interviews, and material sometimes obtained from the biographee's family, publishers, agent, or other associates.

Entries that have not been verified by the biographees or their representatives are marked with an asterisk (*).

Contact the Editor

We encourage our readers to examine the entire *SATA* series. Please write and tell us if we can make *SATA* even more helpful to you. Give your comments and suggestions to the editor:

BY MAIL: Editor, *Something about the Author,* The Gale Group, 27500 Drake Rd., Farmington Hills, MI 48331-3535.

BY TELEPHONE: (800) 347-GALE

BY FAX: (248) 699-8065

Acknowledgments

Grateful acknowledgment is made to the following publishers, authors, and artists whose works appear in this volume.

ALARCON, FRANCISCO X. Gonzalez, Maya Christina, illustrator. From an illustration in *Laughing Tomatoes and Other Spring Poems,* by Francisco X. Alarcon. Children's Book Press, 1997. Poems copyright © 1997 by Francisco X. Alarcon, pictures copyright © 1997 by Maya Christina Gonzalez. All rights reserved. Reproduced by permission of the publisher, Children's Book Press, San Francisco, CA. / Alarcon, Francisco X., photograph by Francisco Dominguez. Reproduced by permission of Francisco Dominguez.

BACA, MARIA. Baca, Maria, illustrator. From an illustration in *Maya's Children: The Story of La Llorona,* by Rudolfo Anaya. Hyperion Books, 1997. Copyright © 1997 by Rudolfo Anaya. Illustrations © 1997 by Maria Baca. All rights reserved. Reproduced by permission of Hyperion.

BORDEN, LOUISE. Lewin, Ted, illustrator. From an illustration in *Paperboy,* by Mary Kay Kroeger and Louise Borden. Clarion Books, 1996. Illustrations copyright © 1996 by Ted Lewin. Reproduced by permission of Houghton Mifflin Company. / Allen, Thomas B., illustrator. From an illustration in *Good-Bye, Charles Lindbergh,* by Louise Borden. Margaret K. McElderry Books, 1998. Illustrations copyright © 1998 by Thomas B. Allen. All rights reserved. Reproduced by permission of Margaret K. McElderry Books, an imprint of Simon & Schuster Children's Publishing Division. / Gustavson, Adam, illustrator. From a jacket of *Good Luck, Mrs. K.!,* by Louise Borden. McElderry Books, 1999. Jacket illustration copyright © 1999 by Adam Gustavson. Reproduced with the permission of Margaret K. McElderry Books, an imprint of Simon & Schuster Children's Publishing Division. / Borden, Louise, photograph by Ayars Borden. Reproduced by permission of Louise Borden.

BUEHNER, CARALYN. Buehner, Mark, illustrator. From an illustration in *I Did It, I'm Sorry,* by Caralyn Buehner. Dial Books, 1998. Pictures copyright © 1998 by Mark Buehner. All rights reserved. Reproduced by permission of Dial Books for Young Readers, a division of Penguin Putnam Inc.

BUEHNER, MARK. Buehner, Mark, illustrator. From an illustration in *Harvey Potter's Balloon Farm,* by Jerdine Nolen. Mulberry Books, 1994. Illustrations copyright © 1994 by Mark Buehner. All rights reserved. Reproduced by permission of Lothrop, Lee & Shepard Books, a division of William Morrow & Company, Inc. / Buehner, Mark, photograph by Caralyn Buehner. Reproduced by permission of Mark Buehner.

CANYON, CHRISTOPHER. Canyon, Christopher, photograph. Reproduced by permission.

CLEMENTS, ANDREW. Selznick, Brian, illustrator. From an illustration in *Frindle,* by Andrew Clements. Aladdin Paperbacks, 1996. Illustrations copyright © 1996 by Brian Selznick. All rights reserved. Reproduced by permission of Simon & Schuster Books for Young Readers, an imprint of Simon & Schuster Children's Publishing Division. / Landis, Joan, illustrator. From an illustration in *Who Owns the Cow?,* by Andrew Clements. Clarion Books, 1996. Illustrations copyright © 1995 by Joan Landis. All rights reserved. Reproduced by permission of Houghton Mifflin Company. / Cassity, Don, illustrator. From a cover of *Gromble's Haunted Halloween,* by Andrew Clements. Simon Spotlight, 1998. Copyright © 1998 Viacom International Inc. Reproduced by permission of Simon Spotlight, an imprint of Simon & Schuster Children's Publishing Division. / Clements, Andrew, photograph. Reproduced by permission.

COOPER, ANN. Emerling, Dorothy, illustrator. From a cover of *In the Forest,* by Ann Cooper. Denver Museum of Natural History Press, in cooperation with Roberts Rinehart Publishers, 1996. Art copyright © 1996 by Dorothy Emerling. All rights reserved. Reproduced by permission of Roberts Rinehart Publishers. / Cooper, Ann, photograph. Reproduced by permission.

COOPER, SUSAN. Wiesner, David, illustrator. From a cover of *The Dark Is Rising,* by Susan Cooper. Aladdin Paperbacks, 1986. Cover illustration copyright © 1986 by David Wiesner. Reproduced with the permission of Aladdin Paperbacks, an imprint of Simon & Schuster Children's Publishing Division. / Smith, Jos. A., illustrator. From an illustration in *Danny and the Kings,* by Susan Cooper. Margaret K. McElderry Books, 1993. Illustrations copyright © 1993 by Jos. A. Smith. All rights reserved. Reproduced by permission of Margaret K. McElderry Books, an imprint of Simon & Schuster Children's Publishing Division. / Burleson, Joe, illustrator. From a cover of *The Boggart and the Monster,* by Susan Coo-

MOSS, MARISSA. From an illustration in *Amelia Writes Again,* by Marissa Moss. Tricycle Press, 1996. Copyright © 1996 by Marissa Moss. All rights reserved. Reproduced by permission of The Pleasant Company. / Toy, Julie, photographer. From a cover of *Rachel's Journal: The Story of a Pioneer Girl,* by Marissa Moss. Silver Whistle, 1998. Copyright © 1998 by Marissa Moss. Cover photograph copyright © 1998 by Julie Toy. Reproduced by permission of Harcourt Brace & Company and Julie Toy.

NOVAK, MATT. Novak, Matt, illustrator. From an illustration in his *Elmer Blunt's Open House.* Orchard Books, 1992. Copyright © 1992 by Matt Novak. All rights reserved. Reproduced by permission of the publisher, Orchard Books, New York. / Novak, Matt, illustrator. From an illustration in his *The Pillow War.* Orchard Books, 1997. Copyright © 1997 by Matt Novak. All rights reserved. Reproduced by permission of the publisher, Orchard Books, New York.

OUGHTON, TAYLOR. Oughton, Taylor, illustrator. From an illustration in *Loon at Northwood Lake,* by Elizabeth Ring. Soundprints, 1997. Copyright © 1997 Trudy Corporation. All rights reserved. Reproduced by permission of Trudy Corporation. / Oughton, Taylor, photograph. Reproduced by permission.

PAUSEWANG, GUDRUN. Pausewang, Gudrun, photograph. © Ravensburger Buchverlag. Reproduced by permission.

PEARCE, MARGARET. Pearce, Margaret, photograph. Reproduced by permission.

PRINGLE, LAURENCE. Palmer, Kate Salley, illustrator. From a cover of *Octopus Hug,* by Laurence Pringle. Boyds Mills Press, 1993. Cover illustration © 1993 by Kate Salley Palmer. Reproduced by permission. / Marstall, Bob, illustrator. From a jacket of *An Extraordinary Life: The Story of a Monarch Butterfly,* by Laurence Pringle. Orchard Books, 1997. Jacket illustration copyright © 1997 by Bob Marstall. All rights reserved. Reproduced by permission of the publisher, Orchard Books, New York. / Potter, Katherine, illustrator. From an illustration in *Naming the Cat,* by Laurence Pringle. Walker and Company, 1997. Illustrations copyright © 1997 by Katherine Potter. All rights reserved. Reproduced by permission. / Garrison, Barbara, illustrator. From an illustration in *One Room School,* by Laurence Pringle. Boyds Mills Press, 1998. Illustrations copyright © 1998 by Barbara Garrison. All rights reserved. Reproduced by permission. / Pringle, Laurence, photograph. Reproduced by permission.

REIM, MELANIE K. Reim, Melanie K., illustrator. From an illustration in *I Was Born a Slave: The Story of Harriet Jacobs,* by Jennifer Fleischner. The Millbrook Press, Inc., 1997. Illustrations copyright © 1997 by Melanie K. Reim. All rights reserved. Reproduced by permission.

ROBINET, HARRIET GILLEM. Nickens, Bessie, illustrator. From a jacket of *Forty Acres and Maybe a Mule,* by Harriet Gillem Robinet. Jean Karl Books, 1998. Jacket illustration copyright © 1998 by Bessie Nickens. Reproduced by permission of Bessie Nickens. / Robinet, Harriet, photograph by M. Louis Robinet. Reproduced by permission of Harriet Robinet.

SACHAR, LOUIS. Schick, Joel, illustrator. From an illustration in *Wayside School Gets a Little Stranger,* by Louis Sachar. Morrow Junior Books, 1995. Illustrations copyright © 1995 by Joel Schick. All rights reserved. Reproduced by permission of Morrow Junior Books, a division of William Morrow & Company, Inc. / Sachar, Louis, photograph. Reproduced by permission.

SHARRATT, NICK. From an illustration in *My Mom and Dad Make Me Laugh,* by Nick Sharratt. Candlewick Press, 1994. Illustrations copyright © 1994 Nick Sharratt. Reproduced by permission of Walker Books Ltd. Published in the U.S. by Candlewick Press, Inc., Cambridge, MA. / Sharratt, Nick, photograph by Caroline Forbes. © Caroline Forbes. Reproduced by permission of Caroline Forbes.

SHINE, ANDREA. Shine, Andrea, illustrator. From an illustration in *The Summer My Father Was Ten,* by Pat Brisson. Boyds Mills Press, 1998. Illustrations © 1998 by Andrea Shine. All rights reserved. Reproduced by permission. / Shine, Andrea, photograph by Vivian Rieger. © Vivian Rieger, 1997. Reproduced by permission of Andrea Shine.

SIERRA, JUDY. Chess, Victoria, illustrator. From an illustration in *Good Night Dinosaurs,* by Judy Sierra. Clarion Books, 1996. Illustrations copyright © 1996 by Victoria Chess. Reproduced by permission of Houghton Mifflin Company. / Hillenbrand, Will, illustrator. From an illustration in *Counting Crocodiles,* by Judy Sierra. Harcourt Brace & Company, 1997. Illustrations copyright © 1997 by Will Hillenbrand. All rights reserved. Reproduced by permission of Harcourt Brace & Company.

SILVERBERG, ROBERT. Silverberg, Robert, at six months old with parents Michael and Helen, photograph; Silverberg, at camp in West Copake, New York, 1953, photograph; Silverberg, with Algis Budrys and Charles Harris, at World Science Fiction Convention, 1956, photograph; Silverberg, circa 1966, photograph by Clifford D. Simak; Silverberg, with Philip K.

Dick at World Science Fiction Convention, Oakland, California, 1968, photograph by David A. Kyle; Silverberg, 1972, photograph by William Rotsler; Silverberg, at science fiction convention, Los Angeles, 1976, photograph; Silverberg, 1982, photograph by Ken M. Sekiguchi; Silverberg, 1993, photograph; Silverberg, with wife Karen, 1998, photograph by Alison V. Haber. All reproduced by permission of Robert Silverberg / Silverberg, Robert, with Nebula Award, 1970, photograph by Jay Kay Klein. Reproduced by permission of Jay Kay Klein.

SINGER, MUFF. Sims, Blanche, illustrator. From an illustration in *The World's Greatest Toe Show,* by Nancy Lamb and Muff Singer. Published by Little Rainbow, an imprint and trademark of Troll Communications, LLC, 1994. Illustrations copyright © 1994 by Blanche Sims. All rights reserved. Reproduced by permission of Troll Communications, LLC. / Singer, Muff, photograph. Reproduced by permission.

SPECK, NANCY. Speck, Nancy, photograph. Reproduced by permission.

STEVENSON, SUCIE. Stevenson, Sucie, illustrator. From an illustration in her *Christmas Eve.* G. P. Putnam's Sons, 1988. Copyright © 1988 by Sucie Stevenson. All rights reserved. Reproduced by permission of G. P. Putnam's Sons, a division of Penguin Putnam Inc. / Stevenson, Sucie, illustrator. From an illustration in *Baby-O,* by Nancy White Carlstrom. Little, Brown, 1992. Text copyright © 1992 by Nancy White Carlstrom. Illustrations copyright © 1992 by Sucie Stevenson. Reproduced by permission of Sucie Stevenson.

STILLERMAN, MARCI. Stillerman, Marci, photograph. Reproduced by permission.

STUTSON, CAROLINE. Hawkes, Kevin, illustrator. From an illustration in *By the Light of the Halloween Moon,* by Caroline Stutson. Lothrop, Lee & Shepard Books, 1993. Illustrations copyright © 1993 by Kevin Hawkes. All rights reserved. Reproduced by permission of Lothrop, Lee & Shepard Books, a division of William Morrow & Company, Inc. / Stutson, Caroline, photograph by Sue Enderlin. Reproduced by permission.

SULLY, TOM. Sully, Tom, illustrator. From an illustration in *Tumbleweed Christmas,* by Alane Ferguson. Simon & Schuster, 1996. Illustrations copyright © 1996 by Tom Sully. All rights reserved. Reproduced by permission of Simon & Schuster Books for Young Readers, an imprint of Simon & Schuster Children's Publishing Division. / Sully, Thomas, "Self Portrait with Ancestor," oil on linen, 1997. Reproduced by permission.

TABACK, SIMMS. Taback, Simms, illustrator. From an illustration in *Two Little Witches,* by Harriet Ziefert. Candlewick Press, 1996. Illustrations copyright © 1996 by Simms Taback. All rights reserved. Reproduced by permission of Walker Books Ltd. Published in the U.S. by Candlewick Press, Inc., Cambridge, MA. / Taback, Simms, illustrator. From an illustration in his *There Was an Old Lady Who Swallowed a Fly.* Viking, 1997. Copyright © Simms Taback, 1997. All rights reserved. Reproduced by permission of Viking, a division of Penguin Putnam Inc. / Taback, Simms, photograph by Marion Goldman. Reproduced by permission of Simms Taback.

WIRTHS, CLAUDINE. Willingham, Fred, illustrator. From an illustration in *Busy Toes,* by C. W. Bowie. Whispering Coyote Press, 1997. Illustrations copyright © 1998 by Fred Willingham. All rights reserved. Reproduced by permission. / Wirths, Claudine, photograph. Reproduced by permission.

WOJCIECHOWSKA, MAIA. Wojciechowska, Maia, with her Aunt Walcia, 1937, photograph; Wojciechowska, training to be bullfighter, 1957, photograph; Wojciechowska, on Harley Davidson, 1958, photograph; Rudakowski, Stas (Maia Wojciechowska's uncle), Lodz, Poland, 1961, photograph; Wojciechowska, with granddaughter Laina and mother Madame Wojciechowska, 1983, photograph; Wojciechowska, with brothers Chris and Zbyszek, 1984, photograph; Rodman, Selden (Maia Wojciechowska's husband), with granddaughter Laina, 1995, photograph; Rudakowska, Andzia (Maia Wojciechowska's aunt), photograph; Rudakowska, Stefania (Maia Wojciechowska's grandmother), photograph; Rudakowski (Maia Wojciechowska's maternal grandfather), photograph; Wojciechowski, Lt. Col. Zygmunt (Maia Wojciechowska's father), photograph; McRae, Oriana Rodman (Maia Wojciechowska's daughter), with her daughter Laina, photograph; Wojciechowska, Maia, with daughter Leonora, photograph. All reproduced by permission of Maia Wojciechowska.

WOLFER, DIANNE. From a cover of *Border Line,* by Dianne Wolfer. Fremantle Arts Center Press, 1995. Reproduced by permission. / Wolfer, Dianne, photograph. Darryl Smith Photographics. Reproduced by permission.

WOODRUFF, JOAN LESLIE. Woodruff, Joan Leslie, photograph by Laura L. Klure. Reproduced by permission of Joan Leslie Woodruff.

WOOLF, PAULA. Woolf, Paula, photograph. Reproduced by permission.

something about the author

ALARCON, Francisco X(avier) 1954-

Personal

Born February 21, 1954, in Wilmington, CA; son of Jesus Pastor and Consuelo Vargas Alarcon. *Education:* Attended East Los Angeles College, 1973-74; California State University, Long Beach, B.A., 1977; Stanford University, M.A., 1979, A.B.D., 1990; attended Universidad Nacional Autonoma de Mexico, 1982.

Addresses

Office—Department of Spanish, University of California at Davis, Davis, CA 95616.

Career

Worked as a dishwasher and grape harvester in the early 1970s; California State University, Long Beach, research assistant in Mexican studies, 1976-77; Milagro Books, Oakland, CA, program director, 1981-82; Computer Curriculum Corporation, Palo Alto, CA, translator, 1984; Golden Gate National Recreation Area, California, park ranger, 1984; University of California, Santa Cruz, lecturer, 1985-92; Monterey Institute of International Studies, lecturer, 1988; University of California, Davis, Department of Spanish, program director for Spanish for Native Speakers, 1992—; Board of Directors, Children's Book Press, 1998—. *Member:* National Poetry Association (board member, 1987—), El Centro Chicano de Escritores (president, 1985—), Mission Cultural Center (board member, 1986—, president,

Francisco X. Alarcon

1986-89), San Francisco Poetry Center (board member, 1988—), Familia Center (board member, 1990-92, secretary, 1990), La Raza/Galeria Posada (board mem-

1

ber, 1993-98; co-coordinator of El Taller Literario, 1993—), PEN West-New Mexico (advisory board member, 1992—), Arts Education and Outreach Committee of the Sacramento Metropolitan Arts Commission (1993-94), American Council on the Teaching of Foreign Languages (ACTFL)-New York (co-chair, Spanish for Native Speakers Special Interest Group).

Awards, Honors

Fulbright fellowship, 1982-83; second prize, *Palabra nueva* contest, University of Texas at El Paso, 1983, for "Los repatriaciones de noviembre"; named Distinguished Alumnus of California State University—Long Beach, 1984; first prize, Chicano Literary Contest, University of California—Irvine, 1984; Prisma Award, CURAS, 1987; California Arts Council, fellowship in poetry, 1989-90; Josephine Miles Literary Award, PEN Oakland, 1993; American Book Award, 1993; Pura Belpre Honor Award for Poetry, American Library Association, 1998; Pellicer-Frost Poetry Prize (second honor mention), Third Binational Border Poetry Contest, 1998.

Writings

FOR CHILDREN; POETRY

Snake Poems: An Aztec Invocation, Chronicle Books, 1992.

Laughing Tomatoes and Other Spring Poems/Jitomates risuenos y otros poemas de primavera, illustrated by Maya Christina Gonzalez, Children's Book Press, 1997.

From the Bellybutton of the Moon and Other Summer Poems, illustrated by Maya Christina Gonzalez, Children's Book Press, 1998.

Angels Ride Bikes and Other Fall Poems/Los angeles andan en bicicleta y otros poemas de otono, illustrated by Maya Christina Gonzalez, Children's Book Press, in press.

OTHER POETRY

Tattoos, Nomad (Oakland, CA), 1985.

(With Rodrigo Reyes and Juan Pablo Gutierrez) *Ya vas, Carnal* (title means "Right on, Brother"), Humanizarte (San Francisco), 1985.

(Co-editor) *Quarry West 26:* "Chicanas y chicanos en dialogo" (anthology), University of California, Santa Cruz, 1989.

Quake Poems, We Press (Santa Cruz, CA), 1989.

Body in Flames/Cuerpo en llamas, translated by Francisco Aragon, Chronicle (San Francisco), 1990.

Loma Prieta, We Press, photographs by Frank Balthis, 1990.

De amor oscuro (title means "Of Dark Love"), translated by Adrienne Rich and Francisco Aragon, illustrated by Ray Rice, Moving Parts (Santa Cruz), 1991.

Poemas Zurdos, Editorial Factor, Mexico City, Mexico, 1992.

No Golden Gate for Us, Pennywhistle Press, 1993.

Cuerpo en llamas has also been published in Swedish and Irish, and *De amor oscuro* has been published in Irish.

OTHER

(With Fabian A. Samaniego and Nelson Rojas) *Mundo 21* (textbook), Houghton Mifflin, 1995.

(Editor, with M. Cecilia Colombi) *La Ensenanza del Espanol a Hispanohablantes: Praxis y Teoria* (college textbook), Houghton Mifflin, 1996.

(Translator) Carmen L. Garza, *In My Family (En Mi Familia)* (picture book), Children's Book Press, 1996.

(Translator) Lynn Moroney and Te Ata, *Viborita de Cascabel* (picture book), illustrated by Mira Reisberg, Children's Book Press, 1996.

(With Fabian Samaniego and Ricardo Otherguy) *Tu mundo* (textbook), Houghton Mifflin, 1997.

(With Fabian Samaniego and Nelson Rojas) *Nuestro Mundo* (textbook), Houghton Mifflin, 1997.

(Translator) Carmen L. Garza, *Magic Windows* (picture book), Children's Book Press, 1999.

Author of introduction to the bilingual edition of Otto Rene Castillo's *Tomorrow Triumphant,* Night Horn (San Francisco), 1984; author of essay "Reclaiming Ourselves, Reclaiming America," in *Without Discovery: A Native Response to Columbus,* edited by Ray Gonzalez, Broken Moon Press (Seattle), 1992.

Alarcon's poetry has appeared in numerous anthologies, including *Palabra Nueva: Cuentos Chicanos,* edited by Ricardo Aguilar, Armando Armengol, and Sergio Elizondo, Texas Western Press (El Paso), 1984, *Lenguas Sueltas: Poemas,* Moving Parts Press, 1994, *Lighthouse Point: An Anthology of Santa Cruz Writers,* edited by Patrice Vecchione and Steve Wiesinger, M. Press Soquel (Santa Cruz), 1987, *Best New Chicano Literature 1989,* edited by Julian Palley, Bilingual Press (Tempe), 1989, *New Chicana/Chicano Writing 1,* edited by Charles M. Tatum, The University of Arizona Press, 1992, *After Aztlan: Latino Poets of the Nineties,* edited by Ray Gonzalez, David R. Godine (Boston), 1992, *Catch a Sunflake,* Macmillan/McGraw-Hill, 1993, *Voices from the Fields: Children of Migrant Farmworkers Tell Their Stories,* interviews and photographs by S. Beth Atkin, Little, Brown, 1993, *Currents from the Dancing River: Contemporary Latino Fiction, Nonfiction, and Poetry,* edited by Ray Gonzalez, Harcourt Brace, 1994, *La poesia actual en espanol (decada 1983-1992). Cuadernos de poesia nueva,* Asociacion Prometeo de Poesia (Madrid), 1994, *Del otro lado,* Fondo Nacional para la Cultura y las Artes, Supplemento de *Blanco Movil,* edited by Eduardo Mosches (Mexico City), 1994, *An Introduction to Poetry,* edited by X. J. Kennedy and Dana Gioia, HarperCollins, 1994, *Saludos! Poemas de Nuevo Mexico/Poems of New Mexico,* Pennywhistle Press (Tesuque), 1995, *Letters to America: Contemporary American Poetry on Race,* edited by Jim Daniels, Wayne State Univeristy Press, 1995, *Paper Dance: 55 Latino Poets,* edited by Victor Hernandez Cruz, Leroy V. Quintana, and Vigil Suarez, Persea Books, 1995, *Strange Attraction: The Best of Ten Years of ZYZZYVA,* edited by Howard Junker, University of Nevada Press, 1995, *The Name of Love: Classic Gay Love Poems,* edited by Michael Lassell, St. Martin's Press, 1995, *POESidA: A Bilingual Anthology of AIDS Poetry from the United States, Latin America, and Spain,* edited by Carlos A. Rodriguez, Ollantay Press, 1995, *La voz urgente: Antologia de literatura chicana en espanol,* edited by Manuel M. Martin-Rodriguez, Editorial Fundamentos, 1995, *Poemcrazy,* edited by Susan G. Wooldridge, Clarkson Potter Publishers, 1996, *Goddess of the Americas/La Diosa de las Americas: Writings on the Virgen of Guadalupe,* edited by Ana Castillo, Riverhead Books, 1996, *Under the Pomegranate Tree: The Best New Latino Erotica,* edited by Ray Gonzalez, Washington Square Books, 1996, and *I Feel a Little Jumpy Around You, A Book of Her Poems & His Poems Collected in Paris,* edited by Noami Shihab Nye and Paul B. Janeczko, Simon & Schuster, 1997.

Contributor to periodicals, including *Alcatraz, Confluencia, Plural, The Berkeley Poetry Review, Metamorfosis, Five Fingers Review, La Opinion, Revista Mujeres, The James White Review, The Guadalupe Review, ZYZZYVA, The Last Word: West Coast Writers, The Bloomsbury Review, The Americas Review, Puerto del Sol, Before Columbus Review: A Quarterly Review of Multicultural Literature, Mocking Bird, Wild Duck, Andelas, Poetry Now, Compost 8, A Journal of Art, Literature, and Ideas, SIC: Vice & Verse,* and *Poetry Flash: The Bay Area's Poetry Review and Literary Calendar.*

Sidelights

As a writer, performer, professor, and activist raised in both Mexico and the United States, Francisco X. Alarcon voices his multicultural upbringing and rich Mexican heritage to younger audiences through his powerful collections of poetry. Deemed as "neither conventional nor traditional, either in the English or Spanish tradition of versification and rhyming" by *Dictionary of Literary Biography* essayist Salvador Rodriguez del Pino, Alarcon encourages readers to contemplate everyday objects or scenes from another perspective.

Born in Wilmington, California, in 1954, Alarcon was raised in both Mexico and the United States, moving from one place to another frequently during his childhood. As a result he was educated in both countries, although he often felt like an outsider in each. Named after his grandfather, Alarcon was mesmerized by his grandfather's tales of old Mexico and the early twentieth-century revolutionary movements. When Alarcon became a young adult, he moved to California—arriving with only five dollars to his name—and initially held a series of low-paying jobs, including a stint as a migrant laborer. In order to earn an American high school diploma, he began an arduous educational journey that

Alarcon's collection of twenty emotive poems for primary graders, written in English and Spanish, celebrates various signs of springtime. (From Laughing Tomatoes and Other Spring Poems, *illustrated by Maya Christina Gonzalez.*)

started in a Los Angeles adult-education program and culminated with three college degrees, including a master of arts degree from Stanford University.

Alarcon first began writing poetry during his college years. While at Stanford he worked for a bilingual newspaper in a job that helped him become involved with the surrounding community and awakened him to the political realities of being Hispanic in the United States. Much of Alarcon's early poetry, taut verses written in Spanish and geared for adults, is a reflection of his mixed heritage and his growing awareness of the social and political implications of the barrio. He lived in a San Francisco neighborhood that was a diverse blend of Latin and Central American peoples with strong ties to their homelands; solidarity with this Hispanic community played an integral role in shaping his voice as a poet. He began reading his work in the numerous hospitable venues for poetry in the Bay Area, enjoying a reputation as a rising young voice on the literary scene.

After he received his graduate degree, Alarcon returned to Mexico as a Fulbright fellow and from there took a trip into Cuba; these experiences introduced him to such prominent Latin American writers as Elias Nandino and helped shape the direction of Alarcon's poetry. His encounter with Nandino—an openly gay writer then in his eighties and finally achieving critical recognition—solidified Alarcon's commitment to maintain honesty about his own sexual orientation in his poetry. The extended trip was a turning point for the young writer's career, helping to shape his literary voice and bringing wider recognition to his work. He became involved with a theater group and appeared frequently in local media coverage of the literary scene in Mexico City. Following his return to California he won several awards for his work, which by then had expanded to include prose and essays, and joined the faculty of the University of California at Santa Cruz as a professor of Chicano literature.

While most of Alarcon's earlier works are for older readers, he reached a new audience, young adults, with *Snake Poems: An Aztec Invocation.* For this work Alarcon drew upon a seventeenth-century manuscript written by a Spanish priest, also named Alarcon. Originally, the priest had chronicled the powerful rituals and beliefs of the Aztecs in their original language in order to provide concrete evidence of their heathenism. The poet Alarcon, however, uses the text to highlight the complexity and beauty of the indigenous people and their spirituality. Added to the translated manuscript are Alarcon's own lyrical and narrative pieces plus his impressions of contemporary Mexican-American culture. Calling the work "unusual" and "powerful" in *Booklist,* Pat Monaghan appreciated the way Alarcon "reveals and revels in his heritage" and hoped for more from the talented poet.

Alarcon connects with an even younger audience—primary graders—with *Laughing Tomatoes: And Other Spring Poems / Jitomates risuenos y otros poemas de primavera.* In his opening words Alarcon tells his readers: "A Poem / makes us see / everything / for the first time." What follows is a collection of short poems, or "quick snapshots of moments in life," according to *School Library Journal* contributor Ann Welton. The text is written in both English and Spanish. As the title indicates, the energetic, colorful poems describe various signs of spring to readers as if they were seeing them for the first time. Janice M. Del Negro, writing in *Bulletin of the Center for Children's Books,* noted that each poem "seems to have something to shout about," while a *Kirkus Reviews* critic called the work an "accessible, open-hearted collection." Alarcon followed *Laughing Tomatoes* with another book of poems for children, *From the Bellybutton of the Moon and Other Summer Poems.*

In the *Dictionary of Literary Biography* essay, Alarcon discusses his literary career and its relationship with his Hispanic heritage, explaining: "I think maybe I'm sort of in the Latin tradition of the poet. There's no difference between the political and the personal, the social and the intimate . . . . It's very common in Latin America to have poets as the collective voice and the person who takes on a certain responsibility in the community."

Works Cited

Alarcon, Francisco X., *Laughing Tomatoes and Other Spring Poems / Jitomates risuenos y otros poemas de primavera,* Children's Book Press, 1997.

Del Negro, Janice M., review of *Laughing Tomatoes: And Other Spring Poems, Bulletin of the Center for Children's Books,* June, 1997, p. 349.

Review of *Laughing Tomatoes: And Other Spring Poems, Kirkus Reviews,* March 15, 1997, p. 458.

Monaghan, Pat, review of *Snake Poems: An Aztec Invocation, Booklist,* March 1, 1992, p. 1191.

Rodriguez del Pino, Salvador, "Francisco Xavier Alarcon," *Dictionary of Literary Biography,* Volume 122: *Chicano Writers,* Gale, 1992, pp. 3-7.

Welton, Ann, review of *Laughing Tomatoes: And Other Spring Poems, School Library Journal,* May, 1997, p. 118.

For More Information See

PERIODICALS

Booklist, June 1, 1997, p. 1707; October 15, 1998.

Kirkus Reviews, July 1, 1998, p. 964.

Publishers Weekly, February 3, 1992, p. 78; July 20, 1998, p. 222.

*   *   *

BACA, Maria 1951-

Personal

Born December 5, 1951; daughter of Eugenio M. (a stone mason) and Isabelle (a homemaker) Romero. *Education:* Attended University of Arizona, 1979, and University of New Mexico, 1986. *Politics:* "Non-partisan." *Religion:* "Native American." *Hobbies and other interests:* Hiking, canoeing, swimming, baseball, sweat lodge.

Addresses

Home and office—299 Placitas N.W., Albuquerque, NM 87107.

Career

Painter and sculptor. Artist in residence for public schools of Albuquerque, NM, and other educational institutions throughout the United States.

Awards, Honors

Grant from National Endowment for the Arts, 1990.

Illustrator

Rudolfo A. Anaya, *Maya's Children: The Story of La Llorona,* Hyperion, 1997.

Work in Progress

A work on ecology, *Nuestra Senora de Ecologia.*

Sidelights

Maria Baca told *SATA:* "When we are born, we are given an amazing gift. It is the gift of the act of creating. Look around. Someone has thought of an idea and brought it into our three-dimensional reality. Not only are we all capable of this, we do it every waking moment of our lives, and we do this in our dreams, too. Then we forget. How do we begin to remind ourselves and each other of the powerful magic each of us possesses? Through rituals. Rituals are ceremonies that help us remember that life is magic. They also help us to celebrate our understanding of this. Many indigenous people still create celebration. By creating symbols like masks, dances, songs, and prayers, we grow beyond our own reality. We begin to see our own reflection in all living things, and we are reminded to honor that which has been given to us—the magic of life.

"My paintings have taught me that much of our culture comes to us not through literal means, but through reflections and symbols that are only partially contained within the intellect. We do not react mechanically to the world. We act by creating symbols, and thus we transcend the physical and move into a dimension of symbolic representation. We are indeed symbolic creatures, and the creative act has everything to do with our symbolic behavior. Knowing this, I have been amazed to witness the nearly complete abolishment of art in our schools."

One night Señor Tiempo was lurking outside the home of Maya's parents. He overheard Maya's mother say, "Our daughter is safe in her home by the lake."

"Yes," Maya's father said. "Perhaps now she has escaped the vengeance of Señor Tiempo."

"Now I know where Maya is hiding," Señor Tiempo said. "I will pay her a visit."

Señor Tiempo disguised himself as a wise old teacher, one who travels the roads and gives good advice. He appeared at Maya's hut, where she and her children were harvesting corn.

Maria Baca's bright illustrations adorn the tale of the jealous god of time who seeks vengeance on the immortal grandchildren of the Sun God. (From Maya's Children: The Story of La Llorona, *retold by Rudolfo Anaya.)*

For More Information See

PERIODICALS
Booklist, May 1, 1997, p. 1500.

*   *   *

BERG, Elizabeth 1948-

Personal

Born December 2, 1948, in St. Paul, MN; daughter of Arthur (in the military) and Jeanne Hoff; married Howard Berg (a marketing director), March 30, 1974 ; children: Julie, Jennifer. *Education:* Attended University of Minnesota; St. Mary's Junior College, A.A.S.

Addresses

Agent—Lisa Bankoff, International Creative Management, 40 West 57th St., New York, NY 10019.

Career

Writer. Critical-care nurse in Massachusetts, until 1985.

Writings

FOR CHILDREN; "FESTIVALS OF THE WORLD" SERIES

Indonesia, Gareth Stevens, 1997.
Mexico, Gareth Stevens, 1997.
Egypt, Gareth Stevens, 1997.
Italy, Gareth Stevens, 1997.
Nigeria, Gareth Stevens, 1998.

Berg has also edited several volumes of the "Festivals of the World" Series.

NOVELS

Durable Goods, Random House, 1993.
Talk before Sleep, Random House, 1993.
Range of Motion, Random House, 1995.
The Pull of the Moon, Random House, 1996.
Joy School, Random House, 1997.
The First Law of Thermodynamics, Random House, 1998.
The Set Point for Happiness, Random House, 1998.
What We Keep, Random House, 1998.

OTHER

Family Traditions: Celebrations for Holidays and Everyday (nonfiction), Reader's Digest (Pleasantville, NY), 1992.

Contributor of short stories to periodicals, including *Family Circle, Ladies' Home Journal, Parents, Redbook,* and *Woman's Day.*

Sidelights

Unlike many novelists, Elizabeth Berg did not decide to become a writer as soon as she put pen to paper as a young girl and wrote her first story. Instead, after graduating from college, she dedicated several years to working as a critical-care nurse near Boston, Massachusetts. Berg's own battle with cancer—and the realization that each moment, precious as it is, should be spent in a fulfilling way—prompted her career change from nurse to writer. Her novels, which include the coming-of-age story *Durable Goods* and its sequel, *Joy School,* have been praised by critics for what *Publishers Weekly* commentator Nicholas A. Basbanes called their "honesty and perception." "If it seems that [Berg] ... is writing with a passion that approaches missionary zeal," Basbanes added, "it is because she has learned, through painful experience, that life is a gift too precious to be taken casually."

Durable Goods introduces readers to twelve-year-old Katie, a Texas preteen living with her older sister and her father, a career army officer. With their mother now dead from cancer, the girls must cope with their father's increasingly more abusive emotional outbursts, and Katie withdraws into her poetry and her friendships. Patrick T. Reardon, writing in Chicago's *Tribune Books,* praised the character of Katie as "strong enough, solid enough, flexible enough to make it through the rough handling of life." He added that Berg's rendering of Katie's relationship with her father is portrayed with "sensitivity rather than sentimentality." *Booklist* contributor Donna Seaman also commended the novel, calling *Durable Goods* "a tender, smart and perfectly constructed little novel, suffused with humor and admiration for youth's great capacity for love and instinct for truth." Judy Silverman, writing in *Voice of Youth Advocates,* asserted: "Beautifully written, strong, and passionate, this book will hold wide appeal."

In *Joy School,* Katie is a year older and her sister has left home to get married. Now living in Missouri, Katie makes several new friends and falls madly in love with a gas station attendant ten years older than she. While her father is still morose and abusive, Katie's new flame treats her infatuation with sensitivity, in a novel that *School Library Journal* contributor Susan H. Woodcock called "a quiet read that lingers in one's thoughts, a true joy." A *Kirkus Reviews* commentator dubbed *Joy School* "a pleasant between-meals snack of the kids-are-great genre: teary, funny, Hallmarkian wise . . . ." Berg readily acknowledges the sentimental quality evident in her works. "I write about people that I wish I were like, but it's always me talking," she maintained in an interview with Basbanes for *Publishers Weekly.* "It's always the same motivation, whatever theme it takes. For me, there will always be life-affirming stuff. I'm a rank sentimentalist, and I make no apologies for it." Berg is also the author of several novels that are more exclusively for adults, including *Talk before Sleep,* which recounts the relationship between two friends as one slowly succumbs to cancer; *The Pull of the Moon,* about a middle-aged woman's journey of self-discovery; and *The Set Point for Happiness.*

Works Cited

Basbanes, Nicholas A., "Elizabeth Berg: A Life-Affirming Sentimentalist," *Publishers Weekly,* August 21, 1995, p. 34.

Review of *Joy School, Kirkus Reviews,* February 1, 1997, p. 155.

Reardon, Patrick, review of *Durable Goods, Tribune Books* (Chicago), June 21, 1993, p. E5.

Seaman, Donna, review of *Durable Goods, Booklist,* April 15, 1993, p. 1491.

Silverman, Judy, review of *Durable Goods, Voice of Youth Advocates,* December, 1993, p. 287.

Woodcock, Susan H., review of *Joy School, School Library Journal,* July, 1997, p. 114.

For More Information See

PERIODICALS

Booklist, March 1, 1997, p. 1108.
Kirkus Reviews, February 15, 1993, p. 163.
New Yorker, July 12, 1993, p. 103.
New York Times Book Review, October 24, 1993, p. 22.
Publishers Weekly, February 22, 1993, p. 81; July 3, 1995, p. 49; February 26, 1996, p. 82.
School Library Journal, November, 1993, p. 148; November, 1994, p. 140.

*   *   *

BETTERIDGE, Anne
See POTTER, Margaret (Newman)

*   *   *

BORDEN, Louise (Walker) 1949-

Personal

Born October 30, 1949, in Cincinnati, OH; daughter of William Lee (president of a sales distributorship) and Louise (Crutcher) Walker; married Peter A. Borden (president of a sales distributorship), September 4, 1971; children: Catherine, Ayars (daughter), Ted. *Education:* Denison University, B.A., 1971. *Politics:* Independent. *Religion:* Methodist. *Hobbies and other interests:* Being an "avid fan of the Cincinnati Reds; writing; tennis; reading; spending summers in Leland, Michigan; spending time with my family and friends; travel."

Addresses

Home—628 Myrtle Ave., Terrace Park, OH 45174.

Career

Meadowbrook School, Weston, MA, teaching assistant, 1971-73; Cincinnati Country Day School, Cincinnati, OH, pre-primary teacher, 1973-74; The Bookshelf (bookstore), Cincinnati, co-owner, 1988-91; writer. Served on the boards of Redeemer Nursery School, Cincinnati Children's Theater, and Hillsdale Alumni Association. *Member:* Society of Children's Book Writers and Illustrators.

Writings

Caps, Hats, Socks, and Mittens: A Book about the Four Seasons, illustrated by Lillian Hoban, Scholastic, 1989.
The Neighborhood Trucker, illustrated by Sandra Speidel, Scholastic, 1990.
The Watching Game, illustrated by Teri Weidner, Scholastic, 1991.
Albie the Lifeguard, illustrated by Elizabeth Sayles, Scholastic, 1993.
Just in Time for Christmas, illustrated by Ted Lewin, Scholastic, 1994.
(With Mary Kay Kroeger) *Paperboy,* illustrated by Ted Lewin, Clarion, 1996.
Thanksgiving Is ..., illustrated by Steve Bjorkman, Scholastic, 1997.
The Little Ships: The Heroic Rescue at Dunkirk in World War II, illustrated by Michael Foreman, Margaret McElderry, 1997.
Goodbye, Charles Lindbergh, illustrated by Thomas B. Allen, McElderry, 1998.
Good Luck, Mrs. K.!, illustrated by Adam Gustavson, McElderry, 1999.

Contributor of poetry to *Christmas in the Stable,* Harcourt (New York City), 1990.

Louise Borden

Sidelights

A former school teacher, Louise Borden has written several books for young readers that take a gentle approach to childhood. A young boy realizes his dream of riding in his favorite truck in *The Neighborhood Trucker,* while in *The Little Ships: The Heroic Rescue at Dunkirk in World War II,* a fisherman's daughter helps come to the aid of Allied soldiers trapped on the beach at Dunkirk. Family traditions are the focus of *Just in Time for Christmas,* which a *Publishers Weekly* contributor described as "a poignant story, sparely and smoothly told." And a young boy has a once-in-a-lifetime encounter with an American hero in *Good-Bye, Charles Lindbergh,* a picture book based on the real-life recollections of Harold Gilpin, who met the famed aviator when Lindbergh landed his plane in a field near Gilpin's Mississippi home. "More than just a retelling," asserted *Booklist* reviewer Shelle Rosenfeld, "the book explores the complex issues of age versus youth, modern technology versus the Old World, innocence versus experience." Rosenfeld added that *Good-Bye, Charles Lindbergh* is "both an interesting glimpse back in time

and a moving story of how the ordinary can suddenly become extraordinary."

Borden was born in Cincinnati, Ohio, in 1949. "Growing up, I had a grandmother who loved history," she recalled in an interview for Simon & Schuster. "In grade school, I enjoyed maps, geography, and fiction and nonfiction relating to history. I was fortunate enough to have several wonderful history teachers during my elementary and secondary school years who nourished that interest. Later, in college, I majored in history. The idea of ordinary people against the backdrop of historical events has always interested me much more than specific dates, facts, and issues." After graduating from college, Borden worked at teaching positions in Weston, Massachusetts and in her hometown of Cincinnati, before indulging in a life-long love of books and becoming co-owner of a bookstore, The Bookshelf, in 1988. Borden's first book, *Caps, Hats, Socks, and Mittens,* was published for Scholastic the following year. "The sound of language and the poet's voice have always fascinated me," she once explained to *SATA,* "and so I think that writing picture books was a natural step for me. The sound and

From **Paperboy,** *written by Borden and Mary Kay Kroeger and illustrated by Ted Lewin.*

rhythm that are inherent in good picture books are a continuing challenge—to craft a text that has its own natural voice, as well as a good story line."

Borden started work on *Caps, Hats, Socks, and Mittens* after her second child began primary school. Her work as an assistant first-grade teacher gave her a good sense of how to write a beginning reader in a way that would help students sound out new words. She sent the book to Scholastic and was pleasantly surprised when they sent back a contract for its publication. Borden was even more pleased when her editor at Scholastic chose artist Lillian Hoban to create the pictures. "Everyone always asks if authors are pleased with the illustration for their books. I cannot now think of my words as separate from Lillian Hoban's wonderful pictures," Borden explained.

The author's second book, *The Neighborhood Trucker,* is the story of Elliot Long, a little boy who loves to watch the trucks roll by his home. His favorite is a cement truck from Sardinia Concrete with the number 44 painted on its side; it is driven by a truckdriver named Slim. "The working title for the book was 'More Trucks Please,'" Borden noted. "I had never looked twice at trucks until our son Ted pulled me into their loud, noisy, exciting world. From an early age, Ted has had a passion for trucks—especially cement mixers. There really *is* a Sardinia Concrete several miles from our village, and there really *is* a Slim—a tall, thoughtful driver who shares a special friendship with Ted. The rest is fiction. And, as I tell children, Ted is not the main character in this book. I am. I am Elliot Long. That's what writers do. We pretend a lot. And we become other people." In a review of *The Neighborhood Trucker* for *Bulletin of the Center for Children's Books,* Roger Sutton called the story "a poetic ... portrait of vocational obsession" and a "good bedtime choice for revved-up trucksters."

The Watching Game, Borden's next effort, describes a game played by four cousins when they visit their grandmother in the country. Each child tries to be the first to spot the fox in the woods and to put out their grandfather's hat so the fox will know it has been seen. *School Library Journal* contributor Patricia Pearl offered a favorable assessment of the book, noting that the story "emphasizes the significant themes of family love and respect for nature." *The Watching Game* actually began as a poem called "Granny's Fox." Borden explained, "There was no watching at all—just a boy who spotted a fox." The story took shape with the advice of Borden's editor. "In the first working drafts of the book I did not name the cousins or give them any characteristics. But names are very important to me. I choose them with care. I want children to remember my characters, to know that they are distinctive and have their own identities."

Borden creates another distinctive character in *Albie the Lifeguard.* In this story, a young boy realizes that his lack of skill as a swimmer will keep him off the local swim team. He decides instead to work lifeguard duty at his backyard swimming pool; by the end of the summer, he has gained the confidence to join his friends in

After meeting Harold Gilpin when he was eighty-three, Borden penned her book for young readers about Gilpin's unforgettable boyhood meeting with Lindbergh in the early days of aviation. (From Good-bye, Charles Lindbergh, *illustrated by Thomas B. Allen.)*

swimming the entire lap-length of his town pool, in a story that "pays tribute to the natural ability of a child to recognize and respect his own timetable and abilities," according to *School Library Journal* contributor Liza Bliss. Also enthusiastic about the story, a *Publishers Weekly* reviewer found *Albie the Lifeguard* "a winning tale that indirectly and elegantly demonstrates the psyche's inventiveness."

The Little Ships is a fictionalized re-creation of an important historical event: the 1940 rescue of 300,000 Allied soldiers from the beach at Dunkirk, France, and to safety in Dover, England, by hundreds of small boats captained by naval officers and brave English fishermen. The story is told from the point of view of an English girl who, dressed as a boy, joins her fisherman father in helping to transport the soldiers. Jon Scieszka, writing in the *New York Times Book Review,* maintained that *The Little Ships* "gives a personal, memorable character to what might otherwise be an abstract chapter of history." Scieszka also praised Borden for the tone of her storytelling, noting that her young heroine "describes her exhaustion, and the spectacle of more than 300,000 Allied troops fleeing from the beach to boats and back to England, in a spare and dramatic child's voice, wonderfully free of patriotic preaching or moralizing."

"Today many teachers are integrating various subjects of the curriculum in wonderful ways," Borden explained in discussing the use of historical fiction in the classroom. "For example, skills in social studies, reading, and language arts can all be taught in a holistic way through the use of good literature. Historical fiction—whether picture books or novels—is widely used to introduce topics in social studies and broaden students' knowledge of social and political history. I think if history is made accessible to young readers in interesting ways, they will discover just how rich it is, rather than viewing history as boring and dry."

Borden's *Good-bye, Charles Lindbergh* is another fictional recreation of an actual event. "I saw a 'Dear Abby' letter in my local paper with the name Lindbergh in the title," the author recalled in her interview. "[This] caught my eye because I admired Anne Morrow Lindbergh's writing. I read the letter from Harold Gilpin of Pine Bluff, Arkansas, that told of his meeting Charles Lindbergh near the Mississippi farm that Gilpin grew up on. I immediately pictured an image of a boy on his horse looking up into the sky to see a biplane. I thought that contrast was remarkable: the ordinary meeting the extraordinary. I filed the newspaper clipping but carried the image inside, hoping to someday find a way to write a book about a Mississippi boy meeting the nation's hero.

"A few years later, when I decided to write the book, I actually tracked down Harold Gilpin. We corresponded via phone and mail for several months, and in January 1995, I flew to Arkansas to meet the Gilpins in person . . . . I then drove 175 miles to Canton, Mississippi, so that I could get a feel for the setting of the book. I returned to Cincinnati, contacted the National Air and Space Museum, researched biplanes, read Anne Morrow Lindbergh's journals, listened to the taped interview of Harold Gilpin that I had made in Pine Bluff, and then began writing the story."

Borden's most recent effort, the picture book *Good Luck, Mrs. K!*, is also based on a real-life experience. Told in the words of a nine-year-old narrator, the story centers on a favorite teacher who is hospitalized with cancer. "It is about an exceptional third-grade teacher and her class," the author notes. "Mrs. K. is a composite of the many wonderful teachers whom I have met during my school visits—this is my way to honor them. The story is also based on a teacher I knew, a great friend, who had cancer. Essentially, it's a book about the joy of teaching and learning."

"I think that I learned the craft of writing through osmosis, because long before I was a writer of books for children, I was a reader," Borden once explained to *SATA*. "And because reading has brought me so much pleasure—has given me most of what I have inside my head and inside my heart—it is a real thrill today to realize that maybe one of my books will hook a child into the same wonderfully rich world that I was drawn to at an early age."

A third-grade class faces up to some tough issues as they send letters and drawings to their beloved teacher, who is hospitalized with cancer. (Cover illustration by Adam Gustavson.)

Works Cited

Review of *Albie the Lifeguard, Publishers Weekly,* May 24, 1993, p. 87.

Bliss, Liza, review of *Albie the Lifeguard, School Library Journal,* June, 1993, p. 70.

Borden, Louise, "A Conversation with Louise Borden, Author of *Good-bye, Charles Lindbergh,*" Simon & Schuster, 1998.

Review of *Just in Time for Christmas, Publishers Weekly,* September 19, 1994, p. 30.

Pearl, Patricia, review of *The Watching Game, School Library Journal,* August, 1991, p. 142.

Rosenfeld, Shelle, review of *Good-Bye, Charles Lindbergh, Booklist,* March 1, 1998.

Scieszka, Jon, review of *The Little Ships, New York Times Book Review,* May 18, 1997, p. 25.

Sutton, Roger, review of *The Neighborhood Trucker, Bulletin of the Center for Children's Books,* December, 1990, p. 79.

For More Information See

PERIODICALS

Booklist, August, 1994, p. 22; March 1, 1997, p. 1162.

Bulletin of the Center for Children's Books, April, 1997, p. 276.
Horn Book, May-June, 1997, p. 302.
Kirkus Reviews, April , 1, 1997, p. 549.
School Library Journal, October, 1990, p. 86.

*   *   *

BOWIE, C. W.
See WIRTHS, Claudine (Turner) G(ibson)

*   *   *

BUEHNER, Caralyn M. 1963-

Personal

Name pronounced "*Bee*-ner"; born May 20, 1963, in St. George, UT; daughter of Melvin H. (a judge) and E. Berenice (Harris) Morris; married Mark E. Buehner (an illustrator), 1983; children: Heidi, Grant, Sarah, Samuel, Laura. *Education:* Attended University of Utah, 1981-83, and Utah State University, 1983-85. *Religion:* Church of Jesus Christ of Latter-Day Saints (Mormon).

Addresses

Home—2646 Alden St., Salt Lake City, UT 84106.

Career

Writer.

Awards, Honors

Children's Choice Award, Children's Book Council, 1994, and Utah Children's Choice Award, 1996, both for *A Job for Wittilda;* Parents' Choice Award, 1996, Notable Book, American Library Association, and *Boston Globe-Horn Book* Honor Award, both 1997, all for *Fanny's Dream;* Utah Children's Choice, 1997, for *It's a Spoon, Not a Shovel.*

Writings

PICTURE BOOKS; ILLUSTRATED BY MARK BUEHNER

The Escape of Marvin the Ape, Dial, 1992.
A Job for Wittilda, Dial, 1993.
It's a Spoon, Not a Shovel, Dial, 1995.
Fanny's Dream, Dial, 1996.
I Did It, I'm Sorry, Dial, 1998.

Work in Progress

Papa Thinks about Mudge (working title), a children's picture book.

Sidelights

Together with her husband, artist Mark Buehner, Caralyn Buehner has created a number of entertaining picture books for young children. From the adventures of an ape who roams the city in *The Escape of Marvin the Ape* to a lonely farm girl's fantasy about marrying a prince in *Fanny's Dream,* Buehner combines interesting plots with a sense of fun to capture the imagination of her young audience. Reviewing Buehner's debut work, *The Escape of Marvin the Ape, Five Owls* contributor Stephen Fraser found evidence of "the beginning of a long career of strong, unusual, and zany books children will love."

Born in St. George, Utah in 1963, Buehner was raised in Salt Lake City, the youngest of five siblings. "Books were always important in our house," she recalled to *SATA.* "My mother rarely had time for her own reading, but we knew that she loved books. I remember sitting on her lap as she read to me, or listened to me read. Sometimes on trips, with the whole family packed into a little motorhome, we would lay in our beds at night while Mom read *Onion John* or *The Boxcar Children* by the dim light of the little propane lantern. One of my treasured memories is of being down in the "big girls'" basement bedroom, listening to my older sister read to us from the P. G. Wodehouse series about the unflappable Jeeves. I know there was much that I didn't understand, being so much younger than the older girls, but because they were convulsed in laughter, so was I. The discovery of a story was exquisite, and I loved books from the time I can remember. I loved going to the library; the wonderful smell and feel of a stack of books to take home and savor. I would curl up by the furnace vent, or in the big corner chair with a snack and a book, and be content for hours. Often I'd go to bed and read under the covers with a flashlight. I read the books my older sisters read. Through books I was exposed to some of the world's greatest literature, and probably some of its worst, but I felt as if I were living a thousand lives more than my own. What a wonder to crawl inside another person's head, and see the world through their eyes!"

Buehner met her future husband, illustrator Mark Buehner, while attending college. "I had no intention of being a writer," she recalled, "but was feeding my love of history and humanities. Mark introduced me to a fascinating world of shape and color, where a story can be told in a single picture." Mark encouraged Caralyn to write her first full-length picture book, *The Escape of Marvin the Ape.* In this book, a large ape walks through his open cage door at the New York City Zoo and wanders the surrounding city, riding the subway, watching a baseball game, and ordering food at a local restaurant, all without so much as a raised eyebrow from the people going about their business around him. A *Publishers Weekly* critic maintained that Buehner's "vocabulary choices and turns of phrase imbue this romp with an appealing sense of wonder."

Buehner's wide-ranging exposure to all types of books inevitably influenced her own writing. And, as the mother of five children, her habit of reading aloud to her family strengthened her sense of a story's rhythm and pacing. *A Job for Wittilda,* Buehner's tale of a middle-

Animals presented with moral dilemmas give children the opportunity to decide which are the right choices in Caralyn M. Buehner's funny quiz book. *(From* I Did It, I'm Sorry, *illustrated by Mark Buehner.)*

aged witch forced to get a job to feed her forty-seven hungry cats, was praised by *School Library Journal* contributor Lauralyn Persson for the "effortless flow" of its "rhythmic language." Equally appreciative of the book, which finds Wittilda competing for a job as a pizza delivery person at Dingaling Pizzas, was a *Publishers Weekly* commentator, who found Buehner's "creation of a witch with a heart of gold" to be comforting, and noted that "equal dashes of adventure, magic and reality provide a captivating mix."

The team of Buehner and Buehner performed a public service to all parents of young children when they created a series of etiquette books that make manners fun. *It's a Spoon, Not a Shovel* and *I Did It, I'm Sorry* provide "a handsome combination of humor, puzzles, and lessons in elementary good behavior," according to *Horn Book* reviewer Ann A. Flowers. Written in a quiz format wherein the reader chooses among three possible courses of action, *It's a Spoon, Not a Shovel* depicts a wide variety of social situations, substituting animals for people faced with such quandaries as what to say to the host of a dinner party when showing up late or how best to react to a disappointing birthday present. Julie Yates Walton of *Booklist* praised the volume for containing "ample spoonfuls of humor" that make the "medicine [go] down very easily." Focusing on ethical questions, *I Did It, I'm Sorry* finds engaging animal characters who decide on correct action when cheating, lying, or ignoring the requests of authority figures would be far easier. "This book brims with the sort of solid values every child should learn: never lie, follow the rules, obey your parents and think of others," noted a *Publishers Weekly* reviewer.

Buehner and her family make their home in Salt Lake City, and she and her husband often visit schools to talk about their work as writer and illustrator, respectively. "Both of us want to bring the magic we felt for books as children to the ones we produce," the author noted. Aside from her writing, Buehner's greatest joys are making time in her busy schedule to spend with her family or to participate in church activities. "Much of my writing time is spent in trying to capture the magic of ordinary days for my children in their own photo-journals," Buehner added, "or fumbling to express my awe and wonder at their existence for myself."

Works Cited

Review of *The Escape of Marvin the Ape, Publishers Weekly,* June 22, 1992, p. 61.

Flowers, Ann A., review of *It's a Spoon, Not a Shovel, Horn Book,* July-August, 1995, p. 476.

Fraser, Stephen, review of *The Escape of Marvin the Ape, Five Owls,* November-December, 1992, p. 34.

Review of *I Did It, I'm Sorry, Publishers Weekly,* April 13, 1998, p. 74.

Review of *A Job for Wittilda, Publishers Weekly,* June 28, 1993, p. 76.

Persson, Lauralyn, review of *A Job for Wittilda, School Library Journal,* January, 1994, p. 87.

Walton, Julie Yates, review of *It's a Spoon, Not a Shovel, Booklist,* June 1, 1995, p. 1774.

For More Information See

PERIODICALS

Booklist, July, 1993, p. 1973; April 15, 1998, p. 1449.

Bulletin of the Center for Children's Books, September, 1996, p. 7.

Horn Book, September-October, 1992, p. 574; July-August, 1996, p. 444.

Kirkus Reviews, September 1, 1992, p. 1138; January 1, 1996, p. 65.

Publishers Weekly, May 20, 1996, p. 258.

School Library Journal, August, 1995, p. 115; April, 1996, p. 105.

* * *

BUEHNER, Mark 1959-

Personal

Name pronounced "*Bee*-ner"; born July 20, 1959, in Salt Lake City, UT; son of Philip H. (a business owner) and Marjorie (Evans) Buehner; married Caralyn M. Buehner (a writer), 1983; children: Heidi, Grant, Sarah, Samuel, Laura. *Education:* Attended University of Utah, 1981-82; Utah State University, B.S., 1985. *Religion:* Church of Jesus Christ of Latter-Day Saints (Mormon). *Hobbies and other interests:* Interior and landscape design.

Addresses

Home—2646 Alden St., Salt Lake City, UT 84106.

Career

Illustrator of children's books. Performs volunteer work with religious organizations and scouting programs.

Awards, Honors

Parents' Choice Award, 1990, for *The Adventures of Taxi Dog;* Children's Choice Award, Children's Book Council, 1994, and Utah Children's Choice Award, 1997, both for *A Job for Wittilda;* Gold Medal, National Parenting Best Books, 1994, Oppenheim Toy Portfolio Platinum Award, 1995, American Library Association (ALA) Notable Book, Kentucky Bluegrass Award, and Maryland Black-eyed Susan Award, all for *Harvey Potter's Balloon Farm;* Parents' Choice Award, 1996, ALA Notable Book and *Boston Globe-Horn Book* Honor Award, both 1997, and Society of Illustrators Silver Medal, all for *Fanny's Dream;* Notable Book, ALA, Best Picture Book designation, *Publishers Weekly,* named Cuffies Favorite Picture Book, and Original Art Silver Medal, Society of Illustrators, all 1997, and Children's Choice, International Reading Association-Children's Book Council, 1998, all for *My Life with the Wave.*

Illustrator

PICTURE BOOKS

Debra and Sal Barracca, *The Adventures of Taxi Dog,* Dial, 1990.

Debra and Sal Barracca, *Maxi the Hero,* Dial, 1991.

Jerdine Nolen, *Harvey Potter's Balloon Farm,* Lothrop, 1994.

Catherine Cowan, *My Life with the Wave,* Lothrop, 1997.

Alice Shertle, *I Am the Cat,* Lothrop, 1999.

PICTURE BOOKS; ALL WRITTEN BY CARALYN BUEHNER

The Escape of Marvin the Ape, Dial, 1992.

A Job for Wittilda, Dial, 1993.

It's a Spoon, Not a Shovel, Dial, 1995.

Fanny's Dream, Dial, 1996.

I Did It, I'm Sorry, Dial, 1998.

Adaptations

The Escape of Marvin the Ape has been adapted for CD-ROM.

Work in Progress

Illustrations for *My Monster Mama Loves Me So,* by Laura Leuck.

Sidelights

Highly regarded illustrator Mark Buehner provides pictures for books written by his wife, Caralyn, and other authors, among them Debra and Sal Barracca, Catherine Cowan, and Jerdine Nolen. Praised for the gentle humor and vibrant color that distinguishes his oil and acrylic art, Buehner has received a host of honors for his work. Reviewing the Barraccas' *Maxi, the Hero, New York Times Book Review* contributor Michael

Mark Buehner

Anderson noted that Buehner's "panoramic pictures vibrate with detail and activity; so much is happening that the pages seem to be straining to speak aloud." Anderson added that the illustrator draws in large, rounded forms "a reassuringly solid universe, for all of its surprises."

Born and raised in Salt Lake City, Utah, Buehner was the youngest of a family that included seven children. "I've been told that I learned to walk by holding a pencil; maybe that's where this illustrating business got started!" Buehner told *SATA.* He also recalls being inspired by his father, who used to draw pictures to entertain his young son while the family sat through Sunday church services. As a boy, he used to make his own "books" by drawing pictures and stapling them together—"but I had no idea that what I was doing would eventually become my line of work. Pulling out pencils, paper, and watercolors was just part of my daily routine."

In school, Buehner had a reputation among his teachers as a good artist, and the praise he received for his drawing skills encouraged him to excel. "I couldn't read as well as the other children," Buehner recalled, "but I remember poring over the illustrations in picture books. I particularly latched onto one small book called *Pierre,* by Maurice Sendak, which I not only read but memorized."

By high school, art had become more than just a hobby. Buehner took his first class in oil painting when he was sixteen, and, by his own admission, "became a convert." He still prefers to work in oils. After graduating from Utah State University in 1985, Buehner and his wife, Caralyn, moved to New York City, where they lived for more than four years. In New York, home to most of the country's major publishing houses, Buehner was given the opportunity to illustrate *The Adventures of Taxi Dog,* a picture book about a dog named Maxi who accompanies his owner, a New York City taxi driver named Jim, on his rounds. The book, written by Debra and Sal Barracca, was praised for illustrations that some commentators compared to the work of Chris Van Allsburg; Buehner's oil-over-acrylic technique "gives each scene a subtle, lively play of light and color," according to *School Library Journal* reviewer John Peters.

With the success of *Taxi Dog* and its sequel, *Maxi the Hero,* Buehner soon found other illustration projects coming his way. His work for Jerdine Nolen's popular *Harvey Potter's Balloon Farm* brought his stylized artwork to the front of bookstore windows. The story of a balloon farmer who teaches his trade to a young African-American girl, *Balloon Farm* features "vivid ... illustrations of balloons with expressive faces in every size, color and shape—frogs, demons, elephants, fish, snowmen—and the animals devilishly hidden on every page," according to Ann A. Flowers of *Horn Book.* Reviewing *Balloon Farm* for *School Library Journal,* Kathleen Whalin hailed Buehner as "a master character painter" whose "rich, rounded paintings"

Using expressive air-brushed paintings, Mark Buehner illustrated Jerdine Nolen Harold's playful story of a balloon farmer who teaches his trade to a young girl. (From Harvey Potter's Balloon Farm.*)*

combine with Nolen's text to create "a most satisfying whole."

In *My Life with the Wave*, Buehner brings his artistic talents to bear on Catherine Cowan's retelling of a story by Octavio Paz. The tale of a young boy who grows to love a powerful ocean wave and determines to possess it for himself by bringing it home, *My Life with the Wave* is enlivened by "acrylic and oil paintings [that] capture the powerful sensuality and surrealism" of Paz's original work, in the opinion of *Horn Book* reviewer Cathryn M. Mercier. Calling the story "a celebration of imagination from beginning to end," *School Library Journal* contributor Wendy Lukehart praised Buehner's technique of "insert[ing] small details with such skill that they do not overpower or detract from the main story."

In addition to illustrating the works of the Barraccas, Nolen, and others, Buehner has also teamed up with his wife, Caralyn Buehner, to create a number of children's picture books that have also proved popular. In the couple's first project for young children, *The Escape of Marvin the Ape*, a zoo escapee's day-long exploration of New York City—which occurs without so much as a raised eyebrow from passersby—is brought to life with colorful pictures that "are lively enough to need no definition," according to *School Library Journal* contributor Karen James. *A Job for Wittilda* finds a scruffy witch forced away from her cauldron to earn money to feed her forty-plus cats. Lauralyn Persson hailed Buehner's illustrations as "a delight" in her appraisal for *School Library Journal*, adding that his work contains "comic touches to discover at every rereading." A *Publishers Weekly* reviewer asserted: "Buehner's sumptuous oil and acrylic paintings exhibit his flair for depicting the play of light and shadow, and for deploying a variety of arresting perspectives." Stephanie Zvirin of *Booklist* praised another of the Buehners' books, a variation of the Cinderella story called *Fanny's Dream*, as "a truly wonderful mix of storytelling and art from a husband-wife team with a fine sense of humor."

Zvirin also offered singular accolades to illustrator Buehner for the detail in his "robust, bucolic pictures, which seem almost to jump off the page."

Works Cited

Anderson, Michael, review of *Maxi, the Hero, New York Times Book Review,* January 5, 1992, p. 23.

Flowers, Ann A., review of *Harvey Potter's Balloon Farm, Horn Book,* July-August, 1994, p. 442.

James, Karen, review of *The Escape of Marvin the Ape, School Library Journal,* October, 1992, p. 80.

Review of *A Job for Wittilda, Publishers Weekly,* June 28, 1993, p. 76.

Lukehart, Wendy, review of *My Life with the Wave, School Library Journal,* August, 1997, p. 129.

Mercier, Cathryn M., review of *My Life with the Wave, Horn Book,* September-October, 1997, p. 555.

Persson, Lauralyn, review of *A Job for Wittilda, School Library Journal,* January, 1994, p. 87.

Peters, John, review of *The Adventures of Taxi Dog, School Library Journal,* June, 1990, p. 96.

Whalin, Kathleen, review of *Harvey Potter's Balloon Farm, School Library Journal,* May, 1994, p. 102.

Zvirin, Stephanie, review of *Fanny's Dream, Booklist,* March 15, 1996, p. 1261.

For More Information See

PERIODICALS

Booklist, April 15, 1994, p. 1541; June 1, 1995, p. 1774; July, 1993, p. 1973.

Horn Book, May-June, 1990, p. 317; September-October, 1992, p. 575; July-August, 1995, p. 476; July-August, 1996, p. 444.

New York Times Book Review, November 9, 1997, p. 24.

Publishers Weekly, April 27, 1990, p. 61; December 21, 1990, p. 14; July 3, 1995, p. 59; May 20, 1996, p. 258.

School Library Journal, August, 1995, p. 115; April, 1996, p. 105.

C

CANYON, Christopher 1966-

Personal

Born October 22, 1966, in Ohio; married; wife's name, Jeanette. *Education:* Attended Columbus College of Art & Design.

Christopher Canyon

Addresses

Office—753 South Third St., Columbus, OH 43206.

Career

Illustrator. *Exhibitions:* Society of Illustrators National Scholarship Competition & Exhibition, New York, 1988; Mazza Collection, University of Findlay, Ohio; James Thurber Center, Columbus, OH, 1995; Riffe Gallery, Columbus, OH, 1997; Museum of Northern Arizona, Flagstaff, 1998.

Awards, Honors

Benjamin Franklin Award for best illustrated book, Publishers Marketing Association, 1996, for *The Tree in the Ancient Forest;* Artist for the 1998 State Reading Program, State Library of Ohio, 1998.

Illustrator

Linda Vieira, *The Ever-Living Tree: The Life and Times of a Coast Redwood,* Walker, 1994.
Carol Reed-Jones, *The Tree in the Ancient Forest,* Dawn Publications (Nevada City, CA), 1995.
Sandra De Coteau Orie, *Did You Hear the Wind Sing Your Name?: An Oneida Song of Spring,* Walker, 1995.
Karin Ireland, *Wonderful Nature, Wonderful You,* Dawn Publications, 1996.
Linda Vieira, *Grand Canyon: A Trail through Time,* Walker, 1997.
Donnell Rubay (reteller of story by John Muir), *Stickeen,* Dawn Publications, 1998.

Work in Progress

Illustrations for three books in a nature series by J. Patrick Lewis, for Mikuni Publishing in Tokyo.

Sidelights

Illustrator Christopher Canyon's passion for drawing began during his early childhood. At the age of ten, his parents bought him a beginner's art kit and signed him up for lessons with a local artist. Canyon's talent at drawing and painting continued to blossom and eventually earned him a full scholarship to the Columbus College of Art & Design, where he studied illustration, painting, and design for four years.

Linda Vieira's *The Ever-Living Tree: The Life and Times of a Coast Redwood* was Canyon's first venture into picture-book illustration. The book traces the story of the 2000-year-long life of a redwood tree. Combining nature with history, Vieira dates the stages of the tree's growth by making references to events such as the building of the Great Wall of China, the birth of the United States, and Neil Armstrong walking on the moon. *Booklist* contributor Carolyn Phelan praised Canyon's picture-book debut, saying: "From the complex but controlled page layout to the subtle shadings of color, Canyon shows promise in this, his first book."

Canyon stayed with the same theme when designing illustrations for Carol Reed-Jones's *The Tree in the Ancient Forest*. Another tree, this time a 300-year-old fir, is the main character in this book-length poem depicting the interdependence of living things in the ancient forests. In the words of *Booklist* reviewer Lauren Peterson, "Canyon's superb double-page illustrations can be appreciated both as fine works of art and as detailed studies of forest flora and fauna."

Continuing with the motif of nature, Canyon collaborated with Sandra De Coteau Orie to produce *Did You Hear the Wind Sing Your Name?: An Oneida Song of Spring.* The story reflects Oneida traditions and is structured as a series of questions evoking the imagery and exploring the sensations of spring. *School Library Journal* contributor Donna Scanlon remarked that "Canyon's lush, vibrant, double-page paintings spill out of their frames and are rich in detail." A reviewer for *Publishers Weekly* also praised Canyon's "dramatic, large-scale paintings, in which animals, insects, birds, and flowers are rendered in impressive detail."

Canyon teamed up with Vieira a second time for the aptly-titled *Grand Canyon: A Trail through Time.* In 1996, he spent a month in the Grand Canyon doing research for this picture-book exploration of the awesome landmark. Canyon's efforts are evident in the realism of his illustrations. Susan Dove Lempke declared in a *Booklist* review: "The pictures are especially striking, complete with the textures, colors, light, and perspective ... all gloriously realized." A *Publishers Weekly* reviewer noted that "Canyon is adept at defining not only the grand vistas but also the close-focus scenery." Canyon also did on-location research for *Stickeen,* the story of the famous naturalist John Muir's explorations of southern Alaskan glaciers. Canyon traveled part of Muir's route in his research for the illustrations for this book.

Canyon takes time out from his busy schedule to visit schools and libraries and speak at conferences. He also provides day-long in-service programs on illustration for children and educators. At these programs, Canyon shares how his own childhood experiences and interest in drawing led him to become a professional artist. Through slides and original artwork, he also shares the creative and technical processes involved in creating a picture book, leading audiences on a step-by-step journey through the creation of one of his illustrations.

Canyon told *SATA:* "As an illustrator of children's books, it is a thrill and a privilege for me to share my experiences, to work with children and educators and to help promote a continuing appreciation and enthusiasm for the arts and children's literature. The goal of my programs is to inspire and motivate the creativity of all people. My mission is to help children and educators recognize the value of the arts not only as a language of personal expression, but also as a language of gaining knowledge of our world, ourselves, and others."

Works Cited

Review of *Did You Hear the Wind Sing Your Name?: An Oneida Song of Spring, Publishers Weekly,* January 9, 1995, p. 63.

Review of *Grand Canyon: A Trail through Time, Publishers Weekly,* November 17, 1997, p. 62.

Lempke, Susan Dove, review of *Grand Canyon: A Trail through Time, Booklist,* February 1, 1998, pp. 916-17.

Peterson, Lauren, review of *The Tree in the Ancient Forest, Booklist,* July, 1995, p. 1881.

Phelan, Carolyn, review of *The Ever-Living Tree: The Life and Times of a Coast Redwood, Booklist,* March 1, 1994, p. 1266.

Scanlon, Donna, review of *Did You Hear the Wind Sing Your Name?: An Oneida Song of Spring, School Library Journal,* April, 1995, p. 128.

For More Information See

PERIODICALS

Publishers Weekly, January 31, 1994, p. 89.

School Library Journal, May, 1994, p. 110; September, 1995, p. 196.

*   *   *

CHAPMAN, Jean

Personal

Born in Sydney, Australia; daughter of George William Arden and Margaret (MacLean) Lycett; married Max B. Chapman (an engineer); children: one son, one daughter. *Education:* Attended National Art School. *Hobbies and other interests:* "My interests? Everything, I suspect, but books are my love, particularly children's books. Beautiful picture books, which are now an art form in their own right, are of special interest and delight. We've books all over the house—on bookshelves, on cupboard tops, on bedside tables and chairs, down the stairs, on the floors and sometimes under the beds. And then I enjoy music, the ballet and history, my family and all kinds of people, but children are the nicest of all."

Addresses

Home—New South Wales, Australia.

Career

Author and scriptwriter. Children's literature adviser in Australia. *Member:* Children's Book Council of Australia (life member), Children's Books History Society, International Board on Books for Young People (IBBY), Australia, Dromkeen Children's Literature Collection (life member).

Awards, Honors

Design Award, Australian Books Publishers Association, 1966, for *The Wish Cat,* and 1979, for *Velvet Paws and Whiskers;* commendations from Children's Book Council of Australia, 1966, for *The Wish Cat,* 1976, for *Tell Me Another Tale,* and 1977, for *The Sugar Plum Christmas Book;* award from Government of Austria, 1970, for a translation of *The Wish Cat;* special commendation, Leipzig Children's Book Fair, 1980, for *The Sugar Plum Christmas Book;* commended Christian Book of the Year, 1982, for *Pancakes and Painted Eggs;* Lady Cutler Award for services to children's literature, 1990.

Writings

Amelia Muddle: Stories, illustrated by Adye Adams, Angus and Robertson (Sydney, Australia), 1963.

Sandy the Cane Train, illustrated by Walter Cunningham, Angus and Robertson, 1966.

The Wish Cat, drawings by Noela Young, photographs by Dean Hay, Angus and Robertson, 1966.

Cowboy, illustrated by John Watts, Angus and Robertson, 1969.

Do You Remember What Happened?, illustrated by Edward Ardizzone, Angus and Robertson, 1969.

James Ruse: Pioneer Wheat Farmer, illustrated by Christine Shaw, Wentworth (Sydney, Australia), 1969.

The Someday Dog, photographs by D. Hay, Angus and Robertson, 1968.

Wombat, illustrated by J. Watts, Angus and Robertson, 1969.

Some Australian Houses, illustrated by N. Young, Wentworth, 1969.

Sun, Wind, and Coral: Australia's Great Barrier Reef, illustrated by Betty Robinson, Wentworth, 1972.

The Dilly Dally Man, illustrated by Susanne Dolesch, Angus and Robertson, 1975.

Tell Me a Tale: Stories, Songs and Things to Do, illustrated by Deborah and Kilmeny Niland, Hodder & Stoughton (Sydney, Australia), 1975.

Tell Me Another Tale: Stories, Verses, Songs and Things to Do, illustrated by D. and K. Niland, Hodder & Stoughton, 1976.

Supermarket Thursday: Six Stories, illustrated by A. Lacis, Thomas Nelson (West Melbourne, Australia), 1977.

The Sugar Plum Christmas Book: A Book for Christmas and All the Days of the Year, illustrated by D. Niland, Hodder & Stoughton, 1977, Children's Press, 1982.

The Sugar Plum Song Book: Christmas Songs, illustrated by D. Niland, Hodder & Stoughton, 1977.

Beware, Take Care!: A Safety Manual for Kids, illustrated by Aart Van Ewijk, Hodder & Stoughton, 1978.

Moon-Eyes, illustrated by A. Lacis, Hodder & Stoughton, 1978, McGraw-Hill, 1980.

Tales to Tell, Hodder & Stoughton, 1978.

Velvet Paws and Whiskers, illustrated by D. Niland, Hodder & Stoughton, 1979, Children's Press, 1982.

Pancakes and Painted Eggs: A Book for Easter and All the Days of the Year, illustrated by K. Niland, Children's Press, 1982.

Pine-Cone Possum, illustrated by A. Lacis, Hodder & Stoughton, 1982.

The Great Candle Scandal, illustrated by Roland Harvey, Hodder & Stoughton, 1982.

Haunts and Taunts: A Book for Hallowe'en and All the Nights of the Year, illustrated by D. Niland, Children's Press, 1983.

Double Trouble: An Old Chinese Tale, illustrated by Maya Winters, Ashton Scholastic, 1984.

(Reteller) *The Tall Book of Tall Tales,* illustrated by D. Niland, Hodder & Stoughton, 1985.

(Compiler) *Cat Will Rhyme with Hat: A Book of Poems,* illustrated by Peter Parnall, Scribner, 1986.

Winkie, illustrated by Bruce Treloar, Hodder & Stoughton, 1986.

Cockatoo Soup, illustrated by Rodney McRae, Hodder & Stoughton, 1987.

The Terrible Wild Grey Hairy Thing, illustrated by Vicky Kitanov, Ashton Scholastic, 1986.

The Wreck of the Georgette, illustrated by Jack Montgomery, Macmillan of Australia, (South Melbourne, Australia), 1987.

The Stolen Pumpkin, illustrated by Pat Sirninger, Macmillan, 1987.

Boss Cat, illustrated by Jack Larkin, Macmillan, 1987.

Glue Stew, illustrated by Paul Borg, Martin Educational (Cammeray, New South Wales), 1987.

Capturing the Golden Bird: The Young Hans Christian Andersen, illustrated by Sandra Laroche, Hodder & Stoughton, 1988.

Blue Gum Ark, illustrated by Sue O'Loughlin, Ashton Scholastic (Sydney, Australia), 1988.

(Selector) *Stories to Share,* illustrated by S. Laroche, Hodder & Stoughton, 1988.

Christmas Fun Book, illustrated by Shirley Peters, Ellsyd (Chippendale, New South Wales), 1988.

Mostly Me, illustrated by S. Peters, Hodder & Stoughton, 1989.

(With Donna Bailey) *We Live in Australia,* illustrated by Gill Tomblin, Macmillan, 1988, published as *Australia,* Steck-Vaughn (Austin, TX), 1990.

My Mum's Afraid of Lions, illustrated by Astra Lacis, Hodder & Stoughton, 1990.

Little Bill Bandicoot: Rhymes and Songs for Australian Children, illustrated by S. Laroche, Lothian, 1992.

The Screaming Demon Ghostie, illustrated by David Cox, Omnibus Dipper (Norwood, South Australia), 1992.

Off to School!: Seven Jumping-Happy Stories, illustrated by Pat Reynolds, Omnibus, 1993.

Grey Cat Magic, illustrated by Margaret Power, Omnibus, 1993.

Pink Stinks, illustrated by V. Kitanov, Angus and Robertson, 1993.

A Day with May Gibbs at Nutcote, illustrated by S. Laroche, Margaret Hamilton (Sydney, Australia), 1993.

Greener Than an Emerald, illustrated by Vilma Cencic, Margaret Hamilton, 1993.

The Flying Damper, University of Queensland Press (St. Lucia, Australia), 1994.

Mamie, Also Known as May Gibbs: A Biography, The May Gibbs Society (Huntleys Pt., New South Wales), 1994.

Nose Trouble, illustrated by Timothy Ide, Omnibus, 1994.

Aboard the Nancy Lee, illustrated by David Cox, Omnibus, 1996.

Favourite Live Thing, University of Queensland Press, 1996.

Ali Baba and the Forty Thieves, illustrated by Di Wu, Margaret Hamilton, 1997.

The Bush Jumper, illustrated by Ali Beck, ABC Books for the Australian Broadcasting Corporation (Sydney, Australia), 1998.

Contributor of scripts to Australian Broadcasting Commission Education Programmes.

Adaptations

Many of the stories from the collection, *Tell Me a Tale,* appeared on *Play School* for Australian television and in a radio program called *Kindergarten of the Air.*

Sidelights

Jean Chapman is known for her books about cats, as well as works that celebrate fairy tales and oral traditions both from around the world and specifically from her native land of Australia. Chapman, the youngest of three daughters, grew up during World War II, when her country was at war for six years with Nazi Germany and the Japanese in the Pacific. By the age of twelve she had decided to become a writer. For a long time she did not know for sure what she would write about, but as a grown woman with a child, she reached a decision: "By luck more than anything else," she once told *SATA,* "I found that I was comfortable writing for young children." Thus while working for the Australian Broadcasting Commission Education Programmes, she continued to write. "I find writing a love-hate thing," she said. "It's an addiction."

Tell Me a Tale: Stories, Songs, and Things to Do, highlights Chapman's comfort with her child audience. Full of suggestions for finger-plays, games, and various methods of participation, this well-received collection includes traditional tales, poems, and songs. Many of the book's stories were adapted for television and radio. Of *Tell Me a Tale,* Margery Fisher in *Growing Point* wrote, "This is the most lively and imaginative of the many recent books offered for infant classroom, playschool or

home." The following year, Chapman followed up that book with *Tell Me Another Tale: Stories, Verses, Songs and Things to Do.* Many of the tales she used were traditional ones, such as Cinderella and Red Riding Hood, and these she combined with activities such as cooking hot dogs. "A pleasing book for the family," concluded a reviewer in *Junior Bookshelf.*

The Sugar Plum Christmas Book, through a series of poems, stories, carols, and crafts depicting Christmas in a variety of countries, focuses on many children's favorite time of year. Patricia Homer of *School Library Journal* suggested that American children might find the large number of British expressions, or "Briticisms," a bit difficult in places, but ended her review by describing the "overall feel of the book" as "one of warmth and gaiety." In similar fashion, *Pancakes and Painted Eggs: A Book for Easter and All the Days of the Year* celebrates Easter, and includes such activities as baking a rabbit cake in honor of the Easter Bunny. Also included are Easter poems and other pieces by notable writers such as William Blake, Samuel Taylor Coleridge, Christina Rossetti, and Oscar Wilde. "On the whole," pronounced Homer in *School Library Journal,* "this is a good collection of Easter treats."

Chapman has indulged her love of cats in a number of books such as *The Wish Cat, Moon-Eyes, Velvet Paws and Whiskers,* and *Cat Will Rhyme with Hat. Moon-Eyes,* described by a reviewer in *Bulletin of the Center for Children's Books* as "a scrawny, half-feral cat," is one of thousands of strays who live in the ancient Forum in Rome. The story depicts the cat's Christmas adventures as she steals food and hides in a church, where a kind priest gives her a home. *Velvet Paws and Whiskers* contains twenty-four short stories, songs, and activities about cats, along with poems. Another of Chapman's cat compilations, *Cat Will Rhyme with Hat,* is, in the words of *Booklist's* Carolyn Phelan, "a fine collection of cat poems." Among the writers represented in *Cat Will Rhyme with Hat* are Mark Twain, T. S. Eliot, and J. R. R. Tolkien. "Readers need not love cats to enjoy these sixty-one poems about them," wrote *School Library Journal's* Judy Greenfield, who called the book "a good read-aloud."

Chapman turned in a somewhat different direction with *Capturing the Golden Bird: The Young Hans Christian Andersen,* for which she went to Andersen's native Denmark to research the life of the man who wrote such classic tales as "The Ugly Duckling" and "The Little Mermaid." A reviewer in *Junior Bookshelf* observed that other writers had told Andersen's life story for children, "but none, I think, has handled the material more succinctly and engagingly than Jean Chapman." The book's concentration, the reviewer continued, is on Andersen's childhood of poverty and indirection, "which [is] so much more interesting and important than the years of fame." *Capturing the Golden Bird* also includes ten of Andersen's most famous tales, each with a short critical essay and bibliographic notes by the author.

Chapman continued to write and publish fiction, such as *My Mum's Afraid of Lions.* Katie, the heroine, has an active imagination, and the six stories contained in the volume follow her through a variety of adventures. For instance, when she is at home sick, missing her friends, she causes a lion on television to come into her room. A *Junior Bookshelf* reviewer called these "charming and apparently artless little tales," going on to describe Chapman's character portrayals as "full of affection without a trace of sentimentality."

In *Little Bill Bandicoot: Rhymes and Songs for Australian Children,* Chapman presented a variety of Australian poems set to music, along with dramatic accompaniment so that children could act out the songs. "This is an attractive book which provides a linguistically helpful collection for use with children," wrote Hugo McCann in *Magpies.* Chapman again experimented with new topics in *Greener Than an Emerald,* which portrays the life of a boy isolated on a tropical island, with a seagull as his only companion. By contrast, *Favourite Live Thing* offers plenty of human interaction as two brothers contend with a summer visit from Nonna, who comes from Italy. Annette Dale-Meiklejohn in *Magpies* called *Favourite Live Thing* "a delightful tale of cross-generational and cross-cultural relationships."

Despite her many topics, Chapman has returned regularly to books about cats, of which *Grey Cat Magic* is an example. Young Kim is bored and lonely because his grandfather tends to fall asleep every afternoon, but when "the little grey cat" comes into his life, everything changes. Moira Robinson of *Magpies* observed that Chapman "writes as though she were in the room telling the story," and as evidence quoted the following: "As soon as Kim edged closer, she [the cat] darted off. Gone, just like that. Into the geraniums!" Robinson called the book "as warm and comforting as crumpets on a winter's afternoon."

Works Cited

Review of *Capturing the Golden Bird, Junior Bookshelf,* April, 1988, p. 98.

Dale-Meiklejohn, Annette, review of *Favourite Live Thing, Magpies,* September, 1996, pp. 31-32.

Fisher, Margery, review of *Tell Me a Tale, Growing Point,* November, 1975, p. 2751.

Greenfield, Judy, review of *Cat Will Rhyme with Hat, School Library Journal,* April, 1987, p. 92.

Homer, Patricia, review of *Pancakes and Painted Eggs, School Library Journal,* April, 1983, p. 111.

Homer, Patricia, review of *The Sugar-Plum Christmas Book, School Library Journal,* August, 1983, pp. 62-63.

McCann, Hugo, review of *Little Billy Bandicoot, Magpies,* September, 1992, p. 24.

Review of *Moon-Eyes, Bulletin of the Center for Children's Books,* October, 1980, p. 28.

Review of *My Mum's Afraid of Lions, Junior Bookshelf,* October, 1990, p. 228.

Phelan, Carolyn, review of *Cat Will Rhyme with Hat, Booklist,* February 15, 1987, p. 894.

Robinson, Moira, review of *Grey Cat Magic, Magpies,* September, 1993, p. 28.

Review of *Tell Me Another Tale, Junior Bookshelf,* August, 1977, p. 215.

For More Information See

BOOKS

Adelaide, Debra, *Australian Women Writers,* Pandora (London), 1988.

Helbig, Alethea K. and Agnes Regan Perkins, *Dictionary of Children's Fiction from Australia, Canada, India, New Zealand, and Selected African Countries,* Greenwood (Westport, CT), 1984.

PERIODICALS

Australian Book Review, September, 1996, pp. 60+.

Booklist, February 15, 1983, p. 774; October 15, 1988, p. 420.

Junior Bookshelf, August, 1980, pp. 186-87.

Magpies, July, 1994, p. 28.

School Library Journal, September, 1980, p. 57; March, 1983, p. 172; July, 1990, pp. 66-67.

Times Educational Supplement, June 6, 1986, p. 54; August 1, 1986, p. 21.

—Sketch by Judson Knight

*   *   *

CLEMENTS, Andrew 1949-
(Andrew Elborn)

Personal

Born May 29, 1949, in Camden, NJ; son of William Denney, Jr. (an insurance executive) and Doris (Kruse) Clements; married Rebecca Pierpont (an actress and homemaker), December 16, 1972; children: John, Nathaniel, George, Charles. *Education:* Northwestern University, B.A. in English literature, 1971; National Louis University, M.A., in elementary education, 1972.

Addresses

Home—Westborough, MA.

Career

Writer, editor, and educator. Sunset Ridge School, Northfield, IL, fourth grade teacher, 1972-74; Wilmette Junior High School, Wilmette, IL, eighth grade teacher, 1974-77; New Trier High School, Winnetka, IL, English teacher, 1977-79. Allen D. Bragdon Publishers, New York, NY, editor, 1980-82; Alphabet Press, Natick, MA, sales and marketing manager, editor, 1982-85; Keller Graduate School of Management, Chicago, IL, director, 1985-87; Picture Book Studio, Ltd., Saxonville, MA, vice-president and editorial director, 1987-93; Christian Science Publishing Society, Boston, MA, editor, 1997-98. Served on executive board of the Children's Book Council, New York, 1983-85; frequent speaker in schools and at writing and education conferences.

Awards, Honors

New York Public Library "100 Titles for Reading and Sharing" list, 1996, Fanfare Book, *Horn Book,* Parents' Choice Honor Book, Christopher Award, and Judy Lopez Memorial Honor Book Award, all 1997, Great Stone Face Book Award, 1997-98, and Chicago Public Library's Best of the Best list, Best Kids Books, *Family Fun Magazine,* and Rhode Island Children's Book Award, 1998, all for *Frindle. Frindle* was also nominated for nearly thirty other awards, including the William Allen White Children's Book Award and the Dorothy Canfield Fisher Book Award.

Writings

FOR CHILDREN

Bird Adalbert, Picture Book Studio, 1985.
Big Al (miniature book), illustrated by Yoshi, Picture Book Studios, 1987.
Santa's Secret Helper, illustrated by Debrah Santini, Picture Book Studio, 1990.
(As Andrew Elborn) *Noah and the Ark and the Animals,* illustrated by Ivan Gantschev, Picture Book Studio, 1991.
Temple Cat, illustrated by Alan Marks, Picture Book Studio, 1991, reissued with pictures by Kate Kiesler, Clarion, 1996.

Andrew Clements

Mother Earth's Counting Book, illustrated by Lonni Sue Johnson, Picture Book Studio, 1992.
Billy and the Bad Teacher, illustrated by Elivia Savadier, Picture Book Studio, 1992.
Who Owns the Cow?, illustrated by Joan Landis, Clarion, 1995.
Bright Christmas: An Angel Remembers, illustrated by Kate Kiesler, Clarion, 1996.
Frindle (a middle grades novel), illustrated by Brian Selznick, Simon and Schuster, 1996.
(Adaptor) *Philipp's Birthday Book,* illustrated by Hanne Turk, North-South Books, 1996.
Riff's BeBop Book, Simon and Schuster, 1996.
Real Monsters Go for the Mold!, illustrated by Matthew Stoddart, Simon and Schuster, 1997.
Things That Go EEK on Halloween, illustrated by George Ulrich, Simon and Schuster, 1997.
Real Monsters Stage Fright, illustrated by Matthew Stoddart, Simon and Schuster, 1997.
Music Time, Any Time!, illustrated by Tom Leigh, Simon and Schuster, 1997.
Double Trouble in Walla Walla, illustrated by Salvatore Murdocca, Millbrook Press, 1997.
Workshop, illustrated by David Wisniewski, Clarion, 1998.
Gromble's Haunted Halloween, Simon and Schuster, 1998.
Hey Dad, Could I Borrow Your Hammer?, illustrated by Jackie Snider, Millbrook Press, 1999.
The Landry News (a middle grades novel), Simon and Schuster, 1999.

READING PROGRAM BOOKS FOR SCHOOLS

Karen's Island, Houghton Mifflin, 1995.
Three Wishes for Buster, Houghton Mifflin, 1995.
Bill Picket: An American Original, Texas Style, Houghton Mifflin, 1996.
Hurricane Andrew, Houghton Mifflin, 1998.
Ham and Eggs for Jack, Houghton Mifflin, 1998.
Life in the Desert, Steck-Vaughn, 1998.
Desert Treasure, illustrated by Wayne Anthony Still, Steck-Vaughn, 1998.
Inventors: Making Things Better, Steck-Vaughn, 1998.
Milo's Great Invention, illustrated by Johansen Newman, Steck-Vaughn, 1998.

Also the translator and/or adaptor of more than a dozen picture books for Picture Book Studio and North-South Books, including *Where Is Mr. Mole?, The Christmas Teddy Bear, Brave as a Tiger, The Beast and the Boy, Little Pig, Bigger Trouble, A Dog's Best Friend,* and *Where the Moon Lives.*

Work in Progress

Circus Family Dog, a picture book for Clarion, and *Razzle Dazzled in Walla Walla,* a picture book for Millbrook Press. Clements is also writing a four-book series of middle grades novels for Simon and Schuster.

Sidelights

Andrew Clements has all the bases covered in the field of children's books. An avid reader as a child, he later taught the joys of reading to students in elementary and

The cow gives the milk that she makes by eating grass.

Clements gives young readers insight into the complicated concept of ownership when he lists the various people having some claim to a farmer's cow. (From Who Owns the Cow?, *illustrated by Joan Landis.)*

high school, then went on to the world of publishing, acquiring, editing, marketing, and developing quality children's books for several publishing houses. In 1985, he decided to contribute his own work to that market, beginning with his first picture book, *Bird Adalbert.* The author of the award-winning *Frindle,* a book about the power of words that *Kirkus Reviews* called "something of a classic," Clements has also attracted a wide readership for his picture books, including the popular *Big Al, Santa's Secret Helper, Temple Cat, Bright Christmas,* and his "Real Monsters" books.

"I've got a special place in my heart for libraries and librarians," Clements told *Something about the Author* (*SATA*). "As a kindergartner in Oaklyn, New Jersey, I confess that I was something of a showoff. I was already a good reader, and I didn't mind who knew about it." With parents who were compulsive readers themselves and who passed on the love of books to their children, it was no surprise at home that Clements should be such an

early reader. At school, however, it was a different story. On his first trip to the school library, Clements chose a thick book on myths. The next day he asked his teacher if he could take it back to the library. "'Is it too hard, dear?' she asked sympathetically," Clements recalled. The teacher's eyebrows shot up when Clements informed her that it was not the difficulty of the book that was the problem. He had already finished it and wanted more. "That event created for me an open invitation to head to the library just about any old time I wanted to. And the librarian was a gem. She kept me well stocked."

Clements made his way through the classics, from A. A. Milne to Robert Louis Stevenson, and from Robin Hood to King Arthur. Later loves included Sherlock Holmes and the Hardy Boys, *Robinson Crusoe, The Swiss Family Robinson,* works by Dumas and Jack London, as well as adventure stories and biographies. "I loved owning books. And I will always love that librarian at my elementary school, because she made me feel like I was the owner of every book. That's one of the greatest things about reading a book—read it, and you own it forever."

Clements attended Northwestern University and then earned a master's degree in education at National Louis University. For seven years thereafter, he taught school, both at the grade school level and high school. "I liked it," Clements told *SATA*. "The kids and I laughed a lot. I enjoyed the hundreds of little conversations every day, the running jokes—I even liked the noise and the craziness of a Friday afternoon right before Christmas vacation. And I loved reading good books with kids— the kids at school and also the four boys my wife and I had at home. As a teacher, it was a thrill to read a book aloud, and see a whole class listen so carefully to every word, dying to know what would happen next. And I was amazed at the wonderful discussions a good book can spark. Good books make good things happen in real life. They can make a big difference. So when I was given the chance to start writing for children, I jumped at it."

That chance began, initially, as an editor of children's books at various publishers, including Alphabet Press and Picture Book Studio, where he not only acquired titles but also helped translate and adapt European picture books for the American market. "I didn't start writing books until I was about thirty-five years old," Clements told *SATA*. "But I began writing a long time before that. And the way I really got started writing was by reading. Before too long I found myself reading something good and saying to myself, 'I wish I had written that!' I think the more good books you read, the better you learn what good writing sounds like and feels

Clements's book, with glow-in-the-dark stickers, is based on characters from the popular "Real Monsters" animated television program. (Cover illustration by Don Cassity.)

like. Every good writer I know started off as a good reader."

One of Clements's most popular titles is his second picture book, *Big Al,* a "simple story about the need for friendship," as Gratia Banta described the book in *School Library Journal.* Big Al of the title is a rather ugly and scary-looking fish who desperately tries to be liked by the smaller fish. When Big Al saves the lives of the little fish, he accomplishes his mission, becoming their fast friend. Noting the illustrator Yoshi's use of silk batik and painting, Banta wrote that the "magnificence" of the illustrations matched "Clements' international story of friendship.... The book offers a welcome sense of something other than western culture."

Other picture books followed. *Santa's Secret Helper* was the first of several Clements Christmas books to date. Illustrated by Debrah Santini, *Santa's Secret Helper* features Mrs. Santa as a stand-in for her exhausted husband, dressed just like Santa and filling stockings with great care. Back at the North Pole, she gets a big hug from her husband. "This story is appealing in its simplicity," noted *Booklist's* Ilene Cooper, who gave high praise to the artwork which keeps the helper's identity a secret until the very end. Another holiday title is Clements's *Bright Christmas: An Angel Remembers,* the story of the Nativity told from the point of view of an angel. *Publishers Weekly* remarked that in "the voice of a seasoned spinner of yarns, Clements imagines a heavenly perspective on the birth of Jesus." Writing in *Booklist,* Shelley Townsend-Hudson described the book as a "lovely blend of words and pictures" which "attempt to explain the idea of eternity...." *School Library Journal* noted that the book was told "in spare, tempered, and reverent prose," and concluded that *Bright Christmas* "is a fine combination of text and illustration that tells a familiar story."

Clements has explored themes ranging from strengthening counting skills to accepting differences to the concept of ownership in his ambitious picture books. A simple task such as learning how to count is transformed by Clements into an exploration "of the diverse wonders of our planet," as Steven Engelfried described *Mother Earth's Counting Book* in a *School Library Journal* review. The seven continents and four oceans of this planet all figure into Clements's counting scheme. *Billy and the Bad Teacher* tells a story of acceptance that "will have students and teachers rolling out of their chairs," according to Jeanne Marie Clancy in *School Library Journal.* Neat and compulsive Billy is initially horrified when he gets the unorthodox Mr. Adams for his new teacher, but slowly comes to love this teacher who makes long division fun and reads *The Swiss Family Robinson* to the class each day. "The story makes a nice point about accepting the foibles of others without hitting readers over the head with it," concluded Clancy.

The concept of ownership comes under scrutiny in *Who Owns the Cow?,* a story about a cow, a farmer, and the many people who come into contact with both. A little

Fifth-grader Nick makes up a new word to irritate his language-arts teacher, but after the neologism has taken hold years later, he finds his teacher has been on his side all along. (From Frindle, *illustrated by Brian Selznick.)*

girl thinks of the cow when she hears its bell; a milkman earns a living by delivering its milk; an artist paints it. So who really owns it? While several reviewers felt this question of ownership might be too philosophical for most young readers, Deborah Stevenson of the *Bulletin of the Center for Children's Books* maintained that *Who Owns the Cow?* is an "offbeat book with an appealing style" that "will puzzle some and become the favorite of others." *Horn Book Guide* called the book "almost ecological in spirit," and a "thoughtful consideration of ordinary cause-and-effect relationships." Relationships also figure in *Temple Cat,* the story of an ancient Egyptian feline who is the lord of a temple but is tired of being pampered. The cat longs simply to be loved, and finds such love in the arms of two children after it has run away. Susan Middleton, writing in *School Library Journal,* asserted that "this endearing tale is sure to find favor wherever cat stories are in demand," while a *Kirkus Reviews* critic remarked that "Clements pens a tale for consummate cat enthusiasts or lovers of antiquity."

A further adventure in the picture book format is *Double Trouble in Walla Walla.* Young Lulu is sent to the principal's office when she cannot stop speaking in a sort of hyphenated slang, in a book that Barbara McGinn in *School Library Journal* dubbed "side-splitting fun." "In this breathlessly verbose tale, a rash of compound nonsense words infects an elementary school," commented a *Publishers Weekly* reviewer, who concluded that "children with a fondness for wordplay may delight in this dizzying romp."

More such wordplay is served up in Clements's first novel for middle graders, *Frindle.* The book was inspired by comments Clements once made when talking to students at a Rhode Island school, "teaching them a little about the way words work," as Clements told *SATA.* "I was trying to explain to them how words only mean what we decide they mean. They didn't believe me when I pointed to a fat dictionary and told them that ordinary people like them and like me had made up all the words in that book—and that new words get made up all the time." To illustrate his point, Clements pulled a pen from his pocket and told the students that they could change the name of this instrument from pen to anything they made up. Clements chose a made-up word, "frindle," and challenged students to start calling it by that name instead of "pen" to see if such a name would stick. "The kids loved that story, and for a couple of years I told that same story every time I went to talk at a school or a library. Then one day in 1990 as I was sifting through my life, looking for a story idea, I wondered what would happen if a kid started using a new word, and other kids really liked it, but his English teacher didn't. So the idea for the book was born."

In the novel, Nick, who always stays one step ahead of his teachers, can usually manage to sidetrack the teacher from assigning homework. However, when he meets Mrs. Granger, his new fifth-grade language-arts teacher, this simple ruse breaks down. To irritate her, he invents the word "frindle" for pen and convinces other kids in the school to use the neologism. Soon the word spreads to the city, the state, the nation, and ten years later "frindle" has even made it into the dictionary. And only then does Nick realize that Mrs. Granger has secretly been rooting for him and his new word all the time. "The chesslike sparring between the gifted Nicholas and his crafty teacher is enthralling," commented a *Kirkus Reviews* critic, who concluded that "this is a captivating tale—one to press upon children, and one they'll be passing among themselves." A *Publishers Weekly* commentator remarked that "dictionary lovers will cotton to this mild classroom fantasy, while readers who have a hard time believing that one person could invent a word out of thin air will be surprised to learn that the word 'quiz' was invented the same way." *Booklist*'s Kay Weisman concluded her review of *Frindle* by noting that the book is sure to be "popular with a wide range of readers [and] will make a great read-aloud as well." In a starred review, Elizabeth S. Watson of *Horn Book* remarked that Clements "has created a fresh imaginative plot that will have readers smiling all the way through, if not laughing out loud." Award committees agreed with the critics: *Frindle* garnered more than thirty award nominations, and won the 1997 Christopher Award.

Clements continues his commitment to the world of children's books with classroom appearances and the writing and/or illustrating of early readers, picture books, and more novels for middle graders. "There has been a lot of talk in recent years about the decline of reading," he told *SATA*, "the overpowering influence of the television and multi-media screens, even a national descent into illiteracy. Everyone is so upset when these ideas are voiced, and everyone feels sure that reading and books are important—but why? Apart from the basic skill of functional or task-related reading, why is there a universal conviction that books and literature are indispensable? I think it's because when we read, we're in charge. That's probably the most significant difference between pagetime and screentime. When we read, we decide when, where, how long, and about what. One of the few places on earth that it is still possible to experience an instant sense of freedom and privacy is anywhere we open up a good book and begin to read."

Works Cited

Banta, Gratia, review of *Big Al, School Library Journal,* June, 1989, p. 86.

Review of *Bright Christmas: An Angel Remembers, Publishers Weekly,* September 30, 1996, p. 90.

Review of *Bright Christmas: An Angel Remembers, School Library Journal,* October, 1996, p. 34.

Clancy, Jeanne Marie, review of *Billy and the Bad Teacher, School Library Journal,* January, 1994, p. 87.

Cooper, Ilene, review of *Santa's Secret Helper, Booklist,* December 15, 1990, pp. 860-61.

Review of *Double Trouble in Walla Walla, Publishers Weekly,* October 13, 1997, p. 74.

Engelfried, Steven, review of *Mother Earth's Counting Book, School Library Journal,* June, 1993, p. 72.

Review of *Frindle, Kirkus Reviews,* July 1, 1996, p. 965.

Review of *Frindle, Publishers Weekly,* July 15, 1996, p. 74.

McGinn, Barbara, review of *Double Trouble in Walla Walla, School Library Journal,* January, 1998, p. 81.

Middleton, Susan, review of *Temple Cat, School Library Journal,* March, 1996, p. 167.

Stevenson, Deborah, review of *Who Owns the Cow?, Bulletin of the Center for Children's Books,* October, 1995, p. 49.

Review of *Temple Cat, Kirkus Reviews,* December 15, 1995, p. 1768.

Townsend-Hudson, Shelley, review of *Bright Christmas: An Angel Remembers, Booklist,* September 1, 1996, p. 136.

Watson, Elizabeth S., review of *Frindle, Horn Book,* November-December, 1996, p. 732.

Weisman, Kay, review of *Frindle, Booklist,* September 1, 1996, p. 125.

Review of *Who Owns the Cow?, Horn Book Guide,* spring, 1996, p. 23.

For More Information See

PERIODICALS

Booklist, February 15, 1985, p. 842; December 15, 1996, p. 734.

Bulletin of the Center for Children's Books, February, 1996, p. 186; October, 1996, pp. 51-52.

Kirkus Reviews, July 1, 1995, p. 944; October 1, 1996, p. 1475.

New York Times Book Review, March 16, 1997, p. 26.

Publishers Weekly, September 14, 1994, p. 31; October 6, 1997, p. 50; April 27, 1998, p. 66.

School Library Journal, July, 1990, p. 59; October, 1994, p. 39; December, 1995, p. 73; November, 1996, p. 87; July, 1998, p. 74.

—*Sketch by J. Sydney Jones*

* * *

COOPER, Ann (Catherine) 1939-

Personal

Born March 18, 1939, in Cumbria, England; daughter of Norman (a teacher) and Cora (a teacher; maiden name, Smith) Dawson; married John Cooper (a physics professor), May 5, 1962; children: Catherine, Michael, Patrick. *Education:* London University, B.Sc. (with honors),

Ann Cooper

Cooper's informational book, from the "Wild Wonders" series on animals and their habitats, features inhabitants and plant life of deciduous forests of the eastern United States. (Cover illustration by Dorothy Emerling.)

1960; attended University of Colorado, 1966-1992. *Hobbies and other interests:* Reading, hiking, camping, travel, photography, and birdwatching.

Addresses

Home and Office—2839 3rd St., Boulder, CO 80304. *Electronic Mail*—wordswild@aol.com.

Career

Bedford College, University of London, and Hammersmith Hospital, London, England, medical research, 1960-65; homemaker, 1965-84; Prosound Music, Boulder, CO, computing, 1984-86; writer, 1988—. Worked as a volunteer teacher in various locations in Colorado. *Member:* Colorado Authors League, Society of Children's Book Writers and Illustrators.

Awards, Honors

Colorado Book Award, 1992, and Parents' Choice Magazine selection, both for *Eagles: Hunters of the Sky;* Parent's Choice Award for *Bats: Swift Shadows in the Twilight.*

Writings

FOR CHILDREN

(With Ann Armstrong and Carol Kampert) *The Wildwatch Book: Ideas, Activities, and Projects for Exploring Colorado's Front Range,* Denver Museum of Natural History and Rinehart, 1990.

Eagles: Hunters of the Sky, Denver Museum of Natural History and Rinehart, 1992.

Bats: Swift Shadows in the Twilight, illustrated by Gail Kohler Opsahl and Marjorie C. Leggitt, Denver Museum of Natural History and Rinehart, 1994.

Owls: On Silent Wings, Denver Museum of Natural History and Rinehart, 1994.

Above the Treeline, illustrated by Dorothy Emerling, Denver Museum of Natural History and Rinehart, 1996.

In the Forest, illustrated by Dorothy Emerling, Denver Museum of Natural History and Rinehart, 1996.

Along the Seashore, illustrated by Dorothy Emerling, Denver Museum of Natural History and Rinehart, 1997.

In the Desert, illustrated by Dorothy Emerling, Denver Museum of Natural History and Rinehart, 1997.

Around the Pond, illustrated by Dorothy Emerling, Denver Museum of Natural History and Rinehart, 1998.

Work in Progress

In the City for Denver Museum of Natural History and Rinehart; nature activity series "Critter Clues"; *Marsh Magic,* a book of poetry for children.

Sidelights

Ann Cooper told *SATA:* "I write out of a passionate concern for all things wild. I'd like to think my books spread a little nature-mania and recruit another generation to take care of earth.

"My love affair with nature began long ago. My father was an avid naturalist. He understood when I got sidetracked by primroses and toads on the way to school. Coming to a new country was a revelation. I wanted to learn everything about the unfamiliar animals and plants. I've spent the last thirty years doing just that on the edge of the Rocky Mountains—now home.

"Writing came when my children were grown and gone and I had time to test a new career. It was a lucky choice that opened up a world of adventure—from mist-netting bats at the bottom of a desert canyon to tramping wild beaches in all weather. But I am an undisciplined writer, I'd much rather spend all my time outdoors—watching."

In *Owls: On Silent Wings,* Cooper brings to young readers her wonder and passion for the natural world. The book displays a wide array of information, stories, and activities for budding nature lovers. Noting the wealth and variety of material in a review for *Appraisal,* librarian Patti Sinclair described *Owls* as a "mini-teaching unit." The book identifies various owls and their habitats, presenting the ecological concerns created by logging in old-growth forests. The reader learns the facts and fiction about the winged creature through scientific information, pictures, Native American stories, and hands-on activities. In her *Appraisal* review, Nancy Payne praised this "colorful scientific writing" for meeting the computer-age challenge to be more "creative and interactive." Ellen W. Chu highly recommended *Owls* in her review for *Science Books & Films* and credits Cooper's book with being the needed stimulus for "children ... to go out and find the real animals and perhaps experience the childhood sense of wonder so necessary to sustaining owls."

Cooper once again presents science as a creative hands-on experience in her award-winning *Bats: Swift Shadows in the Twilight.* Factual information rests side by side with folktales, and readers learn hands-on about a bat's habitat by making a cave diorama. Timothy C. Williams praised the book for its accuracy and clarity in his review for *Science Books and Films,* calling it an "unusual and interesting way to present biological and conservation issues."

Advising readers that you can't judge a book by its cover in her review for *School Library Journal,* Helen Rosenberg found *In the Forest* "chock full of surprises." She especially noted the life-size paw prints superimposed over text, a treasure map of the forest floor, and a "forest sandwich" revealing the layers of animals and habitats. Cooper gives short descriptions of many animals that inhabit the forest ecosystem, including bats, owls, and deer. A *Kirkus Reviews* critic described the book as "effective and charming."

While similar in format to *In the Forest, Above the Treeline* takes place in the alpine tundra of the southern Rocky Mountains. Paw prints mark the snow while the author challenges the reader to identify them. A treasure map on the inside cover shows the different locales in the tundra. Later in the text, numerous inhabitants are identified and their living spaces are explored. Praising Cooper's book as a "learning experience," *Science Books & Films* contributor Robert Leo Smith described Cooper's writing as "what good natural history writing for young people should be: intriguing, accurate, challenging, actively illustrated, well presented, and cleverly designed."

Works Cited

Chu, Ellen W., review of *Owls: On Silent Wings, Science Books & Films,* January-February, 1995, p. 21.

Review of *In the Forest, Kirkus Reviews,* May 1, 1996, p. 686.

Payne, Nancy, review of *Owls: On Silent Wings, Appraisal,* winter, 1995, p. 20.

Rosenberg, Helen, review of *In the Forest, School Library Journal,* August, 1996, p. 134.

Sinclair, Patti, review of *Owls: On Silent Wings, Appraisal,* winter, 1995, p. 19.

Smith, Robert Leo, review of *Above the Treeline, Science Books & Films,* January-February, 1997, p. 18.

Williams, Timothy C., review of *Bats: Swift Shadows in the Twilight, Science Books & Films,* January-February, 1995, pp. 20-21.

For More Information See

PERIODICALS

Bloomsbury Review, July, 1997, p. 21.

Instructor, May, 1996, p. 18.

Kirkus Reviews, May 15, 1997, p. 798.

Kliatt, November, 1994, p. 43.

Parents Choice, April, 1994, p. 25.

School Library Journal, August, 1996, p. 134; August, 1997, p. 146.

*   *   *

COOPER, Susan (Mary) 1935-

Personal

Born May 23, 1935, in Burnham, Buckinghamshire, England; came to the United States in 1963; daughter of

John Richard (an employee of the Great Western Railway) and Ethel May (a teacher; maiden name, Field) Cooper; married Nicholas J. Grant (a scientist and college professor), August 3, 1963 (divorced, 1983); married Hume Cronyn (an actor and playwright), 1996; children (first marriage): Jonathan, Katharine; stepchildren: (first marriage) Anne, Bill (died, 1986), Peter; (second marriage) Tandy. *Education:* Somerville College, Oxford University, M.A., 1956. *Hobbies and other interests:* Music, islands.

Addresses

Home—Connecticut and New York City. *Office*—c/o Margaret K. McElderry, Simon & Schuster, 15 Columbus Circle, New York, NY 10023.

Career

Author, playwright, screenwriter, and journalist. *Sunday Times,* London, England, reporter and feature writer, 1956-63. *Member:* Society of Authors (United Kingdom), Authors League of America, Authors Guild, Writers Guild of America.

Awards, Honors

Horn Book Honor List citation for *Over Sea, Under Stone; Horn Book* Honor List and American Library Association (ALA) Notable Book citations, both 1970, both for *Dawn of Fear; Boston Globe—Horn Book* Award, Carnegie Medal runner-up, and ALA Notable Book citation, all 1973, and Newbery Award Honor Book, 1974, all for *The Dark Is Rising;* ALA Notable Book citation, for *Greenwitch;* Newbery Medal, Tir na N'og Award (Wales), Carnegie Medal commendation, *Horn Book* Honor List, and ALA Notable Book citation, all 1976, all for *The Grey King;* Tir na N'og Award, 1978, for *Silver on the Tree;* Parents' Choice Award (text and illustration), 1983, for *The Silver Cow;* Janusz Korczak Award, B'nai B'rith, and Universe Award runner-up, both 1984, both for *Seaward;* Christopher Award, Humanitas Prize, Writers Guild of America Award, and Emmy Award nomination from Academy of Television Arts and Sciences, all 1984, all for *The Dollmaker;* Emmy Award nomination, 1987, and Writers Guild of America Award, 1988, for teleplay *Foxfire; Horn Book* Honor List citation, 1987, for *The Selkie Girl;* Janusz Korczak Award, B'nai B'rith, 1989, for *Seaward.*

Writings

FOR YOUNG ADULTS; "THE DARK IS RISING" SEQUENCE; FANTASY

Over Sea, Under Stone, illustrated by Margery Gill, Jonathan Cape (London), 1965, Harcourt, 1966.
The Dark Is Rising, illustrated by Alan E. Cober, Atheneum, 1973, illustrated by Lianne Payne, Puffin (London), 1994.
Greenwitch, Atheneum, 1974.
The Grey King, illustrated by Michael Heslop, Atheneum, 1975.

Susan Cooper

Silver on the Tree, Atheneum, 1977, Chatto and Windus, 1977.

OTHER FICTION; FOR YOUNG PEOPLE

Dawn of Fear (historical fiction), illustrations by Margery Gill, Harcourt, 1970, Chatto and Windus, 1972.
Seaward (fantasy), Atheneum, 1983.
(Contributor) *When I Was Your Age,* edited by Amy Ehrlich, Candlewick Press, 1996.
(With Margaret Mahy, Uri Orlev, and Tjomg Khing) *Don't Read This! And Other Tales of the Unnatural* (short stories), Front Street, 1998.

FOR CHILDREN; FANTASIES

Jethro and the Jumbie, illustrated by Ashley Bryan, Atheneum, 1979.
The Boggart, McElderry, 1992.
The Boggart and the Monster, McElderry, 1997.

RETELLINGS; ALL ILLUSTRATED BY WARWICK HUTTON

The Silver Cow: A Welsh Tale, Atheneum, 1983.
The Selkie Girl, McElderry, 1986.
Tam Lin, McElderry, 1991.

PICTURE BOOKS

Matthew's Dragon, illustrated by Jos. A. Smith, McElderry, 1991.
Danny and the Kings, illustrated by Jos. A. Smith, McElderry, 1993.

FOR ADULTS; NONFICTION, EXCEPT AS NOTED

(Contributor) Michael Sissons and Philip French, editors, *The Age of Austerity: 1945-51,* Hodder and Stoughton

(London), 1963, Scribner, 1966. *Mandrake* (science fiction), Jonathan Cape, 1964.

Behind the Golden Curtain: A View of the U.S.A., Hodder and Stoughton, 1965, Scribner, 1966.

(Editor and author of preface) J. B. Priestley, *Essays of Five Decades,* Little, Brown (Boston), 1968.

J. B. Priestley: Portrait of an Author, Heinemann (London), 1970, Harper, 1971.

Dreams and Wishes: Essays on Writing for Children, McElderry, 1996.

PLAYS

(With Hume Cronyn) *Foxfire* (play; first produced at Stratford, Ontario, 1980; produced on Broadway at Ethel Barrymore Theatre, November 11, 1982; also see below), Samuel French, 1983.

(With Cronyn) *The Dollmaker* (teleplay; adaptation of the novel by Harriette Arnow), produced by American Broadcasting Companies, Inc. (ABC), May 13, 1984.

Foxfire (teleplay), produced by Columbia Broadcasting System, Inc. (CBS), December 13, 1987.

To Dance with the White Dog (teleplay), produced by CBS, December 5, 1993.

OTHER

Also author of the teleplay *Dark Encounter,* 1976. Author of introduction to *The Christmas Revels Songbook: In Celebration of the Winter Solstice,* edited by John and Nancy Langstaff, David R. Godine, 1985, also published as *The Christmas Revels Songbook: Carols, Processions, Rounds, Ritual, and Children's Songs in Celebration of the Winter Solstice,* Godine, 1995, and of introduction to *A Revels Garland of Song: In Celebration of Spring, Summer, and Autumn,* edited by John Langstaff, Revels, Inc., 1996. Contributor of concluding essay to *The Phoenix and the Carpet* by E. Nesbit, Dell, 1987, as well as essays to several collections of children's literature criticism. Contributor to numerous magazines and newspapers, including the *Horn Book Magazine,* the *New York Times Book Review, Magpies,* and the *Welsh Review.* Cooper also contributed the narration to the motion picture *George Balanchine's Nutcracker,* Warner Brothers, 1993. Her papers are housed in the Lillian H. Smith collection, Toronto Public Library, Toronto, Ontario.

Adaptations

Cooper's Newbery Medal acceptance speech for *The Grey King* was released as a sound recording by Weston Woods, 1976. *The Dark Is Rising* was released on two audio cassettes by Miller-Brody, 1979, and by Listening Library and Chivers Audio, 1999; *The Silver Cow* was released as a filmstrip in 1985 and as a sound recording in 1986, both by Weston Woods; *The Selkie Girl* was released as a filmstrip and audio cassette, Weston Woods, 1988; *The Boggart* was released on four audio cassettes by the Listening Library, Inc., and Chivers Audio, 1994; *The Boggart and the Monster* was released on three audio cassettes by Listening Library, Inc., and Chivers Audio, 1997.

Work in Progress

Motion-picture adaptations of "The Dark Is Rising" and "The Boggart."

Sidelights

Called "one of the most versatile, popular, and critically acclaimed children's writers of the twentieth century" by Joel D. Chaston in the *Dictionary of Literary Biography,* Cooper is considered an exceptional author for the young whose works—fantasy novels and realistic fiction for young adults and stories, retellings, and picture books for children—reflect her keen insight into human nature, her knowledge of folklore, history, and archeology, and her ability to evoke place with authenticity. Credited with a rich, poetic literary style, she is also well regarded as a writer of fiction, nonfiction, and plays for adults.

Characteristically, Cooper draws on the myths and legends of the British Isles as the basis for her works, and she is often praised for her ability to mesh the real and the fantastic, the ancient and the contemporary. She is best known as the creator of "The Dark Is Rising" sequence, a quintet of epic fantasies for young adults that depicts how a group of modern-day English children become involved in a cosmic battle between good and evil, which Cooper calls the Light and the Dark. As in several of her other books, the sequence features magical experiences that prepare the young protagonists for conflicts that will occur throughout their daily lives. Favorably compared to the fantasies of J. R. R. Tolkien, C. S. Lewis, Ursula K. Le Guin, and Alan Garner, these works are rooted in the mythology of Britain and feature characters from and inspired by Arthurian legend, such as Merlin the great magician and Bran, the son of King Arthur and Guinevere. Cooper is often acknowledged for revealing social concerns within the supernatural events that she depicts. In addition to her pervasive theme of the struggle between good and evil, a theme that the author uses to explore the human potential for both qualities, Cooper addresses such issues as displacement, responsibility and choice, self-awareness, and the coexistence of magic and technology. Although her books include danger, violence, death, and a variety of the manifestations of evil, Cooper is credited with presenting her readers with a positive view of human nature as well as with conclusions that demonstrate the ultimate triumph of good.

Critics laud Cooper as a gifted storyteller and superior craftsman whose works succeed in bringing together the ordinary and the extraordinary while capturing the thoughts and emotions of the young. Writing in *Children's Books and Their Creators,* Anne E. Deifendeifer noted that the "power of her fantasy for children places Cooper firmly among the best of children's authors.... The tremendous scope and intensity of Cooper's work marks her as a modern master of the high-fantasy genre." Commenting on Cooper's "extraordinary prowess as an author of fantasy," *Twentieth-Century Young Adult Writers* contributor Karen Patricia Smith claimed that throughout her books "major themes resurface, allowing the reader to experience and internalize the depth of her commitment to her social ideals as well as to her art." Cooper has been criticized by some reviewers for predictability and use of cliche in some of her books and for unevenness in "The Dark Is Rising" sequence; writing in *School Librarian,* David Rees claimed, "The whole quintet is shallow, relying on a box of magic tricks to disguise the poverty of the author's thinking and imagination." However, most observers view Cooper as the creator of rewarding, fascinating works with great relevance to their audience. Margaret K. McElderry wrote in *Horn Book* that Cooper is "one of the small and very select company of writers who—somehow, somewhere—have been touched by magic; the gift of creation is theirs, the power to bring to life, for ordinary mortals, 'the very best of symbolic high fantasy.' ... Music and song, old tales and legends, prose and poetry, theater and reality, imagination and intellect, power and control, a strong sense of place and

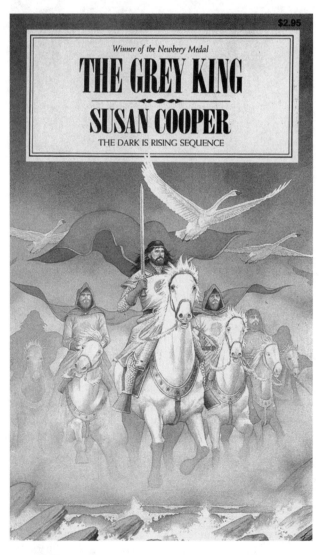

Young Will Stanton fulfills his destiny as an Old One by uncovering the Six Signs of Light necessary to overcome the darkness of evil which is gaining power in the world. (Cover illustration by David Wiesner.)

people both past and present—all are part of the magic that has touched Susan Cooper.... Her journeys add great luster to the world of literature."

Cooper was born in Burnham, Buckinghamshire, an area approximately twenty miles outside of London, to a railwayman and a teacher. In her essay in *Something about the Author Autobiography Series (SAAS),* she described her father John as a gentle person who enjoyed music and drawing and who introduced Susan to traveling. "The trains rushed westward into the big world," Cooper recalled, "and so, in the end, did I, and have seldom stopped traveling since." Her mother Ethel was at "the centre of my life always, until she died. She mattered so much that I don't know how to write about her." Cooper noted that her mother, a teacher, taught her and her brother Roderick "from a head full of poetry and music and high standards, and she and my remarkable high school headmistress between them were the encouraging forces which sent me to Somerville College in the University of Oxford." Roderick Cooper was later to become a popular mystery writer for adults. Cooper noted in *SAAS,* "Where did the writing itself come from—the impulse, the talent? I don't know, of course, but I suspect it may have something to do with my mother's parents, the only grandparents I properly knew." Cooper's grandfather, Frederick Benjamin Field, was a stagestruck Londoner who often took his seven children to the theater and organized elaborate games of charades and dramatic monologues for his grandchildren. He also encouraged young Susan to read his favorite novelists, Dickens, Thackeray, and Wells. Cooper's grandmother, Mary Ellen Davies, was a quiet, loving woman who had come to London at fourteen from the small Welsh village of Aberdovey, a place where Cooper's parents later resided. The Dovey valley, the author wrote, plays "a large part in my books because it has a large part of my heart. Perhaps I am a writer because of my grandmother's Welshness, the Celtic blessing that turns itself often into the words or melody of song."

When Cooper was four years old, World War II broke out in Britain. The war lasted until she was ten. The author has described those years as particularly influential ones. Her parents, Londoners by birth, were affected strongly by the Blitz and its devastation. "[T]hey wanted me to remember," Cooper wrote in *SAAS.* "So I remembered, and years later put my war into a thinly disguised autobiographical novel called *Dawn of Fear.* Unconsciously, I dare say, I have put it into a number of other books as well, for a child raised in wartime is inevitably given a strong sense of Us and Them, the good side (one's own, of course) against the bad. Though I wasn't thinking about Adolf Hitler and his night-bombing Luftwaffe when I began to write fantasies characterising the forces of evil as the Dark, in the shadowy corners of my mind they probably were." By the time she was ten, Cooper had written original plays for a friend's puppet theater, a small illustrated book, and a weekly newspaper. She enjoyed reading, especially the books of E. Nesbit, Arthur Ransome, Rudyard Kipling, John Masefield, and Jack London, and was entranced by poetry and by the rich tradition of mythology of Great Britain. In addition, she listened faithfully to the British Broadcasting Corporation (BBC) radio program "The Children's Hour," which dramatized some of her favorite stories. Like her grandfather, Cooper was also enthralled by the theater, recalling, for example, the awe she felt when she saw her first pantomime at the age of three. At Slough High School, a school for girls, she was encouraged to develop her writing talent. When she graduated, Cooper won a scholarship to Oxford, where she studied English literature and enjoyed what she called in *SAAS* "a calm stretch of such good fortune that I can hardly describe it." While at Oxford, Cooper discovered, as she wrote, "people, scholarship, and myself." She devoured the works of Shakespeare, Milton, and the English Metaphysical poets, heard lectures by J. R. R. Tolkien and C. S. Lewis, and worked for the university newspaper, becoming its first female editor. She also published her first short story and, on her last day at Oxford, submitted a long essay describing her feelings about the end of university life to the editors of the London *Times,* who published it in its entirety.

After her graduation, Cooper worked as a temporary reporter at the London *Sunday Express* before being hired by the *Sunday Times,* where she worked as a news reporter and feature writer for seven years, one of which she spent working for Ian Fleming, the author of the "James Bond" novels. Cooper wrote articles for the *Sunday Times* column "Mainly for Children"; later, she used some of her subjects—King Arthur, medieval castles, Roman Britain, and brass rubbings—in her books for young people. While at the *Sunday Times,* Cooper began writing novels for adults. Her second attempt, the science-fiction novel *Mandrake,* was published in 1964. A dystopian novel in the manner of *Brave New World* and *1984,* the book addresses the concept of evil residing in ordinary people, a theme that the author would later explore in her books for the young. After completing *Mandrake,* Cooper began writing a children's story for a contest offered by E. Nesbit's publisher, Ernest Benn. The contest offered a prize in Nesbit's name for a family adventure story in the tradition of Nesbit's works. This project, Cooper wrote in *SAAS,* "offered the irresistible combination of a challenge, a deadline, and money, and I dived at it in delight." Cooper's story began, she noted, with the invention of "three rather Nesbitish children named Simon, Jane, and Barney Drew, and I sent them on a train journey from London to Cornwall." However, with the introduction of the children's great-uncle Merriman Lyon—actually Merlin the magician—the book transformed into something quite different than its author originally intended. Cooper wrote in *SAAS,* "Merry took over. He led the book out of realism, to myth-haunted layers of story that took me way past a 'family adventure' and way past my deadline. Now I was no longer writing for a deadline or for money. I was writing for me, or perhaps for the child I once was and in part still am." When the book was finished, Cooper cut the first chapter about the railway journey; the result was the

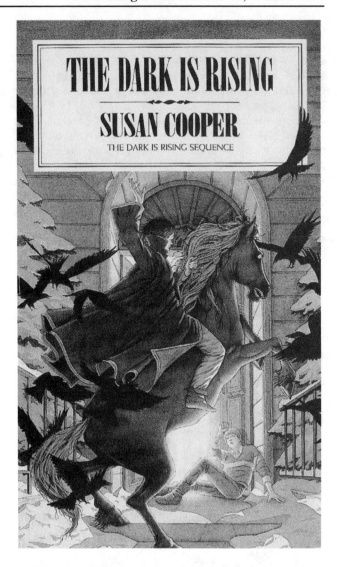

In the fourth novel from her "The Dark Is Rising" quintet, Cooper teams Will Stanton with the son of King Arthur in a quest for a magic harp that will arouse six ancient sleepers who must join in the final battle between the Light and the Dark.

first volume of "The Dark Is Rising" quintet, *Over Sea, Under Stone.*

Rejected by more than twenty publishers before its acceptance by Jonathan Cape, *Over Sea, Under Stone* describes how the Drew children, who have traveled to Trewissick, Cornwall, for a holiday with their scholarly, white-haired great-uncle, use an ancient map that they find in an attic to recover the Holy Grail. Plunged into the battle between good and evil, the children become misled by members of the Dark posing as the local vicar and a pair of tourists and encounter dangerous situations such as the kidnapping of Barney Drew. However, the powers of Great-Uncle Merry and the initiative of the children win a victory for the Light. At the end of the story, the Grail is placed in the British Museum and an ancient magical manuscript—which interprets the writing on the Grail, gives the outcome of the battle between the Light and the Dark, and promises that King Arthur will come again—is sent to the bottom of the sea. Writing in *Growing Point,* Margery Fisher said that "perhaps this is a book with a theme too big for itself, but it is a fascinating book to read and it has considerable literary quality." *School Librarian* contributor C. E. J. Smith commented, "The children are credible and their adventures shift so cunningly from the plausible to the legendary as to be totally absorbing . . . . [T]he final scene on the jagged rocks amid an incoming tide is a feast for any imaginative twelve- or thirteen-year-old."

At the age of twenty-seven, Cooper married American scientist Nicholas Grant, a widower with three children, and moved to Winchester, Massachusetts. As she adjusted to her new life, Cooper continued to write. The London *Sunday Times* hired her to cover American stories, including the trial of Jack Ruby in Dallas. She also began to contribute a weekly column to the *Western Mail,* the national morning newspaper of Wales. Her column, Cooper wrote in *SAAS,* "dealt with every imaginable aspect of American life" and led to a nonfiction book for adults, *Behind the Golden Curtain: A View of the U.S.A.,* in which she explains the differences between the cultures of America and England. She also edited a collection of essays by her friend J. B. Priestley, a notable English novelist, dramatist, and essayist, and later published a biography of Priestley. When Cooper and her husband had two children of their own, Jonathan and Kate, she read them fairy stories, folktales, and verse. While they were asleep or in nursery school, Cooper worked on an autobiographical novel for adults about her childhood. American editor Margaret K. McElderry suggested that the book should be published for children, and in 1970 it was issued as *Dawn of Fear.*

Describing how a young boy is made aware of the horrors of the Second World War, *Dawn of Fear* outlines how Derek Brand—a middle grader who lives in a housing estate in the Thames Valley—learns the meaning of sadness, suffering, and fear when his best friend Peter and his family are killed by German bombs. Drawing parallels between Derek's private war—a rivalry between two gangs of local boys—and the larger one, Cooper is credited with evoking the pain of war while movingly describing the death of a child. A reviewer in *Publishers Weekly* commented, "The gifted author . . . has brought her insight and writing skills to creating another remarkable story." The critic concluded by calling *Dawn of Fear* a "moving chronicle of despair and of courage." Ethel L. Heins of *Horn Book* praised *Dawn of Fear* as "an uncommon kind of war story," and a reviewer in *Junior Bookshelf* claimed, "To date I have not come across a book which makes anything like the same impression."

In her next book for young people, *The Dark Is Rising,* Cooper continues the story she began in *Over Sea, Under Stone.* In this work, Will Stanton, the seventh son of a seventh son, learns on his eleventh birthday that he is the last of the Old Ones, immortal beings who serve the Light and who are committed to keeping the world safe from the Dark. Will undertakes a journey to find

and join together the Six Signs of the Light—wood, bronze, iron, fire, water, and stone—to be used in a final battle against the Dark. In his quest, in which he is guided by the first of the Old Ones, Merriman Lyon, Will encounters evil forces who appear in different forms as he moves back and forth in time. Finally, the Dark rises during a winter filled with violent blizzards and floods, but Will, using both his intuition and the knowledge given him by Merry, successfully joins the Signs of the Light. A reviewer in the *Times Literary Supplement* noted, "With a cosmic struggle between good and evil as her subject, Susan Cooper invites comparison with Tolkien, and survives the comparison remarkably well." Writing in *Book World,* Virginia Haviland noted that the book "is exceptional by any standard," while S. William Alderson of *Children's Book Review* commented that *The Dark Is Rising* "captures and holds one's imagination, almost as if the magic forces within the story were themselves reaching out to spellbind the reader." Ethel L. Heins of *Horn Book* noted the strength of Cooper's writing, which she said "can be as rich and as eloquent as a Beethoven symphony," while Sally Emerson of *Books and Bookmen* concluded that anyone "who fears that they or their children are becoming rigidly sensible should buy this book to enrich imagination and recover wonderment."

First-grader Danny is helped by three self-named "Kings of the Road" when he tries to get a Christmas tree for his needy family. (From Danny and the Kings, *written by Cooper and illustrated by Jos. A. Smith.)*

The sequel to *The Dark Is Rising, Greenwitch,* again features the three Drew children, the protagonists of *Over Sea, Under Stone.* The siblings work with their great-uncle Merry and Will Stanton, the main character from *The Dark Is Rising,* to recover the Holy Grail—which has been stolen from the British Museum by a painter who is an emissary of the Dark—as well as the ancient manuscript that accompanies it. As the children engage in their pursuit, the forces of Wild Magic embodied by the Greenwitch, a tree woman woven by Cornish villagers that is given life by an ocean goddess, come to their defense through the sympathies of middle child Jane Drew. Through her compassion, Jane obtains the manuscript from the Greenwitch, thus allowing the Old Ones to learn about the next part of their quest. Writing in *Growing Point,* Margery Fisher claimed, "Fantasies like this depend most of all on the sheer power of the writing, on the literary synthesis between the sunlit world of here and now and the dark, misty otherwhere from which evil comes. The synthesis is less strong in this new book and the effect less consistent than in the other two books of the five so far published. Nonetheless, it is a compelling story . . . ." A reviewer in the *Times Literary Supplement* predicted, "When Miss Cooper manages to knit her material into a single organic whole her achievement will be great."

The Grey King is often considered the most successful of the "Dark Is Rising" sequence. In this book, Will Stanton has become ill with hepatitis and is sent to the seaside town of Tywyn, Wales, to recuperate. While in Wales, Will learns that he must undertake two quests: the recovery of a golden harp hidden in the nearby hills and the awakening of six ancient sleepers who are to be roused by the sound of the harp for the final battle between the Light and the Dark. Will is joined by Bran Davies, an albino boy who is revealed as the son of King Arthur, and Bran's white sheepdog Cafall. Bound by a preordained fate, the three retrieve the harp, but Will is thrust into a confrontation with the Grey King, an evil Lord of the High Magic who uses ghostly gray foxes and a crazed Welshman, Caradog Pritchard, to carry out his wishes, which include the killing of Cafall. At the conclusion of the novel, the sleepers are raised and preparations begin for the final showdown between the opposing forces. Writing in *Horn Book,* Mary M. Burns called *The Grey King* a "spellbinding tour de force," while Zena Sutherland of *Bulletin of the Center for Children's Books* called it a "compelling fantasy that is traditional in theme and components yet original in conception." Two major fantasists, Natalie Babbitt and Jill Paton Walsh, also commented on *The Grey King.* Writing in the *New York Times Book Review,* Babbitt said, "It is useless to try to recreate the subtleties of Susan Cooper's plotting and language. Enough to say that this volume, like those preceding it, is brimful of mythic elements and is beautifully told." Paton Walsh, writing in the *Times Literary Supplement,* noted the book's "authentic evocative power" and the fact that Cooper "commands, to a rare degree, the power to thrill the reader, to produce a particular tremor of excitement and fear, in response not only to Arthurian magic . . . but rather to haunted places, to landscape deeply embedded in ancient fable, to a sense of secret forces breaking through." In 1976, *The Grey King* was awarded the Newbery Medal and the Tir na N'og Award; it also received a commendation for the Carnegie Medal in the same year.

The final volume of "The Dark Is Rising" sequence, *Silver on the Tree,* brings together the protagonists from the preceding books. In this story, which is again set in Wales, Will Stanton summons the Old Ones for a final battle with the forces of the Dark. Will, Bran, Merriman, and the Drew children travel through time to acquire the weapons needed for combat. At the end of their adventures, which range from incredibly dangerous to extremely beautiful, the children and the Old Ones find the legendary Midsummer Tree, the silver fruit of which determines the victor of the battle. At the end of the novel, the Six Sleepers finally defeat the Lords of the Dark, Will completes his tasks as the last of the Old Ones, and Bran, who is offered immortality, bids a final farewell to his father King Arthur by choosing to remain human. Writing in *Horn Book,* Ann A. Flowers called *Silver on the Tree* a "triumphant conclusion" and "a tour de force," while a reviewer in the *Junior Bookshelf* commented that here, "crafted by the hand of a master, is a story of the ageless battle of good and evil, a book in one of the great traditions of children's literature and destined, perhaps, to become one of the high peaks of that tradition." Writing in *Growing Point,* Margery Fisher commented that the series "has given readers many moments of startled awareness and now that it is complete it deserves more deliberate consideration as a whole." Shirley Wilton of *School Library Journal* noted that Cooper "maintains a masterly control over the complex strands of her story sweeping readers along on a fantastic journey. It is an experience not to be missed and, for Cooper fans, a fitting wrap-up to the unfolding saga."

Following the completion of her fantasy quintet, Cooper began writing stories and picture books for younger children, an audience to whom most of her subsequent books have been directed. The first of these, *Jethro and the Jumbie,* is a story set in, and using the dialect of, the British Virgin Islands, where Cooper had written some of "The Dark Is Rising" series. Blending fantasy and reality, the book describes a small black boy who, promised a fishing trip by his older brother, is upset when his brother cancels out and tells Jethro that he is too weak to accompany him. Despite warnings from friends, Jethro embarks down the "jumbie trail," where the spirits of the dead reside. Jethro meets a jumbie, a shape-shifting spirit who tries to frighten the boy by changing into monstrous creatures. When Jethro refuses to be intimidated, the jumbie dissolves in tears. Taking pity on him, Jethro makes the jumbie his friend and ally, and the jumbie helps Jethro to change his brother's mind. Writing in the *Times Educational Supplement,* Virginia Makins noted, "Real boys and girls are surprisingly rare animals in books that appear for young children. And stories about them that capture the range and depth of young children's emotions and thinking are astonishingly rare. Susan Cooper's *Jethro and the*

Jumbie ... is a winner on both counts." Although a critic in *Kirkus Reviews* commented that, like the jumbie, the story "lacks the fullness of life that would convince you it's real," Zena Sutherland of the *Bulletin of the Center for Children's Books* concluded that the humorous treatment "works beautifully to lift the story, so that it is more than a boy-meets-ghost incident...."

Cooper returned to the genre of young adult fantasy with her novel *Seaward*. Written during a particularly difficult period in which the author dealt with her divorce from Nicholas Grant and the death of both her parents, *Seaward* describes how two teenagers, the girl Calliope (Cally) and the boy Westerly (West), cross the borders of time as they try to reach the sea. Each involved with the private quests that are prompted by the deaths of their respective parents, the protagonists enter the world of Lady Taramis, who is actually Death, and her twin brother Lugan—Life—and encounter many dangers before they reach their destination. At the sea, the teens, who have fallen in love, learn the identity of Taramis and Lugan as well as the fact that Cally is the descendant of a selkie, a seal who can turn into a human. At the end of the novel, Cally decides not to become a selkie and West decides to return to his own world; as a result, the friends are promised that, although they live in different countries, they will meet again and will spend their lives together. Writing in *Horn Book,* Paul Heins called *Seaward* an "uncanny, unconventional fantasy" and concluded that, like the Scottish novelist and poet George MacDonald, Cooper "has endowed the concept of human responsibility—of human choice—with the face of fantasy." M. Hobbs of *Junior Bookshelf* noted that it "is a rare treat to have another novel from Susan Cooper" and concluded that *Seaward* is a "deeply moving, splendid novel, of unearthly beauty, and worthy of its predecessors." Writing in *SAAS,* Cooper commented that *Seaward* is a book "about loving, and death, and life, and there are probably elements in it that I did not put there with conscious intent.... My parents were dead, and my marriage had just broken up. It was an awful time, and writing *Seaward* was one of the things that helped me through it."

The myths and legends of the British Isles have always been an important part of Cooper's novels. In 1983, she published *The Silver Cow: A Welsh Tale,* the first of several volumes of retellings illustrated by English artist Warwick Hutton. A legend that the reteller remembered from childhood explaining why white water lilies float in a Welsh mountain lake, *The Silver Cow* describes how Huw, a talented harpist, receives a silver cow from the magic people of the lake as a gift in return for his skillful playing. The cow and her children give milk so rich that it brings great wealth to Huw's greedy father, Gwilym, who has forbidden his son to play his harp or to attend school so that he can tend to the cows. When the silver cow grows too old to give milk, Gwilym arranges to have her slaughtered; however, a voice from the lake calls the cow and her offspring, and water lilies grow in each place where the cows have disappeared. Writing in *Horn Book,* Mary M. Burns commented that the "lilting text ... captures the enchantment inherent" in the tale and concluded that Huw "is a felicitous addition" to it. Zena Sutherland of the *Bulletin of the Center for Children's Books* noted the "fluent retelling" and concluded that the story "is poignant and firmly structured...."

Another of Cooper's retellings, *The Selkie Girl,* is a story taken from the folktales of Ireland and the Scottish Islands that, like *Seaward,* draws on the legends of seal maidens. The tale outlines how the lonely fisherman Donallan catches the beautiful selkie with whom he has fallen in love by stealing her seal skin so that she cannot go back to the sea. The couple has five children; when the youngest child finds the seal skin and tells his mother where it is hidden, she returns to her home in the water, where she also has five seal children. Before she goes, the selkie promises to meet with her land family once a year and blesses them with fine catches from their fishing. Writing in the *Junior Bookshelf,* Marcus Crouch said, "Here, even in this small exercise, a master story-teller is at work, covering the bare bones of the story with living flesh." Ethel R. Twichell of *Horn Book* concurred, noting that the author "remains faithful to the

The Boggart, a Scottish trickster spirit, offers assistance to the Loch Ness Monster when the creature is trying to elude a scientific investigation. (Cover illustration by Joe Burleson.)

spirit and magic of the story but gives it a fullness and inevitability that only a true storyteller can evoke." Based on a Scottish ballad, *Tam Lin* is the third collaboration between Cooper and illustrator Hutton. The story outlines how Margaret, the spirited daughter of a king, runs away to a forbidden wood where she meets an enchanted knight, Tam Lin. Learning that Tam Lin is under a spell that can only be broken by the love of a mortal, Margaret holds on to Tam Lin on Midsummer's Eve as the fairy queen who cast the spell on him transforms him into a wolf, a snake, a deer, and a red-hot bar of iron; through Margaret's love, the enchantment of Tam Lin is broken. Writing in *Horn Book,* Ethel L. Heins called *Tam Lin* "a beautifully paced literary fairy tale, told and pictured with precision and restraint." Helen Gregory of *School Library Journal* noted that Cooper's version of the tale "is alive with dialogue." Critics also acknowledged the feminist slant that Cooper brought to her retelling.

Originally written as a bedtime story for one of the author's grandchildren, *Matthew's Dragon* is a picture book with pictures by Jos. A. Smith about how young Matthew meets a tiny dragon who emerges from the pages of a book. After battling the neighborhood cat, Matthew and the dragon—who grows as big as a house—fly into the sky, where they meet all of the dragons from storyland before returning home to bed. A reviewer in *Publishers Weekly* called *Matthew's Dragon* "another display of impressive storytelling" as well as "an inspired pairing of author and illustrator." Susan Fromberg Schaeffer, writing in the *New York Times Book Review,* concluded that the book "lets the dragon and the imagination soar." Smith also provided the illustrations for *Danny and the Kings,* a realistic picture book with echoes of the Bible story about the Three Wise Men. Danny, a small boy who lives in a trailer with his widowed mother, is proud to be one of the Three Kings in his school's Christmas play but desperately wants a Christmas tree. When a truck driver accidentally smashes the tree that Danny's friend has given him, the driver takes the boy to a diner where he tells his story to the trucker's two friends, who call themselves the Kings of the Road. Danny is successful in his Christmas pageant; when he gets home, he is welcomed by a beautiful tree decorated with lights that had been used to decorate the three trucks. Writing in *Bulletin of the Center for Children's Books,* Betsy Hearne said, "[S]ome holiday books deserve year-round attention and not many of them feature the elements that make this one so appealing.... At the risk of sounding sexist and classist, it's hard to find working-class boy-books, so put this one on your Christmas list for next year." Writing in *Booklist,* Deborah Abbott noted, "in spite of the predictability of the plot, the genuine warmth of the season glows through the smooth text."

With *The Boggart,* a humorous fantasy for middle graders, Cooper created one of her most popular books. The title character, a Scottish trickster spirit, has lived in Castle Keep as a companion of the Mac Devon clan, who are the recipients of its lighthearted practical jokes. When the last Mac Devon passes away, the Boggart is grief-stricken until the Volnik family of Toronto—distant relatives of the Mac Devons—come to the castle that they have inherited. After arrangements are made for the castle's sale, the boggart is accidentally shipped back to Canada in an old desk. Emily Volnik and her younger brother Jessup, a computer whiz, recognize the spirit's presence when it starts playing practical jokes on the family, tricks that become dangerous when they begin to involve electricity. Although the children have become fond of the mischievous sprite, they realize that it needs to return home to Scotland, so, in conjunction with their Scottish friend Tommy, they ship the spirit back to its castle on diskette via a computer game created by Jessup. Writing in the *New York Times Book Review,* Rafael Yglesias commented, "The plot of a mysterious and possibly ancient being befriending modern kids and making trouble in their world will be familiar to any reader who has seen 'Gremlins' or 'E. T.,' but that doesn't make its working out in *The Boggart* any less suspenseful or, in one lovely scene at a theater in Toronto, surprising and moving." The critic concluded, "The inevitable failure of a spirit to coexist with our dreary practical world isn't a new theme, although in *The Boggart* it seems fresher than ever." Calling the boggart a "fascinating character, sly, ingenious, and endearing—as long as he belongs to someone else," Ann A. Flowers of *Horn Book* noted that what "is most admirable is Susan Cooper's seamless fusion of the newest technology and one of the oldest forms of wild magic." Writing in *Five Owls,* Gary D. Schmidt noted that Cooper makes "rich distinctions between the bustle of Toronto and the quiet of Scotland, between the new technology and the Old Magic, between imagination and pseudo-scientific pretension." Schmidt concluded, "The result is a delightful and quick read, with a conclusion perhaps not as high and noble and cosmic as that of *Silver on the Tree* but in its own way just as satisfying and just as complete."

The lovable imp returns in *The Boggart and the Monster,* a story in which the trickster and the Volnik children, who have come to stay at Castle Keep, help Nessie—the Loch Ness monster who is the boggart's cousin—elude a scientific investigation. Writing in the *New York Times Book Review,* Jim Gladstone maintained: "Cooper sets up a provocative elision of technological, natural, emotional and spiritual forces. Not that children will necessarily notice. The story is swiftly plotted and densely populated, zipping along with the speed of a video game." Stephanie Zvirin of *Booklist* concluded, "[The] plot has plenty of sparkling complications, and there are some fresh, funny faces to round out the cast of well-drawn old friends. The clever premise and great characters will leave kids clamoring for more."

Cooper has often written in books and magazines and has spoken to groups about both the genre of fantasy and her own literary career. In 1996, she published *Dreams and Wishes: Essays on Writing for Children,* a collection of fourteen essays drawn from various speeches in which she explores the craft of writing, outlines the nature of fantasy, and recalls her experiences as an author and reporter. Writing in *Voice of Youth Advo-*

cates, Mary Ann Capan commented, "Through these major speeches, the reader gains insight into the author's personal life as well as her creative process." A critic in *Publishers Weekly* called *Dreams and Wishes* "essential reading not just for fans of Cooper or of fantasy novels, but for devotees of children's literature." Citing one of Cooper's anecdotes, the reviewer wrote that when a hurricane destroyed the author's family vacation home, her college-age son Jonathan nervously asked his mother if his favorite books from childhood, stories by the English writer Richmal Crompton, were unharmed. "I suspect," the critic concluded, "that under similar circumstances many other children might inquire worriedly about the safety of their Susan Cooper titles."

Works Cited

Abbott, Deborah, review of *Danny and the Kings, Booklist,* October 15, 1993, p. 451.

Alderson, S. William, review of *The Dark Is Rising, Children's Book Review,* September, 1973, p. 112.

Babbitt, Natalie, review of *The Grey King, New York Times Book Review,* November 28, 1975, pp. 10, 12.

Burns, Mary M., review of *The Grey King, Horn Book,* October, 1975, p. 461.

Burns, Mary M., review of *The Silver Cow: A Welsh Tale, Horn Book,* June, 1983, pp. 287-88.

Capan, Mary Ann, review of *Dreams and Wishes: Essays on Writing for Children, Voice of Youth Advocates,* August, 1996, p. 187.

Chaston, Joel D., essay in *Dictionary of Literary Biography,* Volume 161: *British Children's Writers since 1960,* Gale, 1996, pp. 69-82.

Cooper, Susan, essay in *Something about the Author Autobiography Series,* Volume 6, Gale, 1989, pp. 67-85.

Crouch, Marcus, review of *The Selkie Girl, Junior Bookshelf,* April, 1988, pp. 77-78.

Review of *Dawn of Fear, Junior Bookshelf,* August, 1972, p. 241.

Review of *Dawn of Fear, Publishers Weekly,* August 31, 1970, p. 279.

Deifendeifer, Anne E., essay on Cooper in *Children's Books and Their Creators,* edited by Anita Silvey, Houghton Mifflin, 1995, p. 169.

Review of *Dreams and Wishes: Essays on Writing for Children, Publishers Weekly,* May 27, 1996, p. 81.

Emerson, Sally, review of *The Dark Is Rising, Books and Bookmen,* October, 1973, pp. 130-31.

Fisher, Margery, "Arthurian Echoes," *Growing Point,* September, 1965, pp. 545-55.

Fisher, Margery, review of *Greenwitch, Growing Point,* January, 1975, pp. 2555-56.

Fisher, Margery, "Dual Worlds," *Growing Point,* March, 1978, p. 3277.

Flowers, Ann A., review of *The Boggart, Horn Book,* May-June, 1993, p. 330.

Flowers, Ann A., review of *Silver on the Tree, Horn Book,* December, 1977, pp. 660-61.

Gladstone, Jim, "Magical Mysteries," *New York Times Book Review,* May 18, 1997, p. 29.

Review of *Greenwitch, Times Literary Supplement,* July 5, 1974, p. 721.

Gregory, Helen, review of *Tam Lin, School Library Journal,* May, 1991, p. 88.

Review of *The Grey King, Times Literary Supplement,* June 15, 1975, p. 685.

Haviland, Virginia, "A Child's Garden of Ghosts, Poltergeists, and Werewolves," *Book World—The Washington Post,* July 8, 1973, p. 13.

Hearne, Betsy, review of *Danny and the Kings, Bulletin of the Center for Children's Books,* February, 1994, p. 184.

Heins, Ethel L., review of *The Dark Is Rising, Horn Book,* June, 1973, p. 286.

Heins, Ethel L., review of *Dawn of Fear, Horn Book,* October, 1970, p. 477.

Heins, Ethel L., review of *Tam Lin, Horn Book,* May-June, 1991, pp. 340-41.

Heins, Paul, review of *Seaward, Horn Book,* February, 1984, pp. 59-60.

Hobbs, M., review of *Seaward, Junior Bookshelf,* April, 1984, p. 80.

Review of *Jethro and the Jumbie, Kirkus Reviews,* February 1, 1980, p. 120.

Makins, Virginia, "Blithe Spirits," *Times Educational Supplement,* June 20, 1980, p. 44.

Review of *Matthew's Dragon, Publishers Weekly,* July 12, 1991, p. 65.

McElderry, Margaret K., "Susan Cooper," *Horn Book,* August, 1976, pp. 367-72.

Paton Walsh, Jill, "Evoking Dark Powers," *Times Literary Supplement,* December 5, 1975, p. 1457.

Rees, David, "Susan Cooper," *School Librarian,* September, 1984, pp. 197-205.

Schaeffer, Susan Fromberg, "There's No Escaping Them," *New York Times Book Review,* November 10, 1991, p. 53.

Schmidt, Gary D., review of *The Boggart, Five Owls,* May-June, 1993, p. 117.

Review of *Silver on the Tree, Junior Bookshelf,* April, 1978, pp. 99-100.

Smith, C. E. J., review of *Over Sea, Under Stone, School Librarian,* December, 1965, p. 358.

Smith, Karen Patricia, essay in *Twentieth-Century Young Adult Writers,* edited by Laura Standley Berger, Gale, 1994, pp. 150-52.

Sutherland, Zena, review of *The Grey King, Bulletin of the Center for Children's Books,* November, 1975, p. 41.

Sutherland, Zena, review of *Jethro and the Jumbie, Bulletin of the Center for Children's Books,* January, 1980, p. 91.

Sutherland, Zena, review of *The Silver Cow: A Welsh Tale, Bulletin of the Center for Children's Books,* March, 1983, p. 124.

Twichell, Ethel R., review of *The Selkie Girl, Horn Book,* November-December, 1986, pp. 731-32.

Wilton, Shirley, review of *Silver on the Tree, School Library Journal,* December, 1977, p. 48.

Yglesias, Rafael, "The Gremlin on the Floppy Disk," *New York Times Book Review,* May 16, 1993, p. 23.

Zvirin, Stephanie, review of *The Boggart and the Monster, Booklist,* March 1, 1997, p. 1162.

For More Information See

BOOKS

Children's Literature Review, Volume 4, Gale, 1982, pp. 41-49.

Cooper, Susan, "Escaping into Ourselves," *Celebrating Children's Books: Essays on Children's Literature in Honor of Zena Sutherland,* edited by Betsy Hearne and Marilyn Kaye, Lothrop, 1981.

Cooper, Susan, in a publicity release from Atheneum Publishers, 1985.

Cooper, Susan, essay in *Speaking for Ourselves: Autobiographical Sketches by Notable Authors of Books for Young Adults,* Volume 1, edited by Donald Gallo, National Council of Teachers of English, 1990.

PERIODICALS

Booklist, September 15, 1997, p. 226.

Book World, July 7, 1996, p. 15.

Horn Book, August, 1976, pp. 367-72; January-February, 1997, p. 83.

Journal of Youth Services, spring, 1997, p. 305.

School Library Journal, May-June, 1997, p. 315.

—*Sketch by Gerard J. Senick*

D–E

DONEY, Todd L. W. 1959-

Personal

Born July 27, 1959, in Chicago, IL; married (divorced); children: Reid, Jesse. *Education:* William Rainey Harper College, associate degree in art, 1979; American Academy of Art, associate degree in technology with a major in graphic art, 1982.

Addresses

Home—Morristown, NJ.

Career

American Academy of Art, Chicago, IL, illustration instructor, 1984-87; Jack O'Grady Advertising Arts, 1985-86; freelance illustrator, 1986—; Joe Kubert School of Cartoon and Graphic Art, Inc., advertising illustrator instructor, 1997—. Participated in demonstration workshops, 1984-90. *Exhibitions:* Works have been exhibited at the Society of Illustrators Annual Exhibition, 32, 34 and 38; Arts for the Parks Annual Exhibition, 1990, 1991, and 1993-95; "The Original Art Show," Society of Illustrators, 1996; "Flora," Macculloch Hall Historical Museum, 1998; and "One Man Show," Brickton Gallery and Art Center, 1998. *Member:* Society of Illustrators.

Awards, Honors

Notable Trade Book in the Field of Social Studies, National Council of Social Studies Children's Book Center, and Children's Books of the Year, Outstanding Merit, Child Study Children's Book Committee, both for *Red Bird.*

Illustrator

Lewis Lazare, *Ernie Discovers Excellence: A Children's Story for Businessmen of All Ages,* Turnbull & Willoughby, 1984.

Richard Mann, *The Wonderful Father Book,* Turnbull & Willoughby, 1985.
(With Greg Sauers) Lennie Rose, *Parties with Panache,* Turnbull & Willoughby, 1986.
Joseph A. Altsheler, *Kentucky Frontiersmen: The Adventures of Henry Ware, Hunter and Border Fighter,* Voyageur, 1988.
Alan Schroeder, *The Stone Lion,* Scribner, 1994.
(Reteller) Marian Horosko, *Sleeping Beauty: The Ballet Story,* Atheneum, 1994.
Barbara Mitchell, *Red Bird,* Lothrop Lee & Shepard, 1996.
Charlotte F. Otten, *January Rides the Wind: A Book of Months,* Lothrop Lee & Shepard, 1997.
Jonathan London, *Old Salt, Young Salt,* Lothrop Lee & Shepard, 1997.

Sidelights

Todd L. W. Doney once commented in a Lothrop, Lee, & Shepard publicity piece: "I can't remember when I started drawing, but it was early. In fact, I won a drawing contest at the age of three. I don't remember what I drew (I was told later that it was Casper the Friendly Ghost and his family), but I do remember the first-place prize, which was a rocking horse.

"The art college of my choice was the American Academy of Art in Chicago. Under the guidance of some of the most talented artists in Chicago, I decided to become an illustrator.

"After graduating in 1982, I obtained my first commission, a football illustration for a major monthly magazine. I have been working as an illustrator ever since."

Before illustrating a book, Doney likes to spend time observing and taking photographs of his subject matter. As part of his preparation for doing the oil paintings for *Red Bird,* he went to the Nanticoke powwow, and when working on *January Rides the Wind: A Book of Months* he spent time with a group of kids, creating scenes for the book from their activities. Doney commented: "There's a special energy—a vitality—that seems to

Todd L. W. Doney carefully observed a group of children and recorded their seasonal activities to create illustrations for Charlotte F. Otten's book of poems about each month of the year.(From January Rides the Wind: A Book of Months.*)*

transfer to the art when you've witnessed the scene yourself."

The Stone Lion, written by Alan Schroeder, recalls a traditional Tibetan tale of two brothers, one (Drashi) being good—the other (Jarlo) evil. When they each encounter a magical stone lion at the top of the mountain, the lion responds accordingly, punishing the greedy Jarlo and rewarding Drashi's kindheartedness with a bucket full of gold and silver. "Doney's softly focused representational art captures both the majesty of the mountainous land and the intimacy of the characters' exchanges," wrote a critic for *Publishers Weekly.* Likewise, Margaret A. Chang praised Doney's artistry in her review for *School Library Journal,* claiming the "full-color, painterly illustrations offer sweeping vistas of the Himalayas as a back drop to the action."

Set in Delaware, *Red Bird,* written by Barbara Mitchell, describes young Katie's weekend experience of the annual Nanticoke powwow, a celebration she shares with her multi-generational family. Native drumming welcomes Red Bird (Katie's Nanticoke name) and her family as they arrive at the powwow on a Delaware farm. Here, in beaded leather dress, Red Bird enjoys the singing, dancing, and stories that fill these special days with her people. In a review for *School Library Journal,* writer Lisa Mitten declared this picture book "unique" because of its coverage of an "Eastern" powwow and because Doney's illustrations are "accurate oil paintings rather than photos." She goes on to say: "The warm and woodsy double-page art is right on target in conveying the sights of powwows along the East Coast." Observed Leone McDermott, a critic for *Booklist,* "the pictures of sunlit dancers in richly detailed ceremonial garb" are "most striking." A *Publishers Weekly* reviewer singled out a picture spread of the Nanticoke before the white settlers came, describing it as "moving and exquisite."

Twelve short poems, each accompanied by a Doney oil painting, make up the illustrations for the picture book *January Rides the Wind: A Book of Months,* written by Charlotte Otten. Poems and pictures summon outdoor scenes and seasons related to each month. Children fill the pages—doing what children do when spring arrives or winter fills with snow. Truly a collaboration between author and illustrator, critics could not describe one without the other. Kathleen Whalin, critic for *School Library Journal* declared that the "combined effect of text and art is stunning." Together, they form a "glowing, sensual salute to the seasons," according to Whalin. In praise of the book, Susan Dove Lempke in her *Booklist* review claimed: "The paintings evoke intense feelings just as the poems capture the spirit of a moment," noting how writer and artist "together created a deeply satisfying celebration of the changes in nature."

Works Cited

Chang, Margaret A., review of *Stone Lion, School Library Journal,* May, 1994, p. 110.
Lempke, Susan Dove, review of *January Rides the Wind: A Book of Months, Booklist,* October 15, 1997, p. 403.

McDermott, Leone, review of *Red Bird, Booklist,* May 1, 1996, p. 1512.
Mitten, Lisa, review of *Red Bird, School Library Journal,* June, 1996, p. 106.
Review of *Red Bird, Publishers Weekly,* May 20, 1996, p. 259.
Review of *Stone Lion, Publishers Weekly,* January 17, 1994, p. 434.
Whalin, Kathleen, review of *January Rides the Wind: A Book of Months, School Library Journal,* October, 1997, p. 121.

For More Information See

PERIODICALS

School Library Journal, March, 1989, p. 197; November, 1994, p. 98; October, 1996, p. 102.
Booklist, October 15, 1996, p. 436.*

* * *

DOYLE, Brian 1935-

Personal

Born August 12, 1935, in Ottawa, Ontario, Canada; son of Hulbert (a government worker and customs broker) and Charlotte (a homemaker and poet; maiden name, Duff) Doyle; married Jacqueline Aronson (a homemaker and government worker), December 26, 1960; children: Megan, Ryan. *Education:* Carleton University, B.J. and B.A., 1957; also completed course work for M.A. at Ottawa University.

Addresses

Home—118 Ossington Ave., Ottawa, Ontario, Canada K1S 3B8.

Career

Author, playwright, scriptwriter, educator. Teacher at Glebe Collegiate Institute (high school) and Ottawa Technical High School, Ottawa, Ontario; became head of English department at Glebe Collegiate and served on both the Ottawa Board of Education and the faculty of Queen's University, Kingston, Ontario. Worked variously as a journalist, waiter, taxi driver, driving instructor, office worker, bricklayer, and jazz singer. *Military service:* Canadian Naval Reserve, 1955-56. *Member:* James Joyce Society of Ottawa (chairman).

Awards, Honors

Book of the Year Award, Canadian Library Association, 1983, for *Up to Low,* and 1989, for *Easy Avenue;* three times runner-up, Governor General's Literary Award, Canada Council; Mr. Christie's Book Award, Canadian Children's Book Centre and Communications Jeunesse, 1990, for *Covered Bridge;* Vicky Metcalf Award, Canadian Authors Association, 1991, for body of work; Book of the Year Award, Canadian Library Association, 1997, and Mr. Christie's Book Award, 1997, for *Uncle*

Brian Doyle

Ronald; finalist, Hans Christian Andersen Author Award, International Board on Books for Young People, 1998.

Writings

FICTION; FOR YOUNG ADULTS

Hey, Dad!, Groundwood Books (Toronto), 1978.
You Can Pick Me Up at Peggy's Cove, Groundwood Books, 1979.
Up to Low, Groundwood Books, 1982.
Angel Square, Groundwood Books, 1984, Bradbury Press (New York), 1986.
Easy Avenue, Groundwood Books, 1988.
Covered Bridge, Groundwood Books, 1990.
Spud Sweetgrass, Groundwood Books, 1992.
Spud in Winter, Groundwood Books, 1995.
Uncle Ronald, Groundwood Books, 1996.
Dam Lies, Groundwood Books, 1998.

OTHER

Author of plays for children. Contributor of articles and short stories to newspapers and magazines, including the Toronto *Globe and Mail* and *Fiddlehead.* Doyle's works have been translated into French and published in Braille editions.

Adaptations

You Can Pick Me Up at Peggy's Cove was made into a film directed by Don McBrearty and into a video released by Beacon Films, Inc., in 1982. CNIB released sound recordings of *You Can Pick Me Up at Peggy's Cove* in 1984, *Angel Square* in 1985, *Easy Avenue* in 1994, and *Covered Bridge* in 1995; *Easy Avenue* was also released as a sound recording by the Library Services Branch, Vancouver, British Columbia, in 1994. *Meet the Author: Brian Doyle* was released as a short film in 1987. *Angel Square* was made into a film directed by Ann Wheeler and released by the National Film Board of Canada, Edmonton, Alberta, 1990.

Sidelights

Considered one of Canada's most distinguished authors of young adult literature and books for middle graders, Doyle is acclaimed as an exceptional creator of realistic fiction as well as a brilliant comic writer whose works reflect his insight and sensitivity in depicting the moral dilemmas of the young. His books, which are set in both historical and contemporary periods and often incorporate autobiographical elements, are often considered unique in the field of Canadian juvenile literature for their concentration on the inner lives of their characters, for their experimental nature, and for their exploration of mature, often epic themes. Praised as a storyteller and creator of character as well as an accomplished literary stylist, Doyle has been compared to such authors as Charles Dickens, J. D. Salinger, Kurt Vonnegut, and Judy Blume and is regarded as a favorite writer by Canadian young people. Characteristically, the author uses regional settings—including the area in and around his home of Ottawa—and rounded portrayals of Canadian communities to provide the foundation for his explorations of such themes as the relationships between parents and children, the power of love, the acceptance of death and loss, and the need for tolerance. Central to Doyle's works is his focus on the maturation process of his young male and female protagonists: his characters learn to find balance in their often chaotic lives by facing personal strife and social injustice and by drawing on their inner strength. Writing in *Children's Books and Their Creators,* Sarah Ellis noted that these young narrators "describe their world with a wry, eye-rolling awareness of its hypocrisies and real evils, but they are never cynical, bitter, or solipsistic. The enclosing narrative voice of the books is warm and tolerant, emotionally vulnerable."

Although his works contain death—including murder and suicide—as well as child and spousal abuse, drunkenness, and violent racial strife, Doyle underscores his books with humor and optimism; his stories acknowledge the imperfections and tragedies of the human condition while stressing such attributes as goodness, healing, and redemption. The author's humor, which ranges from black to slapstick to whimsical, is considered one of his most appealing features and is often present in his characterizations, especially of the outrageous, larger-than-life personages who play supporting roles in his stories. As a writer, Doyle favors fast-moving plots and an intimate narrative style that is considered both spare and elegant; his works—which reflect the author's love of wordplay and the tall tale as well as his frequent use of the three-word paragraph—also include puns, songs, colloquialisms, headlines, jingles, and recipes. Writing in *Books for Young People,* Eva Martin called Doyle "one of the most daring and experimental writers of young-adult novels. He deals with the most sensitive of issues—race, violence, anti-social activity of all sorts—with a tongue-in-cheek humor that never denigrates the human spirit.... Thanks to writers like Doyle, Canada, in spite of the lion to the south, has developed a literature for young adults that is as unique as it is universal." Writing in *Magpies,* Agnes Nieuwenhuizen concluded, "Perhaps Doyle's most extraordinary feat is that there is never a sense of design or message or moralising. What shines through his work is a breath of vision and tolerance and a quirky exuberance and curiosity even in the face of adversity and resistance."

Born in Ottawa, Doyle grew up in two locations: an ethnically diverse section of the city where he spent the school year and a log cabin on the Gatineau River near Low, Quebec, about forty miles north of town, where he spent his summers. Doyle's memories of his parents, siblings, and neighbors as well as the landscape and atmosphere of his youthful environment have greatly influenced his writing, as has his experience as a father of two children; as Agnes Nieuwenhuizen described it in *Magpies,* "Family is at the centre of Doyle's life and work," while Ann Vanderhoof of *Quill and Quire* added, "His family, his memories of his adventures as son and as parent, provide the jumping off point for his fiction." Doyle credits his father Hulbert and his paternal grandfather for nurturing his instincts as a storyteller: he once told *Something about the Author (SATA),* "I loved sitting around listening to my father and my grandfather. Both of them were wonderful storytellers, and they didn't tell stories so much as they just talked." Doyle noted that his grandfather was "constantly reciting verse—songs and poems, ballads mostly—about this adventure and that adventure. My father wasn't a literary person, although he was the best raconteur I ever met. If in my work there is a kind of sound, that's where it comes from, rhythms inherited from sitting around listening to my father's family exchanging their world vision." Doyle's mother Charlotte Duff Doyle also influenced his development as a writer: "My mother," he told *SATA,* "was a literary person. She was not a verbal person at all. However, she wrote well and wrote privately. She was very private, but she'd show her poetry to me." Doyle's mother wrote the poem "Sea Savour," which begins the author's second novel *You Can Pick Me Up at Peggy's Cove.*

In his comments to *SATA,* Doyle said, "I'm always surprised at how much I can feel, so I must have been the kind of kid that paid attention. I'm surprised at myself all the time at how much I can remember. I must have been all eyes and ears." The author grew up in a difficult home environment: his father was cruel when

he drank and his mother, who cared for a retarded daughter as well as for the rest of the family, was often overwhelmed. Doyle told *SATA* that he "wasn't much of a student" until he reached college; however, he did enjoy reading comic books and works such as *Heidi* and *The Adventures of Huckleberry Finn.* When he was about ten years old, Doyle decided that he wanted to be a writer. "The first writing I did was in the snow," he told *SATA.* "I wrote 'Gerald is a bastard,'" referring to a boyhood friend. When Hulbert Doyle discovered what his son had written, he took him in the house, and, the author remembered, "put a piece of paper down on the table and gave me a pencil. Then he said, 'Say some more, but don't write it in the snow because he'll see it.'" When he was in the eighth grade, Doyle's older sister Pamela, a sixteen-year-old with Down's Syndrome, passed away; Doyle's memories of Pamela, and his recollection of the toll her caretaking took on his mother, led to his inclusion of several characters with disabilities in his books. While in high school at

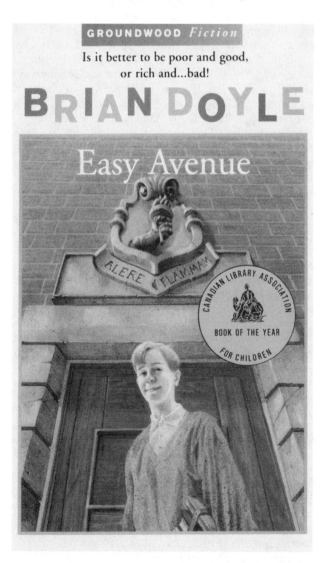

In Doyle's award-winning novel for young adults, orphan Hubbo O'Driscoll fabricates an identity to win acceptance into an exclusive club. (Cover illustration by Ludmilla Temertey.)

Ottawa's Glebe Collegiate Institute, Doyle began submitting short stories to magazines, some of which came back with personal rejection letters. Doyle played football, won medals in gymnastics, and published poetry in the yearbook; he also fought, stole, and skipped school. He recalled in his essay in *Something about the Author Autobiography Series (SAAS)*, "Once, on a Christmas exam in geometry, I got three out of a hundred. Three percent. Then something very peculiar happens. On the Easter exam, I got 99 out of a hundred! How can that be? It's as though I just suddenly woke up! The teacher is convinced I cheated." Later, he is nominated for head boy, but has his name taken off the list by the vice-principal, who, the author recalled, "[s]ays I'm a show-off. And I'm a bum. And I'll never amount to anything. And my shirt is always hanging out of my pants. When he says this I realize I've been a pain for six years. But what he says about 'never amounting to anything.' That hurts."

After graduating from Glebe Collegiate, Doyle attended Carleton College in Ottawa, where he majored in journalism and met Jackie Aronson, the woman he was later to marry. He read novels, plays, and poetry by prominent Canadian writers as well as by such authors as Homer, Shakespeare, Twain, Joyce, Hemingway, Salinger, and Dylan Thomas while working dozens of jobs to pay for college; just before graduation, he won a prize for a paper he wrote on the Gatineau River Valley. After graduation, Doyle became a reporter for the Toronto *Telegram* but left after a short time to teach high school in Ottawa; he also completed the course work for a master's degree in literature at Ottawa University but left before writing his thesis. Doyle continued his writing during this time, becoming a columnist for a community paper and publishing a short story in the literary magazine *Fiddlehead*. He and his wife adopted two children, Megan and Ryan, and became involved in local theater; Doyle began writing well-received plays for his students and also became somewhat of a celebrity when one of his articles on the ineffectuality of teacher training was quoted in the Toronto *Globe and Mail*. Asked to return to his alma mater Globe Collegiate, Doyle became head of the English department and continued to write well-received student plays, including ten musicals and a satirical parody of *Hamlet*. He retired from teaching in 1991.

Doyle published his first book for young readers, *Hey, Dad!*, in 1978. A story for middle graders that he wrote for his daughter Megan, *Hey, Dad!* uses the journey motif—both literal and symbolic—to represent the growing maturity of its young protagonist. In an interview with Agnes Nieuwenhuizen in *Magpies*, Doyle remembered, "I wanted to write a very personal tale about and to my ten-year-old daughter. She was not reading very much and I was hunting around for reading material but didn't much like what was around . . . . We had gone on a family trip across Canada and had both kept journals, so I strung together an episodic chronicle about our trip. I made it funny, but included stuff she had been grappling with. Stuff about time and mortality." Doyle followed *Hey, Dad!* with *You Can Pick Me*

Up at Peggy's Cove, another story for middle graders that he wrote for his son Ryan. He recalled in *SATA,* "I wrote [the books] for them and, at the time, they were at that age—the good age, where I thought I knew them really well and, in fact, I did. I don't think I ever knew anybody as well as I did my daughter when she was that age. I felt like I was right inside her skin. So writing *Hey, Dad!* and *You Can Pick Me Up at Peggy's Cove* was an attempt to capture that knowledge before it went away."

In *Hey, Dad!*, Doyle describes how thirteen-year-old Megan, who shares her name with the author's daughter, grows beyond her childhood self-absorption and begins to question the connection between love and death during a family trip from Ottawa to Vancouver. Writing in *In Review*, Irma McDonough commented, "Here is a new author with a new approach to realistic writing for young people. Doyle has written a junior novel we have been waiting for—one that is not a trend book or a social

When Spud Sweetgrass witnesses a crime, he draws upon his Native-American heritage to summon the courage to notify the authorities. *(Cover illustration by Marion Stuck.)*

documentary; rather, a novel that will reinforce young people's tender feelings and gently encourage them to find their own answers to the age-old questions." In *Peggy's Cove,* young narrator Ryan—who shares his name with the author's son and is the brother of Megan from *Hey, Dad!*—is sent to stay in the Nova Scotia fishing town of Peggy's Cove, a popular tourist attraction, after his father deserts the family during a mid-life crisis. Thinking that his dad will return if he gets into trouble, Ryan starts stealing from tourists; however, his friendship with fisherman Eddie and his mute partner Wingding leads him to self-knowledge and, eventually, to heroism. Writing in *In Review,* Mickie McClear commented that Doyle "has that rare gift of insight which enables him to breathe life into his portrayals of adolescents," while Jon C. Stott of *The World of Children's Books* concluded that *Peggy's Cove* is a "sensitive and compelling story which will continue to find readers for many years to come."

After completing his second novel, Doyle thought that he was through writing books for children. However, his editor at Groundwood Books, Peggy Aldana, directed him to mine his own childhood for inspiration. The result was *Up to Low,* Doyle's first young adult novel and the first to be set in the Gatineau Hills in Quebec. Based on the author's boyhood experiences at his family's cabin, *Up to Low* takes place during the early 1950s and features teenage narrator Young Tommy, a boy who has recently lost his mother. Tommy travels to the town of Low with his father and his father's friend Frank, an alcoholic. On their way, the group stops at many taverns, where the men tell Tommy about Mean Hughie, the meanest man in Gatineau, who has vanished into the wilderness to die of cancer. When the companions reach Low, a town that Doyle portrays as filled with comic residents, Tommy is awestruck by the beauty of Mean Hughie's eighteen-year-old daughter Baby Bridget, a girl with striking green eyes whose arm was cut off accidentally by a binding machine. The teens embark on a journey to find Mean Hughie, and the strength of their love provides spiritual healing for both Tommy and Bridget, who reconciles with her father before he dies. Writing in *Quill and Quire,* Joan McGrath noted that *Up to Low* "is something special among books for young adults," while Mary Ainslie Smith of *Books in Canada* called it "Doyle's best novel yet."

In his next book, *Angel Square,* Doyle again features Young Tommy as narrator but changes his setting to the multicultural Lowertown area of urban Ottawa. On his way home from school, Tommy crosses Angel Square, a place where fights between French Canadian, Irish Catholic, and Jewish kids take place daily. When anti-Semitism results in the critical injury of the father of his best friend, Sammy Rosenberg, Tommy fights back against racial hatred in Lowertown and finds the culprit by working with a network of his Jewish, Irish, and French Canadian friends; as Agnes Nieuwenhuizen noted, the children "get together to deal with an adult situation." Writing in *Quill and Quire,* Paul Kropp called *Angel Square* "a real triumph of young adult writing," while a reviewer in *Children's Book News*

Set one hundred years in the past, Doyle's novel relates the story of twelve-year-old Mickey, who escapes from an abusive father to reside with warm and welcoming Uncle Ronald.(Cover illustration by Ludmilla Temertey.)

concluded, "Through Tommy's eyes we see the absurdity of racism and the hope that at least one child will understand our differences. This is Brian Doyle's best and guarantees an enjoyable yet sobering read for all." Doyle told *SATA* that *Angel Square* is "very close to what my youth was, as close as I can conjure up anyway.... I think that *Angel Square* was hard to relax with, because it touched on some pain." Doyle includes a portrait of his retarded sister Pamela, who shares her name with the character in the novel. The author commented, "There's a little bit of her in each book—anybody who's handicapped in any way. I had trouble going all out with her memory, because it was painful, but some of it got in there in *Angel Square.*"

In *Uncle Ronald,* Doyle features a character introduced in *Up to Low,* "Crazy Mickey," who is Young Tommy's hundred-year-old great-grandfather. Now one hundred and twelve, Mickey narrates the events of the winter he was twelve. The son of a drunken, abusive father, Mickey is smuggled by his mother onto a train that takes him from Ottawa into the Gatineau Hills, where he is to stay with his Uncle Ronald and his middle-aged aunts, the O'Malley girls. Mickey's relatives prove to be warm and welcoming, and he bonds with his uncle's horse Second Chance Lance. Fascinated by the stories about the exploits of the locals, Mickey joins in their attempt to outsmart the government bailiffs trying to collect back taxes. Underpinning the story is Mickey's fear that his father will try to come and collect him and his newly arrived mother; when he does, the man meets a violent end when he falls under the wheels of a train while trying to steal Second Chance Lance. Writing in *Horn Book,* Martha Parravano called *Uncle Ronald* a "not-to-be-missed read—for the evocation of setting, for the genuine feel of the lively local stories, and for the sheer joy of Doyle's prose." Observed Mary-Ann Stouck in *Canadian Children's Literature,* "This book is mainly remarkable for the warmth and compassion, never descending into sentimentality, with which it treats Mickey and his troubles." Maureen Garvie of *Quill and Quire* concluded that, although it may not be the Doyle book for kids to begin with, "for the young reader who has acquired a taste for Doyle, *Uncle Ronald* is vintage."

Easy Avenue, a novel for young adults, introduces narrator Hubbo O'Driscoll, a poor orphan who is left in the care of a very old, very kind distant relative known only as Mrs. Driscoll. Hubbo becomes involved with Fleurette Featherstone Fitchell, a fellow resident of the Uplands Emergency Shelter who is the daughter of a Lowertown prostitute. When he enters Glebe Collegiate Institute—the high school that Doyle attended and where he later taught—Hubbo becomes caught between the people from the shelter and the elite Glebe students. When he gets a job as the companion to a wealthy elderly woman and begins to receive money from a mysterious benefactor, Hubbo fabricates an identity that is acceptable to the snobbish members of an exclusive club that he wishes to join. At the end of the novel, Hubbo realizes his loyalties and tears up his application for club membership. Compared to *Great Expectations, Easy Avenue* was called "a delightful mix of comedy, irony, and sentiment" by Pamela Young and others in *Maclean's Magazine.* Writing in *Canadian Children's Literature,* Lionel Adey concluded, "for his sometimes grim, sometimes amusing, but never unwholesome tale, Mr. Doyle deserves handsome royalty cheques in today's dollars."

Covered Bridge is the second of Doyle's stories about Hubbo. Set in 1950 and based on what Doyle called in *SAAS* "my first real job doing adult work," the novel outlines how Hubbo, who has moved to a farm in the small Quebec community of Mushrat Creek, becomes the part-time caretaker of a wooden covered bridge that has become a memorial to the tragic romance of two lovers, Ophelia and Oscar. Ophelia, who suffered from a brain tumor, jumped from the bridge to her death; her suicide caused the local priest to ban her from being buried in consecrated ground. When the bridge is slated for demolition in the name of progress, Hubbo works to preserve it, and in the process helps to correct the moral injustice regarding Ophelia, whose ghost he has seen. Writing in *Quill and Quire,* Sandra Martin noted, "Brian Doyle has a delicious way with metaphors. He writes

lean nostalgic tales in spare elegant prose, but not even the lustre of his lacquered sentences can camouflage the fact that *Covered Bridge* is a short story tarted up as a novel, or at best an episode that belongs in a longer work.... Doyle is too good a writer to settle for sketches when it's clear he could flesh out his characters and stories and write a classic Canadian novel." Agnes Nieuwenhuizen called *Covered Bridge* a "hauntingly beautiful tribute to conserving and respecting old things."

Doyle's two books about John "Spud" Sweetgrass, a half-Irish, half-Ojibway teen who is nicknamed for his ability to cook the perfect french fry, are considered somewhat of a departure from his earlier works. Comic mysteries for young adults written in a staccato style, *Spud Sweetgrass* and *Spud in Winter* involve a young protagonist who is trying to come to terms with his father's death, with his boss's shady business dealings, and a gang-style slaying that he has witnessed. In the first book, Spud and his friends Connie Pan and Dink the Thinker attempt to discover who is dumping grease from Spud's french-fry stand into the Ottawa River. A critic in *Kirkus Reviews* commented, "Replete with laughs, tears, and twists, plus a young hero to admire and a cardboard villain to hate, this will slide down effortlessly, like all proper snacks." Connie Tyrrell Burns of *School Library Journal* noted that the author "paints a vivid, touching portrait of one boy's coming-of-age.... Doyle captures perfectly adolescent thoughts and feelings, and writes of them with humor and tenderness." In *Spud in Winter,* Spud draws on his Native heritage to find the courage to name a Mafiosi killer. Writing in *Quill and Quire,* Mary Beaty commented, "The Spud books are divertimenti: enjoyable, but not as memorable as Doyle's other works.... *Spud in Winter* may have a short life span—or it may morph into nostalgia. A reasonable purchase for Adrian Mole or Al Capsella fans and a definite match for the first Spud book." In her review of both volumes in *Bulletin of the Center for Children's Books,* Deborah Stevenson noted, "What really makes these books sparkle is Doyle's writing.... [T]hese will offer readers some literary northern light." Writing in *Canadian Children's Literature,* Jim Gellert acknowledged that the "Spud" books blend "humour and a recognizable Canadian setting to provide a convincing, realistic context in which Doyle probes contemporary social themes and issues."

In his interview in *SATA,* Doyle noted, "There is a perception that young people are worried about menstruation, divorce, masturbation, hitchhiking—subjects that just carloads of kids' books are written about. These are not the concerns of young people at all as far as I'm concerned. They are the concerns of adults who have young people. Kids' concerns are classical concerns: Am I brave? Am I a hero? Am I honest? Do I love this person? Am I afraid? Am I admired? Am I weak? Am I strong? These are their concerns, and that's what I write about." He added, "As a child, I recall sitting around listening to the adults in my life talking anyway. They never left me out, and they didn't explain or anything either. I think that's how I would like to treat kids that are around me, put it out there, let them figure it out." He noted, "Kids at ten know a lot—they're very wise, although they're not slippery, not good enough liars yet. A ten-year-old boy or girl is as smart as she'll ever get or he'll ever get. So it's with that kind of belief I'm comfortable making the ten-year-old's insights as deep as I want." Later, Doyle commented, "It seems to me that laughter and tears are the two most important reactions to life. They're essential for someone to live an ordinary existence." In an interview with Agnes Nieuwenhuizen in *Magpies*, he observed that, in his novels, laughter and tears are often very close. "One seems to change into the other by some kind of automatic gear. When things get sad in life or writing, I become funny. Very funny situations make me cry. In my writing I don't have to think to get all the bits converging: the humour, the tensions, the sadness, the laughter. I have inherited this ability from my father's side of the family."

Works Cited

Adey, Lionel, "Doyle for the Early Teens," *Canadian Children's Literature,* number 54, 1989, pp. 71-72.

Review of *Angel Square, Children's Book News,* Toronto, December, 1984, p. 3.

Beaty, Mary, review of *Spud in Winter, Quill and Quire,* March, 1995, p. 75.

Burns, Connie Tyrrell, review of *Spud Sweetgrass, School Library Journal,* September, 1996, p. 224.

Doyle, Brian, telephone interview with Sonia Benson for *Something about the Author,* Volume 67, Gale, 1992, pp. 67-74.

Doyle, Brian, essay in *Something about the Author Autobiography Series,* Volume 16, Gale, 1993, pp. 127-41.

Ellis, Sarah, essay on Doyle in *Children's Books and Their Creators,* edited by Anita Silvey, Houghton Mifflin, 1995, p. 210.

Garvie, Maureen, review of *Uncle Ronald, Quill and Quire,* October, 1996, p. 49.

Gellert, Jim, "Spud Does Ottawa—Again," *Canadian Children's Literature,* winter, 1995, p. 80.

Kropp, Paul, "Growing Up Is Hard to Do: Leaving the Boy Behind," *Quill and Quire,* November, 1984, p. 18.

Martin, Eva, "'Easy Avenue' Is Vintage Doyle," *Books for Young People,* October, 1988, pp. 12, 18.

Martin, Sandra, review of *Covered Bridge, Quill and Quire,* October, 1990, p. 13.

McClear, Mickie, review of *You Can Pick Me Up at Peggy's Cove, In Review: Canadian Books for Children,* August, 1980, p. 45.

McDonough, Irma, review of *Hey, Dad!, In Review: Canadian Books for Children,* autumn, 1978, p. 57.

McGrath, Joan, "A Clutch of Juvenile Novels with No-Nonsense Plots," *Quill and Quire,* November, 1982, p. 26.

Nieuwenhuizen, Agnes, "Looking Deeply but not Far: An Interview with Brian Doyle," *Magpies,* November, 1994, pp. 11-13.

Parravano, Martha, review of *Uncle Ronald, Horn Book,* May-June, 1997, p. 318.

Smith, Mary Ainslie, review of *Up to Low, Books in Canada,* February, 1983, pp. 32-33.

Review of *Spud Sweetgrass, Kirkus Reviews,* March 1, 1996, p. 372.

Stevenson, Deborah, review of *Spud Sweetgrass* and *Spud in Winter, Bulletin of the Center for Children's Books,* July-August, 1996, p. 367.

Stott, Jon C., "A Second Baker's Dozen: Our Selection of the Best Canadian Books of 1980," *World of Children's Books,* Volume VI, 1981, pp. 27-33.

Stouck, Mary-Ann, review of *Uncle Ronald, Canadian Children's Literature,* summer, 1998, pp. 67-68.

Vanderhoof, Ann, "Prankster, Teacher, Writer: Brian Doyle Is Up to Good," *Quill and Quire,* December, 1982, p. 27.

Young, Pamela, and others, "Tidings of Fun," *Maclean's Magazine,* December 26, 1988, p. N6.

For More Information See

BOOKS

Children's Literature Review, Volume 22, Gale, 1991, pp. 27-34.

Twentieth-Century Young Adult Writers, St. James, 1994, pp. 189-91.

PERIODICALS

Booklist, June 1, 1996, pp. 1696-97.

Bulletin of the Center for Children's Books, July, 1996, p. 367; February, 1997, p. 203.

Canadian Children's Literature, number 64, 1991, pp. 90-91.

Canadian Materials, March, 1991, p. 88.

—Sketch by Gerard J. Senick

*　　　*　　　*

EDMUND, Sean
See PRINGLE, Laurence (Patrick)

*　　　*　　　*

ELBORN, Andrew
See CLEMENTS, Andrew

*　　　*　　　*

ELISHA, Ron 1951-

Personal

Born December 19, 1951, in Jerusalem, Israel; son of David (a builder) and Haya (Bash) Elisha; married Bertha Rita Rubin (an administrator), December 6, 1981; children: Raphael, Abby. *Education:* University of Melbourne, M.B., B.S., 1975. *Politics:* "None (tending to anarchy)." *Religion:* Atheist. *Hobbies and other interests:* Music, carpentry.

Ron Elisha

Addresses

Home and office—2 Malonga Ct., North Caulfield, Victoria 3161, Australia. *Agent*—Sandy Wagner, 12/44A Bayswater Rd., Kings Cross, New South Wales 2011, Australia.

Career

General practitioner of medicine, Melbourne, Australia, 1977—. *Member:* International PEN, Australian Writers Guild, Fellowship of Australian Writers.

Awards, Honors

Awgie Awards, Australian Writers Guild, 1982, 1984 and 1992; Gold Award, best screenplay, Houston International Film Festival, 1990.

Writings

CHILDREN'S BOOKS

Pigtales, illustrated by Craig Smith, Random House Australia, 1994.
Too Big, illustrated by Cathy Netherwood, Random House Australia, 1997.

PLAYS

In Duty Bound, Yackandandah Playscripts (Montmorency, Australia), 1983.
Two, Currency Press (Sydney, Australia), 1985.
Einstein, Penguin (Ringwood, Australia), 1986.
The Levine Comedy, Yackandandah Playscripts, 1987.
Safe House, Currency Press, 1989.
Esterhaz, Currency Press, 1990.
Pax Americana, Yackandandah Playscripts, 1990.
Choice, Currency Press, 1994.

OTHER

Contributor to periodicals.

Work in Progress

One children's book, *Ferry Tales;* four plays, *Jesus' Blood, Acts of Dog, Affairs of the Heartless,* and *Wandering Gentile;* three novels, *The Hangman's Table, Paris,* and *Paper Cuts;* six screenplays, *Money, Seven Hills to Happiness, Saviours, Critters, Star Quality,* and *Star Crossed.*

Sidelights

Ron Elisha told *SATA:* "My main motivation in writing for children is to create something that adults and children can read together, without boring the pants off either.

"I believe that it's never too early for children to be introduced to the concept of irony, a sorely undervalued commodity in writing for the young. I don't believe that endings need necessarily be either neat or happy, nor do I feel that children should be led to believe that the world is just or makes sense.

"I *do* believe that we should avoid the dumbing-down of children's literature that is being forced upon us by frightened editors. It's time that we, as writers, did our part to ensure that those who come after us are provided with the equipment they will need to express themselves. True expression requires precision. Precision requires both vocabulary and grammar. A child doesn't attain either without being stretched by the books he or she reads."

For More Information See

BOOKS

McNaughton, Howard, essay on Elisha in *Contemporary Dramatists,* 5th edition, edited by K. A. Berney, St. James Press, 1993.

PERIODICALS

Magpies, March, 1995, p. 24.

G

Donald R. Gallo

1938-

As a teenager growing up in Paterson, New Jersey, I did not read anything that was not required of me in school. That is, I did not read novels or other school-type books. I did read the *Boy Scout Manual, Boys' Life* magazine, and anything associated with my outdoor Scouting activities. But I almost never sat down to read for what we call "pleasure." Reading was too boring for me.

Some adults, especially educators and politicians, attack television because they say it is a passive activity while reading is an active one. Ha! I couldn't think of anything more passive than reading when I was a kid. Playing football, exploring new forest trails, deep sea fishing ... *that* is active. Reading was just imagining things; I wanted to DO those things. I preferred hiking, camping out, building model bridges, carving totems, bird-watching, tying knots, building campfires. My accomplishments earned me an Eagle Scout badge, and I was named the Outstanding Scout in my council when I was in high school.

Sports also captured my attention. Not watching but playing: baseball (until I got beaned—it was before Little Leaguers had to wear helmets), softball, track, football, stickball, street basketball. Because I was a fairly good athlete and was physically mature for my age, I was quite successful. In my junior year of high school I ran the bases (indoors) faster than anyone else at Eastside High School. Later that same year, our football team, on which I played offensive tackle and defensive linebacker, went undefeated for the first time in the school's history, and we won the state divisional championship.

Of course, because I did not read very much, I was not a very good writer. I *wanted* to write. But I had no idea how to do it well. Once when I was about ten or twelve, my parents took the family on a vacation to the Delaware

Donald R. Gallo

Donald, almost two years old. "My favorite photo of me as a cute little kid (the car belonged to a friend of my parents),"
Paterson, New Jersey, 1940.

Water Gap, with side trips to places like Roadside America where there was an enormous display of model trains that I can still envision. Not one train but several, all in bright colors, criss-crossing at lighted intersections, passing one another on parallel tracks, whistles blaring as they entered model towns or approached trestles and tunnels. Wanting to remember the excitement and reproduce the activity that I saw that day, I grabbed a notebook—it had an Indian head on the cover—and started to write: "We went to Roadside America today. Saw lots of trains. It was fun." What a letdown. I didn't know how to capture those details. The vision was clear in my head but I couldn't find the words to reproduce it.

Furthermore, my spelling was atrocious and my vocabulary quite limited. Because I was generally a bright student, the authorities at Eastside High School placed me in an Honors English class for the first semester of ninth grade. Not only couldn't I keep up with my better-read and more culturally-experienced colleagues, but I consistently failed the weekly vocabulary quizzes. Every one of them. Of course, like many students who are just given a list of ten words and told to look them up, I went through the motions of writing down definitions and using the words in simple, meaningless sentences, but I never really connected the meanings with the words. And because most of them were words I had never seen before (words like *supercilious*) and never expected to use, I was unmotivated and I consequently failed the quizzes. I was placed in a regular English class after that. "Not working up to his potential," they told my parents.

Later, in college, when I complained to my Freshman Composition instructor that no matter what I did to improve my writing, the highest grade I ever got was C+, he said: "Face it, Gallo, you'll probably never be better than a C writer."

Now I have a PhD, I have written and edited textbooks for teachers, my name is on the covers of more than a dozen books for teenagers, and I have published articles in numerous professional journals. How did I get here from there?

While my parents didn't provide any academic direction other than to make sure I did my homework, they always encouraged and supported me while they provided me with a secure and generally happy home life. In fact, my mother was somewhat over-protective. I believe it was the combination of having such a secure home life and wanting to break away from my mother's smothering attention that allowed me to leave home and try new experiences. The highlights of my teenage years seemed to be going away to summer camp, living for a couple of weeks each summer with my great aunt and uncle in Brooklyn, going away on family vacations, camping out with fellow Scouts, and, later, going away to college.

I was the first in my family to attend college. None of my relatives had much formal education. My father's parents had been factory workers, my mother's father was a police officer in town, and my maternal grandmother had always been a housewife. My mother's parents lived with us from when I was five years old, so it was my very gentle Nana who took care of me and my younger sister when our parents were working. She was the type of person who had a kind word for everyone, and whenever there was a problem, she smoothed it over, assuring me that everything would "work out to the good in the end."

My mother had dropped out of school after the tenth grade and gone to work. She was an information operator for the New Jersey Bell Telephone Company. (Once I dialed Information for a phone number and my mother answered!)

My Italian father, who had been brought to America by his parents when he was nine, had quit school during the ninth grade to help support his family when his father died. For most of his adult life, my father worked for the Pioneer Ice Cream division of the Borden Company, transferring containers of ice cream from the huge freezers to delivery trucks, spending half his working hours at below-zero temperatures. The shop, as he called it, was only a few short blocks from our house, so I would often ride my bike there to visit my dad. It wasn't just the father/son relationship that drew me there, of course; it was the ice cream.

The dock workers always kept a stash of whatever had spilled from broken containers: ice-cream bars, popsicles, Dixie cups, specialty items at holidays, like ice cream in the shape of turkeys or Santa Claus. I got to pick whatever I was in the mood for, and it was free. Sometimes I was allowed to walk with my dad through the factory, and if they were pouring freshly made ice cream into five-gallon containers, one of the workers would hold a small paper plate under the spout, then hand me a towering pile of cherry vanilla, butter pecan, peach in summer, or maybe French vanilla to eat with a small, flat wooden spoon. No experience could ever be better: a young boy with his dad and all the ice cream he could eat!

Both my parents worked extra hours to send me to college. But I didn't know what I wanted to do in life. Being a writer would never have occurred to me. Even now, looking back forty-some years, I am still amazed to see what I have become. And although I eventually became an English teacher, I did not, like most teachers, always want to teach. No librarian had ever influenced me. There were no books except a Bible and a dictionary in our house. No teachers in my high school made a major difference in my intellectual life, though several of them tried. I remember Mr. Friedman, probably the best English teacher I had in high school, recommending that I read Heming-way's *The Old Man and the Sea* because I liked deep-sea fishing (my great-uncle owned a fishing boat out of Sheepshead Bay in Brooklyn, and I worked for him during part of each summer when I was in high school). Good effort from Mr. Friedman. Unfortunately I couldn't identify with old Santiago nor with the kind of fishing he did. I finished the novel but was bored for most of it.

Partly because I earned some of my best grades in math in high school, my father hoped I'd be an engineer—the highest-paying profession back in 1956. But that didn't interest me. I was not only undecided, I hadn't even narrowed my options to a few possibilities. Finally, after two sets of aptitude tests showed me what I already knew—that I loved the outdoors—I applied and was accepted to the New York State College of Forestry at Syracuse University. Can you imagine—forestry!? I liked what I was exposed to there, but I didn't know how to study very well,

and so I failed freshman chemistry and didn't do well in forest botany, and was on the verge of academic probation as the end of my first year approached. But something else was going on in my life during that year, and it caused me to reshape and redirect my studies.

Throughout my teen years, I had always been involved in church activities: singing in the choir, attending youth group activities, teaching Sunday School. At Syracuse University I got involved in a Y group that provided an opportunity for a few of us to help out in local Presbyterian churches that were without their own ministers. Before that year was over, I found myself doing Bible readings, leading prayers, and even preaching sermons to small congregations in rural churches in upstate New York. Those experiences suggested a new direction for my life: I came to believe that I should be a minister.

I transferred to Hope College, a small but good liberal arts college in Holland, Michigan, that my home church helped support. In addition to occasional courses in religion, church music, and New Testament Greek, I chose to major in English because literature seemed more interesting than math and science and easier than history and philosophy. To that point, though, I still had not connected in any way with literature or writing.

Dr. Jim Prins and a couple of well-read roommates helped change that. Prins was a prince of a teacher. He projected a love of literature and a concern for his students like no other person I had ever met before, and he exposed me to Hawthorne, Hemingway, Steinbeck, Sartre, Camus, Zola, Dostoyevsky and others while my roommates introduced me to *Catcher in the Rye*. Wow! I had finally

Donald as an Eagle Scout, 1952.

"As Assistant Camp Director," about 1956.

matured enough so that I was ready for those books. I fell in love with Hemingway's writing and his macho image. I read *The Old Man and the Sea* again and adored it. I was in that skiff with Santiago; I struggled beside him to land that magnificent fish; I raged at the sharks that attacked the marlin lashed to the boat; and I fell into bed exhausted with the old man in the end, knowing that even though we may have been beaten, we would never be defeated. Literature had finally come alive for me.

As I read more and more, my writing improved. Surprise! During my junior year I got so involved with the poetry of e. e. cummings that a term paper I wrote about him and his poetry not only earned me a grade of A but also won the college essay award and a check for $25. I was stunned. After that, the editor of the college newspaper asked me to write a column on religious issues. Although my spelling was still quite poor, my writing career began at that point.

Nearing graduation, I was accepted at two different seminaries. But a variety of disturbing experiences within the Church during the previous years had made me question the honesty of several of the clergymen whom I was close to. I saw too much hypocrisy, too much slanting of the truth, too little regard for human issues, along with a bit of racism, and I decided that organized religion was not the place I wanted to be.

But where did I want to be? I was weeks away from college graduation and had no career! As an older teenager as well as during college summers I had worked as a camp counselor and nature director, had painted houses, packed boxes, unloaded trucks, installed air-conditioners, made pizzas, tutored math, worked on a fishing boat, and ministered to a mission church on the Omaha Indian Reservation in Nebraska. But I certainly was not interested in doing any of those things for the rest of my life. Fortunately, there was a last minute announcement posted on the career counselor's bulletin board about a new

graduate program at Oberlin College, funded by the Ford Foundation, where a student like me could earn a Master of Arts degree and a teaching certificate in one year. Thinking that perhaps I could save souls through literature instead of through religious activities, I applied and was accepted.

A year later, after a generally successful academic year but a horrifying student teaching experience in a large city high school where some of my students were older than I, I landed a fantastic job teaching English in Westport, Connecticut, one of the nation's best school systems back in the 1960s. The parents of many of my students were famous writers, photographers, newspaper editors, artists, radio broadcasters, and executives in major companies headquartered in New York City.

In addition to reading madly in order to keep up with the superior students in my junior high school classes, I also learned to write better. In part that was due to my trying to teach students how to write more effectively, though many of my students were already better writers than I. Part was also due to the response of my department chairperson, Annette Silverstone, who returned a memo I had sent her, all my misspelled words circled in red, with a note at the bottom saying, "If you intend to be an English teacher, you had better learn to spell." I was deeply embarrassed, and from that day on, I began to use a dictionary to check every word I was not absolutely sure about.

My writing also improved because one of my college roommates—Stuart Wilson—continued to send me wonderfully descriptive letters. I admired Stu's writing style and tried to write back in a similarly descriptive way. Slowly I got better at it, eventually realizing what my writing was lacking when I had tried to describe my visit to Roadside America years earlier.

While teaching at Westport's Bedford Junior High School, I was given two opportunities that I now view as significant in my development as a writer and editor: With no background whatsoever in journalism, I volunteered to produce a monthly newsletter for the Westport Education Association, doing everything from writing to layout to typing, duplicating, and distributing it. And I was asked to be the faculty advisor for the school's prize-winning literary magazine, *Image*. The students there were amazingly talented, needing little more than encouragement from me, though I did my best to help them polish their already-good writing. In addition to producing a first-rate publication, the literary magazine group also sponsored a writing contest that was judged by professional writers who worked at the Famous Writers' School housed just down the street. Informal advice from some of those professionals was invaluable to me as well as to the student writers.

Although these positions improved my editing and writing skills, I still did not view myself as a writer.

When I married (for the first time), one of the conditions set by my wife was that we go to graduate school, she for her master's in nursing and I for a sixth year certificate. We chose Syracuse University because the people there gave both of us opportunities to support ourselves through grants and assistantships. While there, I found learning to be much easier than previously, mostly because I knew what I was doing and I was reading and studying to find answers to real teaching problems. I had always felt I was doing the right things in my classroom, but I never knew the theories behind the procedures I used, or had research evidence to support what I wanted to do next. Now I was learning what I needed to know. I earned more A's in that first year than I had in my entire academic career before that. When my wife completed her master's degree and started working in the area, I continued my studies and a year later completed a lengthy dissertation for a PhD degree. We found jobs in Colorado and moved to a house in a suburb of Denver.

In the publish-or-perish academic world at the University of Colorado, I was expected to write. But I didn't have to be told; I *wanted* to write. I had things to say; I wanted other teachers to know what I had been learning and was continuing to discover. I also had a mentor from my doctoral program—Dr. Margaret Early—whose example I wanted to follow, though I was determined never to work as many hours a day as she did. (I didn't succeed at that.)

While at Syracuse, one of the important things I discovered was literature for young people. I had begun to read young adult books in 1967, the same year that S.E. Hinton published *The Outsiders* and Robert Lipsyte published *The Contender.* After I completed my doctorate in 1968, I continued to read the new books in that field as they came out: *The Pigman, Go Ask Alice, Dinky Hocker Shoots Smack!, A Day No Pigs Would Die.* I loved the realism and immediacy of those novels; the language sounded like real teenagers talking; the issues "spoke" to kids. These were the kinds of books I might have read if they had been available when I was a teenager.

Although I focused a great deal of my scholarly activities on the teaching of developmental reading skills

Graduation Day, Hope College, Michigan, 1960.

and writing skills in secondary schools at that time, I slowly began to shift my attention to books for teenagers. Over the next few years, and especially after I left the University of Colorado and took a job at Central Connecticut State University in New Britain, Connecticut, I continued to read YA books voraciously and to survey students about their reading interests and habits. In addition to observing teenagers when I was supervising student teachers in area schools, I asked my university students to bring junior and senior high school students to our class once each semester where we interviewed them. Thus I was able to keep up with what teenagers were reading and how they reacted to what teachers did with books in the local school systems. As my own two kids grew to be teenagers, I also was able to keep track of what they read (and did not read), how their teachers involved them in (or turned them off to) literature, what kinds of writing assignments they had, etc.

While I was keeping tuned in to contemporary teenagers, I had opportunities over the years to hone my skills as an editor and a writer. In 1976, I volunteered to serve as editor of the *Connecticut English Journal,* a publication of the Connecticut Council of Teachers of English that had not been published regularly in previous years. With good advice from *Arizona English Bulletin* editor Ken Donelson at Arizona State University, I sent a letter to a lot of educators across the country, inviting them to write articles for our journal. Except for the final typing prior to duplication, this was another one of those jobs where I was responsible for everything except typing: from editing, layout, and proofing to delivering the manuscript to the printer, sticking on address labels, and mailing the finished copies to council members and subscribers. The journal became quite successful: eight of the ten issues I edited were purchased by the National Council of Teachers of English for national distribution.

One of my two favorite issues was on teaching young adult literature, as you can imagine it would be. The other favorite was the Spring 1977 issue for which I wrote to a number of famous authors who lived in Connecticut, asking them to write something—anything, from a full-blown essay to just a postcard—about how they thought writing should be taught in junior and senior high schools. A few of them did not answer—after all, they were famous writers who had no idea who I was, and they probably had no interest in writing something for an academic journal they had never heard of. I also had no money to pay for their work. One novelist quite bluntly told me she did not write for anyone without being paid for her time. A few, like A.E. Hotchner, said they were too busy with other work; he was leaving shortly for Italy to interview Sophia Loren. (How could I compete with Sophia!?) But those who did send me things—for free—made an impressive list in the issue's table of contents. Among them were a Newbery Award winner and five Pulitzer Prize winners. The issue included essays by Arthur Miller, John Hersey, William Manchester, Barbara Tuchman, Eugene V. Rostow, Hal Borland, Malcolm Cowley, Paul Horgan, Mary Stolz, Elizabeth George Speare, and William Styron. Though they disagreed with one another on specifics, their advice made for interesting reading. The only thing they were unanimous about was that to be any kind of a writer, a person needs to be a reader first.

During my five years of working with a variety of authors from the complementary worlds of education and publishing, I honed my editing skills, lost all fear (well, most, anyway) of dealing with famous people, and learned to be more tactful in my criticisms.

During those same years, I was fortunate to meet a number of authors at conferences of English educators: Richard Peck, Paula Danziger, Walter Dean Myers, Bette Greene, Robert Cormier, Robert Lipsyte, Judie Angell, and others, along with a few editors, most importantly George Nicholson, then Editor-in-Chief at Dell Publishing Company. I didn't just meet these people as an observer. I met the first of them because I was a friend of the person running the conference session and was asked to help out. I picked up Richard Peck at the train station; I bought coffee for Bette Greene and tried to ease her fears before she gave her talk; I met Walter Dean Myers at the airport and invited him for a drink before he retired for the night. A year or two later, I arranged for several authors to speak at the annual Connecticut English teachers' conference, and then invited them for dinner at my home. Not only was I delighted to spend time with such interesting people, but also my son Brian and stepdaughter Chris were thrilled to meet authors such as Robert Lipsyte, Paula Danziger, Robin Brancato, and Robert Cormier.

While continuing my teaching at the university and trying to keep up with as much young adult literature as I could, it slowly occurred to me in the early 1980s that while most schools required students to read short stories, there were only a handful of books of short stories written by young adult novelists. Those collections had each been written by a single author: Joan Aiken, Norma Fox Mazer, Lois Ruby, Nicholasa Mohr, and Robert Cormier. In the few existing collections for high school readers that did feature a variety of authors, such as *Point of Departure: 19 Stories of Youth and Discovery* edited by Robert S. Gold, most of the stories had been reprinted from adult maga-

zines, such as the *New Yorker* and *Esquire*—certainly not magazines that the average teenager ever reads. Why weren't there any collections of good short stories about teenagers that were written by people whose novels were being read by teenagers? It seems the answer was that no one had yet tried to assemble such a collection.

So I asked several of the authors I had met if they would be interested in writing a story for a new, landmark collection, and most of them said they would. In fact, Robert Cormier immediately sent me the only story he had ever written that had not already been published elsewhere: "In the Heat." I proposed the project to George Nicholson at Dell, and he thought the idea was splendid. Two years later, in 1984, *Sixteen: Short Stories by Outstanding Writers for Young Adults* was published. That collection is now viewed as a milestone in young adult literature, and the Young Adult Services Division of the American Library Association lists *Sixteen* as one of the 100 Best of the Best Books for Young Adults published between 1967 and 1992.

As soon as we saw that *Sixteen* was a success—even more successful than the publisher or I had thought possible—we began work on a second collection. That came to be called *Visions*. Then a third: *Connections*.

The procedures were the same for these volumes as for the first one: I sent letters to as many as forty-five authors, starting with the most famous people in the field, inviting them to write a story for my next book. A few authors never answer my invitation. Some, like Judy Blume and Paula Danziger (whose work I would love to have in one of my books) told me they are not comfortable writing short stories and do not care to try, thank you. Robert Cormier had already given me (for *Sixteen*) the last short story he said he'd ever write; he says he enjoys the novel form too much to write in any other form. Some authors say they appreciate the invitation but are too busy with other projects to meet my deadline.

Of the group of authors who respond positively to my invitations, some never find time to finish (or even start) a story for me. By the proposed deadline for submissions, I usually end up with twenty-some manuscripts. Of those, a few have always been knockout stories that bowl me over, make me want to call up a friend and say "Listen to this. This is great!" Richard Peck's now famous "Priscilla and the Wimps" (in *Sixteen*) is one such story. Robert Lipsyte's "The Defender" (in *Ultimate Sports*), Fran Arrick's "The Good Girls" (in *Visions*), Annette Curtis Klaus's "The Hoppins" (in *Short Circuits*), and Will Weaver's "The Photograph" (in *No Easy Answers*) are others.

Sometimes an author sends me a story that I like, but it is too different from the rest of the stories I've already received, or it might be on a theme similar to that of another submitted story that I like better, so I return it, with thanks, because it doesn't fit. In many of those instances, the author sells that story elsewhere. In one case, the writer believed in her rejected story enough to write several other stories and package them into a book as a collection about kids from a specific high school. Good for her!

On rare occasions, an author has sent me a story that is, for a variety of reasons, not effectively written. I don't mean it needs work; if a story seems pretty good but needs some revising, I will work with the writer to make it a better story. I mean it's a pretty poor story. And that always

"At 11,500 feet near Loveland Pass, Colorado," about 1972.

Gallo at Mystic Seaport, Connecticut, about 1992.

surprises as well as disappoints me: to read a story by some famous writer that is so far below par I have to reject it. How do you tell a prize-winning, highly-regarded author that you think her or his story stinks? I don't. I usually go with the excuse that the story doesn't quite fit what we have been looking for.

We have always budgeted for up to sixteen stories in each collection. As editor, I have the final say in which selections get included in any of my books. I am grateful to my editors for always respecting my judgment, even when in rare instances they have disagreed with one of my choices. Usually, I do not make the most difficult choices alone. While putting together *Sixteen,* I duplicated most of the manuscripts and asked six teachers in local middle and high schools to share them with a class or two. The students loved the opportunity to tell me their reactions. For subsequent collections, I've relied on the teenage children of friends as well as colleagues for their opinions of stories I have not been sure about.

For *No Easy Answers,* I selected two submitted stories in manuscript form and, with the permission of the authors, my wife read them to her two tenth-grade English classes. The following day, I spent a class period with each group, listening to their reactions and recommendations. I then e-mailed the students' comments to the authors, who made revisions accordingly. The authors appreciated the instant feedback, and the students felt special to know their opinions were respected.

Although my first three collections were well received, some librarians and people who divide their bibliographies into categories didn't know where to fit *Sixteen, Visions,* and *Connections,* except under the general category of Short Stories. It's also easier to sell a book if you can say what it's about. The stories in my first collections were about a variety of topics. A narrower focus was sensible, so the next book became *Short Circuits,* a collection of thirteen horror/supernatural stories. Incidentally, there was no intent to print only thirteen stories; I

received only thirteen usable manuscripts. (That book, though quite a good seller as well as a Junior Library Guild selection, has gone out of print, but I hope to be able to get it back in print soon.)

Short Circuits was followed by *Join In,* the most challenging collection I've done. Multicultural literature had become the latest buzzword in the educational business, and a book of stories featuring American teenagers from a variety of ethnic backgrounds seemed like a worthwhile project. But where to find enough good writers for such stories? Most novelists who write for young adults are white. And the most famous of the writers who are not white are always in great demand. Thus, most of the authors I invited said they were too busy to write something for this collection. I found as many as I could—including Julius Lester, Lensey Namioka, Maureen Crane Wartski, and Rudolfo Anaya—then turned to white writers who had already published novels that included well-drawn ethnic characters, such as Linda Crew whose highly regarded *Children of the River* features a Cambodian refugee teenager and her family. As a result, *Join In* includes original stories about American teenagers who are African American, Puerto Rican, Vietnamese, Chinese, Japanese, Cuban, Lebanese, Laotian, Chicano, and Pueblo Indian.

Because sports is one of the most popular subjects in books, especially for boys, my next collection has a sports theme. Beginning with authors such as Chris Crutcher, Robert Lipsyte, and Thomas Dygard who had previously published novels about athletes, I assembled a stellar line-up. The sixteen stories in *Ultimate Sports* deal with basketball, football, running, tennis, fishing, sailing, boxing, wrestling, racquetball, and the triathlon, as well as with the Interscholastic Galactic mind game of the future. The title for this book, by the way, was chosen by the votes of several classes of middle school and high school students as well as college students in a teacher preparation program.

The next book capitalized on the national interest in the moral development of children. I invited authors to write stories about teenagers facing moral dilemmas and dealing with the consequences of their decisions. It was crucial that these authors avoid preaching or suggesting pat answers to complex human problems. Authors as diverse as Ron Koertge, Rita Williams-Garcia, Monica Hughes, and Graham Salisbury wrote thought-provoking stories about such topics as peer pressure, computer blackmail, academic cheating, drug use, gang violence, and unwanted pregnancy. On my wife CJ's recommendation, we titled this collection *No Easy Answers: Short Stories About Teenagers Making Tough Choices.*

In addition to those short story collections for teenage readers, I compiled and edited two other types of collections for kids. For one, I invited a different group of authors to write stories for younger readers, those in grades four through eight, since no one at that point had ever published a book of new short stories specifically for that age group. The oldest character in *Within Reach: Ten Stories* is thirteen.

An interesting and disturbing thing occurred with this collection. It was never advertised in any special way by the publisher and it got reviewed in only a few journals. One of those reviews, ignoring the publishing information that accompanied the book, listed it for grades seven to twelve and did not give it a very enthusiastic recommendation. *I* wouldn't give it a very high recommendation for older teens either! That's the wrong audience.

For whatever reasons, this collection sold poorly, was never issued in paperback, and went out of print in a short while. Maybe the stories weren't very good, you are thinking. That's the troubling part: many of these wonderful stories by people such as Judie Angell, Carol Snyder, Pam Conrad, Larry Bograd, and Ardath Mayhar have been reprinted in magazines and textbooks and on CD-ROMs, attesting to their quality and value. So the stories live on even though the book doesn't exist anymore.

The other project was the production of a unique collection of one-act plays for young people. Because novelists who write for teenagers almost always use a lot of dialog and a minimum of description, I believed it would not be very difficult for some of those same people to write a short play for teenagers. Two of the authors I asked, in fact, had already written and published plays: Sandy Asher and Cin Forshay-Lunsford.

Three publishers turned down my proposal for this book, one of them because the editorial director didn't think that novelists were capable of writing well in such a different genre. But Marilyn Kriney at HarperCollins liked the idea, and *Center Stage: One-Act Plays for Teenage*

Readers and Actors was born. Since its premier, several of the ten plays from *Center Stage,* such as Sandy Asher's "Working Out," Jean Davies Okimoto's "Hum It Again, Jeremy," Walter Dean Myers' "Cages," and Robin Brancato's "War of the Words" have been reprinted in literature textbooks and performed on high school stages across the country as well as in Canada. Compared to my short story collections, not many teachers know about this book, but those who do use it continually tell me how much they appreciate it. There is a need for plays such as these for middle and high schools, but there has not been enough perceived interest for a publisher to do another collection like this.

Most anthologies, whether of plays or short stories, are formed by reprinting works from other publications. The stories in all of my collections, in contrast, have all been new creations, published for the first time in my books. In turn, many of the works first published in my collections, as I have noted, have been reprinted in magazines such as *Seventeen, Read, Scholastic Scope,* and *Cicada* as well as in several reading and literature anthologies used in middle and high schools.

In a couple of cases, the authors later expanded their stories into novels, as Jean Davies Okimoto did: "Moonbeam Dawson and the Killer Bear" (from *Connections*) became *The Eclipse of Moonbeam Dawson* eight years later. In some instances, the opposite has occurred: a scene or a character from a novel has been reworked by the author into a short story.

For example, in M. E. Kerr's novel *Night Kites,* the brother of the narrator, a young homosexual man dying of AIDS, is trying to write a story but can't seem to get much beyond the first page. Once she had completed the novel, Kerr then continued and finished the story her character had begun. That became "The Sweet Perfume of Goodbye" that I published in *Visions.* And from his 1995 novel *Ironman,* Chris Crutcher extracted the main character Bo Brewster and made him a secondary character in his short story "Superboy" that he wrote for *Ultimate Sports.* One story from one of my books even became a movie: Chris Crutcher's "A Brief Moment in the Life of Angus Bethune" (from *Connections*), though the title became just *Angus* and the content of the story was changed radically in the process. It's a thrill for me to see these spin-offs occurring just because I have invited someone to write something for one of my books.

These projects have also given some authors a chance to try something different. Instead of writing a sports-oriented story like I expected, Robert Lipsyte turned to science fiction. By writing "Future Tense" for *Sixteen* and having such fun with it, Lipsyte later wrote other stories and a novel in the same genre. Chris Crutcher had never written a short story before I invited him to write something, and he came up with "Angus Bethune." He says that he enjoyed the form so much that he wrote several additional stories and published them in his own collection, fittingly called *Athletic Shorts.* Similarly, Jeanie Okimoto, who had never written a play until I invited her to write one for *Center Stage,* was so pleased with the outcome that she has decided to work on other plays.

"As it says, the Temple of Heaven in Beijing, China,"
June, 1993.

The author at his former home office in Connecticut, 1996.

One of the most rewarding parts of my job is having the opportunity to read a brand new story that no one besides the author has ever seen. When I'm putting together a new collection and the deadline for submissions is approaching, I anxiously await the arrival of the mail truck each day. Opening the mailbox, I reach in and grin when I see a large tan envelope. It may be postmarked from New York City, Palo Alto, Seattle, Houston, Bemidji, or Santa Fe; occasionally the colorful stamps indicate the package has been mailed from Canada, England, Scotland, Switzerland, New Zealand, or, once, Singapore. I carefully tear open the envelope and begin to read. And when my attention is grabbed on the first page, I know this is going to be a great story.

My first reading of any story is for appreciation. The next couple of readings are to confirm the general structure of the story and to note any places that don't make perfect sense. Along the way I fix any mechanical errors I notice: misspellings, improper use of punctuation, subject-verb agreement, etc.—the same kinds of mechanical errors English teachers mark in students' papers. Some authors—Richard Peck, for example—are nearly flawless in their writing. A few others—who shall remain nameless, of course—have never learned the difference between *it's* and *its,* or they consistently place commas and periods outside the ends of quotation marks instead of inside them. But

that's why editors are needed. And because I never catch all of the little things, before the book goes to the printer there is always a copy editor at the publishing house whose keen eyes catch every tiny problem I may have missed.

Because I have experienced what it feels like to have editors change pieces of my writing without my permission—not just sentence structures but the meaning of entire paragraphs—I never change anything in anyone's writing (except for mechanical errors) without the writer's approval. When there are problems in a story—such as missing details that could make a scene more convincing, or sentences or paragraphs that could be reorganized to make the meaning clearer—I try to recommend one or more ways to repair the problem. I may even suggest a different beginning or the omission of an entire section.

Knowing how much students dislike a teacher telling them their work is not as perfect as they think it is, kids in schools I visit usually ask me how those authors react to my criticisms. I am happy to tell students that in more than two decades of doing this job, as far as I know, no author has ever gotten seriously angry at me over changes that I have recommended. In fact, most of them usually thank me for recommending those changes or for catching errors they had failed to notice, because their story or essay is always improved by those changes.

Recently, for example, I recommended that prize-winning author Graham Salisbury begin his story "Waiting for the War" (that will appear in *Time Capsule*) with some action instead of the lengthy description of the setting he had written. He balked at first. So I gently reminded him that teenagers, especially boys for whom his story would be especially appealing, would never get to the action if they weren't attracted by the initial description. I acknowledged that the information provided in his opening was important but it could be integrated elsewhere in the story. Yesterday (as I'm writing this), his revised story arrived in my mailbox with a note: "Okay, you win!" he wrote. "I cut the page-and-a-half intro and started with the boys in action. Actually, I like it this way. It's tighter. It's just hard to shoot your babies, you know?"

Certainly it's hard to cut out parts we like, especially when we have spent so much time on them. But none of us are writing for ourselves. We're writing for the enjoyment of others. And we all get too close to our own creations to see their flaws. That's why we all need someone else's perspective of our writing. I tell students that if most professional writers can't see some of their own mistakes, they, as middle school or high school and college students, would be wise to get other readers to check over their stories and their essays as well as their homework assignments before handing them to teachers.

My correspondence with authors about their stories used to be handled through the U.S. mail and by telephone. Now more than half of my correspondence with authors, agents, and publishers is done through e-mail. For my most recent collection of short stories, actually, eight of the ten authors are on the Internet. On some days I might correspond with authors in California, Wisconsin, Massachusetts, New York, and Ireland, ask for advice from colleagues in Texas and Connecticut, check some facts through Alta Vista on the World Wide Web, and print hard copies of all of it from my PowerMac 6500 on my Epson

Stylus Color 800 printer. When I started doing these books in the early '80s, I typed everything on a Royal manual typewriter, using carbon paper to make copies. I continue to be amazed at how much easier it is to write and, especially, revise and communicate with authors and publishers now. When it used to take two to three weeks between my sending an author suggestions for revisions and the author making those revisions and sending them back to me, now it can be done in one or two days. In some cases, it's done the same day. I believe that computers and the Internet are among the greatest inventions of my lifetime (after Haagen-Dazs chocolate chocolate chip ice cream, that is).

Although I have not written short stories or plays for any of my books, it has been my job to write the introduction to each book as well as the introductions to each story, and the biographical sketches of each author. I also write some of the information that appears on the inside flaps of the hardcover's dust jacket. Even though this is not very imaginative writing, creativity is necessary for organizing the information so that it is interesting and readable.

In addition to editing journals for teachers and collections of short stories and plays for teenage readers, I have edited and written two books for teachers. One of the books is a collection of essays about teaching reading and writing, called *Authors' Insights: Turning Teenagers into Readers and Writers,* with chapters written by some of the same writers who have done short stories for my collections. Among the authors are Harry Mazer, Norma Fox Mazer, Robert Cormier, William Sleator, Gloria D. Miklowitz, and Todd Strasser, writing about the value of classics, motivating students to read, the value of science fiction, the effects of censorship, and writing workshops. There is some excellent writing in there, as well as numerous thoughtful ideas and practical suggestions for teaching literature and writing.

The second book is called *From Hinton to Hamlet:Building Bridges Between Young Adult Literature and the Classics* that I wrote with Sarah K. Herz, a former middle school and high school English teacher from Westport, Connecticut. We wrote this book for all those teachers, especially in high schools, who do not use young adult literature. Many teachers have never read any of it; too many of them have terrible opinions of it from what they *think* YA literature is. At the same time, many of their students are slogging painfully through *Great Expectations, The Scarlet Letter,* or *The Great Gatsby* without much understanding beyond what the teacher tells them, and certainly without any pleasure. We recommend pairing young adult books with specific classics, along with a more student response-centered approach.

The book was difficult to write because we had to integrate a variety of theoretical approaches and research findings with practical student-centered activities that enhanced students' reading experiences, then recommend a number of alternative books whose themes were similar to those of the commonly required classics. But this was a truly collaborative effort, with Sarah writing the first drafts of some chapters and me revising and expanding them. Then I wrote other chapters and Sarah polished them. We

Gallo and his wife CJ, 1997.

constructed the bibliographies and the index during marathon sessions on her back porch.

Some of my work has been for both teachers and students. In 1989 Twayne published *Presenting Richard Peck,* a book they asked me to write about Peck's life and writings. I was fortunate to be assigned this well-known author, because he is such an interesting person, witty and talented, and he writes one excellent novel after the other. The down side of doing Peck is that he has written so much, and not just YA novels. He's produced several short stories, a few poems, a couple of novels for adults, and numerous articles for teachers and librarians. Although the work was always enjoyable, reading and rereading everything he had written and then analyzing all of it took an enormous amount of time. Writing the book was the easy part. What I found most enjoyable, in addition to interviewing Richard Peck for many hours in his New York City apartment, was the research itself: it was the first extensive library research I had done since my doctoral studies.

In the late 1980s, John Lansingh Bennett, then senior editor for publications at the National Council of Teachers of English, challenged me to compile a collection of the biographies of the most famous authors who write for young adults. The goal was to produce a book that was informative, readable, easily handled (unlike those huge library biographical sources), and inexpensive.

In order to do that, I first needed to determine who the top authors were. So I surveyed a group of educators who were leaders in the field of books for young people. Richard Peck suggested that instead of writing all those biographies myself or having a small group of colleagues do it, I should ask the authors to write about themselves. It was a wise and helpful suggestion, which I immediately followed.

I therefore sent a letter of invitation to one hundred authors, asking them to write a brief autobiography and send me a photo and a bibliography of their publications. The resulting responses became *Speaking for Ourselves: Autobiographical Sketches by Notable Authors of Books for Young Adults.* Not all one hundred authors responded. A couple never answered, even after repeated letters. One wrote that she didn't "do stuff like that." Two told me they would not write without being paid. The book thus contains the autobiographies of eighty-seven authors, from Joan Aiken and Lloyd Alexander to Jane Yolen and Paul Zindel.

Three years later, to add new up-and-coming stars as well as authors not included in the first volume, I compiled a companion book featuring eighty-nine additional writers, which we called *Speaking for Ourselves, Too: More Autobiographical Sketches by Notable Authors of Books for Young Adults.* In addition to describing the backgrounds of these authors, these autobiographies provide advice for young writers as well as explanations of the diverse writing processes these authors employ.

Throughout my career I have also written and edited a variety of teacher guides for different commercial publishers, written reading lessons and teaching materials for the seventh and eighth grade books in the Harcourt Brace Bookmark Reading Program (now out of print), selected a good portion of the literature for the D.C. Heath Middle Level Literature Program, and published dozens of articles about reading, teaching literature, teaching writing, and censorship in professional journals and chapters in several books.

What haven't I done? Whenever I present a workshop or lead a book discussion session with teenagers, teachers, or librarians, someone usually asks me when I'm going to publish a collection of my own stories. The answer is "Probably never." I've never been interested in writing a short story. Or a novel. Oh, I'd like to have written a novel; doing it is something quite different.

Creating fiction does not come easily for me, if it comes at all. In college I took a short-story writing course and earned a B, but I think my professor was being generous. The stories I wrote then were distinctly unimaginative, stiff, and not at all memorable. Not only did I not save any of them, but I can't even recall now what they were about. Perhaps someday I will try writing fiction.

In the meantime, I currently have enough ideas for new short story collections to keep me busy for the next five years, and more ideas for nonfiction books and articles than I will ever have time to write. It makes me chuckle to recall that as a teenager I spent countless hours trying to think of something to write whenever a teacher assigned a story or an essay. How many times I cried out in frustration: "There's nothing to write about!"

In 1997 I remarried, took early retirement from my teaching position at Central Connecticut State University, and moved with my new wife, CJ, to a new house on a small pond in a suburb of Cleveland, Ohio, where I now spend most of my time writing and editing. (As I am typing this, several Canada geese are cruising across the pond in front of my office window.) In addition to cooking and gardening, I like to travel as often as possible, taking photographs of the most scenic sites. I've been through Europe, parts of Greece, several Caribbean islands, Mexico, China and Hong Kong, Canada, on a safari in Kenya, and in every state except North Dakota, Mississippi, Arkansas, and Hawaii. I also teach an occasional class in young adult literature, consult for school systems, lead a monthly discussion group with teachers and librarians on books for young people, and am working on several writing projects.

Having now published seven collections of short stories for teenagers, I have written a picture book called *The Wonders of Walls* that I am seeking a publisher for, and am trying to work out the kinks in a series of informational books for younger readers about parts of the body. As I write this, I am also waiting for several authors to send me their stories for my next collection that will consist of ten historical stories about American teenagers, each story set in a different decade of the twentieth century. I'm writing a fairly lengthy introduction to each decade that provides the historical background for each story, including some tasty tidbits, such as the year Snickers candy was first sold, when oreo cookies were first marketed, and how Velcro was discovered. *Time Capsule: Stories About Yesterday for Today* is due to be published at the end of 1999 or in early 2000.

As you can see, I was a very late bloomer. But since I first blossomed, my output has been pleasingly abundant. I hope my growing season will last a long time.

Writings

EDITOR; FOR YOUNG ADULTS

Sixteen: Short Stories by Outstanding Writers for Young Adults, Delacorte, 1984.

Books for You: A Booklist for Senior High Students, National Council of Teachers of English, 1985.

Visions: Short Stories by Outstanding Writers for Young Adults, Delacorte, 1987.

Connections: Short Stories by Outstanding Writers for Young Adults, Delacorte, 1989.

Speaking for Ourselves: Autobiographical Sketches of Notable Authors of Books for Young Adults, National Council of Teachers of English, 1990.

Center Stage: One-Act Plays for Teenage Readers and Actors, HarperCollins, 1990.

Short Circuits: Thirteen Shocking Stories by Outstanding Writers for Young Adults, Delacorte, 1992.

Speaking for Ourselves, Too—More Autobiographical Sketches by Notable Authors of Books for Young Adults, National Council of Teachers of English, 1993.

Within Reach: Ten Stories, HarperCollins, 1993.

Join In: Multiethnic Short Stories by Outstanding Writers for Young Adults, Delacorte, 1993.

Ultimate Sports: Short Stories by Outstanding Writers for Young Adults, Delacorte, 1995.

No Easy Answers: Short Stories about Teenagers Making Tough Choices, Delacorte, 1997.

FOR ADULTS; NONFICTION

Reading Rate and Comprehension, 1970-1971 Assessment, National Assessment of Educational Progress, 1972.

Recipes, Wrappers, Reasoning and Rate, A Digest of the First Reading Assessment, National Assessment of Educational Progress, 1974.

Presenting Richard Peck, Twayne, 1989.

Authors' Insights: Turning Teenagers into Readers and Writers, Boynton/Cook-Heinemann, 1992.

(With Sarah K. Herz) *From Hinton to Hamlet: Building Bridges between Young Adult Literature and the Classics,* Greenwood, 1996.

Has also served as editor for the *Connecticut English Journal,* and as author and consultant for anthologies and textbooks including *Heath Middle Level Literature Program* and *Bookmark Reading Program.*

GERBER, Perren 1933-

Personal

Hebrew name, Pesach Gerber; born November 21, 1933, in Chicago, IL; son of Isadore (a garment worker) and Fannie (Bass) Gerber; married Sandra Lipa, 1958 (divorced, 1980); married Patricia Ann Torlich (a nurse and legal consultant), 1985; children: Ian Marcus, Bena Guida. *Education:* Attended School of the Art Institute of Chicago, Chicago Academy of Fine Art, and School of Visual Arts, New York City. *Politics:* Independent. *Religion:* Jewish. *Hobbies and other interests:* Fishing, photography, on-site sketching and painting.

Addresses

Home and office—2183 Graystone Parkway, Grayson, GA 30017. *Electronic mail*—pgerber @ mindspring.com.

Career

Owner of a company that designed and manufactured displays and exhibits, 1962-82; currently freelance designer for national companies that sell collectible items. Artist and sculptor, with work represented in galleries across the United States. *Military service:* U.S. Army, Infantry and Corps of Engineers, 1956-58.

Perren Gerber

Illustrator

Sashi Fridman, *The Living Letters,* Merkos L'inyouei Chinuch (Brooklyn, NY), 1996.

Marci Stillerman, *Nine Spoons: A Chanukah Story,* Hachai Publications (Brooklyn, NY), 1998.

Work in Progress

A series of children's books based on classic radio series of the 1940s.

Sidelights

Perren Gerber told *SATA:* "At age sixteen I sold my first piece of commercial art. In the nearly fifty years since, I have worked in a great many areas of the commercial and fine art world. With extremely few exceptions, I've enjoyed it all—particularly the variety and the learning processes necessitated by the changes.

"I have worked as a cartoonist, illustrator, technical illustrator, and designer. This last designation covered subject matter both plentiful and diverse: designing museum and commercial exhibits and displays, 'collectibles,' commercial interiors, et cetera. While doing this, I have also worked as an animator, model builder, commercial and fine art sculptor, and most recently, a children's book illustrator.

"I started a shop meant to be a one-man design and fabrication company. Twenty years later there were twenty-one full-time employees working with more than a hundred part-timers and freelance specialists. In 1983 the company was bought by a much larger company. Within three years, what we had taken twenty years to build was gone.

"It was at this point that I determined my mode of work would be what it has been to this day. I work out of three different areas of my home: a conventional art studio, a custom-built sculpture studio, and a compact shop area where small projects and prototypes can be made.

"I consider myself very fortunate. At age sixty-five, I am busier and more productive than ever. I take on only the projects that interest me and only from people I enjoy working with. The variety of work includes almost all of the areas mentioned above, and I look forward to the next requested project I've never done before."

*   *   *

GIBBONS, Gail (Gretchen) 1944-

Personal

Born August 1, 1944, in Oak Park, IL; daughter of Harry George (a tool and die designer) and Grace (Johnson) Ortmann; married Glenn Gibbons, June 25, 1966 (died May 20, 1972); married Kent Ancliffe (a builder), March 23, 1976; children: (stepchildren) Rebecca, Eric. *Education:* University of Illinois, B.F.A., 1967.

Addresses

Home—Corinth, VT, 05039. *Agent*—Florence Alexander, 80 Park Ave., New York, NY 10017. *Office*—Goose Green, Corinth, VT 05039.

Career

Freelance writer and illustrator of children's books, 1975—. WCIA-Television, Champaign, IL, artist, 1967-69; WMAQ-TV, Chicago, IL, promotions and animation artist, 1969; Bob Hower Agency, Chicago, IL, staff artist, 1969-70; WNBC-Television, House of Animation, New York, NY, staff artist, 1970-76; United Press International, New York City, freelance artist, 1977—.

Awards, Honors

New York City Art Director Club award, 1979, for *The Missing Maple Syrup Sap Mystery;* American Institute of Graphic Arts award, 1979, for *Clocks and How They Go;* National Science Teachers Association/Children's Book Council Award, 1980, for *Locks and Keys,* and 1982, for *Tool Book;* certificate of appreciation from U.S. Postmaster General, 1982, for *The Post Office Book: Mail and How It Moves;* American Library Association Notable Book award, 1983, for *Cars and How They Go,* and 1985, for *The Milk Makers;* *Washington Post* Children's Book Guild Award, 1987, for contribution to nonfiction children's literature; National Council of Social Studies Notable Children's Trade Book in the Field of Social Studies, 1983, 1987, 1989, 1990, and 1992; National Science Teachers Association's Outstanding Science Trade Books for Children, 1983, 1987, 1991, 1998; International Reading Association Children's Choice Award, 1989 and 1995; American Bookseller Pick of the Lists, 1992.

Gail Gibbons

Writings

SELF-ILLUSTRATED NONFICTION CHILDREN'S BOOKS, UNLESS NOTED

Willy and His Wheel Wagon, Prentice-Hall, 1975.

Salvador and Mister Sam: A Guide to Parakeet Care (fiction), Prentice-Hall, 1976.

Things to Make and Do for Halloween, F. Watts, 1976.

Things to Make and Do for Columbus Day, F. Watts, 1977.

Things to Make and Do for Your Birthday, F. Watts, 1978.

The Missing Maple Syrup Sap Mystery (fiction), Warne, 1979.

Clocks and How They Go, Crowell, 1979.

Locks and Keys, Crowell, 1980.

The Too Great Bread Bake Book, Warne, 1980.

Trucks, Crowell, 1981.

The Magnificent Morris Mouse Clubhouse (fiction), F. Watts, 1981.

Tool Book, Holiday House, 1982.

The Post Office Book: Mail and How It Moves, Crowell, 1982.

Christmas Time, Holiday House, 1982.

Boat Book, Holiday House, 1983.

Thanksgiving Day, Holiday House, 1983.

New Road!, Crowell, 1983.

Sun Up, Sun Down, Harcourt, 1983.

Department Store, Crowell, 1984.

Fire! Fire!, Crowell, 1984.

Halloween, Holiday House, 1984.

The Seasons of Arnold's Apple Tree, Harcourt, 1984.

Tunnels, Holiday House, 1984.

Check It Out: The Book about Libraries, Harcourt, 1985.

Lights! Camera! Action! How a Movie Is Made, Crowell, 1985.

Fill It Up! All about Service Stations, Crowell, 1985.

The Milk Makers, Macmillan/Collier, 1985.

Playgrounds, Holiday House, 1985.

Flying, Holiday House, 1986.

From Path to Highway: The Story of the Boston Post Road, Crowell, 1986.

Happy Birthday!, Holiday House, 1986.

Up Goes the Skyscraper!, Four Winds, 1986.

Valentine's Day, Holiday House, 1986.

Deadline! From News to Newspaper, Crowell, 1987.

Dinosaurs, Holiday House, 1987.

The Pottery Place, Harcourt, 1987.

Trains, Holiday House, 1987.

Weather Forecasting, Four Winds, 1987.

Zoo, Crowell, 1987.

Dinosaurs, Dragonflies and Diamonds: All about Natural History Museums, Four Winds, 1988.

Farming, Holiday House, 1988.

Prehistoric Animals, Holiday House, 1988.

Sunken Treasure, Crowell, 1988.

Easter, Holiday House, 1989.

Catch the Wind!: All about Kites, Little, Brown, 1989.

Marge's Diner, Crowell, 1989.

Monarch Butterfly, Holiday House, 1989.

Beacons of Light: Lighthouses, Morrow, 1990.

Weather Words and What They Mean, Holiday House, 1990.

How a House Is Built, Holiday House, 1990.

The Puffins Are Back!, HarperCollins, 1991.

From Seed to Plant, Holiday House, 1991.

Surrounded by Sea: Life on a New England Fishing Island, Little, Brown, 1991.

Whales, Holiday House, 1991.

The Great St. Lawrence Seaway, Morrow, 1992.

Sharks, Holiday House, 1992.

Recycle! A Handbook for Kids, Little, Brown, 1992.

Say Woof!: The Day of a Country Veterinarian, Macmillan, 1992.

Stargazers, Holiday House, 1992.

Caves and Caverns, Harcourt Brace, 1993.

Frogs, Holiday House, 1993.

Pirates: Robbers of the High Seas, Little, Brown, 1993.

The Planets, Holiday House, 1993.

Puff—Flash—Bang!: A Book about Signals, Morrow, 1993.

Spiders, Holiday House, 1993.

Christmas on an Island, Morrow, 1994.

Country Fair, Little, Brown, 1994.

Emergency!, Holiday House, 1994.

Nature's Green Umbrella: Tropical Rain Forests, Morrow, 1994.

St. Patrick's Day, Holiday House, 1994.

Wolves, Holiday House, 1994.

Bicycle Book, Holiday House, 1994.

Knights in Shining Armor, Little, Brown, 1995.

Planet Earth/Inside Out, Morrow, 1995.

The Reasons for Seasons, Holiday House, 1995.

Sea Turtles, Holiday House, 1995.

Cats, Holiday House, 1996.

Deserts, Holiday House, 1996.

Dogs, Holiday House, 1996.

Music Maker, Simon and Schuster, 1996.

Click!: A Book about Cameras and Taking Pictures, Little, Brown, 1997.

Gulls . . . Gulls . . . Gulls, Holiday House, 1997.

The Honey Makers, Morrow, 1997.

The Moon Book, Holiday House, 1997.

Paper, Paper Everywhere, Harcourt Brace, 1997.

Marshes and Swamps, Holiday House, 1998.

Soaring with the Wind: The Bald Eagle, Morrow, 1998.

Yippee-Yay!: A Book about Cowboys and Cowgirls, Little, Brown, 1998.

The Art Box, Holiday House, 1998.

Penguins!, Holiday House, 1998.

Snow, Morrow, 1999.

The Quilting Bee, Morrow, 1999.

Exploring the Deep, Dark Sea, Little, Brown, 1999.

Behold—the Dragon!, Morrow, 1999.

Pigs, Holiday House, 1999.

The Pumpkin Book, Holiday House, 1999.

How You Were Born, Simon & Schuster, forthcoming.

Santa Claus, Morrow, forthcoming.

ILLUSTRATOR

Jane Yolen, *Rounds about Rounds*, F. Watts, 1977.

Judith Enderle, *Good Junk*, Dandelion Press, 1979.

Catharine Chase, *Hot & Cold*, Dandelion Press, 1979.

Catharine Chase, *My Balloon*, Dandelion Press, 1979.

Catharine Chase, *Pete, the Wet Pet*, Dandelion Press, 1979.

Catharine Chase, *The Mouse at the Show*, Dandelion Press, 1980.

Donna Lugg Pape, *The Mouse at the Show*, Elsevier/Nelson, 1981.

Joanna Cole, *Cars and How They Go,* Crowell, 1983.
Frank Asch, *Baby in the Box,* Holiday House, 1989.

Adaptations

Several of Gibbons's books have been made into filmstrips and cassettes, including *Thanksgiving Day, Christmas Time,* and *Valentine's Day,* all by Live Oak Media; *Dinosaurs* and *Check It Out! A Book about Libraries* have been made into filmstrips and cassettes by Listening Library. Reading Rainbow has featured a number of her books, including *The Milk Makers* and *Sunken Treasure.*

Sidelights

The author-illustrator of more than one hundred nonfiction children's books, Gail Gibbons has informed an entire generation about the mysterious workings of clocks and locks, detailed the plethora of trucks and trains in the world, and taken young readers behind the counters of department stores, post offices, and fire departments. Her brightly illustrated books have introduced further legions of readers to the world of sharks and sea turtles, and have educated still others to the mechanics of everything from weather to building a skyscraper. Name a topic—milk, paper, news-reporting, puffins—and you can be fairly sure Gail Gibbons has published an award-winning book on it with her trademark crisp text and vibrant design.

In 1987, Gibbons won the *Washington Post*-Children's Book Guild Award for Nonfiction, the judges noting that "The enormous breadth of subjects that Gail Gibbons has brought to life is astonishing," and that her books "are free-flowing fountains of information." As Jennifer Crichton of *Publishers Weekly* once remarked, "[Gibbons] writes and illustrates books that demystify life's everyday workings for readers in the five-to-nine age range." This is a niche that Gibbons has staked out for herself, one of the first author-illustrators to bring vitality and visual excitement into children's nonfiction books. Ideas for Gibbons's books come from many sources: suggestions from her husband, from editors, from children at schools where she is speaking, but mostly from her own insatiable curiosity, from the childish glee we all had in asking "Why?" or "How does that work?"

Born in Oak Park, Illinois, in 1944, Gibbons showed artistic talents at an early age. As she wrote in an entry for *Something about the Author Autobiography Series* (*SAAS*), "there has always been a need for me to put words down on paper and draw and paint pictures. This began at a very young age." Perhaps this need was in part inspired by her father, a tool-and-die designer who as a young man won a scholarship to Chicago's prestigious Art Institute, but turned it down because his parents thought it foolish for a young man to pursue a career in the arts. Already by age five, when Gibbons attended kindergarten, teachers noticed her knack for things artistic. "It seemed to be the happiest messing around with crayons, paints, or clay," Gibbons recalled

in *SAAS.* Her love of painting and drawing increased throughout school; she became known as the class artist and by age ten she created a little book about a pet dog—such an animal was denied her by the rules of the apartment house where she lived. Another youthful project was the recreation—on paper—of time spent on a Wisconsin farm with a friend. "I found myself writing and drawing pictures of what I loved and where I wanted to be," Gibbons wrote in *SAAS.* "It became a form of expressing myself."

She and her best friend would regularly take mass transit into nearby Chicago, visiting the Art Institute, other museums, and the public library. Books became a passion for the young Gibbons as well, and each night she would read long past the time for lights-out. By high school, she had found a refuge in art, for she was a shy teenager who found it "a fight to try to fit in." Upon graduation, there was little question what she would do. She applied and was accepted to the University of Illinois where she studied art. "I consider myself quite fortunate because I never had to debate with myself as to what I wanted to do with my life," Gibbons noted in *SAAS.* "The answer was always there. I wanted to be a writer and artist."

Gibbons, who lives part-time on an island off the coast of Maine, wrote and illustrated this tale of a close-knit lobster-fishing community and their Christmas celebration.

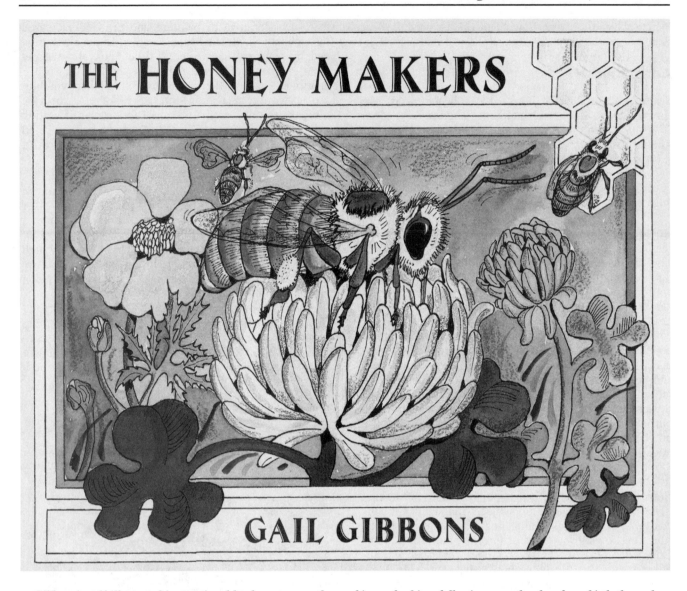

Gibbons's self-illustrated instructional book centers on the workings of a hive, following a worker bee from birth through its many occupations.

College was a revelation to Gibbons, and she was particularly inspired by one of her instructors, a professional illustrator of children's books. "He became sort of an idol to me. I couldn't believe that his work was printed into very fine-looking books." She also grew closer and closer to a young man she had begun dating in high school, and when Gibbons was twenty-one she and Glenn Gibbons were married. Helping to support the household while her husband finished his degree, Gibbons took her first job in television, working for a local station in Champaign, Illinois, as a TV artist, doing set design, animations, and on-air graphics.

When the couple moved to Chicago, Gibbons continued her television work with WMAQ-TV and also worked at an advertising agency. In 1969, they moved to New York, where Gibbons worked for WNBC-TV creating graphics for news shows and the occasional "Saturday Night Live" and "Today Show." In 1971, she became the graphic artist for the NBC children's program, "Take

a Giant Step," and continued with it as the show became "Talk with a Giant." During her stint on this show, she first thought of creating children's books, inspired by the children she was working with on air. She was also freelancing while at NBC, creating television graphics for United Press International.

However, in 1972, Gibbons's life took a radical turn. Her husband died in an accident, and she took several years to put herself back in order emotionally. During this time, she began work on her first children's book, picking an agent out of the yellow pages at random. After taking a look at Gibbons's portfolio, the agent encouraged her to get to work on a book. As she set to work on a book illuminating set theory for youngsters, Gibbons discovered that her years in television came in very handy. "The bright colors I use come from my television background," Gibbons explained to *Booklist's* Stephanie Zvirin in an interview. "A television image is only on the screen for about ten seconds so it has to be very readable and simple." And expanding on this point, Gibbons told Crichton in her *Publishers Weekly* interview that when she was working in television, a lot of people still had black-and-white sets, so that the artist had to be careful to use contrasting colors. "I can't put red next to black, for instance, because on black-and-white, the colors will come out a uniform gray. Bold, flat colors lend themselves to simplicity." Such bright, flat colors and visual simplicity have become the Gibbons trademark.

Though Gibbons's first book, *Willy and His Wheel Wagon,* became a Junior Literary Guild selection, critical reception was not all that positive. Nor was it for several of Gibbons's early works, which included more

fictional approaches to nonfiction subjects as well as activity books for holidays. But Gibbons was not noticing reviews; she had moved out to Cape Cod part-time, commuting to New York several days a week, and fallen in love with the man from whom she rented her Massachusetts cottage. In 1976, she was married to Kent Ancliffe, and with her two new stepchildren the family moved to Vermont where they built a house on two hundred and forty acres. In 1979, Gibbons met Caroline Ward, who was in charge of the children's book exhibit center of the Vermont Libraries. Ward told her of the need for bright, exciting nonfiction for children and suggested that Gibbons turn her hand to nonfiction solely. A bit of market research convinced Gibbons this was a good idea, and the result of it all was *Clocks and*

Gibbons's picture book teaches young readers about supplies and tools for creating art, and gives basic information about color. (From The Art Box, *written and illustrated by Gibbons.)*

How They Go, Gibbons's first book in her new, simplified style which did not attempt to tell a story, but to explain concepts as clearly and vividly as possible.

Of that book, *Booklist*'s Barbara Elleman commented that "Inside movements of the weight and spring clock seemingly tick into action with Gibbons's concisely worded text and clean line work over bold, contrasting colors." Ann A. Flowers, in *Horn Book,* called *Clocks and How They Go* an "admirable example of the kind of book that explains for the young reader how mechanical things work." The recipient of several awards, *Clocks and How They Go* set the tone for Gibbons's new style and led the way to scores of other books describing in simple text and clear illustration how things work. *Locks and Keys* followed the next year, a book that traces the history of such devices and shows the workings of various locks. Karen Jameyson, writing in *Horn Book,* noted that Gibbons "has once again skillfully combined a concise, clear text with explicit, attractive illustrations

to acquaint young readers with a mechanical subject." More things mechanical were served up in *Tool Box,* in which "Gibbons presents clear, attractive, and colorful drawings of common hand tools," according to Richard J. Merrill writing in *Science Books.* A further title dealing with everyday objects is *Paper, Paper Everywhere,* detailing the uses and manufacturing process of paper. Of that title, a *Publishers Weekly* contributor commented that "Gibbons's works have been honored as innovations that entertain and teach children about things encountered in daily life."

Exploring businesses and the world of commerce, Gibbons has illustrated the workings of post offices, diners, and newsrooms, among others. In *The Post Office: Mail and How It Moves,* she explained the behind-the-counter activities of postal workers in a "bright and cheerful" format, according to George A. Woods in the *New York Times Book Review.* "Text and pictures greatly simplify a complex operation and reveal

Gibbons's factual text and powerful illustrations educate young readers about the bald eagle and efforts to save it from extinction.

the postal system to be most expeditious," Woods concluded. In *Department Store,* Gibbons tackled the workings of large-scale retail enterprises. According to Barbara S. Worth in *Children's Book Review Service,* "Gibbons has done a remarkable job of bringing order and organization to a complex topic," with *Department Store.* The work processes of a rural potter were presented in *The Pottery Place,* a book that supplies an "appealing introduction to pottery making for the preschool and elementary-school-aged child," according to Nancy Vasilakis writing in *Horn Book.* In a lightly fictionalized format, Gibbons illustrates the workings of a small restaurant in *Marge's Diner,* a book that *School Library Journal* contributor Mary Lou Budd found to be a "delightful, charming presentation of how a hometown diner operates." Gibbons takes young readers literally behind the headlines in *Deadline!: From News to Newspaper,* a book in which she "explains in simple format the incredible amount of activity generated by a busy staff during six hours in the office of a daily newspaper," according to Martha Rosen in *School Library Journal.* "The colorful, cartoon-like illustrations reinforce the message of the text," Rosen noted.

Production processes were also investigated in books about how apples grow, how honey is made, and how milk gets from the cow to the supermarket. *The Seasons of Arnold's Apple Tree* does double service in showing the change of seasons as well as the development of apples on the tree. *School Library Journal* reviewer Harriet Otto commented that it "shows the close relationship between a boy and an apple tree," and went on to note that Gibbons's "colorful double-page spreads depict the changing seasons." More "manufacturing" was investigated in *The Honey Makers,* a book looking at the workings of a hive, following a worker bee from birth through its many jobs. Reviewing that title in *Booklist,* Kay Weisman stated that "Gibbons' signature full-color artwork makes each page a visual delight, and numerous inset captions and labels add to the wealth of knowledge found in the text." With *The Milk Makers,* Gibbons created "an attractive, informative book on milk production for young readers," according to Eldon Younce in *School Library Journal.* "*Milk Makers* is a perfect introduction for the class trip to a dairy farm or dairy plant and should also have great appeal for younger children," remarked Elizabeth S. Watson in *Horn Book.*

Few topics have escaped Gibbons's practiced eye. Cowboys and cowgirls come under her lens in *Yippee-Yay!,* a book focusing on the thirty-year period following the Civil War in the Wild West. "Following her own tried-and-true layout, she has given youngsters yet another useful historical introduction to a popular topic," wrote John Sigwald in a *School Library Journal* review of the book. Environmentalism took its turn in the handbook for children, *Recycle!,* and one of the most popular modes of transportation for children was examined in *Bicycle Book. Booklist* critic Carolyn Phelan commented that *Bicycle Book* was one of Gibbons's "more engaging picture books" and one that introduces

the history as well as design and care of bikes with clear, colorful illustrations in a "satisfying book."

Gibbons's magpie curiosity finds subjects in everything she does. When she and her husband bought a house on a Maine island, she turned her attention to things of the sea, producing a book on lighthouses, *Beacons of Light;* on sea animals, including *Whales* and *The Puffins Are Back;* and life on such an island, *Surrounded By the Sea: Life on a New England Fishing Island.* She has looked at holidays from Halloween to St. Patrick's Day, at means of transport from trucks to boats, even at children's beloved dinosaurs and knights, and examined occupations from that of a veterinarian to a farmer. Kites caught her fancy, and books on wind and weather resulted. Stargazing, sharks, zoos, skyscrapers, and museums all have been fodder for her books.

"Nonfiction requires a tremendous amount of research," Gibbons noted in *SAAS.* "I want it to be accurate and up-to-date information." She gets such information from libraries, from experts in the fields she is writing about, and from personal experience. While writing *The Great St. Lawrence Seaway,* she and her husband took a trip up that waterway. Such personal experience evidences itself in her work with attention to the telling detail. Research is the first step in a process that could take several months for each title. Once she gets her research done, she writes the text, a process that can take up to fifteen revisions. After the text comes a dummy, a fake copy of the format of the book with line sketches for illustrations. Once this is approved and typeset text arrives, she goes about the actual illustrations, using either watercolors, acrylics, colored pencils, or a process called preseparation with which she achieves her bright, flat colors. "I usually am working on a number of books all at the same time," Gibbons wrote in *SAAS.* "I might be illustrating one, researching another, and working on the writing of another." Additionally, Gibbons regularly visits schools where she talks with both children and educators.

"Whenever I am speaking to children, teachers, and librarians, I always stress how much I feel that nonfiction is important," Gibbons concluded in *SAAS.* "I am constantly impressed in seeing what is happening in schools and libraries around the country. There is a sincere excitement about good literature coming from these places. I like to encourage others to write, hoping that it will be as exciting and rewarding to them as it has been to me."

Works Cited

Budd, Mary Lou, review of *Marge's Diner, School Library Journal,* September, 1989, p. 226.

Crichton, Jennifer, "Picture Books That Explain," *Publishers Weekly,* July 27, 1984, pp. 88-89.

Elleman, Barbara, review of *Clocks and How They Go, Booklist,* November 1, 1979, p. 448.

Flowers, Ann A., review of *Clocks and How They Go, Horn Book,* December, 1979, p. 676.

Gibbons, Gail, essay in *Something about the Author Autobiography Series,* Volume 12, Gale, 1991, pp. 71-82.

Jameyson, Karen, review of *Locks and Keys, Horn Book,* December, 1980, p. 653.

Merrill, Richard J., review of *Tool Box, Science Books,* January-February, 1983, p. 149.

Otto, Harriet, review of *The Seasons of Arnold's Apple Tree, School Library Journal,* December, 1984, p. 70.

Review of *Paper, Paper Everywhere, Publishers Weekly,* February 18, 1983, p. 129.

Phelan, Carolyn, review of *Bicycle Book, Booklist,* December 1, 1995, p. 630.

Rosen, Martha, review of *Deadline!: From News to Newspaper, School Library Journal,* June-July, 1987, p. 82.

Sigwald, John, review of *Yippee-Yay!: A Book about Cowboys and Cowgirls, School Library Journal,* March, 1998, p. 195.

Vasilakis, Nancy, review of *The Pottery Place, Horn Book,* November-December, 1987, pp. 758-59.

Watson, Elizabeth S., review of *The Milk Makers, Horn Book,* July-August, 1985, pp. 463-64.

Weisman, Kay, review of *The Honey Makers, Booklist,* March 15, 1997, p. 1245.

Woods, George A., review of *The Post Office Book: Mail and How It Moves, New York Times Book Review,* September 26, 1982, p. 31.

Worth, Barbara S., review of *Department Store, Children's Book Review Service,* Spring, 1984, p. 122.

Younce, Eldon, review of *The Milk Makers, School Library Journal,* April, 1985, p. 78.

Zvirin, Stephanie, "The Booklist Interview: Gail Gibbons," *Booklist,* December 1, 1994, pp. 676-77.

For More Information See

BOOKS

Authors of Books for Young People, Scarecrow Press, 1990.
Children's Books and Their Creators, Houghton Mifflin, 1995.
Children's Literature Review, Volume 8, Gale, 1985.
Sixth Book of Junior Authors and Illustrators, H. W. Wilson, 1989.

PERIODICALS

Appraisal, fall, 1998, pp. 14-15.
Booklist, April 1, 1991, p. 1570; October 15, 1992, p. 433; October 15, 1993, p. 446; October 1, 1995, p. 322; November 1, 1995, p. 473; March 15, 1998, p. 1245.
Bulletin of the Center for Children's Books, January, 1990, pp. 109-10; March, 1990, p. 159; March, 1992, p. 179; February, 1994, p. 186; May, 1996, p. 301; July, 1997, p. 394.
Horn Book, March-April, 1990, p. 220; November-December, 1991, p. 757; March, 1996, p. 231.
Kirkus Reviews, April 15, 1991, pp. 543-44; March 15, 1992, p. 393; January 15, 1997, p. 141; September 15, 1997, p. 1457.
Publishers Weekly, May 19, 1997, p. 77.
School Library Journal, May, 1990, p. 96; April, 1991, p. 111; April, 1992, p. 105; December, 1993, p. 104; April, 1994, pp. 118-19; October, 1995, p. 125; September, 1996, p. 196; January, 1997, p. 100; May, 1997, p. 119; September, 1997, p. 202; April, 1998, p. 116.*

—*Sketch by J. Sydney Jones*

*　　*　　*

GILMAN, Phoebe 1940-

Personal

Born April 4, 1940, in New York, NY; immigrated to Canada, 1972; daughter of John (a salesman) and Hannah (Slatoff) Gilman; married Emanuel Deligtisch (divorced); married Brian Bender (a computer consultant); children: (first marriage) Ingrid, (second marriage) Melissa, Jason. *Education:* Attended Art Students' League, and Hunter College, 1957-59; studied under Ernst Fuchs at Bezalel Academy, Jerusalem, Israel, 1968. *Religion:* Jewish. *Hobbies and other interests:* Ice skating, movies, and reading.

Addresses

Office—c/o Scholastic, 175 Hillmount Rd., Markham, Ontario L6C 1Z7, Canada.

Career

Freelance artist, author, and illustrator, 1967—; Ontario College of Art, Canada, fine arts instructor, 1975-90. *Exhibitions:* Gilman's work has been on display at Old Jaffa Gallery, Tel Aviv, 1970-71, Le Theatre du P'tit Bonheur, Toronto, Canada, 1973; Galerie Heritage, Toronto, 1974; Prince Arthur Gallery, Toronto, 1982; Mabel's Fables, 1991; Art Gallery of Peterborough, 1991; Art Gallery of Algoma, 1993. *Member:* Canadian Society of Children's Authors, Illustrators, and Performers; Canadian Children's Book Center (board member, 1992-97); Canadian Writers' Union.

Awards, Honors

Merit Award, Art Directors Club of Toronto, 1984, for *The Balloon Tree;* Ruth Schwartz Children's Book Award, Ontario Arts Council and Canadian Booksellers Association, and Sydney Taylor Book Award, Association of Jewish Libraries, both 1993, both for *Something for Nothing;* Vickey Metcalf Award, Canadian Authors Association, 1993, for entire body of work.

Writings

AUTHOR AND ILLUSTRATOR (UNLESS OTHERWISE INDICATED)

The Balloon Tree, Scholastic Canada (Toronto), 1984, Firefly, 1995.
Jillian Jiggs, Scholastic Canada, 1985, Scholastic, 1988.
Little Blue Ben, Scholastic Canada, 1986, Scholastic, 1989.
The Wonderful Pigs of Jillian Jiggs, Scholastic Canada, 1988, Scholastic, 1989.

Phoebe Gilman

Grandma and the Pirates, Scholastic Canada, 1990, Scholastic, 1990.
(Adaptor) *Something from Nothing,* Scholastic, 1990.
(Jean Little and Maggie De Vries) *Once Upon a Golden Apple,* Viking (Ontario, Canada), 1991.
Jillian Jiggs to the Rescue, Scholastic Canada, 1994, Scholastic, 1994.
The Gypsy Princess, Scholastic Canada, 1995, Scholastic Press, 1997.
Pirate Pearl, Scholastic Canada, 1998.

The Balloon Tree, Jillian Jiggs, The Wonderful Pigs of Jillian Jiggs, Grandma and the Pirates, Something from Nothing, The Gypsy Princess, and *Pirate Pearl* have all been translated into French. *Something from Nothing* has also been translated into Japanese and Spanish.

Adaptations

The Balloon Tree, Jillian Jiggs, Grandma and the Pirates, Something from Nothing, and *The Gypsy Princess* have been issued in audio cassette format.

Sidelights

Phoebe Gilman told *SATA:* "I wonder if being creative has anything to do with being extremely gullible. My husband kids me about this all the time. He says that you can tell me anything and my first reaction is usually ... '*WOW! Isn't that amazing!*' I am used to moving about

in my imagination without barriers; inhabiting a 'what if' world where anything is possible. I walk between the worlds of possibility and fact, weaving them together, a bit from here salted with a bit from there.

"When I finish writing something, I can't wait till someone reads it. I anxiously await a response. I want to hear them chuckle and laugh out loud over what I've written. I want to touch them in some way. Sharing stories, we come to understand our world and ourselves. When we enter the world of another's imagination, we come back a little different, a little changed. I like to think of books as windows through which the creator allows you to peer into the soul. Or, to quote the immortal Emily Dickinson: '*This is my letter to the world....*'

"If you want to know who I am, read what I have written, for it is through my work that I am continually revealing myself. If you smoosh together all the characters I've created, you'll come up with a fairly accurate picture of who I am ... a messy, creative creature, like *Jillian Jiggs,* who once dreamed of being a princess like Cinnamon in *The Gypsy Princess,* and who now lives happily ever after ... weaving stories out of my life just as Joseph did in *Something from Nothing.*"

Born in New York City, Phoebe Gilman grew up in the Bronx, taking advantage of an extensive library system. "My mother loved to read," she recalled, "so it was only natural that my brothers and I got our own library cards as soon as we were able to print out names. My favorite books were fairy tales. When the pictures didn't match the images that the words had painted in my head, I would cover them up with my hands." This early exposure to picture books in some ways inspired Gilman's interest in art, an occupation she later found suitable to her passion for travel. "One of the nice things about being an artist," she said, "is that it is a very portable profession. I have lived for extended periods of time in both Europe and Israel." In fact, she seemed headed toward a career as an artist rather than a writer, but as she once said, "I prefer the words to the pictures, which is a little odd.... It still surprises me to be called a writer." According to Gilman, her daughter Ingrid provided her with the impetus to begin writing: "When her balloon burst on a tree branch, I wished the tree would magically sprout balloons. It didn't ... what sprouted was an idea in my head. Why not write a story about a tree that blossoms balloons?" That, she said, was how she came to write her first book. "It was not how I came to be published," she continued. "That took fifteen years and umpty-zillion rejection slips to accomplish."

That first picture book appeared as *The Balloon Tree* in 1984. The classic tale of a princess locked in a tower by an evil captor, *The Balloon Tree* follows the story of Princess Leora, captured by an archduke who seizes control of the kingdom while her father, the king, is away. The Princess Leora wants to send a message to her father, and the only way to do so is by sending up a balloon from her tower. However, the archduke has seized all the balloons in the kingdom—all but one from which a helpful wizard is able to create a tree that spawns millions of balloons. Frieda Wishinsky, writing in *Quill & Quire,* called *The Balloon Tree* "appealing and well-crafted ... a gentle, lighthearted tale." Murray J. Evans, in a *Canadian Children's Literature* review, paid special attention to the artwork: "What sets the book apart is its spectacular illustrations so reminiscent of a medieval illuminated manuscript." "While the story entertains," concluded Evans, "... the illustrations of Gilman's book persistently fascinate and often amuse."

Gilman's character Jillian Jiggs made her first appearance in a book by the same name, published in 1985. Writing in *Canadian Children's Literature,* Lisa Mac-Naughton attested to the popularity of the book, claiming that "Jillian Jillian Jillian JIGGS! is a chant heard frequently among children in child care centres." In 1988 Jillian was back, in *The Wonderful Pigs of Jillian Jiggs.* This time she had developed an industry of sorts, making little stuffed pigs and selling them. The only problem is that she loves her pigs too much to part with them. However, this leads her to a crafty solution, sharing her sewing skills with friends. MacNaughton suggested that the idea of a money-making business would particularly appeal to older readers.

One day his mother said to him, "Joseph, where is your button?"
Joseph looked. It was gone!

Retelling a traditional Jewish folktale, Gilman relates the story of young Joseph, whose tailor grandfather transforms a precious baby blanket into various items for the boy to treasure as he grows older. (From Something from Nothing, *written and illustrated by Gilman.)*

Appearing in 1986, *Little Blue Ben* is, as Wishinsky noted in *Quill & Quire,* a "warm, inviting book" about three lovable elfin creatures who share a blue house: Ben, his brother Blue Cat, and their mother Blue Hen. A dispute with Blue Cat over a dish of shish-kebabed eggs leads the two youngsters into a competitive game of hide-and-seek. "Children will enjoy searching for Little Blue Ben," claimed Wishinsky, while a critic in *Canadian Children's Literature* praised *Little Blue Ben* as "a delightful book for four- to six-year-olds."

Grandma and the Pirates finds the young heroine Melissa going to battle with pirates to rescue her grandmother and Oliver the parrot. Instead of trying to escape from the amusingly gruesome pirates, the three prisoners decide to take a different approach to freedom. In addition to admiring the blend of text and illustration, *Canadian Materials* reviewer Jane Robinson lauded Gilman's gentle prose, "as rhythmic as the waves," and Kathleen Corrigan, contributor to *Canadian Children's Literature,* observed that "Phoebe Gilman not only knows a good story, she knows how to write it well and draw it superbly."

A retelling of an old Yiddish tale, *Something from Nothing,* resurrects an old story and with it a vanished way of life in the small Jewish towns that once dotted Eastern Europe. In the story, young Joseph is saddened when he must give up a favorite blanket, decorated with stars, when it becomes frayed and worn; but his grandfather helps Joseph keep his precious blanket by remaking it as a jacket. When this too wears out, the grandfather successively reshapes it as a vest, and later a tie. Each time, the amount of fabric becomes smaller, until ultimately it is only a button, which Joseph then loses. Meanwhile, a family of mice living in a hole in the wall have begun to acquire an ever-expanding wardrobe of star-spangled clothes. *Something from Nothing* makes use of "pleasing rhythm and repetitive language," according to Norma Charles in *Canadian Materials.* In a *Booklist* review, Stephanie Zvirin found the book visually pleasing, pointing out "The red-gold tones of the background and the rich browns of the artwork" which "lend a feeling of warmth that perfectly replicates the flavor of this sweet, funny tale."

Gilman reintroduced her spunky character Jillian Jiggs in the 1994 work *Jillian Jiggs to the Rescue.* In this episode, Jillian's little sister Rebecca is frightened because of a bad dream about a monster. The ever-resourceful Jillian designs a "monster machine," which will catch and shrink the monster. Thinking they have trapped the monster, the two girls try to squash it, but to everyone's surprise, the monster turns itself into a cat! As with its predecessors, this installment in the Jillian Jiggs saga is also told in rhyme. Joanne Findon, writing in *Quill & Quire,* called it "a delightful sequel to the other Jillian Jiggs books," showing readers how "Rebecca is able to confront her fears and take positive action against them." Once again, the book's visual aspects received praise as well: "Gilman's use of vivid colours and intricate detail in each scene," wrote J. R. Wyten-

When the King galloped into the courtyard he could see the Archduke screaming at the Princess. "You spoiled everything," he was shouting at her. "It isn't fair! *I* want to be King!"

In Gilman's tale of a princess held by an evil captor, the young girl enlists the help of a wizard, who supplies her with balloons to send a message to her father. (From The Balloon Tree, *written and illustrated by Gilman.)*

broek in *Canadian Literature,* "make the book a visual feast and enhance the text in many ways."

As *The Balloon Tree* had covered territory familiar to fairy tale readers, *The Gypsy Princess* reinvents elements of stories which carry the moral that "The grass is always greener on the other side of the fence," or "There's no place like home." The gypsy girl Cinnamon wishes she could be a princess and live in a castle, but when her dream comes true, she realizes she was most happy when she was with her family. To get back home, she must surrender all the trappings of her royal life, including her slippers and crown, a decision she has trouble making. "Gilman extends characterization through her use of facial expressions," wrote Susan S. Verner in a *Bulletin of the Center for Children's Books* review, while *Quill & Quire* contributor Janet MacNaughton concluded, "This is truly an admirable book."

Works Cited

Charles, Norma, review of *Something from Nothing, Canadian Materials,* September, 1992, pp. 207-208.

Corrigan, Kathleen, review of *Grandma and the Pirates, Canadian Children's Literature,* 1991, pp. 114-15.

Evans, Murray, J., review of *The Balloon Tree, Canadian Children's Literature,* 1985, pp. 145-48.

Findon, Joanne, review of *Jillian Jiggs to the Rescue, Quill & Quire,* March, 1994, p. 80.

Review of *Little Blue Ben, Canadian Children's Literature,* 1987, p. 94.

MacNaughton, Janet, review of *The Gypsy Princess, Quill & Quire,* December, 1995, p. 37.

MacNaughton, Lisa, review of *The Wonderful Pigs of Jillian Jiggs, Canadian Children's Literature,* 1990, pp. 111-113.

Robinson, Jane, review of *Grandma and the Pirates, Canadian Materials,* November, 1990, p. 267.

Verner, Susan S., review of *The Gypsy Princess, Bulletin of the Center for Children's Books,* March, 1996, p. 267.

Wishinsky, Frieda, review of *The Balloon Tree, Quill & Quire,* February, 1985, pp. 10-11, 14.

Wishinsky, Frieda, review of *Little Blue Ben, Quill & Quire,* December, 1986, pp. 14-15.

Wytenbroek, J. R., review of *Jillian Jiggs to the Rescue, Canadian Literature,* winter, 1995, p. 205.

Zvirin, Stephanie, review of *Something from Nothing, Booklist,* September 1, 1993, p. 64.

For More Information See

PERIODICALS

Booklist, September 15, 1990, p. 178; February 1, 1997, pp. 945-46.

Bulletin of the Center for Children's Books, February, 1994, pp. 186-87.

Canadian Children's Literature, 1993, pp. 52-54; winter, 1997, pp. 78-81.

Canadian Literature, winter, 1992, pp. 189-90.

Horn Book, November-December, 1993, pp. 770-73.

Publishers Weekly, September 20, 1993, p. 72.

Quill & Quire, October, 1985, p. 22.

School Library Journal, January, 1991, p. 72; March, 1997, p. 152.

—*Sketch by Judson Knight*

*   *   *

GLEASON, Katherine (A.) 1960-

Personal

Born October 9, 1960, in Boston, MA; daughter of Andrew Mattei (a college professor) and Jean (a college professor; maiden name, Berko) Gleason. *Education:* Brown University, B.A., 1982; Yale University, M.A., 1985. *Politics:* Democrat.

Addresses

Home—199 East Seventh St., No. 2D, New York, NY 10009. *Electronic mail*—kag475@aol.com.

Career

Greenroom Enterprises (film production company), Astoria, NY, production associate, 1987-88; Michael Rowan Group (marketing and survey research firm), New York City, associate, 1988-90; *Womanews,* New York City, contributing editor, 1989-91; *Lingua Franca,* Mamaroneck, NY, managing editor, 1991-92; Lucas/

Katherine Gleason

Evans Books, Inc., New York City, projects coordinator, 1992-94; freelance writer and editor, New York City, 1994—.

Writings

Origami Ornaments, Troll Communications, 1995.
Flying Origami, Troll, 1996.
Scary Origami, Troll, 1996.
Native American Literature, Chelsea House, 1996.
Native American Art, Scholastic, 1996.
Clay Pots: A Native American Craft Kit, illustrated by Meryl Henderson and Eleanor Kwei, Troll, 1997.
Leap Frog Origami, Troll, 1997.
Kirigami Christmas Tree, Troll, 1998.
Paper Magic: The Art of Origami, illustrated by Meryl Henderson, Troll, 1998.

Creator of craft kits with instructions, including *Egyptian Treasure Box,* illustrated by Eleanor Kwei, Troll Communications, 1997; *Frame Your Friends: Make Your Own Mini Photo Frames,* design by Gen Shibuya, Troll, 1998.

For More Information See

PERIODICALS

School Library Journal, March, 1997, p. 200; April, 1997, p. 149.

*   *   *

GOLD, Alison Leslie 1945-

Personal

Born July 13, 1945, in New York, NY; daughter of William (a college professor) and Shirley (a board of education supervisor) Greenwald; divorced; children: Thor. *Education:* Attended University of North Carolina, 1962-64, and Mexico City College, 1964-65; New School for Social Research, B.A., 1968. *Hobbies and other interests:* Travel abroad.

Addresses

Home—Santa Monica, CA. *Agent*—Charlotte Sheedy, 41 King St., New York, NY 10014.

Career

Writer.

Awards, Honors

Christopher Award, 1987, and merit of distinction, International Center for Holocaust Studies, Anti-Defamation League, 1987, both for *Anne Frank Remembered: The Story of the Woman Who Helped to Hide the Frank Family.*

Writings

FOR CHILDREN

Memories of Anne Frank: Reflections of a Childhood Friend, Scholastic, 1997.

OTHER

(With Miep Gies) *Anne Frank Remembered: The Story of the Woman Who Helped to Hide the Frank Family,* Simon & Schuster, 1987.
(With Nha Ca and Le Van) *Kieu Chinh: Hanoi, Saigon, Hollywood,* Than Huu (Orange, CA), 1991.
Clairvoyant: The Imagined Life of Lucia Joyce: A Novel, Hyperion, 1991.
The Devil's Mistress: The Diary of Eva Braun, the Woman Who Lived and Died with Hitler: A Novel, Faber and Faber (Boston, MA), 1997.

Also a writer for television and radio. Contributor of reviews to periodicals, including *Los Angeles Times.*

Adaptations

Anne Frank Remembered was adapted for an Emmy-award winning television film by William Hanley and broadcast by CBS as *The Attic: The Hiding of Anne Frank,* in 1988.

Sidelights

Recognized for her biographies and historical fiction, Alison Leslie Gold attained international acclaim with her first work, *Anne Frank Remembered: The Story of the Woman Who Helped to Hide the Frank Family,* written with Miep Gies. Gies and her husband, Jan, are the individuals who hid Anne Frank and her family in their home in Nazi-occupied Amsterdam. After its publication in 1987, *Anne Frank Remembered* won the prestigious Christopher Award and was adapted for film. Starring Mary Steenburgen as Gies, the television movie aired on CBS as *The Attic: The Hiding of Anne Frank* and received an Emmy Award. Gold has also written about other women, including the infamous Eva Braun, Adolf Hitler's mistress, and Lucia Joyce, the daughter of celebrated Irish author James Joyce. More recently, Gold has again featured Frank in her first book for children, *Memories of Anne Frank: Reflections of a Childhood Friend.*

Written for middle graders, *Memories of Anne Frank* offers readers a new perspective on Frank's short life, relating her interactions with Hanna Pick-Goslar—a survivor of the Holocaust and Frank's childhood friend and neighbor in Amsterdam. Referred to as Hanneli and Lies in Frank's diary, Pick-Goslar met Frank at age four and remained friends with her until the Frank family suddenly disappeared. For a long time the Goslars, as well as others, thought the family had escaped to Switzerland. It was not until a year after the Goslars themselves were sent to the Nazi concentration camp Bergen-Belsen that they discovered Frank was in the next camp. The two girls met a few brief times, secretly

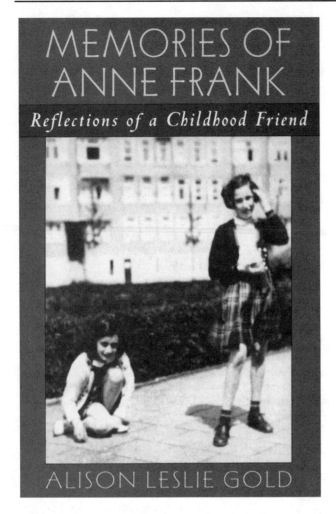

In Alison Leslie Gold's biography of Hannah Goslar, who was a childhood friend of Anne Frank, young readers are offered an affecting picture of how two young girls' lives were profoundly and tragically changed by the Holocaust.

whispering through a barbed wire fence, before Frank's death.

Critics have praised Gold for shedding new light on the life of Frank and for effectively communicating the horrors of the Holocaust to a younger audience. As Betsy Hearne maintained in the *Bulletin of the Center for Children's Books,* "This straightforward account ... extends the information we have about Frank; and ... deepens our knowledge of her situation through Pick-Goslar's own experiences of living in Nazi-occupied Amsterdam and of surviving both transit and concentration camps." A *Publishers Weekly* commentator observed that while the relationship between Frank and Pick-Goslar has been explored previously in books for adults, "the poignancy of Gold's book rests in its sensitive evocation of Goslar's youthful reactions to the war and its destruction of her family and community." Reviewing *Memories of Anne Frank* in *Booklist,* Hazel Rochman asserted that the book "reads like a haunting version of what Anne's life could have been."

Gold, who is also a writer for television, radio, and various periodicals, once explained that she is "always looking for meaningful stories to be brought to the world, especially ones with European origins."

Works Cited

Hearne, Betsy, review of *Memories of Anne Frank: Reflections of a Childhood Friend, Bulletin of the Center for Children's Books,* November, 1997, p. 85.
Review of *Memories of Anne Frank: Reflections of a Childhood Friend, Publishers Weekly,* July 7, 1997, p. 69.
Rochman, Hazel, review of *Memories of Anne Frank: Reflections of a Childhood Friend, Booklist,* September 1, 1997, p. 113.

For More Information See

PERIODICALS

Instructor, October, 1997, p. 27.
New York Times Book Review, May 10, 1987, p. 7.
Publishers Weekly, April 3, 1987, p. 60.
School Library Journal, November, 1997, p. 128.

* * *

GRAY, Nigel 1941-

Personal

Born April 9, 1941, in Aughafatten, Northern Ireland; married Yasmin Hamid, April 29, 1978; children: Sara, Jo, Sam. *Education:* University of Lancaster, B.A., 1971. *Politics:* Libertarian. *Religion:* Atheist.

Career

Actor, writer, teacher of creative writing, editor, and photographer, 1971—. Founder, editor, and publisher of *Fireweed* (quarterly journal of socialist and working-class arts), 1975; writer-in-residence for East Midlands Arts, 1977-80. Former manual laborer.

Writings

FOR YOUNG READERS

(With David Craig) *The Battle Against the Giant* (two-act play), produced in London at Unity Theatre, 1974.
My Cat, Macmillan, 1975.
(Contributor) Sheila Elkin, editor, *More Stories from Playschool,* Pan Books, 1976.
The Deserter (novel), illustrated by Ted Lewin, Harper (New York City), 1977.
It'll All Come Out in the Wash, illustrated by Edward Frascino, Harper, 1979.
Grannie's Holiday, An Earwig in the Ear, Lunch Break (three plays for slow readers), Hutchinson, 1979.
The Job (rock musical), produced at Arts Centre Theatre, Northampton, England, 1981.

Murphy (radio play), produced at RTE, Dublin, 1982, British Broadcasting Corporation (BBC), London, 1983.

(Contributor) Josie Karavasil, editor, *School's O.K.,* Evans, 1982.

Shots, Kinderbuchverlag (Berlin), 1982, Lutterworth (Cambridge), 1986.

(With Margaret Wilson) *The Dog Show,* Cygnet Books (Nedlands, Australia), 1986.

I'll Take You to Mrs. Cole!, illustrated by Michael Foreman, Andersen, 1985, Bergh Publishing Group (New York City), 1986.

The One and Only Robin Hood, illustrated by Helen Craig, Walker, 1987, Joy Street Books (Boston, MA), 1987.

Carrot Top, Orchard Books, 1987.

Fly, illustrated by Mike Dodd, Macdonald (London), 1987, illustrated by Craig Smith, Cygnet Books, 1994.

The Garden Dragon and the Lovely Lily, illustrated by Yann le Goaec, MacDonald, 1987.

A Balloon for Grandad, illustrated by Jane Ray, Orchard Books, 1988.

A Country Far Away, illustrated by Philippe Dupasquier, Orchard Books, 1988.

Pigs Can't Fly, illustrated by Carme Sole Vendrell, Andersen Press, 1990.

Little Pig's Tale, illustrated by Mary Rees, Walker, 1990, Macmillan, 1990.

The Grocer's Daughter, illustrated by David Mackintosh, University of Queensland Press (St. Lucia, Australia), 1994.

Keep on Chomping!, illustrated by Philippe Dupasquier, Andersen, 1993.

Sharon and Darren, illustrated by Cathy Wilcox, Young Lions, 1993.

Running Away from Home, illustrated by Gregory Rogers, Andersen, 1995, Crown Publishers (New York City), 1996.

The Frog Prince, illustrated by Allan Langoulant, Cygnet Books, 1996.

Full House, illustrated by Bob Graham, Happy Cat (Manningtree, England), 1998.

Jake and the Mermaid, International Specialized Book Services, 1998.

The Deserter and *A Country Far Away* have been translated into other languages, including German, Dutch, and Urdu.

OTHER

The Silent Majority: A Study of the Working Class in Post-War British Fiction, Vision Press (London), 1973.

(Contributing editor) *Green and Pleasant Land,* British Withdrawal from Northern Ireland Campaign, 1974.

(Contributor) D. Craig and Margot Heinemann, editors, *Experiments in English Teaching,* Edward Arnold, 1976.

(Contributor) Peter Colenette, editor, *Winter's Tales 23,* Macmillan, 1977.

(Editor) *Lung Cancer Prevention: Guidelines for Smoking Control,* International Union Against Cancer (Geneva, Switzerland), 1977.

Come Close (poems), illustrated by Ken Sprague, Journeyman Press, 1978.

(With D. Craig) *The Rebels and the Hostage* (novel), Journeyman Press, 1978.

(Editor) *Write Thru the Year,* Northampton Press, 1980.

(Editor) *Phoenix Country,* Journeyman Press, 1980.

Life Sentence, Sinclair Browne (London), 1984.

(Compiler) *The Worst of Times: An Oral History of the Great Depression in Britain,* preface by Richard Hoggart, Barnes & Noble (Totowa, NJ), 1985.

Happy Families, Macmillan, 1985.

Woodland Management for Pheasants and Wildlife, David & Charles (Newton Abbot, England), 1986.

(Adaptor) Anne Cheetham, *Black Harvest,* additional material by Jan Dean, Collins Educational, 1986.

(With Clive Scruton) *Private Eye of New York,* Black (London), 1991.

Adaptations

More Stories from Playschool was produced as a television series by the British Broadcasting Corporation (BBC) in 1976; *The Rebels and the Hostage* was produced as a play in Northampton, England, at Lings Theatre, April 6, 1979.

Sidelights

Nigel Gray, whose early writings deal with political and racial unrest, grew up in divided Northern Ireland. In a country where Catholics and Protestants were at odds with one another, he was the son of a Protestant farm laborer and a Catholic kitchen maid. Gray has described himself as a "hopeless" student who found his vocation as a writer "quite by accident." During the Vietnam War in the late 1960s and early 1970s, he took part in a peace mission to Southeast Asia, and while there was so moved by the events of the war that he was "forced to write." An author who works in a variety of styles and genres, Gray has identified himself as a "'Jack of all trades' and, consequently, 'master of none.'"

In one of his earliest novels for young readers, *The Deserter,* Gray approached the subject of violence in Northern Ireland head-on. The title character, a British soldier named Dave who is fleeing an assignment as part of his country's peacekeeping force, is taken in and befriended by four children named Terry, Lucy, Chris, and Andy, the story's narrator. Andy's and Chris's parents, who are not married, also help Dave with gifts of money and food, and cover for the children when they lie to the police regarding Dave's whereabouts. Zena Sutherland of the *Bulletin of the Center for Children's Books* noted that "the story is ... strong in its messages of nonviolence and parental love," and though the parents "live together without legal sanction ... they are wise and loving...." Several other reviewers, however, questioned aspects of the book's message. "Nigel Gray," wrote a critic in *Junior Bookshelf,* "makes the harbouring of Dave seem exciting enough.... Dave, mind, is a very persuasive character and the children are impressionable." But, the reviewer asked, is it wise to encourage children to aid someone in committing an illegal act such as deserting from the armed forces? Jack Forman of *School Library Journal* also rejected the political standpoint, but concluded that "American readers will find this involving and will readily identify with the pre-teen heroes."

Just as Gray's experiences as a young person played a part in the writing of *The Deserter,* his personal life also influenced *Shots.* Gray's wife Yasmin is black, from the African nation of Sudan. "She is the most gentle, caring, good person I ever met," Gray once told *SATA,* but "[she] has been spat on in the street." *Shots* is the story of a black woman, Samia, who is involved with a white Englishman. Though their multiracial neighborhood accepts the relationship between Samia and the father of her children Sarah and Joe, tragedy strikes when Samia's house is deliberately set aflame with her and her children in it. Though the story involves violence, the title does not refer to gunshots, but to shots from Sarah's camera, with which she is able to provide evidence against the guilty parties. "It is a sad reflection," wrote a reviewer in *Junior Bookshelf,* "that this fast-moving, well-written story may well bear a close resemblance to the real lives that some of our young people live." Margery Fisher of *Growing Point* observed that the dialogue and interaction between the racially varied cast of characters—West Indian, Irish, Pakistani, Sikh, and English—is much more important than the book's action. "This is Any

Sam's anger at his father prompts the boy to run away from home, until loneliness causes him to return. (From Running Away from Home, *written by Gray and illustrated by Gregory Rogers.)*

City in our own time," she wrote, "impressively re-created through the interaction of a few individuals." Robin Barlow in *School Librarian* noted that writers of books about multiracial subjects tend either to "trivialise matters" or to build "a set of relationships which do not clearly illustrate the relevant issues to young people. Nigel Gray has not fallen into either of these traps."

Many of Gray's other works are far more lighthearted, and less politically charged, than *The Deserter* and *Shots.* True to his self-description as a jack of all trades, he has written a wide array of books. For instance, *It'll All Come Out in the Wash* is as gentle as *The Deserter* and *Shots* are intense. In the story, a nervous mother hovers over her daughter, who as a result tends to make mistakes and spill things; but whenever the mother tells the girl's father about her worries over their daughter, he has the same answer: "Don't worry, Love, that's how she learns. And it'll all come out in the wash." According to Zena Sutherland of the *Bulletin of the Center for Children's Books,* "the light touch, the child-oriented message, and the element of disaster-humor that so appeals to young children contribute to a pleasant read-aloud story."

The Dog Show, in which a group of dogs holds a contest with a cat as judge, is even more whimsical. "[T]he reader is allowed a wry chuckle at both the choice of winner and the rationale behind the judge's selection," wrote Annette Dale-Meiklejohn in *Magpies.* In *I'll Take You to Mrs. Cole!,* something that seems frightening turns out to be good. Whenever he does anything wrong, a boy is repeatedly threatened by his mother with the words in the book's title; but one day when he runs away from home, he finds himself strangely drawn to Mrs.

Today we played soccer. I scored a goal.

In his imaginative picture book, Nigel Gray depicts unexpected similarities between the lives of a white boy in a British suburb and a black boy in an African village. (From A Country Far Away, *illustrated by Philippe Dupasquier.)*

Cole's house. As it turns out, she is friendly and welcoming, and invites him to come in and play with her large and happy family of children. "While somewhat over the top," wrote a critic in *Publishers Weekly,* "Gray's story is sympathetic, humorous and a rollicking read-aloud."

The One and Only Robin Hood reinterprets a classic story, combining it with the nursery rhyme "Sing a Song of Sixpence." Thus Maid Marian becomes a maid in the king's laundry, and bakes the four-and-twenty-black-birds for His Majesty's table. On each spread are questions for readers to answer, such as "Who was in the counting house counting out the money?" A *Publishers Weekly* reviewer noted, "Gray's retelling of the legend is cast appropriately in the question-and-answer format of medieval ballads sung by troubadours in the English countryside" during the same time period in which Robin Hood's adventures are set.

With *A Balloon for Grandad,* Gray brought in semi-autobiographical elements, but used a much lighter touch than he had in *The Deserter* or *Shots.* The protagonist of this book is named Sam, and his grandfather, Abdualla, lives far away in a tropical country which could be Sudan. When Sam loses a balloon and watches in sadness as it goes floating up into the sky, his father tells him that the balloon is simply going to Grandad far, far away. Thus "One of childhood's most common tragedies," observed a critic in *Kirkus Reviews,* "is converted into an imaginative adventure." The balloon, Sam's dad tells him, will float "high over the sparkling blue-green sea where silver fish leap from the waves; high over the hot yellow sand of the desert where scorpions, and spitting spiders, and sidewinder snakes hide from the heat.... And sandgrouse will peck at it ... and falcons will fall on it, and hawks will fly after it, and vultures with their big hooky beaks and their sharp talons will tear at it, but the dry desert wind will help it to dodge and weave and nothing will harm it." Ilene Cooper in *Booklist* promised that "The lilting, evocative text will charm young listeners, who will respond to a story about a grandparent who is far away, and to the overall affectionate tone."

In *A Country Far Away,* Gray and illustrator Philippe Dupasquier explored similar ideas, depicting odd similarities between the lives of a white boy in a British suburb and a black boy in an African village. Thus the words "Today it rained—so we went swimming" are accompanied by images of the African child swimming in the water hole, which has filled up after a long drought; and of the English child at an indoor pool, where he has gone because it is too wet to play outside. "The simple idea which inspires this book," wrote a reviewer in *Children's Bookshelf,* "is well executed, intriguing the reader by the contrasts and similarities in two widely separated lives." Beth Herbert of *Booklist* concluded that *A Country Far Away* "provides a thought-provoking vision of our shrinking world."

Little Pig's Tale, with its "all-pig cast," wrote Kay McPherson in *School Library Journal,* "exhibits a strong

understanding of the interests of youngsters." In the book, Little Pig wants to give his mother a present for her birthday. A *Publishers Weekly* critic commented, "The obvious choices—a spaceship, an orchard, glittering jewels—prove too difficult to procure." Therefore, Little Pig finally decides to wrap himself, and of course this makes his mother happier than anything he could have given her. In *Running Away from Home,* a six-year-old boy decides to run away from home, so he packs what Susan Dove Lempke in *Booklist* called "important items—marbles, Winnie the Pooh ... his stuffed gorilla and his pillow." But when he comes back home for his toothbrush, and his parents offer him a piece of cake, he agrees to stay. It is a book, wrote Trevor Dickinson in *School Librarian,* that will "ring many happy bells with readers of all ages."

Works Cited

Review of *A Balloon for Grandad, Kirkus Reviews,* November 1, 1988, p. 1604.

Barlow, Robin, review of *Shots, School Librarian,* May, 1987, pp. 149-50.

Cooper, Ilene, review of *A Balloon for Grandad, Booklist,* December 1, 1988, p. 648.

Review of *A Country Far Away, Junior Bookshelf,* February, 1989, p. 14.

Dale-Meiklejohn, Annette, review of *The Dog Show, Magpies,* July, 1996, p. 26.

Review of *The Deserter, Junior Bookshelf,* October, 1979, p. 278.

Dickinson, Trevor, review of *Running Away from Home, School Librarian,* May, 1996, p. 56.

Fisher, Margery, review of *Shots, Growing Point,* November, 1986, p. 4717.

Forman, Jack, review of *The Deserter, School Library Journal,* October, 1977, pp. 111-12.

Herbert, Beth, review of *A Country Far Away, Booklist,* November 15, 1989, p. 665.

Review of *I'll Take You to Mrs. Cole!, Publishers Weekly,* March 30, 1992, p. 105.

Lempke, Susan Dove, review of *Running Away from Home, Booklist,* August, 1996, p. 1907.

Review of *Little Pig's Tale, Publishers Weekly,* October 26, 1990, pp. 66-67.

McPherson, Kay, review of *Little Pig's Tale, School Library Journal,* February, 1991, pp. 69-70.

Review of *The One and Only Robin Hood, Publishers Weekly,* September 11, 1987, pp. 91-92.

Review of *Shots, Junior Bookshelf,* February, 1987, p. 40.

Sutherland, Zena, review of *The Deserter, Bulletin of the Center for Children's Books,* February, 1978, p. 92.

Sutherland, Zena, review of *It'll All Come Out in the Wash, Bulletin of the Center for Children's Books,* January, 1980, p. 109.

For More Information See

PERIODICALS

Australian Book Review, June, 1996, p. 63.

Bulletin of the Center for Children's Books, February, 1989, pp. 147-48.

Junior Bookshelf, February, 1986, p. 15; April, 1988, p. 83; April, 1989, p. 61; April, 1996, p. 59.
Kirkus Reviews, August 1, 1989, p. 1157; May 15, 1996, p. 744.
Magpies, May, 1996, p. 38.

—Sketch by Judson Knight

*   *   *

GUILE, Melanie 1949-

Personal

Surname rhymes with "tile"; born October 10, 1949, in County Durham, England; daughter of Leslie Allen (a psychiatrist) and Marjorie (a teacher of the handicapped) Guile; children: Paul, Melissa, Saskia. *Education:* University of Melbourne, B.A. (with honors) M.A., and Diploma in Education. *Politics:* "Labour/Green." *Hobbies and other interests:* Gardening, cats, walking, swimming, sketching.

Addresses

Home—47 Tongue St., Yarraville, Victoria 3013, Australia. *Electronic mail*—m.guile@rmit.edu.au.

Career

University of Melbourne, Parkville, Australia, lecturer on English literature, 1972-88, lecturer on children's literature, 1988-94; Royal Melbourne Institute of Technology, Melbourne, Australia, instructional designer and educational editor, 1980 and 1995—.

Writings

Revenge of the Green Genie (junior fiction), illustrated by Clare Watson, Scholastic Australia (Sydney), 1996.
(Contributor) *St. Catherine's: A Centenary Celebration, 1896-1996,* Helicon, 1996.
Mr. Venus—Computer Wizard (junior fiction), Scholastic Australia, 1997.

Contributor of columns and reviews to *Magpies,* an Australian journal of children's literature.

Work in Progress

A novel for young people "about a cantankerous granny who dies and returns to the family as a ghost."

Sidelights

Melanie Guile told *SATA:* "From the age of seven I knew I wanted to write stories. We had a wonderful teacher—a Miss Christianson—who used to pin great colorful, detailed posters to the blackboard and encourage us to weave stories around them. I also remember that, when you had finished your other work, you were allowed to read special books. They were nothing to look at on the outside—just blank red covers—but inside they were Cicely May Barker's 'Flower Fairy' books! I love them still.

"Because everyone knew you couldn't make a living by writing books, people suggested that I might be a journalist, and for many years that's what I said I would become. But at high school and university, my love of literature took another twist and I became a university lecturer—enthusing other people about great works of literature. The academic study of literature does nothing for one's own writing, alas—in fact quite the reverse. In my case, I rediscovered the confidence to write when I had my second baby. I thought: 'Well, here's someone who won't judge too harshly!' I wrote my first (unpublished) children's novel in the few weeks after her birth, and to my great joy, my children are still my greatest fans.

"I wrote several rather dull and serious books before I hit on the idea of humor—and it seemed to like me! Now, I concentrate on comic stories for middle-to-upper primary-age readers. I always try to put lots of magic into them as well. Magic and humour seem a good combination, because I want to write books that reluctant readers will enjoy. It was a great moment for me when, at an author talk I was giving at a school, an intellectually disabled boy showed huge enthusiasm for my book *Revenge of the Green Genie.* His aide told me the boy had written his first-ever story, inspired by my book. I want children to love books—mine or anyone else's—and to find delight in them, as this boy did.

"Because I hate rewriting, I tend to write fast and not rework very much at all. I know this is not a good model for young writers to follow, but I suppose I'm too impatient to draft and redraft. The hardest part is thinking up the plot—something I'm not good at. I have so little time in my busy life to write that each book takes at least a year. One day I hope to be able to devote a set number of days a week to my writing but, at the moment, it's whenever I can snatch a spare day or weekend.

"I read other modern children's writers, and I'm lost in admiration—particularly for some Australian authors and illustrators. They are very honest, no-nonsense writers. It's a great advantage to work in children's writing because the kids won't let you get away with anything false, and they require a good story. Too many adult authors seem to have great talent but not enough to say.

"To aspiring writers I would say the usual things: read lots of good books of the kind you want to write. Write about what you know. The more writing you do, the better you'll get. Don't give up. But I'd also say something I don't hear writers saying much: that you do need a basic talent for words, and this needs to be coupled with a practical determination. Calm persistence goes a long way and is certainly more useful than inspiration. Finally—listen to advice, but above all trust your own voice."

H

HANSEN, Brooks 1965-

Personal

Born March 29, 1965, in New York, NY; son of Peter Emil (a television executive) and Whitney (an artist; maiden name, Brooks) Hansen. *Education:* Harvard University, B.A. *Religion:* "Catholic/Swedenborgian."

Addresses

Agent—Amanda Urban, International Creative Management, 40 West 57th Street, New York, NY 10019.

Career

Writer.

Writings

FOR CHILDREN; SELF-ILLUSTRATED

Caesar's Antlers, Farrar, Straus & Giroux, 1997.

OTHER

(With Nick Davis) *Boone* (a novel), Summit, 1990.
The Pilgrimage of Gustav Uyterhoeven, Harcourt, 1993.
The Chess Garden, illustrated by Miles Hyman, Farrar, Straus & Giroux, 1995, published as *The Chess Garden; or The Twilight Letters of Gustav Uyterhoeven,* Sceptre (London), 1995.
Perlman's Ordeal: A Novel, Farrar, Straus & Giroux, in press.

Sidelights

Brooks Hansen is best known for two unique novels that have garnered critical acclaim for their sheer inventiveness. In *Boone,* he and collaborator Nick Davis create an imaginary biography of an artist that mimics the oral history genre. According to *New York Times Book Review* contributor Alfred Corn, one of the best realized pretenses in this faux biography is the authors' ability to mimic the language of their own contemporaries and convincingly present it as Boone's own idiom. *The Chess Garden* is a complex fantasy written by Hansen that involves the game of chess, an imaginary country, and a series of letters from Dr. Uyterhoeven, serving in a prisoner of war camp during the Boer War, to his wife in Dayton, Ohio. "The novel," noted Steven Poole in the *Times Literary Supplement,* "is a wonderfully bewitching compendium of stories, germinated in Arthurian legend, Poe and Carroll." *New York Times Book Review* contributor Jay Parini asserted that "comparisons to Nabokov and Calvino are doubtless in order," adding that "*The Chess Garden* stands by itself, a marvel of attention to the things of this world, and worlds beyond."

Hansen achieved similar success with *Caesar's Antlers,* his first novel for young readers. Dubbed by *Booklist* reviewer John Peters as a "poignant animal story" complete with "larger-than-life characters," this unusual tale centers on themes of courage, hope, and love, as a kind reindeer and a family of sparrows join forces to search for their loved ones. The story begins in Norway with a pair of sparrows named Bette and Piorello, who have just added two young ones to their nest. Their happy situation quickly changes, however, when Piorello accidentally flies into a window, injuring himself. Fortunately, Elsbeth, a young girl visiting her grandmother, finds him and nurses him back to health. But Elsbeth decides to keep Piorello as a pet and takes him with her to boarding school in England. Bette, determined to find Piorello, moves her nest into the antlers of newly found friend Caesar, a gentle reindeer on his own mission to find the two herders who raised him. After a difficult and often treacherous journey, Caesar finds the herdsmen, just as one of them is dying. And after a failed attempt to return home with a flock of geese, the sparrow Piorello is eventually reunited with his family on Christmas Eve.

"Natural and supernatural mix freely in this deeply felt winter's tale, warmed by Caesar's steady heart and the sparrow's unfaltering love," observed Peters. A *Publishers Weekly* commentator praised the book's "eloquent descriptions of the Nordic regions ... and heart-felt

CAESAR'S ANTLERS
Brooks Hansen

A kind reindeer and a family of sparrows search for their loved ones in Brooks Hansen's touching self-illustrated story for young readers. (Cover illustration by Tom Pohrt.)

expressions of self-sacrifice." The critic also noted that Hansen's pen-and-ink drawings "add just the right touch to his delicate prose." *New York Times Book Review* contributor Mark Oppenheimer found *Caesar's Antlers* a "touching and at times gripping story," and praised Hansen for "the book's full-blooded characters and moral sense." Maeve Visser Knoth of *Horn Book* asserted that "Hansen's first novel for children is lyrical and old-fashioned in the best ways."

Works Cited

Review of *Caesar's Antlers, Publishers Weekly,* October 13, 1997, p. 76.
Corn, Alfred, review of *Boone, New York Times Book Review,* August 5, 1990, p. 14.
Knoth, Maeve Visser, review of *Caesar's Antlers, Horn Book,* January-February, 1998, p. 73.
Oppenheimer, Mark, review of *Caesar's Antlers, New York Times Book Review,* April 19, 1998, p. 33.
Parini, Jay, review of *The Chess Garden, New York Times Book Review,* September 24, 1995, p. 14.

Peters, John, review of *Caesar's Antlers, Booklist,* October 1, 1997, p. 329.
Poole, Steven, review of *The Chess Garden, Times Literary Supplement,* June 23, 1995, p. 26.

For More Information See

PERIODICALS

Kirkus Reviews, August 15, 1997, p. 1305.
Publishers Weekly, June 26, 1995, p. 86.
School Library Journal, November, 1997, p. 118.

* * *

HOBAN, Lillian 1925-1998

OBITUARY NOTICE—See index for *SATA* sketch: Born May 18, 1925, in Philadelphia, PA; died of heart failure, July 17, 1998, in New York, NY. Illustrator and author of children's books. Hoban is best known as an author and illustrator of best-selling HarperCollins "I Can Read" Books that depict the joys and concerns of early childhood. Educated at the Philadelphia Museum School of Art, Hoban studied dance with modern dance pioneer Martha Graham, and performed as a dancer during the 1950s. She was self-taught as an illustrator, and began writing her first children's stories after the births of her own four children. In 1964 she illustrated *Bread and Jam for Frances* and *A Baby Sister for Frances,* the first two of the popular "Frances" books written by her husband, Russell Hoban, and featuring a little anthropomorphic badger and her community of friends. Hoban illustrated a number of other stories written by Russell Hoban, and provided pictures for the texts of many other popular children's writers as well, among them Miriam Cohen, Johanna Hurwitz, Marjorie Weinman Sharmat, daughter Julia Hoban, and Louise Borden. Hoban's first work as both author and illustrator, *Arthur's Christmas Cookies,* was published in 1972. She wrote and illustrated several further books featuring her character Arthur the chimpanzee, including *Arthur's Honey Bear, Arthur's Pen Pal, Arthur's Halloween Costume,* and *Arthur's Loose Tooth.* The eleventh of the "Arthur" stories, *Arthur's Birthday Party,* was published posthumously. In addition to the Arthur books, Hoban wrote and illustrated other children's books, among them *Stick-in-the-Mud Turtle, Grandparents' Houses, The Case of the Two Masked Robbers,* and *Silly Tilly and the Easter Bunny.* Hoban and her husband Russell divorced in 1975. They shared a Christopher Award and a Lewis Carroll Shelf Award for *Emmet Otter's Jug-Band Christmas,* for which Lillian Hoban provided the illustrations.

OBITUARIES AND OTHER SOURCES:

PERIODICALS

New York Times, August 2, 1998, p. A42.

OTHER

Obituary provided by HarperCollins publishers, July 23, 1998.

HOBAN, Tana

Personal

Born in Philadelphia, PA; daughter of Abram T. (an advertising manager for the *Jewish Daily Forward*) and Jennie (maiden name, Dimmerman) Hoban; married Edward Gallob (a photographer), 1939 (divorced, 1982); married John G. Morris (journalist), 1983; children: (first marriage) Miela (daughter). *Education:* Graduate of School of Design for Women (now Moore College of Art), 1938.

Addresses

Home—56, Rue des Tournelles, 75003 Paris, France.

Career

Children's author and illustrator, photographer, and artist. Freelance artist, doing advertising and magazine illustration, Philadelphia, PA, beginning 1940; later became a professional photographer. Instructor in photography and graphics at the Annenberg School of Communications, University of Pennsylvania, 1966-69, and at New York University, 1974-76; visiting lecturer at numerous schools throughout the United States, 1974-84. With her husband, Edward Gallob, has been partner-owner of the Hoban-Gallob Studio, Philadelphia, 1946—. Lecturer to school children, teachers, and librarians in Alaska, Arkansas, Connecticut, Minnesota, Mississippi, Nebraska, New York, Ohio, Pennsylvania, Texas, Virginia, and Wisconsin, and in Canada and Europe. Producer of films, *Catsup,* 1967, *Where Is It?,* and *One Little Kitten,* both 1980, and *Panda, Panda* and *Dancing Zoo Zebra,* both 1987. *Exhibitions:* Photographs have been exhibited in one-woman shows at Neikrug Gallery, New York City, 1980, Photographs Unlimited, New York City, 1982, Galerie Agathe Gaillard, Paris, France, 1985, Espace Van Gogh, Arles, France, 1989, and Please Touch Museum, Philadelphia, 1990; work has also been included in a group exhibition with work by artists Margaret Bourke-White, Esther Bubley, Dorothea Lange, and Helen Levitt at Museum of Modern Art, New York City, 1949, Art Alliance, Philadelphia, 1950. Work also included in the following exhibitions: "The Family of Man," Museum of Modern Art, New York City, 1955, White House Conference of Children and Youth, Washington, D.C., 1960, and Print Club of Philadelphia, 1965; "What Is Man?, Museum of the Philadelphia Civic Center, 1966; "Les Enfants," Galerie Agathe Gaillard, Paris, France, 1984, and Elaine Benson Gallery, Bridgehampton, New York City, 1985. Tana Hoban's photographs are in the permanent collections of the Museum of Modern Art, Kerlan Collection of University of Minnesota, De Grummond Collection of University of Southern Mississippi, Musee Carnavalet, Paris, Bibliotheque Nationale, Paris, Mediatheque d'Arles, and Please Touch Museum. Photographs have also appeared in magazines, including *Life, Look, McCall's, Ladies Home Journal,* and *Harper's Bazaar.*

Member: American Society of Magazine Photographers, Authors Guild, Authors League of America, P.E.N.

Awards, Honors

John Frederick Lewis fellowship, 1938; received gold medal award from Chicago Art Directors, 1958, New York Art Directors, 1962 and 1963, and Philadelphia Art Directors, 1962 and 1963; named one of ten top women photographers by Professional Photographers of America, 1959; Golden Eagle Award from Council on International Nontheatrical Events, 1967, for *Catsup; Look Again!* was a *New York Times* Choice of Best Illustrated Children's Books of the Year, 1971, and a Children's Book Showcase Title, 1972; *Count and See* was a *New York Times* Choice of Best Illustrated Children's Books of the Year, 1972, and a Children's Book Showcase Title, 1973; *Circles, Triangles, and Squares* was a runner-up in the Fourth Annual Children's Science Competition and received honorable mention award from New York Academy of Sciences, both 1975; *Is It Red? Is It Yellow? Is It Blue?* received citation from Brooklyn Art Books for Children, certificate of excellence from American Institute of Graphic Arts, was named an American Library Association (ALA) notable book and an International Reading Association—Children's Book Council children's choice book, all 1979; *Take Another Look* was named an ALA notable book, 1981; certificate of excellence from American Institute of Graphic Arts, 1982, for *A, B, See;* award for non-fiction from Washington Children's Book Guild, 1983; *Round and Round and Round* was named an ALA notable book, 1983; Drexel Citation from Drexel University, 1983, for body of creative work; *New York Times* Notable book award, 1984, for *I Walk and Read;* honorable mention, New York Academy of Sciences, 1985, for *Is It Rough? Is It Smooth? Is It Shiny?;* ALA notable book and *Boston Globe/Horn Book* Special Award, both 1985, named to *Horn Book*'s Fanfare List, 1986, all for *1,2,3;* George G. Stone Recognition of Merit Award, 1986, for entire body of work; honorable mention award, New York Academy of Sciences, 1986, for *Is It Larger? Is It Smaller?;* honorable mention, New York Academy of Sciences, 1986, for *Shapes, Shapes, Shapes;* Special International Award (Geneva, Switzerland), 1987, for entire body of work; *New York Times* Best Illustrated Book Award, 1988, for *Look! Look! Look!;* Parents' Choice Foundation Award, 1990, for *Of Colors and Things;* Parents' Choice Picture Book Award and *Boston Globe* Nonfiction Honor book, both 1990, for *Shadows and Reflections.*

Writings

JUVENILES; SELF-ILLUSTRATED

Shapes and Things, Macmillan, 1970.
Look Again!, Macmillan, 1971.
Count and See, Macmillan, 1972.
Push, Pull, Empty, Full: A Book of Opposites, Macmillan, 1972.
Over, Under, and Through, and Other Special Concepts, Macmillan, 1973.

Tana Hoban offers young readers photographs of various common objects and poses the challenge of categorizing each item. (From Animal, Vegetable, or Mineral?, *written and illustrated with photos by Hoban.*)

Where Is It?, Macmillan, 1974.

Circles, Triangles, and Squares, Macmillan, 1974.

Dig/Drill, Dump/Fill (Junior Literary Guild selection), Greenwillow, 1975.

Big Ones, Little Ones, Greenwillow, 1976.

Is It Red? Is It Yellow? Is It Blue?, Greenwillow, 1978.

One Little Kitten, Greenwillow, 1979.

Take Another Look, Greenwillow, 1981.

More Than One, Greenwillow, 1981.

A, B, See, Greenwillow, 1982.

Round and Round and Round, Greenwillow, 1983.

I Read Signs, Greenwillow, 1983.

I Read Symbols, Greenwillow, 1983.

I Walk and Read, Greenwillow, 1984.

Is It Rough? Is It Smooth? Is It Shiny?, Greenwillow, 1984.

1,2,3, Greenwillow, 1985.

What Is It?, Greenwillow, 1985.

Is It Larger? Is It Smaller?, Greenwillow, 1985.

A Children's Zoo, Greenwillow, 1985.

Shapes, Shapes, Shapes, Greenwillow, 1986.

Panda, Panda, Greenwillow, 1986.

Red, Blue, Yellow Shoe, Greenwillow, 1986.

26 Letters and 99 Cents, Greenwillow, 1987.

Dots, Spots, Speckles, and Stripes, Greenwillow, 1987.

Look! Look! Look!, Greenwillow, 1988.

Of Colors and Things, Greenwillow, 1989.

Shadows and Reflections, Greenwillow, 1990.

Exactly the Opposite, Greenwillow, 1990.

All about Where, Greenwillow, 1991.

Look Up, Look Down, Greenwillow, 1992.

Spirals, Curves, Fanshapes, and Lines, Greenwillow, 1992.

Dig, Drill, Dump, Fill, Greenwillow, 1992.

White on Black, Greenwillow, 1993.

Black on White, Greenwillow, 1993.

Who Are They?, Greenwillow, 1994.

Who Is That?, Greenwillow, 1994.

Tana Hoban's What Is It?, Greenwillow, 1994.

Tana Hoban's Red, Blue, Yellow Shoe, Greenwillow, 1994.

Colors Everywhere, Greenwillow, 1995.

Animal, Vegetable, or Mineral?, Greenwillow, 1995.

Just Look, Greenwillow, 1996.

Look Book, Greenwillow, 1997.

Construction Zone, Greenwillow, 1997.

So Many Circles, So Many Squares, Greenwillow, 1998.

More, Fewer, Less, Greenwillow, 1998.

Cubes and Cones, Greenwillow, 1999.

Let's Count, Greenwillow, 1999.

ADULT BOOKS

(Self-illustrated) *How to Photograph Your Child,* Crown, 1955.
(Contributor) *Encyclopedia of Photography,* Greystone Press, 1963.

ILLUSTRATOR

Edna Bennett, *Photographing Youth,* Amphoto, 1961.
Edith Baer, *The Wonder of Hands,* Parents' Magazine Press, 1970.
Charlotte Zolotow, *The Moon Was the Best,* Greenwillow, 1993.
Miela Ford, *Little Elephant,* Greenwillow, 1994.

Adaptations

Where Is It? and *One Little Kitten* were adapted for film in 1980; *Panda, Panda* was adapted for film in 1987.

Sidelights

Tana Hoban is an award-winning photographer who transformed a successful career in photojournalism into an even more successful one as a creator of children's concept books. "Trying to find fresh laudatory adjectives to describe Tana Hoban's photographs is like finding new phrases to describe the sunset," wrote *Horn Book's* Mary M. Burns in a review of Hoban's *Just Look.* "The best ones have already been used."

Named one of the top ten women photographers of America in 1959, with her work on the covers of magazines and hanging in museums, Hoban turned to children's nonfiction in 1970, starting with her *Shapes and Things.* Hoban created a body of more than fifty books which, "by presenting difficult concepts through familiar objects and surroundings, allow children to look at their world with fresh eyes," according to Jane Botham in *Children's Books and Their Creators.* Hoban uses simple, everyday shapes and objects in her photographs, but portrays them in subtle ways, new to the eye. As Botham went on to note, "No other photographer extends a child's world or expands imagination through everyday experiences as does Hoban." Her usually wordless picture books have been called lively and spontaneous and provide vibrant introductions for the very young both to the world of concepts and to books in general.

Through photos of machines, Hoban familiarizes young readers with construction and demolition. (From Construction Zone, *written and illustrated with photos by Hoban.)*

Born in Philadelphia of Russian parents in the second decade of the twentieth century, Hoban grew up in the country, in Lansdale, Pennsylvania. "Somehow I have always felt more European than American," Hoban wrote in *Something about the Author Autobiography Series* (*SAAS*), "perhaps because my parents were Russian immigrants." Her father, who became the advertising manager for the *Jewish Daily Forward,* one of the leading Jewish newspapers of its day, was also in love with the theater, and passed on his passion for the arts to his oldest daughter. It was he who enrolled his daughter in art classes as a little girl, insisting that she should have her own career. Such influences were obviously passed on to her younger brother, Russell Hoban, also, for he became the well known author of the "Frances" series of children's books and of such unconventional adult novels as *Riddley Walker* and *Turtle Diary.*

Though growing up in the country and attending the typical red brick school, Hoban and her siblings had something of an uncommon youth. Her father was a socialist, more Russian than American, who as Hoban noted in *SAAS,* "always cut a dashing figure." He kept bees and pigeons, and was noted as much for his unusual beliefs as for his hard work. "My parents had a way of making everything seem special," Hoban wrote in *SAAS.* "When my father brought me a gift—even a little bracelet—he led me to believe that it was very rare, that he had found it by searching around the world. And when he told me I was wonderful, I believed that, too."

Hoban developed an early love for illustration, and by the eighth grade had already determined it would be her focus in life. She had not yet discovered photography. By the time of high school graduation in 1934, she had moved on to painting and design. At a graduation party her father gave her, she met the man who was to become her future first husband, Edward Gallob, an actor in the drama guild which her father sponsored. But for the time there was no talk of marriage; Hoban enrolled in the School for Design, now known as Moore College of Art. In her last semester at school, she was introduced to photography, something that Gallob too was passionately involved in.

Midway through her studies, Hoban's father died of pneumonia, and her mother suddenly had to earn a living. Hoban, along with her sister, became a sales assistant in her mother's children's shop while also continuing her studies. Upon graduation, she won a fellowship in painting which took her to Europe. Upon her return, she married Gallob and started work as a freelance artist for magazines and advertising. An early success was an illustrated Christmas cover for the *Saturday Evening Post.*

Slowly, however, Hoban began to focus more on photography. Her early work was in children's portraits for display in her mother's shop. "I decided to specialize in children because they were less self-conscious than adults," Hoban noted in *SAAS.* "I wanted natural, spontaneous responses." Her work soon began appearing in magazines and in advertising campaigns, and her name became associated with that of other famous women photographers such as Margaret Bourke-White and Dorothea Lange. After the birth of her own daughter, Hoban's pictures of children became even more popular, for this personal focus added to her work. In one year alone her pictures adorned the covers of sixteen magazines. Hoban experimented with film and also taught a course in photography as communication at the prestigious Annenberg School at the University of Pennsylvania.

By the late 1960s, Hoban wanted to branch out again—this time she chose children's books. Her first titles were an exploration of form and shape. Looking for the uncommon in the common, she published *Shapes and Things,* which *Publishers Weekly* highly praised, stating that the "world of shapes and things will never look the same again, thanks to Tana Hoban." In this book, Hoban took such everyday objects as paper clips, combs, and eggbeaters, and found new perspectives with her photographs. *Kirkus Reviews* called this first book "an apparently simple, actually subtle aesthetic exercise," and concluded that Hoban's "images are both material and dematerialized, and the familiar yields a startling beauty."

Hoban employed cut-out pages in *Look Again!* to make young and old viewers alike take a new gaze at the textures of familiar objects such as sea shells and small animals. A square hole centered on a white page focuses attention on one aspect of a familiar object; only when the page is turned is the entire object revealed. Vertical stripes are revealed to be part of a zebra, for example, in this book which a *Publishers Weekly* reviewer called a "rich visual experience." A critic in *Kirkus Reviews* noted that "No words come between the photographs and the child," and that Hoban "uses her camera eye to reveal and relate as nothing else does." Hoban enlarged on this visual exercise with her *Look! Look! Look!, Take Another Look, Just Look,* and the *Look Book.* Reviewing *Just Look* in *School Library Journal,* Helen Rosenberg noted that the illustrator's colorful images, "always beautiful in their simplicity and clarity," enabled children to be newly conscious of their surroundings. Rosenberg concluded that "the pure design . . . opens up youngsters' imaginations to many possibilities."

Hoban's first books were done primarily in the studio, and then she learned of an experiment done at the Bank Street School in which young children were given cameras, and turned the viewfinders on their own neighborhoods with astounding results. Looking at the world through the tiny viewfinder, these children saw it anew, and Hoban began to ask herself what she was not seeing in her own world. "I deliberately set out to rediscover the city," she wrote in *SAAS,* "to find the things that had become so familiar that I no longer saw them." A row of garbage cans inspired her *Count and See,* an "instructive and entertaining learn-to-count book," according to a *Publishers Weekly* reviewer. Writing in *Horn Book,* Anita Silvey concluded that *Count and See* was "outstanding in comparison with the

Simple geometric shapes are introduced in Hoban's **So Many Circles, So Many Squares,** *self-illustrated with the author's photographs.*

many dismal, unattractive counting books in print." Other counting, number, and alphabet books from Hoban include *1, 2, 3, A, B, See,* and *26 Letters and 99 Cents.*

Hoban has concentrated primarily on picture books that give a child a sense of concepts and verbal relationships. Each of her books has the added advantage of fresh perspective, of enabling the viewer to see something new in the world. Starting with black and white photographs, she has expanded her work into color photos, many of urban scenes, both in New York and in Paris, where she went to live with her second husband in the mid-1980s. "Before we came here," Hoban noted in *SAAS,* "I wasn't at all sure that I would be able to continue doing my books. I thought perhaps I would paint again. Instead, my book production increased." Hoban has more than fifty children's books to her credit, dealing with shapes, numbers, the alphabet, colors, and such concepts as opposites, sizes, space, and amounts.

Push, Pull, Empty, Full is a black-and-white book dealing with opposites. Here, simple text is illustrated by pictures on facing pages. Reviewing this book in *Bulletin of the Center for Children's Books,* Zena

Sutherland called it "Very simple, perfectly clear, and most attractive," concluding that "this is a book that may well stimulate small children to think about other terms of comparison." More opposites were served up in *Exactly the Opposite,* "One of Tana Hoban's best concept books," according to Sutherland. Ellen Fader, writing in *Horn Book,* noted of the same title that the "prolific and gifted photographer again dazzles with her images" and concluded that "this book is another winner from an artist with a seemingly unlimited imagination."

Over, Under, and Through, and Other Spatial Concepts continued this concept-oriented approach, as did *All about Where* which explores location with fifteen prepositions. Of her colors book, *Is It Red? Is It Yellow? Is It Blue?,* Denise M. Wilms remarked in *Booklist* that it was "Imaginative, useful, and fun to look at." The world of light and color was further explored in the award-winning *Shadows and Reflections, Of Colors and Things, Red, Blue, Yellow Shoe,* and *Colors Everywhere.* Reviewing *Shadows and Reflections* in *School Library Journal,* Marylin Iarusso commented that Hoban's "imaginative, wordless book of color photographs is a visual treat." Recognition books by Hoban also employ the use of light: contrast is emphasized with black silhouettes on white in her *Black on White,* and the same technique is employed in *What Is That?,* a board book for toddlers.

Shapes and sizes also get the Hoban treatment in a plethora of titles, among which are *Is It Larger? Is It Smaller?, Circles Triangles, and Squares, Dots, Spots, Speckles, and Stripes, Spirals, Curves, Fanshapes, and Lines,* and *So Many Circles, So Many Squares.* Reviewing the last title in *School Library Journal,* Stephani Hutchinson declared that "This is one of Hoban's best books on shapes yet." *Booklist*'s Carolyn Phelan called *So Many Circles, So Many Squares* "Another attractive, open-ended book from an exceptional photographer."

"A photograph, like a painting, can simply record an incident or, in the hands of a photo-artist, it can interpret, extend, contrast, and develop real insight," observed Charlotte S. Huck in her classic textbook *Children's Literature in the Elementary School.* "Instead of interposing itself between readers and the subject," Patricia Dooley pointed out in *School Library Journal,* "the lens of Hoban's camera seems to strip whatever might have kept them from really seeing the captured object."

Such a rediscovery of the everyday is no accident. As Hoban wrote in an entry for *Fourth Book of Junior Authors and Illustrators,* "My books are about everyday things that are so ordinary that one tends to overlook them. I try to rediscover these things and share them with children. But there is more to each picture than a first look reveals. I always try to include something new, something to reach for."

Works Cited

Botham, Jane, *Children's Books and Their Creators,* edited by Anita Silvey, Houghton Mifflin, 1995, p. 314.

Burns, Mary M., review of *Just Look, Horn Book,* May-June, 1996, p. 324.

Review of *Count and See, Publishers Weekly,* May 1, 1972, p. 50.

de Montreville, Doris, and Elizabeth D. Crawford, editors, *Fourth Book of Junior Authors and Illustrators,* H. W. Wilson, 1978, pp. 178-79.

Dooley, Patricia, review of *Of Colors and Things, School Library Journal,* April, 1989, p. 83.

Fader, Ellen, review of *Exactly the Opposite, Horn Book,* November-December, 1990, p. 758.

Hoban, Tana, essay in *Something about the Author Autobiographical Series,* Volume 12, Gale, 1990, pp. 157-75.

Huck, Charlotte S., "Picture Books" in her *Children's Literature in the Elementary School,* third edition, Holt, Rinehart and Winston, 1979, p. 120.

Hutchinson, Stephani, review of *So Many Circles, So Many Squares, School Library Journal,* March, 1998, p. 196.

Iarusso, Marilyn, review of *Shadows and Reflections, School Library Journal,* May, 1990, p. 97.

Review of *Look Again!, Kirkus Reviews,* February 15, 1971, p. 168.

Review of *Look Again!, Publishers Weekly,* May 3, 1971, p. 55.

Phelan, Carolyn, review of *So Many Circles, So Many Squares, Booklist,* March 1, 1998, p. 1138.

Rosenberg, Helen, review of *Just Look, School Library Journal,* April, 1996, p. 126.

Review of *Shapes and Things, Kirkus Reviews,* June 15, 1970, p. 637.

Review of *Shapes and Things, Publishers Weekly,* July 20, 1970, p. 70.

Silvey, Anita, review of *Count and See, Horn Book,* August, 1972, p. 361.

Sutherland, Zena, review of *Push, Pull, Empty, Full, Bulletin of the Center for Children's Books,* November, 1972, p. 43.

Sutherland, Zena, review of *Exactly the Opposite, Bulletin of the Center for Children's Books,* October, 1990, p. 30.

Wilms, Denise M., review of *Is It Red? Is It Yellow? Is It Blue?, Booklist,* January 1, 1979, p. 750.

For More Information See

BOOKS

Children's Literature Review, Volume 13, Gale, 1987, pp. 98-113.

Contemporary Photographers, third edition, St. James Press, 1995.

Literature for Thursday's Child, Science Research Associates, 1975, pp. 243-306.

PERIODICALS

Booklist, November 15, 1992, p. 602; May 1, 1995, p. 1577; August, 1995, p. 1952; April 1, 1997, p. 1335.

Bulletin of the Center for Children's Books, April, 1991, p. 195; March, 1995, p. 238; June, 1996, p. 339; April, 1997, p. 284.

Five Owls, July-August, 1989, p. 88.

Horn Book, May-June, 1990, p. 350; May-June, 1991, pp. 346-47; November-December, 1994, p. 720; July-August, 1995, p. 483; May-June, 1996, p. 324; September-October, 1997, p. 591.

Los Angeles Times Book Review, March 25, 1990, p. 8.

New York Times Book Review, September 19, 1993, p. 36; June 11, 1995, p. 43.

School Library Journal, August, 1993, p. 145; November, 1994, p. 82; March, 1997, p. 175; August, 1997, p. 135.*

—*Sketch by J. Sydney Jones*

J

JOHNSON, Meredith Merrell 1952-

Personal

Born September 28, 1952, in Witchita, KS; daughter of Theodore Kermit (an industrial engineer) and Margaret Jane (in state politics; maiden name, Hotchkiss) Merrell; married Larre Dean Johnson (a copywriter), September 2, 1972; children: Casey Merrell, Matthew McKendrey. *Education:* Art Center College of Design, graduated with honors.

Addresses

Home—5228 Palm Dr., La Canada Flintridge, CA 91811. *Office*—Ogilvy & Mather Advertising, 11766 Wilshire Blvd., Los Angeles, CA 90025.

Career

Hallmark Cards, Kansas City, MO, illustrator, 1970-72; Della Femina Travisano, Los Angeles, CA, art director, 1979-82; Foote Cone Belding, Los Angeles, art director, 1982-85; Ogilvy & Mather, Los Angeles, art director, senior partner, 1985—.

Illustrator

FOR CHILDREN

Lanczak Williams and Susan Lewis, *My First Vocabulary,* Price Stern Sloan, 1985.

Lanczak Williams and Susan Lewis, *My First Spelling Book,* Price Stern Sloan, 1985.

Roger Burrough, *Little Cloud,* Price Stern Sloan, 1986.

Roger Burrough, *Very Tall, Very Small,* Price Stern Sloan, 1986.

Josh and Dottie McDowell, *Pizza for Everyone,* Chariot Books (Elgin, IL), 1988.

B. B. Hiller, *Rent a Third Grader,* Scholastic, 1988.

Jerry Spinelli, *The Bathwater Gang,* Little, Brown, 1990.

Eve Merriam, *What Can You Do with a Pocket?,* DLM, 1990.

Donna Jo Napoli, *Soccer Shock,* Dutton, 1991.

Sharron Lucky, *Sing Along with the Whales,* DLM, 1991.

Elizabeth Skoglund, *Alfred McDuff Is Afraid of the War,* Tyndale, 1991.

Tracey Moncure and Dawn Schiller, *Itsy Bitsy Spider,* DLM, 1991.

Sheri Brownrigg, *All Tutus Should Be Pink,* Scholastic, 1992.

Meredith Merrell Johnson

Johnson illustrated Debbie Dadey's stories about the adventurous Marty.

Jerry Spinelli, *The Bathwater Gang Gets Down to Business,* Little, Brown, 1992.

Sheri Brownrigg, *Best Friends Wear Pink Tutus,* Scholastic, 1993.

Teddy Slater, *N-O Spells No!,* Scholastic, 1993.

Vicki Cobb and Kathy Darling, *Wanna Bet?,* Morrow, 1993.

Beverly Lewis, *Six Hour Mystery,* Augsburg, 1993.

Linda Lee Maifair, *Brothers Don't Know Everything,* Augsburg, 1993.

Beverly Lewis, *Mountain Bikes and Garbanzo Beans,* Augsburg, 1993.

Linda Lee Maifair, *No Girls Allowed,* Augsburg, 1993.

Esther Allen Peterson, *Spy Machine,* Augsburg, 1993.

Carole Greene, Linda Schullman and Rika Spungin, *Emerald Forest Matching Game,* DLM, 1993.

P. J. Petersen, *The Sub,* Dutton, 1993.

Denise Ortman Pomeraning, *Operation Melody,* Augsburg, 1994.

Grace Maccarone, *Soccer Game,* Scholastic, 1994.

Beverly Lewis, *Mystery at Midnight,* Augsburg, 1995.

Ellen Javernick, *Mrs. Polliwog's Problem Solving Service,* Augsburg, 1995.

Joanne Rocklin, *How Much Is that Guinea Pig in the Window?,* Scholastic, 1995.

Elaine Moore, *Peanut Butter Trap,* Troll, 1996.

Eva Moore, *Day of the Bad Haircut,* Scholastic, 1996.

Candice Ransom, *Teacher's Pest,* Troll, 1996.

Marylin Kaye, *Jill's Happy Un-Birthday,* Pocket, 1996.

Marylin Kaye, *Teammates,* Pocket, 1996.

Marylin Kaye, *Happy Winter Holidays,* Pocket, 1996.

Debbie Dadey, *Marty the Millionaire,* Willowisp, 1997.

Debbie Dadey, *Marty the Mudwrestler,* Willowisp, 1997.

P. J. Petersen, *Can You Keep a Secret?,* Dutton, 1997.

P. J. Petersen, *My Worst Friend,* Dutton, 1998.

Melanie Babendrier, *Club Trouble,* Willowisp, 1998.

Lynea Bowdish, *A Friend for Caitlin,* Willowisp, 1998.

Sindy McKay, *Ben and Becky Get a Pet,* Treasure Bay, 1998.

Sindy McKay, *Ben and Becky and the Haunted House,* Treasure Bay, in press.

Marilyn Sachs, *JoJo and Winnie,* Dutton, in press.

FOR CHILDREN; ALL WRITTEN BY JOAN SINGLETON PRESTINE

Sometimes, I'm Afraid, Price Stern Sloan, 1987.

When Someone Special Dies, Price Stern Sloan, 1987.

Me First, Price Stern Sloan, 1987.

My Parents Go on a Trip, Price Stern Sloan, 1987.

I Want This, and This, and This, Price Stern Sloan, 1987.

Love Me Anyway, Price Stern Sloan, 1987.

FOR CHILDREN; ALL WRITTEN BY BOB McGRATH

The Shoveler, Price Stern Sloan, 1989.
I'm a Good Mommy, Price Stern Sloan, 1989.
Mr. Sneakers, Price Stern Sloan, 1989.
Dog Lies, Price Stern Sloan, 1989.
Me, Myself, Price Stern Sloan, 1989.
You're a Good Daddy, Price Stern Sloan, 1989.

FOR CHILDREN; ALL WRITTEN BY YVETTE LODGE

When I Learn to Dress Myself, Meridian, 1990.
When I Learn to Tell Time, Meridian, 1990.
When I Learn to Subtract, Meridian, 1990.
When I Learn to Write, Meridian, 1990.
When I Learn to Add, Meridian, 1990.

*FOR CHILDREN; ALL WRITTEN BY MARJORIE AND
ANDREW SHARMAT*

Field Trip, Harper & Row, 1990.
Haunted Bus, Harper & Row, 1991.
Bully on the Bus, Harper & Row, 1991.
Secret Notebook, Harper & Row, 1991.
Cooking Class, Harper & Row, 1991.

FOR CHILDREN; ALL WRITTEN BY STEVEN KROLL

New Kid in Town, Avon, 1992.
Playing for Favorites, Avon, 1992.
The Slump, Avon, 1992.
The Streak, Avon, 1992.
Pitching Trouble, Avon, 1993.
Second Chance, Avon, 1993.
Pride of the Rockets, Avon, 1993.

OTHER

Illustrator of book covers for a variety of publishers,
including Price Stern Sloan, Macmillan, and Dutton;
contributor of illustrations to *Spider* and *Cricket* magazines.

For More Information See

PERIODICALS

Booklist, May 1, 1993, p. 1585.
School Library Journal, April, 1992, p. 118; July, 1993, pp.
86-87; August, 1993, p. 170; January, 1998, p. 90.

*   *   *

JOHNSON, Sylvia A.

Personal

Born in Indianapolis, IN. *Education:* Graduated from
Marian College, IN; University of Illinois, M.A.

Career

Writer. Worked as a book and freelance editor in
Minneapolis.

Awards, Honors

New York Academy of Sciences special award, 1983,
for *Apple Trees, Beetles, Crabs, Frogs and Toads, Inside*
*an Egg, Ladybugs, Mosses, Mushrooms, Penguins,
Potatoes, Silkworms,* and *Snails.*

Writings

FOR YOUNG PEOPLE

"Lerner Wildlife Library" series (including *Animals of the
Deserts, Animals of the Grasslands, Animals of the
Mountains, Animals of the Polar Regions, Animals of
the Temperate Forests,* and *Animals of the Tropical
Forests*), illustrated by Alcuin C. Dornisch, Lerner,
1976.
The Wildlife Atlas, illustrated by A. C. Dornisch, Lerner,
1977.
(With Jim Hargrove) *Mountain Climbing,* photographs by
John Yaworsky, Lerner, 1983.
(With Alice Aamodt) *Wolf Pack: Tracking Wolves in the
Wild,* Lerner, 1985.
(With Louis B. Casagrande) *Focus on Mexico: Modern Life
in an Ancient Land,* photographs by Phillips Bourns,
Lerner, 1986.
(With Kunihiko Hisa) "Discovering Dinosaurs" series
(including *The Dinosaur Family Tree, How Did
Dinosaurs Live?,* and *What Were Dinosaurs?*) Lerner,
1990.
Albatrosses of Midway Island, photographs by Frans
Lanting, Carolrhoda Books, 1990.
Roses Red, Violets Blue: Why Flowers Have Colors,
photographs by Yuko Sato, Lerner, 1991.

*For the "National Science Book" series, Sylvia A.
Johnson penned several award-winning titles that were
lauded for their lucid texts and abundant diagrams and
photographs. (Cover photo by Masana Izawa.)*

A Beekeeper's Year, photographs by Nick Von Ohlen, Little, Brown, 1994.

Raptor Rescue!: An Eagle Flies Free, photographs by Ron Winch, Dutton, 1995.

Ferrets, Carolrhoda Books, 1996.

Tomatoes, Potatoes, Corn, and Beans: How the Foods of the Americas Changed Eating around the World, Atheneum, 1997.

Mapping the World, Atheneum, 1999.

"NATURAL SCIENCE" SERIES, PUBLISHED BY LERNER PUBLICATIONS

Penguins, 1981.

Beetles, photographs by Isao Kishida, 1982.

Crabs, photographs by Atsushi Sakurai, 1982.

(With Jane Dallinger) *Frogs and Toads,* photographs by Hiroshi Tanemura, 1982.

Inside an Egg, photographs by Kiyoshi Shimuzi, 1982.

Ladybugs, photographs by Yuko Sato, 1982.

Mushrooms, photographs by Masana Izawa, 1982.

Silkworms, photographs by Isao Kishida, 1982.

Snails, photographs by Modoki Masuda, 1982.

Mosses, photographs by Masana Izawa, 1983.

Apple Trees, photographs by Hiroo Koike, 1983.

Potatoes, photographs by Masaharu Suzuki, 1984.

Coral Reefs, photographs by Shohei Shirai, 1984.

Mantises, photographs by Satoshi Kuribayashi, 1984.

Wasps, photographs by Hiroshi Ogawa, 1984.

Bats, photographs by Modoki Masuda, 1985.

Rice, photographs by Noburo Moriya, 1985.

Morning Glories, photographs by Yuko Sato, 1985.

Snakes, photographs by Modoki Masuda, 1986.

Tree Frogs, photographs by Masuda, 1986.

Chirping Insects, photographs by Yuko Sato, 1986.

How Leaves Change, photographs by Sato, 1986.

Fireflies, photographs by Satoshi Kuribayashi, Lerner, 1986.

Elephant Seals, photographs by Frans Lanting, 1989.

Hermit Crabs, photographs by Kazunari Kawashima, 1989.

Water Insects, photographs by Modoki Masuda, 1989.

Wheat, photographs by Masaharu Suzuki, 1990.

Johnson has also adapted books from translation for "The Animal Friends" series, Carolrhoda Books, and co-authored, with Karlind T. Moller and Clark D. Starr, *A Parent's Guide to Cleft Lip and Palate,* University of Minnesota Press, 1990.

Sidelights

Sylvia A. Johnson is a prolific author of science and nature books whose topics range from wolves to mushrooms. She has written many well-received titles in Lerner's "Natural Science Books" series as well as such popular individual titles as *A Beekeeper's Year, Raptor Rescue!: An Eagle Flies Free,* and *Tomatoes, Potatoes, Corn, and Beans: How the Foods of the Americas Changed Eating around the World.* Reviewing her *Wolf Pack* in the *Bulletin of the Center for Children's Books,* one writer called Johnson's work "scientific without being pedantic ... full of engrossing, well-selected information." It is Johnson's ability to simplify without

eviscerating that has made her a popular writer of children's science and nature books.

Johnson, who has also worked as a freelance book editor in Minneapolis, has done most of her writing for the Minneapolis-based Lerner Publications. Her first work was six titles in the "Lerner Wildlife Library" series: *Animals of the Deserts, Animals of the Grasslands, Animals of the Mountains, Animals of the Polar Regions, Animals of the Temperate Forests,* and *Animals of the Tropical Forests.* Each title in the series briefly describes the geographic region in terms of both climatic conditions and flora and fauna. Johnson then focuses one-page descriptions on ten representative animals from each region, such as the giant panda in the mountain regions, or the anteater in the tropical forests. "The text is short," noted Barbara Elleman of *Booklist,* "its emphasis is limited to the physical characteristics, such as camouflage or eating habits, which enable the animal to survive in its particular environment...." Reviewing *Animals of the Deserts,* Marjorie E. Smith commented in *Appraisal* that the book "is an easy way

Johnson follows Minnesota beekeeper John Wetzler through four seasons of labor while she explains the tending of the hives and the extracting and packaging of the honey. (From A Beekeeper's Year, *illustrated with photos by Nick Von Ohlen.)*

to introduce a study of the desert, animals, conservation, the effects of lack of water on plant and animal life, and much more." Linda L. Mills, writing about the series in general in *School Library Journal,* maintained: "Unusual for their division of animals by climate, these books are geared for the older intermediate grades but could also be used by advanced third graders." The titles were later condensed into a one-volume work, *The Wildlife Atlas.*

Johnson next turned her hand to more than two dozen volumes in the Lerner "Natural Science Book" series, which features scientific terminology in boldface type with appended glossaries that further define words. Each title deals with a particular life-form, from penguins to mosses, and each is illustrated with diagrams and close-up, color photographs. Some of these titles have original text by Johnson, while others were adapted by her from translations of Japanese originals. Her first book in the series, *Penguins,* features a text that "should appeal not only to budding naturalists but to all children (and grownups) who are captivated by the unique birds at home in the icy Antarctic," according to a reviewer in *Publishers Weekly.* This same reviewer concluded that *Penguins* is an "outstanding addition" to the Lerner series. Terry Lawhead, reviewing Johnson's *Beetles* and *Silkworms* in *School Library Journal,* commented: "I hope this series goes on forever. There is some lovely writing.... The attention to highly accurate anatomy, life cycles and detailed close-up photographs never ceases to amaze me." Lawhead concluded that "this series has singlehandedly uplifted the credibility of science books...." Elisabeth LeBris praised Johnson's *Bats* in *School Library Journal,* calling it an "excellent book" and one which "no library should be without." Martha T. Kane, writing in *Appraisal,* dubbed *Bats* "a beautiful book" and commented that it "will hold its readers spellbound." The lumbering amphibians of California's Ano Nuevo Island are examined in Johnson's *Elephant Seals,* a "winning addition" to the Lerner series, according to *School Library Journal* contributor Kathryn Weisman. "Johnson's book will appeal to browsers as well as report writers and should be a part of most natural history collections," Weisman concluded.

Plants also have their place in the "Natural Science Book" series, and Johnson contributed many titles to their study. Reviewing Johnson's *Mosses* in *Horn Book,* Sarah S. Gagne observed that the "reproductive cycle of moss ... is so well illustrated that one can form mental images of the structures and so readily follow the cycle." William D. Perkins commented in *Appraisal* that "in *Mosses,* the author has done an excellent job of packaging information in manageable bits which build upon one another to give the reader a solid sense of what is important about these fascinating plants." Nancy Curtin observed in *School Library Journal* that Johnson's *Apple Trees* offers fine detail on the fertilization and development of the apple, and that though other books have looked at the same topic, "none cover the subject better." Other plants that Johnson examines in the series include the potato, rice, and wheat. "Here is everything anyone always wanted to know about potatoes, but didn't even know enough to ask," noted Eldon

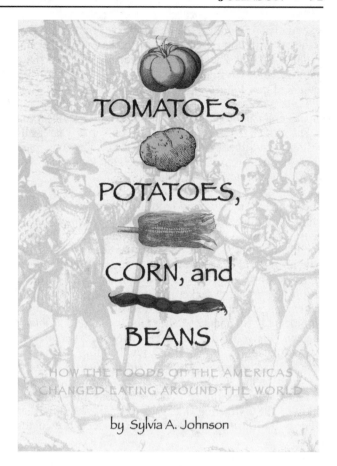

Johnson's educational book explains how the culinary habits of people all around the world were altered by the discovery and exportation of certain foods from the Americas.

Younce in a *School Library Journal* review of *Potatoes.* "The text is well written and the color photography is excellent," Younce concluded. "An informative book about a very versatile vegetable." Summing up the series in general, *Booklist's* Elleman called it "lucid" and "handsomely photographed," while Althea L. Phillips dubbed it "an extremely attractive and well-written series" in *Appraisal.*

Johnson has also contributed volumes to the "Carolrhoda Nature Watch" series, including *Albatrosses of Midway Island* and *Ferrets.* The former title captures "the mystery of the world's largest flighted bird," according to a *Kirkus Reviews* critic, who concluded that the book is "informative, funny; a delight for nature browser or bird lover." The possibility of keeping ferrets as pets is explored in *Ferrets.* Ellen M. Riordan, writing in *School Library Journal,* noted that "good quality, full-color photographs accompany a clear, readable text in this comprehensive book...." A *Kirkus Reviews* contributor concluded a review of *Ferrets* by stating that the "presentation of information is straightforward and easy to follow."

Johnson has also written several individual titles on various topics in nature and science. Her *Wolf Pack: Tracking Wolves in the Wild* explains that wolves, essentially wild dogs, display all the traits that we associate with domesticated dogs—including loyalty and social cohesion. They are structured in packs and mate for life. Lee Jeffers Brami, writing in *Appraisal*, remarked that Johnson's *Wolf Pack* "conveys these facts and many others through simple, flowing prose and superb color photographs." Cynthia M. Sturgis observed in *School Library Journal* that Johnson's text was "well-written" and the combination of text, diagrams, and photographs "make this an excellent candidate for school or public library collections."

Bees, eagles, and common foods of the Americas are the subjects of three further Johnson titles. *A Beekeeper's Year* focuses on the work of a Minnesota beekeeper, tracing the man's labors through the seasons from the time he gets rid of the protective winter trappings on the hives in April until he seals them up again in autumn. "From the arresting jacket photograph to the recipes on the last page of the text, this is a most intriguing book," commented Stephanie Zvirin in a starred *Booklist* review. "Pair this with books on honeybee behavior and physiology, and you may find a few budding apiarists in your midst," Zvirin concluded. *Horn Book*'s Margaret A. Bush called *A Beekeeper's Year* "informative" and "useful," commenting particularly on Johnson's descriptions of the extracting and packaging of the honey as well as the introduction of a foreign queen bee to the hive.

Johnson told the story of one eagle, patient S-137, at an animal rescue center in St. Paul, Minnesota, in her *Raptor Rescue! An Eagle Flies Free*. The victim of a gunshot wound, this bald eagle recovered and was released back into nature. Along with this true tale, Johnson also related the story of raptors in general and how they are endangered by the encroachment of humans. "Flowing text and striking close-ups present the rehabilitation of a bald eagle," commented Tippen McDaniel in *Appraisal*, while Susan Dove Lempke noted in *Booklist* that *Raptor Rescue!* combines "the appeal of an animal book, a veterinary career book, and a conservation book...."

With *Tomatoes, Potatoes, Corn, and Beans,* Johnson showed how the eating habits of people all over the world were changed by the discovery and exportation of these foods from the Americas. "Johnson blends history, botany, geography, folklore, cookery, and art in a fascinating account of how Columbus' 'discovery' in 1492 began an exchange of foods between the Americas and the Old World that improved the lives of millions," Hazel Rochman commented in *Booklist*. The foods from the Americas in fact turned out to be of greater value than any of the gold or silver for which explorers were searching. Johnson also included peppers and peanuts in her stew to create a book, according to Lois McCulley in *School Library Journal*, that is "useful for social-history collections as well as any library needing information about the history of foodstuffs." Writing in *Voice of Youth Advocates*, Joyce Hamilton observed that Johnson's book "contains information that will be difficult to find elsewhere," and also noted that "the numerous anecdotes, such as those on the origination of peanut butter and potato chips, are entertaining."

Works Cited

Review of *Albatrosses of Midway Island, Kirkus Reviews,* January 1, 1990, p. 47.

Brami, Lee Jeffers, review of *Wolf Pack, Appraisal,* summer, 1986, p. 39.

Bush, Margaret A., review of *A Beekeeper's Year, Horn Book,* September-October, 1994, p. 612.

Curtin, Nancy, review of *Apple Trees, School Library Journal,* April, 1984, pp. 115-16.

Elleman, Barbara, review of "Lerner Wildlife Library" series, *Booklist,* September 1, 1976, p. 39.

Elleman, Barbara, review of "Natural Science Book" series, *Booklist,* September 1, 1981, p. 43.

Review of *Ferrets, Kirkus Reviews,* June 1, 1997, p. 874.

Gagne, Sarah S., "Views on Science Books," *Horn Book,* June, 1984, p. 370.

Hamilton, Joyce, review of *Tomatoes, Potatoes, Corn, and Beans, Voice of Youth Advocates,* December, 1997, pp. 334-35.

Kane, Martha T., review of *Bats, Appraisal,* fall, 1986, pp. 58-59.

Lawhead, Terry, review of *Beetles* and *Silkworms, School Library Journal,* November, 1982, p. 80.

LeBris, Elisabeth, review of *Bats, School Library Journal,* February, 1986, p. 86.

Lempke, Susan Dove, review of *Raptor Rescue!, Booklist,* September 15, 1995, p. 155.

McCulley, Lois, review of *Tomatoes, Potatoes, Corn, and Beans, School Library Journal,* May, 1997, p. 146.

McDaniel, Tippen, review of *Raptor Rescue!, Appraisal,* winter, 1996, pp. 31-32.

Mills, Linda L., review of "Lerner Wildlife Library" series, *School Library Journal,* September, 1976, p. 118.

Review of *Penguins, Publishers Weekly,* May 22, 1981, p. 76.

Perkins, William D., review of *Mosses, Appraisal,* spring-summer, 1984, pp. 52-53.

Phillips, Althea L., review of "Natural Science Book" series, *Appraisal,* winter, 1983, pp. 65-66.

Riordan, Ellen M., review of *Ferrets, School Library Journal,* August, 1997, p. 148.

Rochman, Hazel, review of *Tomatoes, Potatoes, Corn, and Beans, Booklist,* April 15, 1997, p. 1415.

Smith, Marjorie E., review of *Animals of the Deserts, Appraisal,* winter, 1977, pp. 24-25.

Sturgis, Cynthia M., review of *Wolf Pack, School Library Journal,* January, 1986, p. 69.

Weisman, Kathryn, review of *Elephant Seals, School Library Journal,* March, 1989, p. 192.

Review of *Wolf Pack, Bulletin of the Center for Children's Books,* December, 1985, pp. 69-70.

Younce, Eldon, review of *Potatoes, School Library Journal,* November, 1984, p. 126.

Zvirin, Stephanie, review of *A Beekeeper's Year, Booklist,* March 15, 1994, p. 1348.

For More Information See

PERIODICALS

Appraisal, summer, 1989, p. 46; summer, 1990, pp. 70-71; winter, 1992, pp. 35-36.
Booklist, December 1, 1991, p. 693.
Bulletin of the Center for Children's Books, December, 1991, p. 94; July-August, 1994, pp. 361-62; July-August, 1997, p. 399.
Horn Book, January-February, 1996, p. 91.

Kirkus Reviews, November 15, 1986, p. 1730; September 15, 1991, p. 1223; February 15, 1997, p. 301.
School Library Journal, March, 1987, p. 160; July, 1990, p. 80; October, 1995, p. 148.*

—Sketch by J. Sydney Jones

*   *   *

JONES, Volcano
See MITCHELL, Adrian

K

KEEGAN, Marcia 1943-

Personal

Born May 23, 1943, in Tulsa, OK; daughter of Otis Clair and Mary Elizabeth (Collar) Keegan. *Education:* University of New Mexico, B.A., 1963.

Addresses

Home—Weehawken, NJ.

Career

Freelance writer and photographer. *Member:* American Society of Magazine Photographers, Art Directors Club.

Writings

SELF-ILLUSTRATED (WITH PHOTOGRAPHS)

The Taos Indians and Their Sacred Blue Lake, Messner, 1971, reprinted with a foreword by Stewart L. Udall, Clear Light (Santa Fe, NM), 1991.
Mother Earth, Father Sky: Navajo and Pueblo Indians of the Southwest, Grossman, 1974.
(Editor) *We Can Still Hear Them Clapping,* Avon, 1974.
Pueblo and Navajo Cookery, Earth Books (Dobbs Ferry, NY), 1977.
Oklahoma, Abbeville, 1979.
Pueblo Boy: Growing up in Two Worlds, Dutton, 1981.
New Mexico, Skyline, 1984.
Pueblo People: Ancient Tradition, Modern Lives, Clear Light, 1997.
Pueblo People: Place, Space, and Balance, Clear Light, 1997.

ILLUSTRATOR, WITH PHOTOGRAPHS

Richard Margolis, *Only the Moon and Me,* Lippincott, 1969.
(And editor) *Teachings of His Holiness the Dalai Lama,* Clear Light, 1981.
Jamake Highwater, *Moonsong Lullaby,* Lothrop, 1981.

The Dalai Lama of Tibet, *Ocean of Wisdom: Guidelines for Living,* foreword by Richard Gere, Clear Light, 1989.
(With others) *Enduring Culture: A Century of Photography of the Southwest Indians,* Clear Light, 1990.
Ancient Wisdom, Living Traditions: Himalayan Culture in Song, Verse, and Picture, edited and translated by Lobsang Lhalungpa, Clear Light, 1997.

Sidelights

Photographer and author Marcia Keegan has created several books for children that introduce a diversity of cultures and life experiences. Reflecting the author's love for the American Southwest, several of Keegan's books, which include *Mother Earth, Father Sky: Navajo and Pueblo Indians of the Southwest* and *The Taos Indians and Their Sacred Blue Lake,* focus on the land now inhabited by such Native American people as the Navajo and Pueblo. Also reflecting Keegan's interest in native cultures is her photo-essay for younger readers, *Pueblo Boy: Growing up in Two Worlds,* first published in 1981.

Pueblo Boy focuses on Timmy, a ten-year-old boy of the Tewa tribe who lives with his family in San Ildefonso Pueblo, on the outskirts of Santa Fe, New Mexico. By following Timmy in his daily routine, Keegan shows students how Native American traditions have become integrated with American culture: computers are available at school, while at home Timmy lives in almost the identical style of adobe hut that has been home to his family for over a century. Praising Keegan for highlighting cultural differences in her "interesting and readable" text, Maeve Visser Knoth maintained that author's "clear, colorful photographs . . . will attract an enthusiastic audience." A *Kirkus Reviews* critic called *Pueblo Boy* "an authentic glimpse of the positive side of Pueblo life."

In addition to her many writings on Native American peoples and culture, Keegan has also traveled outside the American Southwest to document subjects for her photo-essays and books. In *We Can Still Hear Them Clapping,* she captures the sunset years of vaudeville, interviewing and photographing many now-elderly performers in such famous New York City vaudeville revues as *Ziegfield's Follies.* A *Booklist* critic hailed *We Can Still Hear Them Clapping* as "a moving tribute to the trouper spirit," and a *Publishers Weekly* commentator called Keegan's work "a lovely book, stylish, dignified, executed with feeling." Keegan also provides the photographs for two volumes of spiritual inspiration by Tibet's Dalai Lama.

Works Cited

Knoth, Maeve Visser, review of *Pueblo Boy: Growing up in Two Worlds, Horn Book,* July-August, 1991, pp. 579-80.

Review of *Pueblo Boy: Growing up in Two Worlds, Kirkus Reviews,* May 15, 1991, p. 673.

Review of *We Can Still Hear Them Clapping, Publishers Weekly,* September 15, 1975, p. 60.

Review of *We Can Still Hear Them Clapping, Booklist,* January 1, 1976, p. 610.

For More Information See

PERIODICALS

Bloomsbury Review, November, 1990, p. 27.
Booklist, May 1, 1991, p. 1708.
Bulletin of the Center for Children's Books, April, 1991, p. 196.
Five Owls, January 1991, p. 52.
New York Times Book Review, November 5, 1972, p. 20; October 19, 1975, p. 7.
School Library Journal, September, 1991, p. 190.

*   *   *

KENT, Deborah Ann 1948-

Personal

Born October 11, 1948, in Little Falls, NJ; daughter of Gordon L. and Doris M. (Vandermay) Kent; married Richard Conrad Stein (a writer), December 15, 1979; children: Janna. *Education:* Oberlin College, B.A., 1969; Smith College, M.S.W., 1971; Instituto Allende, M.F.A., 1976.

Addresses

Home—5817 N. Nina Ave., Chicago, IL 60631. *Agent*—Amy Berkower, Writer's House, Inc., 21 West 26th St., New York, NY 10010.

Career

Writer. University Settlement, New York, NY, social worker, 1971-75. Worked with Centro de Crecimiento, San Miguel de Allende, Mexico, 1977-80.

Writings

FOR YOUNG PEOPLE

Belonging: A Novel, Dial, 1978.
Cindy, Scholastic, 1982.
That Special Summer, Silhouette, 1982.
Jody, Scholastic, 1983.
Te Amo Means I Love You, Bantam, 1983.
Heartwaves, Ace, 1984.
Honey and Spice, New American Library, 1985.
Love to the Rescue, Scholastic, 1985.
Ten-Speed Summer, Bantam, 1985.
Talk to Me, My Love, Dell, 1987.
Taking the Lead, Bantam, 1987.
One Step at a Time, Scholastic, 1989.
Why Me?, Scholastic, 1992.
Benjamin Franklin: Extraordinary Patriot, Scholastic, 1993.
The American Revolution: "Give Me Liberty, or Give Me Death!", Enslow Publishers, 1994.
The Vietnam War: "What Are We Fighting For?", Enslow Publishers, 1994.
Mexico: Rich in Spirit and Tradition, Marshall Cavendish, 1995.
Salem, Massachusetts, Silver Burdett, 1995.
Dorothy Day: Friend to the Forgotten, William B. Eerdmans (Grand Rapids, MI), 1996.

Deborah Ann Kent

(With Kathryn A. Quinlan) *Extraordinary People with Disabilities,* Children's Press, 1996.
China: Old Ways Meet New, Marshall Cavendish, 1996.
Too Soon to Say Goodbye, Scholastic, 1997.
Only Way Out, Scholastic, 1998.
Lexington and Concord, Children's Press, 1998.
Hillary Rodham Clinton, Children's Press, 1998.
Jane Means Appleton Pierce, Children's Press, 1998.

"AMERICA THE BEAUTIFUL" SERIES

Massachusetts, Children's Press, 1987.
New Jersey, Children's Press, 1987.
Louisiana, Children's Press, 1988.
Pennsylvania, Children's Press, 1988.
Colorado, Children's Press, 1989.
Ohio, Children's Press, 1989.
Connecticut, Children's Press, 1990.
Maryland, Children's Press, 1990.
South Carolina, Children's Press, 1990.
Delaware, Children's Press, 1991.
Iowa, Children's Press, 1991.
Washington, D.C., Children's Press, 1991.
Puerto Rico, Children's Press, 1992.
New Mexico, Children's Press, 1999.
Maine, Children's Press, 1999.

"CORNERSTONES OF FREEDOM" SERIES

Jane Addams and Hull House, Children's Press, 1992.
The Titanic, Children's Press, 1993.
The Freedom Riders, Children's Press, 1993.
Yellowstone National Park, Children's Press, 1994.
The White House, Children's Press, 1994.
The Vietnam Women's Memorial, Children's Press, 1995.
The Star-Spangled Banner, Children's Press, 1995.
The Lincoln Memorial, Children's Press, 1996.
African Americans in the Thirteen Colonies, Children's Press, 1996.
The Disability-Rights Movement, Children's Press, 1996.
The Battle of Lexington and Concord, Children's Press, 1997.
Thurgood Marshall and the Supreme Court, Children's Press, 1997.

"CITIES OF THE WORLD" SERIES

Rio de Janeiro, Children's Press, 1996.
Tokyo, Children's Press, 1996.
Beijing, Children's Press, 1996.
New York City, Children's Press, 1996.
Amsterdam, Children's Press, 1997.
Dublin, Children's Press, 1997.
San Francisco, Children's Press, 1997.
St. Petersburg, Children's Press, 1997.
Boston, Children's Press, 1998.
Buenos Aires, Children's Press, 1998.
Madrid, Children's Press, 1999.

"HOW WE LIVED IN EARLY AMERICA" SERIES

Colonial New England, Marshall Cavendish, 1999.
The Middle Colonies, Marshall Cavendish, 1999.
The Southern Colonies, Marshall Cavendish, 1999.

OTHER

Contributor to *Disabled U.S.A.* and *Journal of Visual Impairment and Blindness.*

Sidelights

A versatile and prolific author, Deborah Ann Kent has written scores of well-received books for young people in a variety of genres. The success of her 1978 debut, the semi-autobiographical novel *Belonging,* sparked a flurry of activity during the 1980s, as Kent penned a number of novels for middle graders and young adults and eventually ventured into the writing of biographies and other nonfiction as well. These later works include histories such as *The American Revolution, The Vietnam War,* and *China: Old Ways Meet New,* documentary studies such as *Extraordinary People with Disabilities* and *The Disability-Rights Movement,* biographies of *Dorothy Day* and *Hillary Rodham Clinton,* and a look at a number of famous institutions and other popular subjects, among them *The White House, The Lincoln Memorial,* and *The Titanic.* Many commentators have offered favorable assessments of Kent's work. Anita Palladino, writing in *School Library Journal,* called *The American Revolution* "an agreeably unbiased presentation," while Valerie Childress dubbed *The Vietnam War* "a good overview" in a commentary for that same journal. In another review of *The Vietnam War, Voice of Youth Advocates* contributor Anne Liebst praised Kent for "a concise and factual account" and a "valuable introduction" to the war.

"I grew up in Little Falls, New Jersey, about fifteen miles from Manhattan," Kent once told *SATA.* "My parents were both very education-oriented, and there

Kent's **African Americans in the Thirteen Colonies,** *a title from the "Cornerstones of Freedom" series, examines the slave trade of the seventeenth and eighteenth centuries in America.*

Helen Keller, pictured here with Anne Sullivan, is included in Kent's compilation of biographies featuring a wide variety of famous figures from history who have overcome adversity. (From Extraordinary People with Disabilities, *written by Kent with Kathryn A. Quinlan.)*

were always plenty of books around for my brothers and me to discover.

"I have been totally blind all my life. Fortunately for me, New Jersey practiced 'mainstreaming' long before it was required by federal law, and I was able to attend public schools from the time I entered eighth grade. Some of my experiences in making the transition from a special class for blind kids to a regular class provided the background for my first young-adult novel, *Belonging*.

"I've been interested in writing for as long as I can remember. My father used to make up stories with us, assigning each of us the roles of various characters, and we would record these little plays on tape for posterity. When I was six I received honorable mention in a story contest sponsored by *Highlights* (magazine), and they printed my story, 'The Animal Parade.'

"I continued to write stories through high school and college, but became increasingly discouraged by the warnings of teachers and counselors that nobody makes a living as a writer in this day and age. I determined to do something more practical with my life, and putting dreams of becoming an author aside, earned a master's degree in social work.

"I worked as a social worker for four years at the University Settlement House on New York's Lower East Side. Although it was often frustrating, I really enjoyed my job and the people I met through my work. I continued writing short stories, but I found that the settlement house took most of my time and energy.

"When I had been at the University Settlement for four years, I spent my summer vacation in the town of San Miguel de Allende, Mexico. I fell in love with the charming colonial town, its narrow cobblestone streets and the warmth and spontaneity of the Mexican people. San Miguel had long attracted artists and writers from Europe and the United States, and I sensed that it could provide me with just the atmosphere I needed if I wanted to devote myself to writing full time. I resigned from my job and returned to San Miguel, intending to stay there for a year. As it turned out, it was five years before I moved back to the States again.

"I began my first book as a project in a writers' workshop, but got so much encouragement that I actually completed and revised the book. I hadn't consciously planned to write a novel for teenagers, but by the time I finished the first chapter, I realized that the book was best suited for a young audience.

"After *Belonging* was accepted for publication, I wondered what I should write next. Meg, the heroine in *Belonging,* is blind but I didn't want to be categorized as a writer who could deal only with blind characters. So I was excited when my agent suggested that I try writing a romance novel for teenagers. My first romance, *Cindy,* grew out of my experiences in Mexico. It is the story of an American girl who spends a year in Mexico with her family, and must struggle with cultural differences when she falls in love with a Mexican boy.

"Most of my books are inspired by people I have known and places I have lived. For example, *That Special Summer* takes place in a resort community on a lake, not very different from Green Pond, New Jersey, where my family used to spend several weeks each summer. Although I still do not wish to write exclusively about people who are blind, I feel at the same time that blind people, and people with other disabilities, should be presented more positively in books. So several of my books do have disabled teenagers as minor or major characters."

Kent teamed up with Kathryn A. Quinlan for the nonfiction study *Extraordinary People with Disabilities,* which features biographies of a wide variety of famous individuals who have suffered from blindness (John Milton, Stevie Wonder), deafness (Beethoven), or both (Helen Keller), as well as people such as President Franklin D. Roosevelt, a victim of the debilitating disease polio. Carol F. Creedon, writing in *Science Books & Films,* called *Extraordinary People with Disabilities* a "splendid book," and noted the diversity of the people featured: "They include African Americans, Latinos, Asians, and Native Americans, as well as Caucasians; forty percent are women. Whatever a given student's interests (sports, war, heroism, art, science, music, literature, ballet, activism, and more), he or she will find in this book several people with disabilities with whom to identify." Besides the biographies of some fifty people, there are a number of essays on related topics, including one on the subject of euthanasia. Creedon asserted: "Throughout, the authors' style is engaging and lively, with only the necessary amount of technical terminology." *School Library Journal* contributor Martha Gordon called the book "a fine combination of biography and the history of the disability-rights movement."

Kent has also written for the "Cornerstones of Freedom" series, published by Children's Press. Her work in this series includes a biography of reformer Jane Addams, as well as *The Freedom Riders,* which portrays the civil-rights activists who helped bring an end to racial segregation in the South during the 1960s. Bonnie Siegel, writing in *School Library Journal,* maintained that Kent's *Freedom Riders* "expands a subject usually given one or two lines in existing material." Of *The Lincoln Memorial,* another volume in the series, *School Library Journal* contributor Pamela K. Bomboy wrote, "As in other titles in the series, an enormous amount of complex history is broken down into highly readable and accurate text."

Works Cited

Bomboy, Pamela K., review of *The Lincoln Memorial, School Library Journal,* February, 1997, p. 92.

Childress, Valerie, review of *The Vietnam War: "What Are We Fighting For?",* School Library Journal, November, 1994, p. 127.

Creedon, Carol F., review of *Extraordinary People with Disabilities, Science Books & Films,* April, 1997, pp. 76-77.

Gordon, Martha, review of *Extraordinary People with Disabilities, School Library Journal,* March, 1997, pp. 177-78.

Liebst, Anne, review of *The Vietnam War: "What Are We Fighting For?", Voice of Youth Advocates,* February, 1995, p. 359.

Palladino, Anita, review of *The American Revolution: "Give Me Liberty, or Give Me Death!," School Library Journal,* July, 1994, p. 110.

Siegel, Bonnie, review of *The Freedom Riders, School Library Journal,* August, 1993, p. 176.

For More Information See

PERIODICALS

Booklist, January 1, 1990, p. 917; June 1, 1996, p. 1692; November 1, 1996, p. 493; March 1, 1997, p. 1158.

School Library Journal, September, 1992, p. 267; March, 1994, p. 230; November, 1994, p. 127; January, 1996, p. 119; June, 1996, p. 132; August, 1996, p. 172; September, 1996, pp. 217-18; October, 1996, p. 134; February, 1997, p. 118; March, 1997, pp. 177-78; June, 1997, p. 139.

Voice of Youth Advocates, February, 1990, p. 344.

KLEMM, Barry 1945-

Personal

Born June 10, 1945, in Melbourne, Australia; son of Francis Verdun Klemm (a truck driver) and Ruby Hanna Maud Wickson (a machinist). *Education:* Attended Latrobe University and University of Melbourne.

Addresses

Home—644 Rathdowng St., North Carlton 3054, Australia. *Electronic mail*—almost @ mpx.com.au. *Agent*—c/o AMC Pty. Ltd., P.O. Box 1034, Carlton 3053, Australia.

Career

Writer. *Military service:* Australian Army, Royal Australian Regiment, 1966.

Writings

The Tenth Hero (novel), Addison Wesley Longman (Melbourne, Australia), 1997.

Last Voyage of the Albatross (novel), Addison Wesley Longman, 1998.

Author of film and television scripts, as well as radio plays.

Sidelights

Barry Klemm told *SATA:* "I enjoyed an array of abandoned careers before resorting to literature. I was a crane jockey, insurance clerk, combat soldier, advertising officer, computer programmer, cleaner, stage hand, postman, sports ground manager, builder's labourer, and taxi driver."

*   *   *

KRASNO, Rena 1923-

Personal

Born December 4, 1923, in Shanghai, China; son of David (a writer) and Aida (in business; maiden name, Kriger) Rabinovich; married Hanan Krasno, August 30, 1949; children: Dafna, Maya. *Education:* French Municipal College, earned Certificat d'Etudes, Brevet Superieur, and Baccalaureate (Philosophy Section); studied for 3 years at the Faculty of Medicine at the Jesuit Aurora University (later called Shanghai School of Medicine #2), in Shanghai, China, during World War II. *Religion:* Jewish. *Hobbies and other interests:* Fluent in English and French (active), Russian and German (passive), and Hebrew and Spanish.

Addresses

Home—255 S. Rengstorff #106, Mountain View, CA 94040.

Career

Has worked as a simultaneous interpreter for international organizations such as the United Nations Educational, Scientific, and Cultural Organization (UNESCO), the International Labour Organization (ILO), the Food and Agricultural Organization (FAO), and the Olympic Committee, and others, in Europe and Asia. Served as Honorary Chancellor of Austria in Seoul, Republic of Korea. Sino-Judaic Institute, in charge of public affairs, member of board of directors, member of editorial board, and frequent contributor to the Institute's publication, *Points East.*

Krasno is one of the primary subjects of *Exil Shanghai,* a documentary film by Ulrike Ottinger of Berlin, and she participated in the making of *Sanctuary Shanghai* made by filmmaker Chen Yifei of the Shanghai Yifei Culture and Film Communication Company. In 1998, *Sanctuary Shanghai* was broadcast on Chinese Television (Shanghai).

Awards, Honors

Medal of honor, French government, Shanghai, for Studies.

Writings

(Coauthor) *The Banana Also Has a Heart* (children's book of Filipino legends, in Hebrew), Keter (Jerusalem, Israel), 1972.
Strangers Always: A Jewish Family in Wartime Shanghai, Pacific View (Berkeley, CA), 1992.
Kneeling Carabao and Dancing Giants: Celebrating Filipino Festivals (children's nonfiction), illustrated by Ileana Lee, Pacific View, 1997.

Articles have appeared in *Jerusalem Post, Japan Times, Korea Times, Korea Herald, Die Presse, Filipino Journal of Education, South African Chronicle,* and others.

Work in Progress

A children's book on the history, customs, festivals, legends, and values of Japan, in the same format as *Kneeling Carabao and Dancing Giants,* for Pacific View.

Sidelights

Rena Krasno is the author of *Kneeling Carabao and Dancing Giants: Celebrating Filipino Festivals,* a children's book that surveys numerous festivals celebrated on the more than seven thousand islands that comprise the Philippines. Krasno's description of the festivals includes their associated legends, recipes, songs, and games. Although Filipino immigrants and their descendants are the second most numerous Asian group living in the United States, there are few books for children about the country or its culture, according to Ilene Cooper, who reviewed *Kneeling Carabao and Dancing*

Rena Krasno

Giants for *Booklist.* Cooper maintained that Krasno's writing is "several notches above [the] typical standard" for series nonfiction. Krasno's book reflects the diversity within Filipino culture itself, which is a blend of vestiges of the cultures of the many descendants of immigrants from China, Spain, the Middle East, and Portugal who populate the islands. A *Kirkus Reviews* commentator called *Kneeling Carabao* "a robust sampler of an obviously rich and varied culture."

Krasno is also the author of *Strangers Always: A Jewish Family in Wartime Shanghai,* an adult book based on the diaries she kept as a college student living in China during World War II. Shanghai was host to thousands of Jewish refugees during the first half of the twentieth century, beginning with those who fled Russian pogroms and the Russian Revolution, and including many who sought refuge during Hitler's anti-Jewish campaigns. Krasno's father arrived in China in 1921. He was the publisher and editor of a weekly in Russian, English, and Yiddish. When the Japanese occupied Shanghai completely, after Pearl Harbor until the end of World War II, the city became a less hospitable place for Jews, and Krasno provides a rare, first-person account of life for this isolated community of Jews under Japanese occupation. Kenneth W. Berger, who reviewed *Strangers Always* for *Library Journal,* described the book as "a remarkable combination of personal experiences and short essays" on the history of the Jewish refugee community in Shanghai.

Works Cited

Berger, Kenneth W., review of *Strangers Always: A Jewish Family in Wartime Shanghai, Library Journal,* November 1, 1992, p. 102.

Cooper, Ilene, review of *Kneeling Carabao and Dancing Giants: Celebrating Filipino Festivals, Booklist,* December 1, 1997, p. 620.

Review of *Kneeling Carabao and Dancing Giants: Celebrating Filipino Festivals, Kirkus Reviews,* September 15, 1997, p. 1459.

For More Information See

PERIODICALS

Publishers Weekly, November 16, 1992, p. 56.

L

LANGLEY, Andrew 1949-

Personal

Born October 26, 1949, in Bath, England; son of Kenneth Edward (an engineer) and Mona Emily Francis (a homemaker) Langley; married Lois Ann Norah d'Esterre (an editor), April 19, 1975; children: Samuel Charles, Rose Alice. *Education:* London University, B.A. (English literature; with honors).

Addresses

Home—8 Chapel Path, Colerne, Wilts SN14 8DL, England.

Career

Children's book author. Penguin Books, London, England, marketing assistant, 1974-78.

Writings

"BEHIND THE SCENES" SERIES; FOR CHILDREN; PHOTOGRAPHS BY CHRIS FAIRCLOUGH

Radio Station, F. Watts, 1983.
Hotel, F. Watts, 1983.
Car Ferry, F. Watts, 1983.
Football Club, F. Watts, 1983.
Supermarket, F. Watts, 1983.
Police Station, F. Watts, 1983.
Post Office, F. Watts, 1985.
Newspapers, F. Watts, 1985.

"ORIGINS" SERIES; FOR CHILDREN

A Cup of Tea, Wayland, 1982.
The Meat in Your Hamburger, Wayland, 1982.
The Paper in Your Home, Wayland, 1982.

"TOPICS" SERIES; FOR CHILDREN

Great Disasters, Wayland, 1985, Bookwright Press, 1986.
Under the Ground, Wayland, 1985, Bookwright Press, 1986.

Television, Wayland, 1986, Bookwright Press, 1987.
Jungles, Wayland, 1986, Bookwright Press, 1987.

"PASSPORT" SERIES; FOR CHILDREN

Passport to Great Britain, F. Watts, 1985, Bookwright Press, 1986.

"FOCUS ON" SERIES; FOR CHILDREN

Focus on Wool, Wayland, 1985.
Focus on Vegetables, Wayland, 1985.
Focus on Timber, Wayland, 1986, published in the United States as *Spotlight on Timber,* Rourke Enterprises, 1987.
Focus on Vegetables, Wayland, 1986.

"SPOTLIGHT ON" SERIES; FOR CHILDREN

Spotlight on Airports, F. Watts, 1987.
Spotlight on Aircraft, F. Watts, 1987.
Spotlight on Dinosaurs, F. Watts, 1987.
Spotlight on Aircraft, illustrated by Peter Bull, F. Watts, 1987, published in the United States as *Aircraft,* Bookwright Press, 1989.
Spotlight on Spacecraft, illustrated by Christopher Forsey, Michael Roffe, and others, F. Watts 1987.
Spotlight on the Moon, illustrated by Christopher Forsey, F. Watts, 1987, published in the United States as *The Moon,* 1988.
Spotlight on Trees, F. Watts, 1987.

"LET'S LOOK AT" SERIES; FOR CHILDREN

Let's Look at Bikes, Wayland, 1988, published in the United States as *Bikes and Motorcycles,* Bookwright Press, 1989.
Let's Look at Trucks, Wayland, 1988, published in the United States as *Trucks,* Bookwright Press, 1989.
Let's Look at Circuses, illustrated by D. Bowles, Wayland, 1989.
Let's Look at Aircraft, Wayland, 1989, published in the United States as *Aircraft,* Bookwright, 1989.
Let's Look at Trains, illustrated by Mike Turner, Wayland, 1989, published in the United States as *Trains,* Bookwright, 1989.

Let's Look at Racing Cars, illustrated by Mike Atkinson, Wayland, 1990, published in the United States as *Racing Cars,* Bookwright, 1990.

Let's Look at Monster Machines, illustrated by Mike Atkinson, Wayland, 1990, published in the United States as *Monster Machines,* Bookwright Press, 1990.

"THE STORY OF" SERIES; FOR CHILDREN

(With Stella Alcantara and Josefina Dalupan Hofilena) *The Story of the Philippines,* World Book International, 1989.

The Story of Singapore, World Book International, 1990.

(With Garry Bailey) *The Story of India,* World Book International, 1990.

"RESOURCES" SERIES; FOR CHILDREN

Copper, Wayland, 1981.

Paper, Wayland, 1991, Thomson Learning, 1993.

Steel, Wayland, 1992, Thomson Learning, 1993.

"HISTORY OF BRITAIN" SERIES; PUBLISHED BY HAMLYN; FOR CHILDREN

The Tudors, 1485 to 1603, Hamlyn, 1993.

The Stuarts, 1603 to 1714, Hamlyn, 1993.

Georgian Britain 1714 to 1837, Hamlyn, 1994.

Victorian Britain, 1837 to 1901, Hamlyn, 1994.

Modern Britain: 1901 to the 1990s, Hamlyn, 1994.

Queen Victoria, illustrated by James Field, Hamlyn, 1995.

The Blitz, 1939-1945, illustrated by John James, Hamlyn, 1995.

The Home Front, Hamlyn, 1995.

Elizabeth I, illustrated by Mark Bergin, Heinemann, 1996.

Shakespeare and the Theatre, illustrated by John James, Heinemann, 1996.

"GREAT EXPLORERS" SERIES; FOR CHILDREN

Discovering the New World: The Voyages of Christopher Columbus, illustrated by Paul Crompton, Kibworth Books (Leicester, England), Chelsea Juniors, 1994.

Exploring the Pacific: The Expeditions of Captain Cook, illustrated by David McAllister, Kibworth Books, Chelsea Juniors, 1994.

The Great Polar Adventure: The Journeys of Roald Amundsen, illustrated by Kevin Barnes, Kibworth Books, Chelsea Juniors, 1994.

Journey into Space: The Missions of Neil Armstrong, illustrated by Alex Pang, Kibworth Books, Chelsea Juniors, 1994.

"100 GREATEST" SERIES; FOR CHILDREN

100 Greatest Tyrants, Dragon's World Children's Books (Limpsfield, England), 1996.

100 Greatest Inventions, Grolier, 1997.

100 Greatest Men, Grolier, 1997.

100 Greatest Women, Grolier, 1997.

100 Greatest Sports Champions, Grolier, 1997.

100 Greatest Manmade Wonders, Grolier, 1997.

100 Greatest Medical Discoveries, Grolier, 1997.

100 Greatest Explorers, Grolier, 1997.

100 Greatest Disasters, Grolier, 1997.

100 Greatest Natural Wonders, Grolier, 1997.

100 Greatest Amazing Animals, Grolier, 1997.

100 Greatest Archaeological Discoveries, Grolier, 1997.

FOR CHILDREN

Explorers on the Nile ("In Profile" series), Silver Burdett, 1981.

Working in the Army: A Guide for Young People, National Extension College, 1983.

The Superpowers, Wayland, 1983.

The First Men Round the World, Wayland, Silver Burdett, 1983.

Ian Botham (biography), illustrated by Karen Heywood, Hamilton, 1983.

Cleopatra and the Egyptians ("Life and Times" series), illustrated by Gerry Wood, Wayland, 1985, Bookwright Press, 1986.

Doctor, photographs by Chris Fairclough, F. Watts, 1985.

Energy, Bookwright Press, 1985.

John F. Kennedy (biography), illustrated by Richard Hook, Wayland, 1985, Bookwright Press, 1986.

Librarian, photographs by Chris Fairclough, F. Watts, 1985.

The Making of the Living Planet, Little, Brown, 1985.

Peoples of the World, Wayland, 1985, Bookwright Press, 1986.

The Army, Wayland, 1986.

Combat Pilot, photographs by Chris Fairclough, F. Watts, 1986.

A Family in the Fifties ("How They Lived" series), illustrated by John James, Wayland, 1986.

The Royal Air Force, Wayland, 1986.

The Royal Navy, Wayland, 1986.

Sailor, photographs by Chris Fairclough, F. Watts, 1986.

Airports, illustrated by James Dugdale and others, F. Watts, 1987.

Cars, F. Watts, 1987.

Genghis Kahn and the Mongols ("Life and Times" series), illustrated by Clyde Pearson, Wayland, 1987.

Travel Games for Kids, illustrated by Alisa Tingley, W. Foulsham, 1987, Berkshire House, 1992.

The World of Sharks, Wayland, 1987, Bookwright Press, 1988.

Twenty Names in Pop Music, illustrated by Gary Rees, Wayland, 1987, Marshall Cavendish, 1988.

Travel Quizzes for Kids, W. Foulsham, 1988.

Twenty Explorers, illustrated by Edward Mortelmans, Wayland, 1988, Marshall Cavendish, 1990.

Twenty Names in Crime, illustrated by Gary Rees, Wayland, 1988.

(With Maira Butterfield) *People,* illustrated by Norman Young, Gareth Stevens Children's Books (Milwaukee, WI), 1989.

Sport, Wayland, 1989.

Sport and Politics, Wayland, 1989, Rourke Enterprises, 1990.

(With Tony Reynolds, Tim Furniss, Nigel Hawkes, Jane Sherwin, and Virginia Tulling) *World Issues* (two volumes), Bowker, 1990.

Trucks and Trailers, Puffin, 1991.

Young Sailor, illustrated by Robin Lawrie and Bob Mathias, Adlard Coles Nautical (London, England), Sheridan House (Dobbs Ferry, NY), 1993.

Grasslands, illustrated by Neil Bulpitt and others, J. Morris, 1993.

The Illustrated Book of Questions and Answers, Kibworth Books, 1993, Facts on File, 1996.

Wetlands, illustrated by Neil Bulpitt and others, J. Morris, 1993.

The Industrial Revolution, Viking, 1994.

The Age of Industry ("See Through History" series), Hamlyn, 1994.

Medieval Life, photographs by Geoff Brightling and Geoff Dann, Dorling Kindersley, Knopf, 1996.

(With Philip de Souza) *The Roman News,* Walker, Candlewick Press, 1996.

Victorian Factories, illustrated by James Field, Heinemann, 1996.

Victorian Railways, illustrated by James Field, Heinemann, 1996.

The Search for Riches, Wayland, 1996, Raintree Steck-Vaughn, 1997.

Shakespeare and the Theatre, illustrated by John James, Heinemann, 1996.

(With Gerald Wood) *Life in a Victorian Steamship,* Heinemann, 1997.

Tudor Palaces, illustrated by Mark Bergin and James Field, Heinemann, 1997.

Food and Farming, Heinemann, 1997.

Hans Christian Andersen, illustrated by Toni Morris, Oxford University Press, 1997.

Alexander the Great: The Greatest Ruler of the Ancient World ("What's Their Story?" series), illustrated by Alan Marks, Oxford University Press, 1997.

Amelia Earhart: The Pioneering Pilot ("What's Their Story?" series), illustrated by Alan Marks, Oxford University Press, 1997.

Oxford First Encyclopedia, Oxford University Press, 1998.

Trade and Transport, illustrated by Mark Bergin, James Field, and John James, Heinemann, 1998.

OTHER

(Editor with John Utting) *The Village on the Hill: Aspects of Colerne History,* Colerne History Group, 1990.

Glenfiddich: Made without Compromise since 1887, photographs by Philip Sayer, Good Books (Melksham, England), 1995.

London Pride: 150 Years of Fuller, Smith and Turner, 1845-1995, Good Books, 1995.

Sidelights

English author Andrew Langley has dedicated his career to writing educational books for children. His early books are mostly straightforward works designed to explain day-to-day facts for young readers. In the "Behind the Scenes" series, for example, the author takes a look at the functions of such places as a hotel, a police station, and a post office; in the "Origins" series, Langley explains where such things as hamburger meat come from. Later in his career, he has written more on subjects from the field that has most interested him: history.

Among these books on historical topics, Langley has written biographies about key figures like John F. Kennedy, about exploration ranging from the voyages of Columbus to the American space program, and about

entire historical time periods, such as the Industrial Revolution and the Victorian Age. Among the latter, Langley has received high praise for his "History of Britain" series, which covers the fifteenth century through modern times. In these works, Langley describes all aspects of British history—social, military, political—thoroughly and in a way that is understandable to young readers. All the books contain illustrations, and there are indices, glossaries, and time charts, too, to help readers navigate through the text. One *Junior Bookshelf* critic called it an "important" series for librarians to have.

Some of Langley's books also look at more distant times, such as his *Medieval Life* and *The Roman News.* In a span of just sixty-four pages, *Medieval Life* gives readers a quick look through the fifth through fifteenth centuries in Europe. While some reviewers felt this historical review did not delve deeply enough, others had high praise for the author's realistic portrayal of times little understood by young readers. Norton Hodges, writing in *School Librarian,* praised in particular how Langley gives credit to the roles of women and Islamic culture in medieval times. The critic concluded, "I can wholeheartedly recommend this book to teachers, librarians and young readers."

In an innovative approach to teaching history to young readers, Andrew Langley and coauthor Philip de Souza cover historical events as if they were articles in a modern-day newspaper. (From The Roman News; *illustration by Christian Hook.*)

From Langley's biography **Amelia Earhart: The Pioneering Pilot,** *illustrated by Alan Marks.*

The Roman News, which Langley co-wrote with Philip de Souza, takes a very creative approach to teaching history to youngsters. The authors cover historical events as if they were articles in a modern-day newspaper. Not only are major events such as the assassination of Julius Caesar and the Spartan invasion covered, but also items of social interest, such as slavery, sports, and clothing fashions. Advertisements and advice columns are thrown in to add extra fun and humor. For example, one article wryly suggests that you should always designate just one room in your home as a vomitorium. The book's "readable style, and interesting selection of subjects, makes it a good introduction to Roman history for older juniors and younger secondary children," suggested a *Junior Bookshelf* reviewer. A *Booklist* contributor similarly said *The Roman News* will "encourage creative projects" and be useful to "students having difficulty with standard textual materials."

Of his interest in teaching about history, Langley told *SATA,* "The study of history is endlessly fascinating and frequently enthralling, but an area of staggering ignorance for a huge number of people (especially Americans). Only by understanding the past can we hope to understand the present. I hope that my books—in a very modern way—aid that understanding."

Works Cited

Review of *Georgian Britain, Junior Bookshelf,* February, 1985, p. 38.

Hodges, Norton, review of *Medieval Life, School Librarian,* August, 1996, p. 112.

Review of *The Roman News, Booklist,* October 1, 1996, p. 345.

Review of *The Roman News, Junior Bookshelf,* December, 1996, p. 270.

For More Information See

PERIODICALS

Appraisal, summer, 1985, p. 49; winter, 1988, p. 67; fall, 1993, pp. 85-86.

Booklist, January 1, 1991, pp. 917, 919.

Bulletin of the Center for Children's Books, October, 1988, p. 45.

Growing Point, January, 1988, p. 4919.

Junior Bookshelf, August, 1994, p. 145; October, 1994, pp. 181-82; August, 1995, pp. 145-46.

Kirkus Reviews, May 15, 1996, p. 746.

Publishers Weekly, August 12, 1996, p. 84.

School Librarian, May, 1988, p. 60.

School Library Journal, February, 1990, p. 96; January, 1995, p. 127; July, 1996, p. 92.

Science Books and Films, May, 1997, p. 120.

Times Educational Supplement, November 25, 1983, p. 29; March 9, 1984, p. 51; June 12, 1985, p. 21.*

*   *   *

LEWIS, J. Patrick 1942-

Personal

Born May 5, 1942, in Gary, Indiana; son of Leo J. and Mary (Cambruzzi) Lewis; married Judith Weaver, August 29, 1964 (divorced, 1983); married Susan Marceau, June 24, 1998; children: (first marriage) Beth, Matthew, Leigh Ann. *Education:* St. Joseph's College, Rensselaer, IN, B.A., 1964; Indiana University–Bloomington, M.A., 1965; Ohio State University, Ph.D., 1974. *Religion:* None.

Addresses

Home—104 Fairview Rd., Chagrin Falls, OH 44022. *Agent*—Ginger Knowlton, Curtis Brown, Lt., 10 Astor Pl., New York, NY 10003.

Career

Otterbein College, Westerville, OH, professor of economics, 1974-1998; Author.

Awards, Honors

Children's Book of the Year, Ohioana Library Association, 1989, for *The Tsar and the Amazing Cow;* individual artist grant for adult poetry, Ohio Arts

J. Patrick Lewis

Council, 1989; Kentucky Bluegrass Award, 1996, for *The Christmas of the Reddle Moon.*

Writings

The Tsar and the Amazing Cow, illustrated by Friso Henstra, Dial, 1988.

A Hippopotamusn't and Other Animal Verses, illustrated by Victoria Chess, Dial, 1990.

Two-Legged, Four-Legged, No-Legged Rhymes, illustrated by Pamela Paparone, Knopf, 1991.

Earth Verses and Water Rhymes, illustrated by Robert Sabuda, Atheneum, 1991.

The Moonbow of Mr. B. Bones, illustrated by Dirk Zimmer, Knopf, 1992.

One Dog Day, illustrated by Marcy Dunn Ramsey, Atheneum, 1993.

(Reteller) *The Frog Princess: A Russian Folktale,* illustrated by Gennady Spirin, Dial, 1994.

July Is a Mad Mosquito, illustrated by Melanie W. Hall, Atheneum, 1994.

The Christmas of the Reddle Moon, pictures by Gary Kelley, Dial, 1994.

The Fat-Cats at Sea, illustrated by Victoria Chess, Knopf, 1994.

Black Swan/White Crow (haiku), woodcuts by Chris Manson, Atheneum, 1995.

Ridicholas Nicholas: More Animal Poems, pictures by Victoria Chess, Dial, 1995.

Riddle-icious, illustrated by Debbie Tilley, Knopf, 1996.

The Boat of Many Rooms, illustrated by Reg Cartwright, Atheneum, 1996.

The La-di-da Hare, illustrated by Diane Bluthenthal, Dial, 1997.

Long Was the Winter Road They Traveled: A Tale of the Nativity, illustrated by Drew Bairley, Dial, 1997.

The Little Buggers: Insect and Spider Poems, illustrated by Victoria Chess, Dial, 1997.

Riddle-lightful, illustrated by Debbie Tilley, Knopf, 1998.

The House of Boo, illustrated by Katya Krenina, Atheneum, 1998.

Doodle Dandies: Poems that Take Shape, illustrated by Lisa Desimini, Atheneum, 1998.

BoshBlobberBosh: Runcible Poems for Edward Lear, illustrated by Gary Kelley, Harcourt, 1998.

At the Wish of the Fish: An Adaptation of a Russian Folktale, illustrated by Katya Krenina, Atheneum, 1999.

The Bookworm's Feast: A Potluck of Poems, Dial, 1999.

The Night of the Goat Children, illustrated by Alexi Natchev, Dial, 1999.

OTHER

(Compiler, with Jan S. Adams and Michael W. Curran) *The USSR Today: Current Readings from the Soviet Press: Selections from the Current Digest of the Soviet Press, from May 16, 1973, to June 25, 1975,* American Association for the Advancement of Slavic Studies (Columbus, OH), 1975.

Contributor of reviews to periodicals, including *New York Times, Nation, Chicago Tribune,* and *San Francisco Chronicle;* contributor of articles and reviews to professional journals.

Sidelights

Among the writers whom J. Patrick Lewis has described as influences are Lewis Carroll, A. A. Milne, and Edward Lear. As a student of the Russian language and culture, Lewis has also been influenced by that nation's folklore, which has played a part in several of his works.

In *The Tsar and the Amazing Cow,* Lewis's first book for young readers, a peasant couple lose their three daughters, but their cow comes to the rescue, telling the peasant Stefan, "Drink the milk, Master ... it is magic." So Stefan and his wife Maria drink the milk, and the next morning they discover that they are years younger. The evil Russian tsar in the capital city of St. Petersburg hears of their magic cow and sends for them, but in the end, the amazing cow outwits the greedy tsar, and Stefan and Maria's daughters are restored to them. Ilene Cooper in *Booklist* called *The Tsar and the Amazing Cow* a "well-told tale," and Margaret A. Bush in *Horn Book* described it as a "spare, well-paced narrative, adroitly embellished with an occasional richness of phrase." Betsy Hearne in the *Bulletin of the Center for Children's Books,* referring to the plot twists whereby the dead daughters are restored while the tsar becomes so young he no longer exists, called the book "a rather sophisticated time fantasy ... compactly plotted and distinctively written."

In *A Hippopotamusn't and Other Animal Verses,* Lewis experimented with words and sounds and meaning to produce a book centered on birds and beasts that Hearne called "[p]layful, clever, and above all, freshly worded." Among the lines that Hearne quoted approvingly were these: "that redheaded woodpecker, / redwooded head-pecker, / rockheaded woodpoker's head." Lewis presents a variety of poetic forms including quatrains, couplets, haiku and limericks. In another poem, Lewis writes, "There's a squishy / Fish critter / Swishing in my / Oyster stew. / Tell me, Oyster, / Mister? Sister? / Girl or Boyster? / Which are you?" Mary M. Burns in *Horn Book* pointed out Lewis's concise descriptions, such as his reference to a tomcat as "Night watchman of corners / Caretaker of naps," and his reference to a vulture and an owl as "God Almighty's stare and scowl." "If there is anyone who doesn't chortle over this book," Burns concluded, "don't bother trying to please him or her—nothing ever will."

Lewis continued the animal theme of the previous book in *Two-Legged, Four-Legged, No-Legged Rhymes,* presenting poems on cats, porcupines, and mosquitoes among others. Hazel Rochman, writing in *Booklist,* noted, "the poem many will go back to is 'Stories,' about a faithful old dog before the hearth ('His tail buffs my shoe'); here the mood is quiet, both physical and fragile." A *Kirkus Reviews* critic called the book "an appealing collection." With *Earth Verses and Water Rhymes,* Lewis's tone became, in the words of Hearne in the *Bulletin of the Center for Children's Books,* "more sober." As an example, she quoted "Lighthouse": "This giant white / Land candle burns / The edges of / The fog by turns." Leone McDermott in *Booklist* also described

Commodore Mouse and Honeypot Bear sail to the island of Oh, where they make the acquaintance of the easygoing La-di-da Hare in Lewis's nonsense rhyme story of friendship and frolic. (From The La-di-da Hare, *illustrated by Diana Cain Bluthenthal.)*

it as a quieter, gentler collection than its predecessors, "A pleasant book for curling up with at home or for reading aloud to a group."

The Moonbow of Mr. B. Bones continues in the folkloric tradition of *The Tsar and the Amazing Cow,* though this time the setting is distinctly American. Mr. B. Bones sells "magic jars with mysterious labels—Sundrops, Snowrays, Moonbows, Rainflakes, and Whistling Wind." He does a brisk business until someone claims that the jars are empty, but when Mr. B. opens a jar, a shining light convinces everyone that his "moonbows" are real. "A fine poet," Rochman wrote in *Booklist,* "Lewis tells the story with a lilting, colloquial rhythm." *School Library Journal* contributor Susan Scheps concluded that, "The folktale qualities of plot and narrative make this a good choice for reading aloud." *One Dog Day* also has a distinctively American setting—a "Coon Dog Race and Corn Feed." Twelve-year-old Jilly Hawkes enters her collie, Poetry, in a dog race, and with some help from a local boy named Twef, Poetry wins. "The story has a slow beginning," noted Christie Sylvester in *Booklist,* "but before too long, readers will be cheering Jilly and Poetry on to victory."

With *The Frog Princess,* Lewis returned to Russian folktales, making use of a story that some reviewers described as "complex." When a tsar commands each of his three sons to shoot an arrow into the forest and marry the woman who retrieves it, his youngest son winds up married to a frog who has brought back his arrow. But this frog is special, and in fact she is a beautiful woman who has been placed under a curse by her father. "Lewis's retelling of this complex Russian tale," wrote *School Library Journal* contributor Linda Boyles "is smooth and easy, lightened by touches of humor."

Another collection of verse, *July Is a Mad Mosquito,* followed. In this one, Lewis includes poems for each month of the year, and describes the months together in a final poem: "January's a polar bear; / February's a mole . . . ." *Bulletin of the Center for Children's Books* critic Roger Sutton wrote that, "The rhythms are catchy and the imagery ever-crisp," and concluded that "the poems are fun to read aloud." Sutton noted that it was a particularly good book with which to introduce children to the changing seasons and months of the year, and though Judy Greenfield in *School Library Journal* observed that many such books exist, she held that "Lewis's sensitive and imaginative voice is a welcome addition to the literature."

The Fat-Cats at Sea is a particularly whimsical tale, in which a group of six sailor cats go off to the Isle of Sticky-Goo to retrieve its famous sticky buns for Her Majesty, the Queen of Catmandoo. They go through the sorts of adventures that readers of sea tales have expected ever since the time of Homer's *Odyssey:* homesickness, hostile vessels, and washing up on the shores of a lotus-like paradise. "The jaunty rhythms and smooth impeccable rhymes flow effortlessly, employing a highly appealing blend of downright silliness and a more sophisticated cleverness," stated a *Publishers*

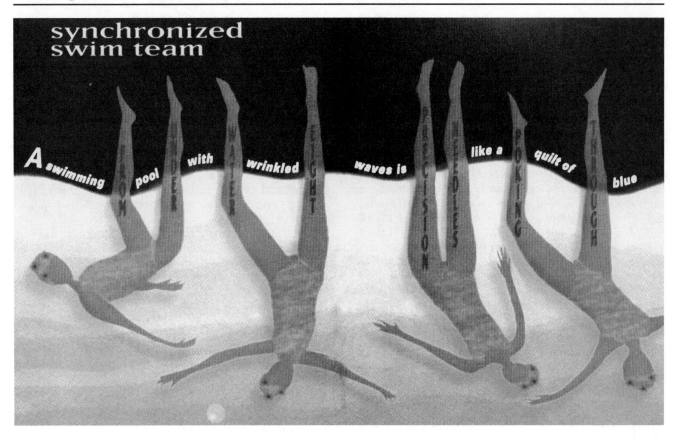

Lewis presents a series of concrete poems, or verse in the form of its subject, in **Doodle Dandies: Poems that Take Shape,** *illustrated by Lisa Desimini.*

Weekly reviewer. By contrast, *Black Swan/White Crow,* a collection of poems in a loose haiku format with woodcut images by Chris Manson, is much more restrained. While not strictly adhering to the stringent haiku form, nonpurists "can expect to find several short poems to their liking" according to *Booklist* reviewer Carolyn Phelan.

Lewis served up more helpings of outlandish humor in *Ridicholas Nicholas: More Animal Poems* and *Riddle-icious,* for which *Bulletin of the Center for Children's Books* gave a special "Big Picture" review by acting editor Deborah Stevenson. "Some books try to *make* language fun," Stevenson wrote. "This one knows it already is and invites readers to share in the revel." The book consists of riddle-poems, such as this one describing a cow: "Standing under summer skies, / Her back end's good for swatting flies. // If there's nothing else to do, / Her front end's good for making moo. // Front to back and in between, / She's the original cream machine." *Riddle-lightful* is a follow-up to *Riddle-icious,* providing thirty-two more simple-to-very-puzzling riddles. "Young wits will congratulate themselves when they figure out the answers to these clever brainteasers," said a critic in *Publishers Weekly.*

Some of Lewis's books feature Biblical themes. *The Boat of Many Rooms,* for instance, tells the story of Noah and his ark through a collection of poems. A reviewer in *Publishers Weekly* applauded the narrative,

commenting, "Lewis employs a wide variety of rhyme scheme and stanza length to convey the bustling energy." *Long Was the Winter Road They Traveled: A Tale of the Nativity,* is in the words of *Booklist*'s Susan Dove Lempke, "A reverent, tender look at the wonders of a night almost 2,000 years ago." *The House of Boo,* on the other hand, is a spooky poem that celebrates a distinctly non-Christian holiday, Halloween.

In *The La-di-da Hare,* Lewis pays tribute to Carroll, Lear, and other influences with an upbeat story that employs much nonsense rhyme. Thus the hare of the title wears a ring of "2-carrot gold," and walks on "Q-Tip toes." A mouse's journey with the Honeypot Bear takes them across "The blue butterflyland [to] / The fabulous Island of Oh." "This unpredictable and spirited romp," concluded a reviewer in *Publishers Weekly,* "blithely echoes classic nonsense poetry." In *Doodle Dandies: Poems that Take Shape,* Lewis presents a series of concrete poems, or verse in the shape of the thing it is describing. In a poem about a giraffe, for example, the word *tail* forms the tail of the giraffe and the word *stilts* is repeated four times to form the giraffe's legs. "These poems take both shape and flight as they soar through the imaginative landscape," enthused Lauren Adams in *Horn Book.* Of Lewis's work with illustrator Lisa Desimini, Adams called it, "A true collaboration of text and art presenting poems that are pictures that are poems...."

In a homage to Edward Lear, one of his sources of inspiration, Lewis created *BoshBlobberBosh,* a set of sixteen poems in various forms about the life of Lear, the unparalleled king of nonsense verse, or "bosh." Lewis explores Lear's childhood as the twentieth child in a family of twenty-one, his job as an art instructor to Queen Victoria, and even Lear's cat, Mr. Foss, makes an appearance. Biographical notes explain the parts of Lear's life from whence the poems are drawn. "The verses are a bit more sweetly whimsical that Lear's angular nonsense," stated Deborah Stevenson in *The Bulletin of the Center for Children's Books,* "but they're enjoyable evocations of the poet's classic contributions, and Lewis has often caught his forerunner's tone." *School Library Journal* contributor Robin L. Gibson thought the collection would work well in tandem with Lear's original work but, "they are strong enough to stand on their own." A reviewer in *Publishers Weekly* approved of the tribute, saying, "Literary chronicles seldom prove as amicable ... and Lear himself would certainly be pleased that Lewis's limericks scan perfectly."

Works Cited

Adams, Lauren, review of *Doodle Dandies, Horn Book,* July-August, 1998, pp. 505-506.

Review of *The Boat of Many Rooms, Publishers Weekly,* January 13, 1997, p. 71.

Review of *BoshBlobberBosh: Runcible Poems for Edward Lear, Publishers Weekly,* October 19, 1998, p. 80.

Boyles, Linda, review of *The Frog Princess, School Library Journal,* September, 1994, p. 209.

Burns, Mary M., review of *A Hippopotamusn't, Horn Book,* May-June, 1990, p. 344.

Bush, Margaret A., review of *The Tsar and the Amazing Cow, Horn Book,* May-June, 1988, pp. 365-66.

Cooper, Ilene, review of *The Tsar and the Amazing Cow, Booklist,* May 15, 1988, p. 1610.

Review of *The Fat-Cats at Sea, Publishers Weekly,* September 5, 1994, p. 111.

Gibson, Robin L., review of *BoshBlobberBosh: Runcible Poems for Edward Lear, School Library Journal,* November, 1998, p. 141.

Greenfield, Judy, review of *July Is a Mad Mosquito, School Library Journal,* April, 1994, p. 120.

Hearne, Betsy, review of *Earth Verses and Water Rhymes, Bulletin of the Center for Children's Books,* January, 1992, p. 132.

Hearne, Betsy, review of *A Hippopotamusn't, Bulletin of the Center for Children's Books,* July-August, 1990, p. 271.

Hearne, Betsy, review of *The Tsar and the Amazing Cow, Bulletin of the Center for Children's Books,* July-August, 1988, pp. 232-33.

Review of *The La-Di-Da Hare, Publishers Weekly,* March 24, 1997, p. 83.

Lempke, Susan Dove, review of *Long Was the Winter Road They Traveled, Booklist,* October 1, 1997, pp. 323-24.

McDermott, Leone, review of *Earth Verses and Water Rhymes, Booklist,* October 1, 1991, p. 320.

Phelan, Carolyn, review of *Black Swan/White Crow, Booklist,* October 15, 1995, p. 406.

Review of *Riddle-lightful, Publishers Weekly,* November 16, 1998, p. 74.

Rochman, Hazel, review of *The Moonbow of Mr. B. Bones, Booklist,* January 15, 1992, p. 952.

Rochman, Hazel, review of *Two-Legged, Four-Legged, No-Legged Rhymes, Booklist,* August, 1991, p. 2150.

Scheps, Susan, review of *The Moonbow of Mr. B. Bones, School Library Journal,* March, 1992, p. 216.

Stevenson, Deborah, review of *BoshBlobberBosh: Runcible Poems for Edward Lear, Bulletin of the Center for Children's Books,* December, 1998, pp. 136-37.

Stevenson, Deborah, review of *Riddle-icious, Bulletin of the Center for Children's Books,* June, 1996, pp. 325-26.

Sutton, Roger, review of *July Is a Mad Mosquito, Bulletin of the Center for Children's Books,* February, 1994, p. 193.

Sylvester, Christie, review of *One Dog Day, Booklist,* April 15, 1993, p. 1515.

Review of *Two-Legged, Four-Legged, No-Legged Rhymes, Kirkus Reviews,* July 1, 1991, pp. 858-59.

For More Information See

BOOKS

Jeffrey S. and Vicky L. Copeland, editors, *Speaking of Poets 2: More Interviews with Poets,* National Council of Teachers of English, 1994.

PERIODICALS

Book Links, July, 1997, pp. 45-48.

Booklist, September 15, 1994, p. 140; December 1, 1995, pp. 638-39.

Bulletin of the Center for Children's Books, February, 1997, p. 212.

Creative Classroom, August, 1998.

Horn Book, March-April, 1996, pp. 216-17; July-August, 1996, p. 475.

Kirkus Reviews, February 1, 1988, p. 202; May 1, 1993, p. 600; July 1, 1998, p. 968; December 15, 1998, p. 1800.

Publishers Weekly, July 18, 1994, p. 244; September 19, 1994, p. 32; October 6, 1997, p. 56; January 18, 1999, p. 338.

School Library Journal, June, 1993, pp. 107-108; September, 1994, pp. 188-89; August, 1998, p. 153.*

—*Sketch by Judson Knight*

*   *   *

LEWIS, Shari 1934-1998

OBITUARY NOTICE—See index for *SATA* sketch: Born January 17, 1934, in New York, NY; died of pneumonia, August 2, 1998, in Los Angeles, CA. Entertainer and author. Lewis's long show business career began when she was a toddler and started taking piano lessons and learning magic tricks from her father, a university professor and part-time magician. Her mother instilled in Lewis a love of music that she carried with her throughout her life. As a youth, Lewis took dance, singing and music lessons, adding the violin to her instrumental repertoire. She attended the High School of

Music and Art in Manhattan, where she sustained a serious ankle injury at age sixteen while dancing in a teen show. Advised by her doctor that a career in dance might no longer be possible, Lewis began experimenting with books on ventriloquism that her father had given her. In 1952 she won the Arthur Godfrey television talent contest with a puppet act and in 1957 was invited to perform on *The Captain Kangaroo Show.* The show's producer asked Lewis if she had any puppets smaller than those she usually used in her performances. She took with her a sock puppet of a lamb that had been lying around and, with a few twitches of her hand, Lewis' best known creation, Lamb Chop, was born.

The delicate, long-lashed puppet was known for her wisecracks and constant interruptions of Lewis and was loved by three generations of fans. Lamb Chop was featured in Lewis' first television show, *The Shari Lewis Show,* which ran on NBC in the early 1960s as well as on *Shari at Six,* which ran on the British Broadcasting Corp. (BBC) in England from 1968 to 1976. Other television shows and specials were aired in the passing decades while Lewis added other much-loved puppets like Hush Puppy and Charlie Horse to her menagerie. Also during that time she ventured into other aspects of entertainment, putting together a Las Vegas act, performing in musicals such as *Damn Yankees* and *Funny Girl,* conducting orchestras, and writing numerous books. Credited with dozens of works for children, Lewis penned books on topics ranging from crafts and magic tricks to four volumes of *Spooky Stuff, Things Kids Collect, The Do It Better Book,* and "one-minute" versions of favorite fairy tales, Greek myths and Bible stories. She returned to television in the early 1990s with *Lamb Chop's Play-Along* on PBS. The show was a hit, garnering five Emmys in as many years. Lewis described herself as an older playmate for children and was producing a new television show, *The Charlie Horse Music Pizza,* at the time of her death.

OBITUARIES AND OTHER SOURCES:

PERIODICALS

Chicago Tribune, August 4, 1998, sec. 1, p. 11.
Los Angeles Times, August 4, 1998, p. B1.
New York Times, August 4, 1998, p. B6.
Times (London), August 8, 1998.
USA Today (electronic), August 4, 1998.
Washington Post, August 4, 1998, p. B4.

*   *   *

LUCADO, Max (Lee) 1955-

Personal

Born January 11, 1955, in San Angelo, TX; son of Jack Terrell and Thelma Esther (Kincaide) Lucado; married Denalyn (first name), August 8, 1981; children: Jenna, Andrea, Sara. *Education:* Abilene Christian University, B.S., 1977, M.A., 1981. *Religion:* Protestant.

Addresses

Office—Oak Hills Church of Christ, 8308 Fredericksburg Rd., San Antonio, TX 78229.

Career

Minister, radio personality, and author of religious fiction and nonfiction; ordained in Church of Christ. Central Church of Christ, Miami, FL, associate minister, 1979-82; Tijunca-lareja de Cristo, Rio de Janeiro, Brazil, missionary, 1983-88; Oak Hills Church of Christ, San Antonio, TX, pulpit minister, 1988—. Lecturer on a daily radio program.

Awards, Honors

Gold Medallion, Evangelical Christian Publishers Association, 1990, for *Six Hours One Friday: Anchoring to the Cross,* 1993, for *Just in Case You Ever Wonder,* 1994, for *Tell Me the Secrets,* and 1995, for *The Crippled Lamb.*

Writings

FICTION; FOR YOUNG PEOPLE

Just in Case You Ever Wonder, illustrated by Toni Goffe, Word (Dallas, TX), 1992.

Max Lucado

(With Jenna, Andrea, and Sara Lucado) *The Children of the King,* illustrated by Toni Goffe, Crossway (Wheaton, IL), 1994.

(With Jenna, Andrea, and Sara Lucado) *The Crippled Lamb,* illustrated by Liz Bonham, Word, 1994.

The Song of the King, illustrated by Toni Goffe, Crossway, 1995.

Alabaster's Song: Christmas through the Eyes of an Angel, illustrated by Michael Garland, Word, 1996.

(With Walt Wangerin) *Christmas by the Hearth: A Treasury of Stories Celebrating the Mystery and Meaning of Christmas,* Tyndale (Wheaton, IL), 1996.

You Are Special, illustrated by Sergio Martinez, Crossway, 1997.

Because I Love You, illustrated by Mitchell Heinze, Crossway, 1998.

Children of the King and *The Song of the King* were also produced on audio cassette by Crossway in 1995.

OTHER FICTION

Tell Me the Story, illustrated by Ron DiCianni, calligraphy by Timothy R. Botts, Crossway, 1992.

Tell Me the Secrets: Treasures for Eternity, illustrated by Ron DiCianni, Crossway, 1993.

The Woodcutter's Wisdom and Other Favorite Stories, Word, 1995.

NONFICTION

No Wonder They Call Him the Savior, Multnomah (Portland, OR), 1986.

God Came Near: Chronicles of the Christ, Multnomah, 1987.

Six Hours One Friday: Anchoring to the Cross, Multnomah, 1989, large print edition published as *Six Hours One Friday: Anchoring to the Power of the Cross,* Walker, 1996.

The Applause of Heaven, Word, 1990, abridged minibook edition, Word, 1993.

In the Eye of the Storm, Word, 1991.

And the Angels Were Silent, Multnomah, 1992; portions republished as *The Final Week of Jesus: Highlights from "And the Angels Were Silent,"* illustrated by Keith Criss, Multnomah, 1994.

He Still Moves Stones, Word, 1993.

Walking with the Savior, Tyndale House, 1993.

On the Anvil, Tyndale House, 1994, large print edition published as *On the Anvil: Stories on Being Shaped into God's Image,* Walker, 1996.

How Hurts Bring Hope, Word, 1995.

How to Study the Bible, Word, 1995.

A Gentle Thunder: Hearing God through the Storm, Word, 1995.

Finding Courage to Overcome Your Past, Word, 1995.

Peace That Defies Pain, Word, 1995.

Finding Joy in the Journey, Word, 1995.

Heaven: God's Highest Hope, Word, 1995.

Stronger in the Broken Places, Word, 1995.

Thirty-One Days of Blessings, Word, 1995.

Tomorrow's Dream, Today's Courage, Word, 1995.

Trusting More, Worrying Less, Word, 1995.

When You Can't Hide Your Mistakes, Word, 1995.

Where Do I Go for Strength, Word, 1995.

A young boy dreams that the ornamental angel sitting atop his Christmas tree comes alive and sings a wonderful song. (From Alabaster's Song: Christmas through the Eyes of an Angel, *written by Lucado and illustrated by Michael Garland.*)

Your Place at God's Table, Word, 1995.

In the Grip of Grace, Word, 1996.

(With J. Countryman) *God's Inspirational Promise Book,* Word, 1996.

(With Charles R. Swindoll and Charles Colson) *The Glory of Christmas: The Most Wonderful Gift of All,* Word, 1996.

The Great House of God: A Home for Your Heart, Word, 1997.

The Cosmic Christmas, Word, 1997.

The Cross: Images and Reflections, Multnomah, 1998.

Heart of Christmas, Thomas Nelson, 1998.

Just Like Jesus: Living in the Heart of the Savior, Word, 1998.

Let the Journey Begin: God's Roadmap for New Beginnings, Word, 1998.

Maxims from Max, Word, 1998.

"LIFE LESSONS" SERIES; ALL PUBLISHED BY WORD

Book of James, 1996.

Book of John, 1996.

Book of Romans, 1996.

Book of Ruth and Esther, 1996.

Book of Hebrews, 1997.

Book of Mark, 1997.

Book of Psalms, 1997.

Genesis, 1997.
Gospel of Acts, 1997.

*"INSPIRATION BIBLE STUDY GUIDES" SERIES; ALL
    PUBLISHED BY WORD*

I and II Peter, 1997.
I Corinthians, 1997.
Revelation, 1997.

OTHER

(Editor) *The Inspirational Study Bible: Life Lessons from
    the Inspired Word of God,* Word, 1995.
(Contributor) *In Search of Wonder: A Call to Worship
    Renewal,* Howard, 1995.

Several of Lucado's works were been produced on audio
cassette by Word in 1997 and have been translated into
Spanish.

Sidelights

Max Lucado, a pastor in his native state of Texas and a
former missionary in Brazil, has become a familiar name
on the best-seller lists in the Christian book category. In
addition to his numerous volumes of meditations,
allegorical stories, and bible study guides, Lucado is also
the author of a number of works for children.

Lucado's first successful book of fiction, *Tell Me the
Story,* earned the author a Gold Medallion award.
Illustrated by Ron DiCianni, this book of Bible stories is
meant to be read aloud by an adult to a child to promote
family discussions on religious values. Its sequel, *Tell
Me the Secrets: Treasures for Eternity,* also features
illustrations by DiCianni and tells the story of a retired
missionary who shares a book of spiritual wisdom with
three children. In the opinion of a *Publishers Weekly*
commentator, *Tell Me the Secrets* is a "lovely story"
which "beautifully combines" the talents of author and
illustrator. Lucado wrote a third volume of family fiction
entitled *When God Whispers Your Name,* a book using
the story form to inspire readers who may not realize
that God has touched them; the narrative includes
Lucado's own experiences in addition to Bible stories.

Lucado has reached a number of young readers directly
through his fiction for children. Two of these works, *Just
in Case You Ever Wonder* and *The Crippled Lamb,* also
brought Gold Medallions for Lucado. Another, *Alabaster's Song: Christmas through the Eyes of an Angel,*
which celebrates the spirit of Christmas, was dubbed a
"pleasant holiday fantasy" by a *Publishers Weekly*
reviewer. In *Alabaster's Song* a young boy dreams that
the ornamental angel sitting atop his Christmas tree
comes alive and sings a wonderful song to the Christ.
Lucado's most recent works for children are *You Are
Special* and *Because I Love You.*

Works Cited

Review of *Alabaster's Song: Christmas through the Eyes of
    an Angel, Publishers Weekly,* January 13, 1997, p. 72.

Review of *Tell Me the Secrets: Treasures for Eternity,
    Publishers Weekly,* November 8, 1993, p. 48.

For More Information See

PERIODICALS

Horn Book Guide, July-December, 1995, p. 37.
Publishers Weekly, June 13, 1994, p. 33.*

*   *   *

LUCASHENKO, Melissa 1967-

Personal

Born August 1, 1967, in Brisbane, Australia; daughter of
Walter (a labourer) and Cecile (a homemaker) Lucas;
married Bill Pennington (a diplomat); children: Gracie,
Charlie. *Education:* Griffith University, B.Comm. (with
honors), 1988. *Politics:* Australian Labor Party. *Religion:* Anglican. *Hobbies and other interests:* Martial
arts, politics, theology.

Melissa Lucashenko

Addresses

Electronic mail—supergin27@bigpond.com.au. *Agent*—c/o University of Queensland Press, P.O. Box 42, St. Lucia, Queensland 4076, Australia.

Career

Foundation for Aboriginal and Islander Research Action, Brisbane, Australia, newspaper editor. Yugambeh Corporation for Culture, member.

Awards, Honors

Dobbie Award, 1998, for *Steam Pigs.*

Writings

Steam Pigs, University of Queensland Press, 1997.
Killing Darcy, University of Queensland Press, 1998.
The Orphan, University of Queensland Press, in press.

Sidelights

Melissa Lucashenko told *SATA:* "I have a black belt in karate and a passionate commitment to social justice and human rights. My heritage is mixed European and Aboriginal, of the Yugambeh tribe in northern New South Wales. I have lived in many parts of Australia, as well as in Tonga, a tiny monarchy in the South Pacific near Fiji."

M

MANGIONE, Gerlando
See MANGIONE, Jerre

* * *

MANGIONE, Jerre 1909-1998
(Gerlando Mangione)

OBITUARY NOTICE—See index for SATA sketch: Born March 20, 1909, in Rochester, NY; died August 16, 1998, in Haverford, PA. Educator and author. The son of Sicilian immigrants, Mangione was born and raised in Rochester, NY, which became the setting of his first book, *Mount Allegro,* an autobiographical work that was released as fiction, much to Mangione's distress, reportedly because the publisher believed it would sell better that way. Originally published in 1943, *Mount Allegro* was reissued several times. Mangione was a staff writer at *Time* in 1931 before he began reviewing books for both the *New York Herald Tribune* and *New Republic.* He joined the Federal Writers' Project as national coordinating editor in 1937 and pursued several jobs in public relations over the course of the next two decades. During that time he also wrote two books, *The Ship and the Flame* and *Reunion in Sicily.* Mangione moved into academics in 1961 when he joined the faculty of the University of Pennsylvania as director of freshman composition. He was named professor emeritus of American literature at the university in 1978. That same year he became founding director of the school's Italian Studies Center. Other works by Mangione include *A Passion for Sicilians: The World Around Danilo Dolci, America is Also Italian,* and *Mussolini's March on Rome.*

OBITUARIES AND OTHER SOURCES:

PERIODICALS

Chicago Tribune, September 6, 1998, sec. 4, p. 6.
New York Times, August 31, 1998, p. A17.

McMORROW, Annalisa 1969-

Personal

Born June 14, 1969, in Philadelphia, PA; daughter of Murray (a writer) and Roberta (a publisher) Suid; married Scott McMorrow (a playwright), June 1, 1996. *Education:* Attended University of California, Los Angeles.

Addresses

Office—P.O. Box 1680, Palo Alto, CA 94302. *Electronic mail*—MMBooks @ aol.com.

Career

Writer and editor.

Writings

Ladybug, Ladybug, illustrated by Marilynn Barr, Monday Morning Books (Palo Alto, CA), 1996.
Twinkle, Twinkle, illustrated by Barr, Monday Morning Books, 1996.
Rub-a-Dub-Dub, illustrated by Barr, Monday Morning Books, 1996.
Daffy-Down-Dilly, illustrated by Barr, Monday Morning Books, 1997.
Rain, Rain, Go Away!, illustrated by Barr, Monday Morning Books, 1997.
Pussycat, Pussycat, illustrated by Barr, Monday Morning Books, 1997.
Amazing Animals! Reading, Writing, and Speaking about Animals, illustrated by Barr, Monday Morning Books, 1998.
Dinosaurs, illustrated by Philip Chalk, Monday Morning Books, 1998.
Mars, illustrated by Chalk, Monday Morning Books, 1998.
Marsupials, illustrated by Chalk, Monday Morning Books, 1998.

Peculiar Plants! Reading, Writing, and Speaking about Plants, illustrated by Barr, Monday Morning Books, 1998.

Storms, illustrated by Chalk, Monday Morning Books, 1998.

Wacky Weather! Reading, Writing, and Speaking about Weather, illustrated by Barr, Monday Morning Books, 1998.

Work in Progress

Books about bats, whales, and bridges.

Sidelights

Annalisa McMorrow told *SATA:* "I grew up in a house filled with all types of books: histories, mysteries, fantasies, and more. This is probably because my father is a writer and my mother is a publisher. They passed their love of books and knowledge on to me.

"Choosing a career in writing was natural. Deciding to write science books for children and teachers was more of a reach. I never liked science in school, but I got the idea that presenting science themes in a fun way could interest children (like me) in the subject matter.

"So far, I've written several books in a science series aimed at children in preschool and kindergarten. I've also written several books for primary graders. When I get fan mail from parents or teachers, I'm thrilled!"

*   *   *

MELVILLE, Anne
See POTTER, Margaret (Newman)

*   *   *

MITCHELL, Adrian 1932-
(Volcano Jones, Apeman Mudgeon, Gerald Stimpson)

Personal

Born October 24, 1932, in London, England; son of James (a research chemist) and Kathleen (a nursery school teacher; maiden name, Fabian) Mitchell; married Celia Hewitt (an actress and bookseller); children: Alistair, Danny, Briony, Sasha, Boty, Beattie. *Education:* "Educated in Hell, in Heaven, and on Earth." *Politics:* Pacifist. *Religion:* "The Arts."

Addresses

Agent—Caroline Sheldon, Londow Farm, Whiteoaks Lane, Shalfleet, PO30 4NU England.

Career

Poet, playwright, novelist. Worked also as a journalist, writing about rock, jazz, books, and television. Works on poetry writing with elementary school children. *Military Service:* "Enforced service" in Royal Air Force; "killed nobody."

Awards, Honors

Co-winner, P.E.N. translation prize, 1966, for *Marat/Sade;* Fellowships at Lancaster, Cambridge, and Nanyang Universities. Honorary Doctorate, North London University.

Writings

FOR CHILDREN

Nothingmas Day, Allison and Busby, 1984.

The Baron Rides Out: The Adventures of Baron Munchausen As He Told Them to Adrian Mitchell, illustrated by Patrick Benson, Walker, 1985.

The Baron on the Island of Cheese: More Adventures of Baron Munchausen, illustrated by P. Benson, Walker, 1986.

The Baron All at Sea: More Adventures of Baron Munchausen, illustrated by P. Benson, Walker, 1987.

Our Mammoth, illustrated by Priscilla Lamont, Walker, 1987.

Our Mammoth Goes to School, illustrated by P. Lamont, Walker, 1987.

Our Mammoth in the Snow, illustrated by P. Lamont, Walker, 1987.

(Compiler) *Strawberry Drums: A Book of Poems with a Beat for You and All Your Friends to Keep,* illustrated by Frances Lloyd, Macdonald Children's, 1989, Delacorte, 1991.

All My Own Stuff (poems), illustrated by F. Lloyd, Simon and Schuster, 1991.

(Editor) *The Orchard Book of Poems,* Orchard Books, 1993.

(Compiler) *The Thirteen Secrets of Poetry,* Simon and Schuster, 1993.

(Reteller) Hans Christian Andersen, *The Ugly Duckling,* illustrated by Jonathan Heale, DK Publishing, 1994.

Gynormous!: The Ultimate Book of Giants, illustrated by Sally Gardner, Orion Children's Books, 1996.

Maudie and the Green Children, illustrated by Sigune Hamann, Tradewind, 1996.

(Reteller) Hans Christian Andersen, *The Steadfast Tin Soldier,* illustrated by J. Heale, DK Publications, 1996.

Balloon Lagoon and Other Magic Islands of Poetry, illustrated by Tony Ross, Orchard Books, 1997.

The Adventures of Robin Hood and Marian, illustrated by Emma Chichester Clark, Orchard Books, 1998.

Twice My Size, illustrated by Daniel Pudles, Bloomsbury, 1998.

PLAYS; FOR CHILDREN

(Lyricist) *George Orwell's Animal Farm,* adapted by Peter Hall, music by Richard Peaslee, Methuen, 1985.

The Pied Piper, Oberon, 1988.

The Wild Animal Song Contest; and, Mowgli's Jungle,
   introduction and activities by Alison Jenkins, Heinemann Educational, 1993.
The Snow Queen, Oberon, 1998.
The Lion, the Witch, and the Wardrobe, Oberon, 1998.

POETRY FOR ADULTS

[Poems] Fantasy Poets No. 24, Fantasy Press, 1955.
Poems, Cape, 1962.
Peace Is Milk, Housmans, 1966.
Out Loud, Cape Goliard, 1968, published as *The Annotated
   Out Loud,* Writers and Readers Publishing Coopera-
   tive, 1976.
Ride the Nightmare: Verse and Prose, Cape, 1971.
(With John Fuller and Peter Levi) *Penguin Modern Poets
   22,* Penguin, 1973.
The Apeman Cometh: Poems, Cape, 1975.
For Beauty Douglas: Collected Poems 1953-1979, pictures
   by Ralph Steadman, Allison and Busby, 1982.
On the Beach at Cambridge: New Poems, Allison and
   Busby, 1984.
(Edited with Leonie Kramer) *The Oxford Anthology of
   Australian Literature,* Oxford University Press, 1985.
Love Songs of World War Three, Allison and Busby, 1989.
Adrian Mitchell's Greatest Hits: His 40 Golden Greats,
   Bloodaxe, 1991.
Blue Coffee: Poems 1985-1996, Bloodaxe, 1996.
Heart on the Left: Poems, 1953-1984, illustrated by Ralph
   Steadman, Bloodaxe, 1997.

PLAYS; FOR ADULTS

(Translator, verse adaptor, with Geoffrey Skelton) Peter
   Weiss, *The Marat/Sade,* adapted by Peter Brooks,
   Atheneum, 1966.
*Tyger: A Celebration Based on the Life and Work of
   William Blake,* Cape, 1971.
Man Friday, music by Mike Westbrook, and *Mind Your
   Head: A Return Trip with Songs,* music by Andy
   Roberts, Methuen, 1974.
(Adapter) Pedro Calderon de la Barca, *The Mayor of
   Zalamea, or, The Best Garrotting Ever Done,* Sala-
   mander Press (Edinburgh, Scotland), 1981.
(Editor) Dylan Thomas, *A Child's Christmas in Wales:
   Christmas Musical,* adapted by Jeremy Brooks, Dra-
   matic Publishing Company, 1984.
(With Berta Freistadt and Deborah Levy) *Peace Plays,*
   Methuen, 1988.
(Adapter) Lope de Vega, *Fuente Ovejuna; Lost in a Mirror
   (It Serves Them Right),* Aris and Phillips, 1989.
(Adapter) Nikolai V. Gogol, *The Government Inspector,*
   Methuen, 1989.
The Patchwork Girl of Oz, Dramatic Publishing Company,
   1994.
(Adapter) P. C. de la Barca, *The Great Theatre of the
   World,* Dramatic Publishing, 1994.
(Editor) P. C. de la Barca, *Life's a Dream,* adapted by John
   Barton, Dramatic Publishing, 1994.
*Plays with Songs: Tyger Two, Man Friday, Satie Day/
   Night, In the Unlikely Event of an Emergency,* Oberon,
   1996.
The Siege: A Play with Songs, music by Andrew Dickson,
   Oberon, 1996.

NOVELS; FOR ADULTS

If You See Me Comin', Cape, 1962, Macmillan, 1962.
The Bodyguard, Cape, 1970, Doubleday, 1971.
Wartime, Cape, 1973, Doubleday, 1975.

OTHER

Also provided seven lyrics for the Peter Brook play, *US.*
Translator and/or editor of various volumes of poems.
Contributor of articles to the *New York Times, New
Statesman, Observer, Sunday Times,* and *Peace News,*
among other periodicals.

Work in Progress

Dancing in the Street, an anthology for teenagers; *The
Heroes,* a play trilogy based on Greek myths, to premier
in Tokyo, 1999.

Sidelights

Adrian Mitchell, British poet and playwright, is an icon
of the Sixties whose performance poetry carried the
message of peace and empowerment of the common
man in that troubled decade. With poetry volumes such
as *Poems, Peace Is Milk,* and *Out Loud,* and plays
including *Tyger, Mind Your Head, Man Friday,* and the
translation/adaptation of Peter Weiss's *Marat/Sade,*
Mitchell carved himself a respected position in the
politicized artistic environment of the 1960s and 1970s.
As Tony Silverman Zinman noted in *Dictionary of
Literary Biography,* all of Mitchell's works "express his
idealistic socialism: his goal is not only to right the

***Young Maudie Hessett finds two Green Children from
Merlin Land and protects them from the scorn and
curiosity of her fellow villagers in Adrian Mitchell's
retelling of the Old English Suffolk country tale.*** *(From*
Maudie and the Green Children, *illustrated by Sigune
Hamann.)*

world's wrongs but also to establish contact with mass audiences."

Increasingly, Mitchell's artistic efforts have turned toward children's literature, and specifically to drama. "Most of my time these days is spent writing stage plays for children," Mitchell told Something about the Author (*SATA*). "One of my favorites was *The Pied Piper* for London's National Theater—another was *The Snow Queen* for the New York State Theater Institute. There should be a children's theater in every town putting on new and old plays for children all the year round, inviting schools to make their own plays for performance." Mitchell has also written volumes of poetry for young readers, has edited volumes of poetry, and has written two series of picture books, one about a prehistoric mammoth that shows up in the modern world, and the other retelling the adventures of that German teller of tall tales, Baron Munchausen.

Mitchell was born in 1932 in London, the son of a research chemist and a teacher. He was educated at Dauntsey's School in Wiltshire. In 1951, he did National Service for a year, and then in 1952 entered Oxford University. During his time at Oxford, Mitchell was heavily influenced by other poets at the university, such as Alistair Elliott; during his last year there he was literary editor of *Isis* magazine and began publishing his own poetry. An early pamphlet of his poems appearing in 1955 included "The Fox," a poem that Zinman noted "is still considered among Mitchell's best and most serious works." Strongly influenced by the poet William Blake, Mitchell later wrote a play about Blake's life.

After Mitchell left Oxford, earning a living became paramount in his life: He worked as a reporter on the *Oxford Mail* for a couple of years and then on the *Evening Standard.* He also wrote television and music reviews for several other magazines and newspapers. All the while Mitchell was also gaining a reputation for his poetry readings and poems, many of which display an interest in song lyrics, especially those of jazz and the blues. However, by 1975, in his volume of poems entitled *The Apeman Cometh,* Mitchell was already displaying a penchant for writing for a youthful audience. In *The Apeman Cometh,* Mitchell includes a section of fifteen poems headed "Mainly for Kids."

Mitchell's first volume of poetry for children, *Nothingmas Day,* appeared in 1984. Margery Fisher, writing in *Growing Point,* noted that Mitchell's poems for children "are entertaining verbal fireworks," including puns, assonances, comic arrangement of lines and "inspired gobbledegook" such as the opening line from "My Last Nature Walk": "I strode among the clumihacken." Fisher concluded that "Mitchell gave space for the melancholy beneath nonsense, for innumerable individual reactions to ordinary matters." A *Junior Bookshelf* reviewer also praised Mitchell's first volume for young readers, observing that the poems have "that turn of phrase, that startling thought, that seductive sound ... so attractive to the young child," and concluding that the book "is a

joy to handle, a delight to read, and a pleasure to look at."

A further Mitchell collection of poetry for children is *All My Own Stuff,* twenty-five poems "showing a variety of tones and moods," according to a writer in *Junior Bookshelf,* who went on to note that "the poetry is full of plays on words." Jocelyn Hanson commented in *School Librarian* that this collection varied from "the silly to the profound," including "funny little verses and couplets, clever and amusing, quick to read and assimilate.... All demonstrate a love of the sound and shape of words." Mitchell's trademark playfulness can be found in lines such as "I am Boj/Organised Sludge and a Thunder-Wedge." Hanson concluded that *All My Own Stuff* "would be useful in demonstrating to children ... how freely words can be used, manipulated and played with within the structures of poetry."

Additionally, Mitchell has collected and edited other poetry anthologies, including *Strawberry Drums* and *The Orchard Book of Poems.* The former is "an engrossing and readable collection of poems," according to a critic in *Junior Bookshelf.* Mitchell collected poems from around the world for *Strawberry Drums:* not only from British poets such as William Blake and Robert Graves, but also from the Navajo people of the American Southwest, the Jakun people of Malaysia, and even from Lennon/McCartney with their lyrics to "Yellow Submarine." The *Junior Bookshelf* reviewer concluded that Mitchell's anthology managed "a freshness that is captivating.... A bubbly, effervescent anthology with golden oldies and new poems side by side." Jane Marino, writing in *School Library Journal,* found this collection to be a "far-flung, eclectic group of thirty poems that invites readers to celebrate words," while Pippa Rann called the book a "pleasingly varied collection," in *School Librarian.* Writing in the introduction to the collection, Mitchell commented that "I chose the poems ... because they are bright and sweet like strawberries. And all of them have a beat—like drums." Rann noted in *School Librarian* that a strength of the book is Mitchell's introduction, in which he demonstrates to young readers how to go about writing a poem for themselves. A further Mitchell poetry anthology is *The Orchard Book of Poems,* a "fresh and beautifully produced collection," according to Pam Harwood in *Books for Keeps.* The anthology compiles poets from John Keats to John Lennon organized into sections such as "The Palace of People" and "The Dazzling City." Harwood went on to call the anthology a "courageous blending of old favourites and new faces...."

Mitchell's inventive word play and sense of the fantastic have also been turned to picture books and plays for children. Among the latter are *The Pied Piper* and *The Snow Queen.* His picture books include the "Baron" and the "Mammoth" series. With the first of these, Mitchell adapted the tall tales about the real-life eighteenth-century German adventurer, Baron Munchausen, whose exploits were fictionalized by R. E. Raspe, to create his own version of events. *The Baron Rides Out* commenced the series, telling of the Baron's forty-eight brothers and sisters, his magical horse, and his ship drawn by seagulls. "Nobody need believe any of this," observed a reviewer for *Junior Bookshelf,* "but the stories are so fantastic that they are fun. Children accept them for what they are and enjoy them." Kenneth Marantz, writing in *School Library Journal,* concluded that "for those who enjoy our Paul Bunyan, this German teller of tall tales will be a special delight." *The Baron on the Island of Cheese* provides "another series of ebullient adventures," according to a *Kirkus Reviews* critic, who concluded: "Mitchell embellishes the nonstop action with delicious asides. This may be the 18th-century verbal equivalent of the Saturday morning cartoons, but it's still fun." Reviewing this second title in the series, Constance A. Mellon noted in *School Library Journal* that "the book is clever, written in the clipped style typical of British humor." Mellon concluded that the book "would be a good extension of the folklore area, and, properly presented, would be of both literary and artistic value to children." A third volume followed, *The Baron All at Sea,* of which Nancy Palmer, writing in *School Library Journal,* commented that "Mitchell has cleaned up the original stories without sanitizing them; plenty of action remains, and nothing feels sapped or bowdlerized." In this third volume, the Baron heroically attempts to help a choir of one thousand Africans return to Timbuktu, a feat that involves a shipwreck and confrontations with wolves and polar bears. "This will be a title of choice for check-out and for reading aloud," Palmer concluded.

Mitchell's second group of picture books include *Our Mammoth, Our Mammoth Goes to School,* and *Our Mammoth in the Snow.* The Gumble twins are at the beach one day when a giant block of ice comes ashore.

Mitchell has been lauded for his faithful yet simplified picture-book retelling of Hans Christian Andersen's tale of a brave, lovesick toy soldier. (From The Steadfast Tin Soldier, *illustrated by Jonathan Heale.*)

As the ice melts, they discover that there is a mammoth inside. Awaking from its long deep-freeze, the mammoth becomes a giant, shaggy means of transport to the twins, carrying them to their house. The twins' unflappable mother accepts the beast into the household, preparing it buttercup pie for sustenance. A *Publishers Weekly* critic noted that "this picture book is both quirky and intriguing," and that "Mitchell's eloquent prose accentuates the story's deadpan humor." The twins subsequently take their mastodon friend with them to school in *Our Mammoth Goes to School.* At first, the animal has a hard time, disliked by the headmaster because of its fleas, but soon the mammoth joins in a school outing and discovers kindred spirits in the elephants at the zoo. "This is another successful example of that familiar genre of the picture book, depicting the appearance of a monstrous monster who eventually becomes everybody's friend," observed William Edmonds in *School Librarian.* Margery Fisher of *Growing Point* maintained that this second volume in the series has an "idiosyncratic text with explosive words and onomatopoeic phrases."

Mitchell has also retold stories from Hans Christian Andersen, including *The Ugly Duckling* and *The Steadfast Tin Soldier.* Reviewing *The Ugly Duckling* in *School Librarian,* Jane Doonan declared, "Here's the art of the backward glance, in a handsome new edition of the old classic.... Adrian Mitchell's poetic retelling retains the sensuous quality of the original descriptions." Writing of *The Steadfast Tin Soldier* in that same journal, Doonan noted that once again Mitchell sticks to the original intent of Andersen, even if simplifying the text. "This is an illustrated book which could take today's children into a very different world," Doonan concluded, "although the theme, exploring the vulnerability of anyone who steadfastly loves another, is timeless." Janice M. Del Negro of the *Bulletin of the Center for Children's Books* commented that *The Steadfast Tin Soldier* "is a remarkably readable interpretation of Andersen's tragic fairy tale." Del Negro concluded: "It's sometimes difficult to make a case for yet another picture-book version of an often-retold fairy tale, but this unique interpretation is its own convincing argument."

Mitchell's imaginative flights have also take him to Sherwood Forest, for his *Adventures of Robin Hood and Marian,* and led him to create a poetry and short story compilation on giants in *Gynormous!* Whatever form Mitchell's work takes, be it poetry, drama, or prose, he retains his original conviction in the transformational power of words. His writing for children has been characterized as unpretentious and simple, and his empathy with young readers is obvious, partly a result of the cruelties he himself experienced attending a large school. For Mitchell, poetry and words are not just means of communication; they can change a reader's perception of the world.

Works Cited

Review of *All My Own Stuff, Junior Bookshelf,* October, 1991, p. 226.

Review of *The Baron on the Island of Cheese, Kirkus Reviews,* September 15, 1986, p. 1451.

Review of *The Baron Rides Out, Junior Bookshelf,* February, 1986, p. 17.

Del Negro, Janice M., review of *The Steadfast Tin Soldier, Bulletin of the Center for Children's Books,* January, 1997, p. 163.

Doonan, Jane, review of *The Steadfast Tin Soldier, School Librarian,* February, 1997, p. 17.

Doonan, Jane, review of *The Ugly Duckling, School Librarian,* November, 1994, p. 144.

Edmonds, William, review of *Our Mammoth Goes to School, School Librarian,* May, 1988, p. 54.

Fisher, Margery, "Sing, Perform or Just Listen," *Growing Point,* January, 1985, p. 4372.

Fisher, Margery, review of *Our Mammoth Goes to School, Growing Point,* May, 1988, p. 4993.

Hanson, Jocelyn, review of *All My Own Stuff, School Librarian,* November, 1991, p. 150.

Harwood, Pam, review of *The Orchard Book of Poems, Books for Keeps,* January, 1997, p. 26.

Marantz, Kenneth, review of *The Baron Rides Out, School Library Journal,* May, 1986, p. 82.

Marino, Jane, review of *Strawberry Drums, School Library Journal,* June, 1991, pp. 96-97.

Mellon, Constance A., review of *The Baron on the Island of Cheese, School Library Journal,* January, 1987, p. 76.

Mitchell, Adrian, *Nothingmas Day,* Allison and Busby, 1984.

Mitchell, Adrian, *All My Own Stuff,* Simon and Schuster, 1991.

Mitchell, Adrian, *Strawberry Drums,* Delacorte, 1991.

Review of *Nothingmas Day, Junior Bookshelf,* February, 1985, p. 43.

Review of *Our Mammoth, Publishers Weekly,* October 30, 1987, p. 68.

Palmer, Nancy, review of *The Baron All at Sea, School Library Journal,* January, 1988, pp. 67-68.

Rann, Pippa, review of *Strawberry Drums, School Librarian,* November, 1989, p. 158.

Review of *Strawberry Drums, Junior Bookshelf,* October, 1989, pp. 229-30.

Zinman, Tony Silverman, "Adrian Mitchell," *Dictionary of Literary Biography, Volume 40: Poets of Great Britain and Ireland Since 1960,* Gale, 1985, pp. 371-79.

For More Information See

BOOKS

The Cambridge Guide to Literature in English, Cambridge University Press, 1988.

Contemporary British Dramatists, St. James Press, 1994.

Contemporary Poets, 6th edition, St. James Press, 1996.

PERIODICALS

Booklist, December 15, 1987, p. 711; March 15, 1992, p. 1330; November 1, 1996, p. 509.

Bulletin of the Center for Children's Books, January, 1988, p. 96.

Junior Bookshelf, October, 1986, p. 183.

School Librarian, November, 1987, pp. 323-24; February, 1992, p. 28; February, 1997, p. 24.

School Library Journal, March, 1988, pp. 171-72; August, 1988, p. 84; July, 1994, p. 73; January, 1997, p. 75.

Times Educational Supplement, May 12, 1989, p. B8; June 8, 1990, p. B16; August 20, 1993, p. 19; July 5, 1996, p. R2; October 3, 1997, p. B6.

—*Sketch by J. Sydney Jones*

* * *

MITCHELSON, Mitch
See MITCHELSON, Peter Richard

* * *

MITCHELSON, Peter Richard 1950-
(Mitch Mitchelson)

Personal

Born May 13, 1950, in Lancaster, England; son of Cedric Albert (a civil servant) and Gladys Lilian (Faulkes) Mitchelson. *Education:* University of Sheffield, B.A. (with honors), 1971. *Politics:* Labour. *Religion:* Church of England.

Addresses

Home—54 Wedgwood House, China Walk Estate, London SE11 6LL, England.

Career

Actor, director, producer, and lecturer in drama. Assessor of Combined Arts for London Arts Board. *Member:* Equity (Actors' Association).

Writings

UNDER NAME MITCH MITCHELSON

(With Jean Hart) *The Lazarus Stone* (play), Rose Banford College, 1995.

The Most Excellent Book of How to Be a Juggler, illustrated by Rob Shone and Peter Harper, Aladdin/Watts, 1997, Millbrook Press (Bridgewater, CT), 1997.

Contributor to *Discovering the Self through Drama and Movement,* edited by Jenny Pearson, published by Jessica Kingsley, 1996.

Work in Progress

Devising street theatre on theme of "newspapers." Children's stories using circus, ecology, and poetry.

Sidelights

Peter Mitchelson, who writes as Mitch Mitchelson, told *SATA:* "The well-spring and motivation of my work has been communication, imagination and the ludic perspective. Co-founding my theatre company Original Mixture I explored the popular forms of story-telling, masks,

Peter Richard Mitchelson

puppetry, clowning and circus. Lecturing on these subjects and physical theatre, I was able to devise and direct shows that integrated stories with live 'rough magic' provided by lively casts of drama and circus students. Other directorial projects enabled me to tackle highly physical productions of Moliere, Goldon, and Aristophanes.

"My training and interest in practising dramatherapy with different client groups has given me a profound sense of the omniprescence and healing nature of art.

"As a 'dramatherapist' I practice a belief in everyone's innate creativity and in the healing power of the arts. As an artist I believe in William Blake's dictum, 'Energy is eternal delight.'"

* * *

MITTON, Tony 1951-

Personal

Born Anthony Robert Mitton, January 10, 1951, in Tripoli, North Africa; son of Stanley (a social worker) and Vera Eileen (Locke) Mitton; married Elizabeth Anne McKellar (a lecturer), January 19, 1991; children: Doris, Guthrie. *Education:* University of Cambridge, B.A. (Honors English), 1973. *Politics:* "Usually vote Labour." *Religion:* Zen Buddhist influence. *Hobbies and other interests:* poetry, story, song, folk culture, also walking, baking, cookery, art, music.

Addresses

Home—41 Sturton Street, Cambridge, CB1 2QG, England. *Agent*—Caroline Walsh, David Higham Associates, 5-8 Lower John St., Golden Square, London, W1R 4HA, England.

Career

Primary teacher, Cambs Lea, United Kingdom, 1975-85, special needs teacher, 1986—. *Member:* Society of Authors.

Awards, Honors

Nottinghamshire Children's Book Award, 1997, for *Royal Raps.*

Writings

Nobody Laughed, Collins Educational (London), 1994.
(Reteller) *Three Tales from Scotland,* illustrated by Joe Rice, Collins Educational, 1995.
Mr Marvel and the Cake, illustrated by Mandy Doyle, Heinemann Educational (Oxford, England), 1996.
Mr Marvel and the Car, illustrated by Mandy Doyle, Heinemann Educational, 1996.
Mr Marvel and the Lemonade, illustrated by Mandy Doyle, Heinemann Educational, 1996.
Mr Marvel and the Washing, illustrated by Mandy Doyle, Heinemann Educational (Oxford, England), 1996.
Big Bad Raps, illustrated by Martin Chatterton, Orchard (London), 1996.
(Reteller) *The Three Billy Goats,* illustrated by Jenny Williams, Heinemann Educational, 1996.
Playtime with Rosie Rabbit, illustrated by Patrick Yee, Simon & Schuster, 1996.
Bedtime for Rosie Rabbit, illustrated by Patrick Yee, Simon & Schuster, 1996.
Royal Raps, illustrated by Martin Chatterton, Orchard, 1996.
Dazzling Diggers, illustrated by Ant Parker, Kingfisher, 1997.
Rosie Rabbit's Birthday Party, illustrated by Patrick Yee, Simon & Schuster, 1997.
Rosie Rabbit Goes to Preschool, illustrated by Patrick Yee, Simon & Schuster, 1997.
Roaring Rockets, illustrated by Ant Parker, Kingfisher, 1997.
Monster Raps, illustrated by Martin Chatterton, Orchard, 1998.
Fangtastic Raps, illustrated by Martin Chatterton, Orchard, 1998.
Where's My Egg?, illustrated by Jane Chapman, Walker, 1998.
Spooky Hoo Hah!, illustrated by Oliver Postgate, Walker, 1998.
Flashing Fire Engines, illustrated by Ant Parker, Kingfisher, 1998.
The Magic Pot, illustrated by Mandy Doyle, Oxford University Press, 1998.
Plum (poems), illustrated by Peter Bailey, Scholastic, 1998.

A Door to Secrets: Riddles in Rhyme, illustrated by David Parkins, Cambridge University Press (Cambridge, England), 1998.

The Seal Hunter, illustrated by Nick Malland, Hippo (London), 1998.

Terrific Trains, illustrated by Ant Parker, Kingfisher, 1998.

There's No Such Thing!, Candlewick Press, 1999.

Work in Progress

Various poetry, verse, and picture book projects; educational texts.

Sidelights

Tony Mitton told *SATA:* "I was born in 1951 in North Africa, the son of a soldier. Until I was nine we lived mostly in Africa, Germany, and Hong Kong. So I didn't really get to know Britain until I was nearly ten. Most of my life I have worked as a primary school teacher. But for the last twelve years, I have only taught for half of the time. At first, I was busy being a parent for the other half of the time, when my children were very young. But now that they are a bit older and go to school, I spend at least two days a week working at my writing. I write poems and stories for school reading books and also for

books you buy in the bookshops. I especially like writing in verse, using rhythm and rhyme. I also very much enjoy planning picture books and writing the words for them. But I need other people to do the pictures. I would like to learn to be an illustrator too, but I like working on the words so much that I don't think I'd make the time to practice. I think as time passes I may start to write more and teach less, if my writing keeps on doing well. But I like going in to school and I think I keep in touch with what a lot of children like by working with them. So for now it seems a good idea to keep on doing both jobs part-time.

"I live in a small house in the middle of Cambridge with my wife and two children, who are nine and thirteen as I write. We also have a sweet cat called Tiggy. I like the town and many of the people, for it's the only place I've ever stayed for a long time. But my wife and I often wish we'd settled somewhere where there are better places for walking, like cliffs and hills with good views of the landscape.

"I honestly think that what I most like doing is writing poems, and working with words in verse. I love fiddling about until I've got it just right (though sometimes I can't). I've always loved reading poems and stories,

Tony Mitton

The ladder rises upward. It reaches for the sky.
A fire engine's ladder stretches up so very high!

Sometimes there's a platform, right up at the top.
It waits beside the window. Then into it you hop.

Mitton's rhyming text and Ant Parker's humorous illustrations offer an informative and fun introduction to fire fighting. (*From* Flashing Fire Engines.)

though these days I find it harder to get proper time for reading, as I'm often busy writing. It's especially hard to find time to read longer books, like novels, so I have to choose carefully to find books that are really worth the time I give to them. I have a great interest in folk and fairy tales and legends, and when I was younger (in my teens) I used to spend a lot of time learning and singing folk and blues songs which I accompanied on the guitar. I think I learned a lot about verse and poetry from doing this, even though writing songs is not quite the same as writing poems.

"I'm not often stuck for ideas with my writing. More often I'm waiting to get the time to get on with something I want to write. Sometimes I get up very early in the morning and do one or two hours writing while most other people are asleep. That's a very good time for me, as my mind's very fresh and clear and no one comes to interrupt. Sometimes, if I have a very good or strong idea, say for a poem, I get a bit frightened to start on it, in case it doesn't turn out well. What I do then is just start writing things down and keep going at it, even if it doesn't go well to start with. That usually works.

"What else do I like doing? Cooking, baking cakes, social meals, and family life. As a family, we talk a great deal about all sorts of things. I love reading to my children and talking to my wife, who knows a lot about books, art, history, and lots more. If I had time to spare I'd like to be in a folk band and play traditional British and Irish folk music.

"When I was about nine, and rather miserable and lonely in a strict little boarding school, I stumbled on a novel during the enforced half-hour of reading after lunch. It was called *Prester John* and was by John Buchan. This is the first novel that I can remember reading for pleasure. It really gripped me. I remember the bereave-

ment of finishing it and being unable to find anything that matched it for me then in power and style. I recently had a similar experience (thirty-seven years later) when I read the first two parts of Philip Pullman's *His Dark Materials* trilogy (*Northern Lights* and *The Subtle Knife*). I'm now waiting for part three to come out, but I don't think Philip Pullman has finished writing it yet.

"My reading of poetry was galvanised by my brother putting a typed copy of a poem by W. B. Yeats up on our bedroom cupboard door. I must have been about thirteen at the time, and he would have been fifteen. The poem was, I believe, the much celebrated 'Lake Isle of Inisfree.' I liked it so much that I got hold of a copy of the Macmillan *Collected Poems of W. B. Yeats*. For a long time my favourite poem was 'The Song of Wandering Aengus.' I still love Yeats's lyric writing, and writing this paragraph has prompted me to get my copy down and dip into it again after a long gap."

For More Information See

PERIODICALS

Junior Bookshelf, October, 1994, p. 166.
School Library Journal, May, 1997, pp. 108-09.

*   *   *

MORGAN, Stacy T(owle) 1959-

Personal

Born in 1959; daughter of Leslie and Alice Towle; married Michael Morgan, 1982; children: four. *Education:* Cedarville College, B.A.; graduate study at Oxford University; Western Kentucky University, M.A. *Hob-*

bies and other interests: Home education, women's issues, music.

Addresses

Home—8790 Randall Dr., Fishers, IN 46038. *Electronic mail*—rubyslip @ in-motion.net.

Career

Park City Daily News, Bowling Green, KY, feature writer, 1983-84; Syracuse University, Syracuse, NY, instructor in English, 1984-85; leader of "home-school cooperatives" in central Indiana, 1993-97; WRVG-FM Radio, affiliated with the public radio series *From a Child's Perspective,* 1998.

Awards, Honors

Named Bowling Green's Business Woman of the Year, 1984.

Writings

The Cuddlers, illustrated by Marvin Jarboe, La Leche League International (Franklin Park, IL), 1993.

"RUBY SLIPPERS" SCHOOL SERIES

Adventures in the Caribbean, illustrated by Pamela Querin, Bethany House (Minneapolis, MN), 1996.
The British Bear Caper, illustrated by Querin, Bethany House, 1996.
Escape from Egypt, illustrated by Querin, Bethany House, 1996.
The Belgium Book Mystery, illustrated by Querin, Bethany House, 1996.
Journey to Japan, illustrated by Querin, Bethany House, 1997.
New Zealand Shake-up, illustrated by Querin, Bethany House, 1997.

Work in Progress

Children's books; adult nonfiction on women's issues.

Sidelights

Stacy T. Morgan told *SATA:* "A good children's book needs to take the reader somewhere. It might be a place where the reader can stay for a while and ponder. It is not necessarily a mystery or an adventure—maybe just a quiet place where the reader feels good and enjoys her surroundings.

"As a children's book writer, I would like to see children's books that address 'moments in time.' Unfortunately, as our society becomes more frenzied, even our stories are too often truncated and void of musicality and wonder. Picture books especially need to be beautifully written and reflective in nature. We need to respect the beauty and sound of words as much as we do the artwork which accompanies them.

"I love books—always have. My very favorite day would consist of reading a novel in the morning, poetry in the afternoon, and a great short story before bed! For me, writing books is just a natural extension of reading them."

*   *   *

MORRIS, Gilbert (Leslie) 1929-

Personal

Born May 24, 1929, in Forrest City, Arkansas; son of O. M. and Jewell Irene (Gilbert) Morris; married Johnnie Yvonne Fegert, May 20, 1948; children: Lynn, Stacy Lee, Alan Blake. *Education:* Arkansas State University, B.A., 1948, M.S.E., 1962; University of Arkansas, Ph.D., 1968; also attended University of Washington-Seattle. *Hobbies and other interests:* Restoring houses.

Career

Ordained Baptist minister, 1950; pastor of Baptist churches in various parts of Arkansas, 1952-58; English teacher at public schools in Reyno, AR, 1958-61; Ouachita Baptist University, Arkadelphia, AR, assistant professor, 1962-70, professor of English, 1970—. *Member:* National Council of Teachers of English.

Writings

"OZARK ADVENTURES/BARNEY BUCK" SERIES

The Bucks of Goober Holler, Tyndale House (Wheaton, IL), 1985.
Barney Buck and the Flying Solar Cycle, WindRider Books (Wheaton, IL), 1985, published as *The Rustlers of Panther Gap,* Tyndale House, 1994.
Barney Buck and the Phantom of the Circus, Tyndale House, 1985, published as *The Phantom of the Circus,* Tyndale House, 1994.
Barney Buck Rides Again!, Tyndale House, 1985, published as *Barney Buck and the Kamikaze Charger,* Tyndale House, 1985.
Barney Buck in Car Number Five, Tyndale House, 1985, published as *Barney Buck and the Rough Rider Special,* Tyndale House, 1985.
Barney Buck and the Wild, Wild Wedding, Tyndale House, 1985, published as *Barney Buck and the World's Wackiest Wedding,* Tyndale House, 1986.

"HOUSE OF WINSLOW" SERIES

The Honorable Imposter, Bethany House (Minneapolis, MN), 1986.
The Captive Bride, Bethany House, 1987.
The Indentured Heart, Bethany House, 1988.
The Gentle Rebel, Bethany House, 1988.
The Saintly Buccaneer, 1988.
The Holy Warrior, Bethany House, 1989.
The Reluctant Bridegroom, Bethany House, 1990.
The Last Confederate, Bethany House, 1990.
The Wounded Yankee, Bethany House, 1991.
The Dixie Widow, Bethany House, 1991.
The Union Belle, Bethany House, 1992.

The Final Adversary, Bethany House, 1992.
The Valiant Gunman, Bethany House, 1993.
The Crossed Sabres, Bethany House, 1993.
The Gallant Outlaw, Bethany House, 1994.
The Jeweled Spur, Bethany House, 1994.
The Rough Rider, Bethany House, 1995.
The Yukon Queen, Bethany House, 1995.
The Iron Lady, Bethany House, 1996.
The Silver Star, Bethany House, 1997.
Voyagers to Freedom, Arrowood Press, 1997.
The Shadow Portrait, Bethany House, 1998.

"RENO WESTERN SAGA" SERIES

The Drifter, Tyndale House, 1986, published as *Reno,* Tyndale House, 1992.
The Deputy, Tyndale House, 1986, published as *Rimrock,* Tyndale House, 1992.
The Runaway, Tyndale House, 1987, published as *Ride the Wild River,* Tyndale House, 1987.
Boomtown, Tyndale House, 1987.
Valley Justice, Tyndale House, 1995.
Lone Wolf, Tyndale House, 1995.

"DANIELLE ROSS MYSTERY" SERIES

Guilt by Association, Revell (Grand Rapids, MI), 1991.
The Final Curtain, Revell, 1991.
Deadly Deception, Revell, 1992.
Revenge at the Rodeo, Revell, 1993.
The Quality of Mercy, Revell, 1993.
Race with Death, Revell, 1994.

"APPOMATTOX SAGA" SERIES

Gate of His Enemies, Tyndale House, 1992.
A Covenant of Love, Tyndale House, 1992.
Where Honor Dwells, Tyndale House, 1993.
Land of the Shadow, Tyndale House, 1993.
The Shadow of His Wings, Tyndale House, 1994.
Out of the Whirlwind, Tyndale House, 1994.
Stars in Their Courses, Tyndale House, 1995.
Wall of Fire, Tyndale House, 1995.
Chariots in the Smoke, Tyndale House, 1997.
Witness in Heaven, Tyndale House, 1998.

"PRICE OF LIBERTY" SERIES; WITH BOBBY FUNDERBURK

A Call to Honor, Word (Dallas, TX), 1993.
All the Shining Young Men, Word, 1993.
The Color of the Star, Word, 1993.
The End of Glory, Word, 1993.
A Silence in Heaven, Word, 1993.
A Time to Heal, Word, 1994.

"CHENEY DUVALL, M.D." SERIES; WITH LYNN MORRIS

The Stars for a Light, Bethany House, 1994.
Shadow of the Mountains, Bethany House, 1994.
A City Not Forsaken, Bethany House, 1995.
Secret Place of Thunder, Bethany House, 1996.
Toward the Sunrising, Bethany House, 1996.
In the Twilight, In the Evening, Bethany House, 1997.
Island of the Innocent, Bethany House, 1998.

"AMERICAN ODYSSEY" SERIES

A Time to Die, Revell, 1994.
A Time to Be Born, Revell, 1994.

A Time to Laugh, Revell, 1995.
A Time to Weep, Revell, 1996.
A Time of War, Revell, 1997.
A Time to Build, Revell, 1998.

"WAKEFIELD DYNASTY" SERIES

The Winds of God, Tyndale House, 1994.
The Sword of Truth, Tyndale House, 1994.
The Fields of Glory, Tyndale House, 1995.
The Shield of Honor, Tyndale House, 1995.
The Ramparts of Heaven, Tyndale House, 1997.
The Song of Princes, Tyndale House, 1997.

"BONNETS AND BUGLES" SERIES

Yankee Belles in Dixie, Moody Press (Chicago), 1995.
The Secret of Richmond Manor, Moody Press, 1995.
Drummer Boy at Bull Run, Moody Press, 1995.
Blockade Runner, Moody Press, 1996.
The Soldier Boy's Discovery, Moody Press, 1996.
Gallant Boys of Gettysburg, Moody Press, 1996.
The Battle of Lookout Mountain, Moody Press, 1996.
Bring the Boys Home, Moody Press, 1997.
Encounter at Cold Harbor, Moody Press, 1997.
Fire over Atlanta, Moody Press, 1997.

"TIME NAVIGATORS" SERIES

The Dangerous Voyage, Bethany House, 1995.
Vanishing Clues, Bethany House, 1996.
Race Against Time, Bethany House, 1997.

"LIBERTY BELL" SERIES

Sound the Trumpet, Bethany House, 1995.
Song in a Strange Land, Bethany House, 1996.
Tread upon the Lion, Bethany House, 1996.
Arrow of the Almighty, Bethany House, 1997.
Wind from the Wilderness, Bethany House, 1998.

"SEVEN SLEEPERS" SERIES

Flight of the Eagles, Moody Press, 1994.
The Gates of Neptune, Moody Press, 1994.
The Sword of Camelot, Moody Press, 1995.
The Caves That Time Forgot, Moody Press, 1995.
Winged Raiders of the Desert, Moody Press, 1995.
Attack of the Amazons, Moody Press, 1996.
Voyage of the Dolphin, Moody Press, 1996.
Empress of the Underworld, Moody Press, 1996.
Escape with the Dream Maker, Moody Press, 1997.
The Final Kingdom, Moody Press, 1997.

"KATY STEELE ADVENTURES" SERIES; WITH ALAN MORRIS

Tracks of Deceit, Tyndale House, 1996.
Imperial Intrigue, Tyndale House, 1996.
The Depths of Malice, Tyndale House, 1998.

"SPIRIT OF APPALACHIA" SERIES

(With Aaron McCarver) *Over the Misty Mountains,* Bethany House, 1996.
(With Aaron McCarver) *Beyond the Quiet Hills,* Bethany House, 1997.
(With Aaron McCarver) *Among the King's Soldiers,* Bethany House, 1998.

"DAYSTAR VOYAGES" SERIES

(With Dan Meeks) *Secret of the Planet Makon,* Moody Press, 1998.

(With Dan Meeks) *Wizards of the Galaxy,* Moody Press, 1998.

Escape from the Red Comet, Moody Press, 1998.

(With Dan Meeks) *Dark Spell over Morlandria,* Moody Press, 1998.

Revenge of the Space Pirate, Moody Press, 1998.

"DIXIE MORRIS ANIMAL ADVENTURE" SERIES

Dixie and Jumbo, Moody Press, 1998.

Dixie and Stripes, Moody Press, 1998.

Dixie and Bandit, Moody Press, 1998.

Dixie and Dolly, Moody Press, 1998.

Dixie and Sandy, Moody Press, 1998.

Dixie and Ivan, Moody Press, 1998.

"CHRONICLES OF THE GOLDEN FRONTIER" SERIES; WITH J. LANDON FERGUSON

Riches Untold, Crossway, 1998.

Unseen Riches, Crossway, 1999.

OTHER

Bunyan (three-act play), produced at Vesper Theater, Arkadelphia, AR, June 6, 1980.

Root Out of Dry Ground: Biblical Characterizations in Verse (poems), illustrated by Caffy Whitney, August House, 1981.

Delaney (detective novel), Tyndale, 1984.

How to Write (and Sell) a Christian Novel: Proven and Practical Advice from a Best-Selling Author, Vine (Ann Arbor, MI), 1994.

(With Bobby Funderburk) *Beyond the River,* Starburst, 1994.

Captain Chip and the March to Victory, Moody, 1994.

Corporal Chip and the Call to Battle, Moody, 1994.

The Remnant, Starburst (Lancaster, PA), 1997.

Those Who Knew Him: Profiles of Christ in Verse, illustrated by Stan D. Myers, Revell, 1997.

Contributor of approximately twenty articles and more than a hundred poems to magazines, including *Texas Review* and *Mississippi Review.*

Sidelights

An educator and ordained minister, Gilbert Morris is an extremely prolific writer who has more *series* to his credit than many authors have books. It is his desire, he has said, to portray "real Christian(s)" in his fiction, not "plaster saint(s)," to show characters "doing a dirty, dangerous job while at the same time trying with at least a partial degree of success to serve God." He has also said that while there are Christians like Elmer Gantry, the dishonest preacher in Sinclair Lewis's novel by that name, there are also heroic figures such as Corrie Ten Boom, who hid Jews in her home in the Netherlands during the Nazi occupation.

One of Gilbert's many series is "House of Winslow," which chronicles the story of a family that spans many generations of American history. The series begins with

The Honorable Imposter, as the patriarch of the Winslow dynasty, Gilbert Winslow, travels from England on the Mayflower. The series continues to trace the growth of the Winslow family throughout the formative years of the American nation, weaving in historical figures and Christian ethics. In *The Indentured Heart,* for instance, Adam Winslow helps a girl come to America as an indentured servant in the mid-1700s. *The Last Confederate,* as its name implies, takes place during the Civil War, when Patience Winslow aids a wounded Union soldier who has appeared on the Winslow plantation. "This book will inspire and capture the imagination of the YA reader," wrote Margaret Ann Fincher in a review for *Voice of Youth Advocates.* "I highly recommend this book for the mystery, excitement and suspense it contains." In *The Yukon Queen,* the era is the 1890s, and a gold rush is taking hold of Alaska, where young Cass Winslow is drawn with his love, Serena.

The "Liberty Bell" series is another historical saga, as is the "Spirit of Appalachia" series. Books in the "Liberty Bell" series, such as *Sound the Trumpet* and *Song in a*

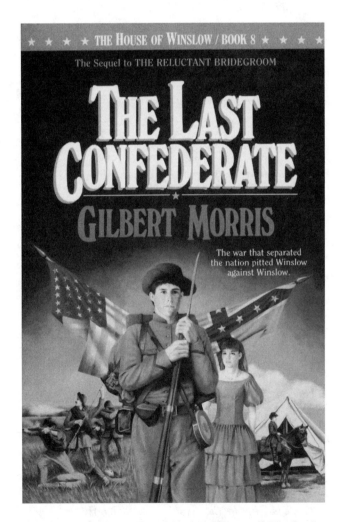

In this book from Gilbert Morris's "House of Winslow" series, which chronicles the story of a family over several decades of American history, Patience Winslow aids a wounded Union soldier who has appeared on her family's plantation during the Civil War.

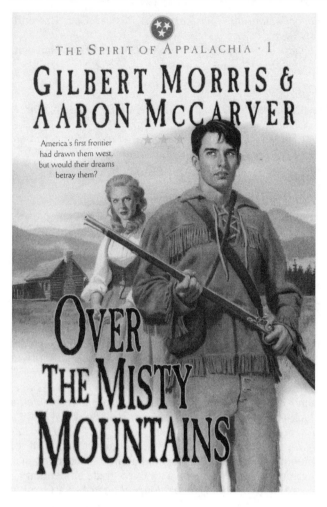

The first title in a series about life on the American frontier, Morris's novel, cowritten with Aaron McCarver, describes the hardships and danger several pioneers face in their struggle for a new life. (Cover illustration by Dan Thornberg.)

Strange Land, feature families united by blood but divided by politics during the American Revolution. For the "Spirit of Appalachia" series, Morris collaborated with Aaron McCarver, dean of Mississippi's Wesley College. That series includes *Over the Misty Mountains,* which *Voice of Youth Advocates* contributor Sheila Anderson called "a good read." Set in the period between 1755 and 1770, *Over the Misty Mountains* tells the story of Jehosaphat Spencer as he makes his way west across the Appalachians from Williamsburg after the death of his wife. The story is, in the words of *Library Journal* contributor Melissa Hudak, "a fast-moving, energetic glimpse of the lives of pioneers."

Other Morris series include "Ozark Adventures," or the "Barney Buck" series as it is sometimes known; the "Reno Western Saga" series; and the "Appomattox Saga" series, set during the Civil War. Morris collaborated with Bobby Funderburk on the "Price of Liberty" series of historical novels; with his daughter Lynn on the "Cheney Duvall, M.D." series; and with his son Alan on the "Katy Steele Adventures" series. He has also written

a half-dozen books for the "American Odyssey" series; many volumes for the "Wakefield Dynasty" series, a family saga like "House of Winslow"; and yet another Civil War series, "Bonnets and Bugles," which includes books such as *Yankee Belles in Dixie, The Battle of Lookout Mountain,* and *Fire over Atlanta.*

Morris doesn't limit himself to historical fiction. Mystery, science fiction and even animal stories, all with a Christian tone, are products of Morris's prolific pen. The "Daystar Voyages" series, cowritten by Morris and Dan Meeks, is science-fiction, and the "Dixie Morris Animal Adventure" series is composed of animal stories such as *Dixie and Jumbo* and *Dixie and Dolly.* The "Danielle Ross Mystery" series portrays a young woman who suddenly finds herself in charge of her father's detective agency after he suffers a heart attack. In *Deadly Deception,* the young heroine takes a job with the Lanzas, a family involved in organized crime. What makes this mystery unusual, according to Diane Goheen in *School Library Journal,* "is the Christian slant; it isn't intrusive, but it does come into play periodically." John Mort of *Booklist* called *Race with Death* "an old-fashioned tale of suspense," and described the "lady preacher" Danielle (or Dani) as "an appealing young woman."

The "Time Navigators" series features time-travelling twins Danny and Dixie, who sail to America aboard the *Mayflower* in *The Dangerous Voyage.* In the words of *Booklist*'s Shelley Townsend-Hudson, the "journey [is] depicted so credibly that readers gain a real sense of the difficult trip." *School Library Journal* contributor Patricia Pearl Dole observed that "the stress on Christian values is successfully and logically integrated." *Vanishing Clues* takes the twins to the time of the French and Indian War. Townsend-Hudson maintained that in this "fast-paced" book, "the problems of the British in fighting a European-style war in the American wilderness are agonizingly portrayed."

In addition to his many series of books for young people, Morris has published *How to Write (and Sell) a Christian Novel: Proven and Practical Advice from a Best-Selling Author.*

Works Cited

Anderson, Sheila, review of *Over the Misty Mountains,* *Voice of Youth Advocates,* December, 1997, p. 320.

Dole, Patricia Pearl, review of *The Dangerous Voyage,* *School Library Journal,* January, 1996, p. 110.

Fincher, Margaret Ann, review of *The Last Confederate,* *Voice of Youth Advocates,* June, 1991, p. 99.

Goheen, Diane, review of *Deadly Deception,* *School Library Journal,* October, 1992, p. 150.

Hudak, Melissa, review of *Over the Misty Mountains,* *Library Journal,* February 1, 1997, p. 66.

Mort, John, review of *Race with Death, Booklist,* November 15, 1994, p. 5740.

Townsend-Hudson, Shelley, review of *The Dangerous Voyage, Booklist,* January 1, 1996, p. 835.

Townsend-Hudson, Shelley, review of *Vanishing Clues,*
Booklist, October 1, 1996, p. 336.

For More Information See

PERIODICALS

Booklist, June 1, 1995, p. 1725; March 1, 1997, p. 1111.
Library Journal, November 1, 1991, p. 67; April 1, 1995,
p. 82; June 1, 1995, p. 98; June 1, 1997, p. 88.
Voice of Youth Advocates, October, 1988, p. 183; October,
1995, p. 221.*

—*Sketch by Judson Knight*

*   *   *

MOSS, Marissa 1959-

Personal

Born September 29, 1959; daughter of Robert (a
engineer) and Harriet Moss; married Harvey Stahl (a
professor); children: Simon, Elias, Asa. *Education:*
University of California, Berkeley, B.A. (art history);
attended California College of Arts & Crafts.

Addresses

Office—c/o Tricycle Press, P.O. Box 7123, Berkeley,
CA 94707.

Career

Author and illustrator. *Member:* Authors Guild, PEN
West, Society of Children's Book Writers and Illustrators, Screenwriters Guild.

Writings

PICTURE BOOKS; ALL SELF-ILLUSTRATED

Who Was It?, Houghton, 1989.
Regina's Big Mistake, Houghton, 1990.
Want to Play?, Houghton, 1990.
After-School Monster, Lothrop, 1991.
Knick Knack Paddywack, Houghton, 1992.
But Not Kate, Lothrop, 1992.
In America, Dutton, 1994.
Mel's Diner, BridgeWater, 1994.
The Ugly Menorah, Farrar, Straus, 1996.

"AMELIA'S NOTEBOOK" SERIES; SELF-ILLUSTRATED

Amelia's Notebook, Tricycle Press, 1995.
Amelia Writes Again, Tricycle Press, 1996.
My Notebook with Help from Amelia, Tricycle Press, 1997.
Amelia Hits the Road, Tricycle Press, 1997.
Amelia Takes Command, Tricycle Press, 1998.
Dr. Amelia's Boredom Survival Guide, American Girl,
1999.
Luv Amelia, Luv Nadia, American Girl, 1999.

FOR CHILDREN; OTHER

True Heart, illustrated by Chris F. Payne, Silver Whistle,
1998.

Rachel's Journal: The Story of a Pioneer Girl, Harcourt,
1998.
Emma's Journal: The Story of a Colonial Girl, Harcourt,
1999.

ILLUSTRATOR

Catherine Gray, *One, Two, Three, and Four—No More?,*
Houghton, 1988.
Dr. Hickey, adapter, *Mother Goose and More: Classic
Rhymes with Added Lines,* Additions Press, 1990.
Bruce Coville, *The Lapsnatcher,* BridgeWater, 1997.

Sidelights

Author and illustrator Marissa Moss has produced
several popular picture books, as well as a series of
beginning readers featuring a young writer named
Amelia. Beginning with *Amelia's Notebook,* Moss
follows her eponymous heroine through her daily
adventures in the fourth grade, as the young protagonist
changes schools, makes new friends, and copes with an
annoying older sister. Moss has captured the imagination
of primary graders with the adventures of her spunky
character, and has tempted them with the opportunity to
"read the secrets a peer records in her journal,"
according to *Publishers Weekly* writer Sally Lodge.
Hand-lettered and bound in a manner that resembles a
black-and-white school composition book, *Amelia's
Notebook* and its companion volumes *Amelia Writes
Again* and *Amelia Hits the Road* are "chock-full of
personal asides and tiny spot drawings" and contain a
"narrative [that] rings true with third-grade authenticity,"
according to *School Library Journal* contributor Carolyn
Noah.

Born in 1959, Moss earned a degree in art history from
the University of California at Berkeley. She told *SATA:*
"I could say I never thought I'd be a writer, only an
illustrator and writing was forced upon me by a lack of
other writers' stories to illustrate. Or I could say I always
wanted to be a writer, but I never thought it was really
possible. As a voracious reader, it seemed too much of a
grown up thing to do, and I'd never be mature enough to
do it. Or I could say I've been writing and illustrating
childrens' books since I was nine. It just took me longer
than most to get published. All these stories are true,
each in their own way."

Moss began her career as a picture book illustrator,
working with author Catherine Gray as well as compos-
ing her own simple texts. One of her first published
efforts as both writer and illustrator, *Who Was It?,*
depicts young Isabelle's quandary after she breaks the
cookie jar while attempting to sneak a between-meals
snack. Praising Moss's watercolor illustrations, *Booklist*
reviewer Denise Wilms also noted that the book's
"moral about telling the truth is delivered with wry,
quiet humor." In *Regina's Big Mistake,* a young artist's
frustration with her own inability compared to the rest of
her classmates is counteracted by a sensitive art teacher,
as Regina is shown how to "draw around" a lumpy sun,
transforming it into a moon. Readers "will enjoy the
solace of having another child struggling to achieve, and

This is my beautiful, new, BLANK notebook, waiting for me to fill it with words and drawings. But I feel as blank and empty as these pages. I mean, I just turned 10 exciting years old, but I feel exactly the same as when I was 9. And I look the same,

same brain, same ideas, same thoughts

me

same old scar from when Cleo threw a toy teapot at me — that's my stupid sister's idea of a tea party!

ears are still not pierced (not till I'm 16, says mom)

same dip under my nose — what is this thing called anyway, and what's it for? to funnel snot into your mouth when you have a runny nose?

Miss Know-It-All Cleo. If she knows so much, how come she can't eat pizza without getting it all over her face? I call her Cheezy chin.

I still had a good birthday, but I expected SOMETHING would change. I thought ten was close to teen — almost a teenager. It's not.

piece o' pizza

gooey, gluey chin

Cleo says no matter how old I am, I'll always be a jerky little sister. And she'll always get to do things first. But she's wrong.

Hand-lettered, illustrated with doodles and sketches, and bound in a manner that resembles a black-and-white school composition book, Marissa Moss's "Amelia's Notebook" series takes her heroine through typical daily events as a primary grader. (From Amelia Writes Again, *written and illustrated by Moss.)*

succeeding," maintained Zena Sutherland of the *Bulletin of the Center for Children's Books. School Library Journal* contributor Ruth Semrau noted that "Moss's crayon cartoons are exactly what is needed to depict the artistic endeavors of very young children."

In *After-School Monster,* Luisa returns home from school one day to find a sharp-toothed creature waiting in her kitchen. Although scared, she stands up to the monster, turning the tables on the creature and evicting him from the house before Mom gets home. While noting that the theme could frighten very small children contemplating being left alone, a *Junior Bookshelf* contributor praised Moss's "striking" full-page illustrations, which feature "an imaginative use of changing sizes." And in an equally imaginative picture book offering, Moss updates the traditional nursery rhyme "Knick Knack Paddywack" with what Sheilamae O'Hara of *Booklist* described as "rollicking, irreverent verse" and "colorful, action-filled" pictures. The author-illustrator's "use of language will tickle all but the tongue tied," added Jody McCoy in an appraisal of *Knick Knack Paddywack* for *School Library Journal.*

"The character of Amelia came to me when I opened a black and white mottled composition book and started to write and draw the way I remembered I wrote and drew when I was nine," Moss told *SATA* about the beginnings of her popular "Amelia's Notebook" series. "By that age I was already a pretty good artist, winner of drugstore coloring contests and determined to grow up to be

Moss's novel, set in 1850, presents the experiences of a girl accompanying her family on a journey along the Oregon Trail on the way to California.

another Leonardo da Vinci." The age of nine was also significant for Moss because that was when she had grown confident enough to send her first illustrated children's book to a publisher. "I don't remember the title, but the story involved an owl's tea party and was in rhymed couplets—bad rhyme I'm sure, as I never got a response from the publisher whose name I mercifully don't recall." Lacking encouragement, Moss left writing for several years, although she continued to tell stories.

The power of storytelling is one of the key themes Moss endeavors to express through her young protagonist, Amelia. "When you write or tell about something," she explained to *SATA,* "you have a kind of control over it, you shape the events, you sort them through, you emphasize some aspects, omit others.... Besides the flights of pure fancy, the imaginative leaps that storytelling allows, it was this sense of control, of finding order and meaning that mattered most to me as a child."

In the Amelia books, the spunky young chronicler dives into activities in a new school after leaving her old friends behind during a family move. "Amelia is droll and funny and not too sophisticated for her years," noted *Booklist* reviewer Stephanie Zvirin, who added that the diarist has a more emotional side too, missing her old friends and full of childhood aspirations about her future. In *Amelia Writes Again,* the heroine has turned ten and has begun a new notebook. In doodles, sketches, and snippets of thoughts, Amelia comments on such things as a fire at school and her inability to pay attention during math class. Everything Moss includes in Amelia's notebooks is true, "or," as Moss tells the groups of students she visits, "is based on the truth. Names have all been changed, because my older sister is mad enough at me already, and some details are altered to make for a better story. So, yes, there really was a fire in my school, but the idea of putting treasures in the newly poured pavement didn't occur to me at the time." Moss wishes it had; instead, she was able to let Amelia do so in *Amelia Writes Again.*

Moss enjoys writing in Amelia's voice because it allows her a flexibility that conventional picture book writing does not. "I can go back and forth between different kinds of writing—the pure invention of storytelling, the thoughtful searching of describing people and events, and the explorations Amelia takes when she writes about noses or numbers, things she notices and writes down to figure out what it is that she's noticing. In the same way that I can go from describing a new teacher to making a story about clouds, Amelia allows me to move freely between words and pictures. I can draw as Amelia draws or I can use *tromp l'oeil* for the objects she tapes into her notebook. I can play with the art as much as I play with the text. The notebook format allows me to leap from words to images and this free flowing back and forth is how I work best. It reflects the way I think—sometimes visually, sometimes verbally—with the pictures not there just to illustrate the text, but to replace it, telling their own story. Often the art allows me a kind of graphic shorthand, a way of conveying what I mean that is much more immediate than words. Kids often ask me which comes first, the words or the pictures. With Amelia, it can be either, and I love that fluidity.

"Amelia is headed in a new direction under her new publisher American Girl. Besides various Amelia products (including, of course, a journaling kit), there are plans for an Amelia CD-ROM (an electronic journal naturally) and an Amelia video, which will expand Amelia's world—and journal—into animation."

In addition to Amelia's notebooks, Moss has begun a new series, this time focusing on young writers from different historical periods. "Like Amelia's notebooks, the pages will seem like real notebook pages," Moss explained to *SATA,* "with drawings and inserted objects on every page, only the main character will be someone from the past." The first book in the series, *Rachel's Journal,* introduces readers to a girl accompanying her family to California in 1850 along the Oregon Trail. Unlike the Amelia books, which were drawn from the author's own memories, Moss had to spend many hours doing research, reading histories, exploring library archives, and pouring over the actual letters and diaries of people who traversed the United States by covered wagon. "It was, for the most part, rivetting reading and I was impressed with what an enormous undertaking, what a leap of faith it was for pioneers to come here," Moss noted. "It was a dangerous trip. Indians, river crossings, storms, and especially sickness were all feared. But I was struck by the difference between how men and women viewed the journey and how children saw it. To kids, it was a great adventure, troublesome at times, tedious and terrifying at others, but ultimately exciting. These children showed tremendous courage and strength of character, and I tried to capture some of that, as well as the exhilaration of travelling into the unknown, in Rachel's journal."

Critics have praised Moss's books for leading younger readers into the art of journal writing. And Moss couldn't be happier. "The many letters I get from kids show that, inspired by Amelia, they, too, are discovering the magic of writing," she told *SATA.* "When readers respond to Amelia by starting their own journals, I feel I've gotten the highest compliment possible—I've made writing cool."

Works Cited

Review of *After-School Monster, Junior Bookshelf,* April, 1993, p. 62.

Lodge, Sally, "Journaling Back Through Time with Marissa Moss," *Publishers Weekly,* August 31, 1998, p. 20.

McCoy, Jody, review of *Knick Knack Paddywack, School Library Journal,* May, 1992, p. 92.

Noah, Carolyn, review of *Amelia's Notebook, School Library Journal,* July, 1995, p. 79.

O'Hara, Sheilamae, review of *Knick Knack Paddywack, Booklist,* July, 1992, p. 1941.

Semrau, Ruth, review of *Regina's Big Mistake, School Library Journal,* January, 1991, p. 79.

Sutherland, Zena, review of *Regina's Big Mistake, Bulletin of the Center for Children's Books,* October, 1990, p. 40.

Wilms, Denise, review of *Who Was It?, Booklist,* November 1, 1989, p. 555.

Zvirin, Stephanie, review of *Amelia's Notebook, Booklist,* April 1, 1995, p. 1391.

For More Information See

PERIODICALS

Booklist, March 1, 1992, p. 1287; October 1, 1994, p. 333; June 1, 1997, p. 1716; November 15, 1997, p. 561.

Bulletin of the Center for Children's Books, November, 1996, p. 108.

Kirkus Reviews, August 15, 1989, p. 1248; August 15, 1990, p. 1171; July 1, 1991, p. 865; July 1, 1996, p. 972.

Publishers Weekly, June 14, 1991, p. 57; September 30, 1996, p. 87; June 16, 1997, p. 61; July 28, 1997, p. 77.

School Library Journal, June, 1992, p. 100; December, 1994, p. 79; July, 1997, p. 60; November, 1997, p. 95.

*   *   *

MUDGEON, Apeman
See MITCHELL, Adrian

N

NATHAN, Amy

Personal

Born in Norfolk, VA; daughter of Martin (a physician) and Patti (a homemaker and actress) Singewald; married Carl F. Nathan (a research physician), 1967; children: Eric, Noah. *Education:* Radcliffe College, B.A. (cum laude), 1967; Harvard Graduate School of Education, M.A.T., 1968; Teachers College, Columbia University, M.A., 1980.

Addresses

Home—5 Edgewood Ave., Larchmont, NY 10538.

Career

Educator, actress, editor, writer. Teacher in various adult education programs in the Boston area, 1968-71; actress in regional theater and Off-Broadway productions, 1971-80; teacher of creative drama at various arts programs in Boston, Washington, and New York City, 1972-80; Scholastic Magazines, associate editor, 1980-81; *Zillions Magazine* (*Consumer Reports for Kids*), associate editor, 1981-94; freelance writer of books and magazine articles for children, 1994—. *Member:* Society of Children's Book Writers and Illustrators, Authors' Guild.

Awards, Honors

Clarion Award, Women in Communication, for *Surviving Homework;* ten Ed. Press Awards for Excellence in Educational Publishing, 1981-95.

Writings

Everything You Need to Know about Conflict Resolution, Rosen, 1996.
Surviving Homework: Tips from Teens, illustrated by Anne Canevari Green, Millbrook, 1996.
The Kids' Allowance Book, illustrated by Debbie Palen, Walker, 1998.

Work in Progress

A book on music for kids, for Oxford University Press.

Sidelights

Amy Nathan has enjoyed several occupations, working as an educator, an actress, and as editor of a children's magazine. As a freelance writer of children's books, she has tackled such subjects as conflict resolution, homework, and allowance in a manner that reviewers have praised as clear, entertaining, and informative. "Information [provided] in a straightforward but sympathetic way" is one of the strengths of Nathan's *Everything You Need to Know about Conflict Resolution,* according to reviewer Karen Herc in *Voice of Youth Advocates.* In this work, the author discusses conflict resolution programs in schools and the role of peer mediators in resolving conflicts between students. The book also suggests specific steps toward conflict resolution, such as practicing listening skills and avoiding accusations in favor of talking about one's own feelings. Included is a section on resources. The work as a whole, was praised by Herc for offering "practical, easily understandable advice."

Nathan turned to students themselves for the answers to questions raised in her next two books, *Surviving Homework* and *The Kids' Allowance Book.* In *Surviving Homework,* the author organizes her information by complaint rather than by chapter, relaying the responses of three hundred high school juniors and seniors to questions about boredom, lack of time, the difficulty of memorizing, and test anxieties. As Rosie Peasley, who reviewed *Surviving Homework* for *School Library Journal,* noted, "the information is presented in a user-friendly, humorous format that will appeal to young people." Jonathan Betz-Zall, who reviewed *The Kids' Allowance Book* for *School Library Journal,* also cited Nathan's appealing prose style, and detected a similarity between the style of *Zillions,* the magazine Nathan had edited for more than ten years, and the "breezy" style of *The Kids' Allowance Book.* In this work, using information from the responses of more than 150 children,

Nathan discusses many allowance-related issues, including: how to convince parents to give an allowance, whether the allowance should be connected to chores, how to negotiate a raise, and how to manage money in general. "With its popular but little-covered topic, logical organization, and attractive style," maintained Betz-Zall, "this book is well worth the investment,"

Works Cited

Betz-Zall, Jonathan, review of *The Kids' Allowance Book,* *School Library Journal,* October, 1998, pp. 157-58.

Herc, Karen, review of *Everything You Need to Know about Conflict Resolution, Voice of Youth Advocates,* June, 1997, p. 136.

Peasley, Rosie, review of *Surviving Homework: Tips from Teens, School Library Journal,* July, 1997, p. 110.

* * *

NOVAK, Matt 1962-

Personal

Born October 23, 1962, in Trenton, New Jersey; son of Theresa (a factory worker; maiden name, Belfiore) Novak. *Education:* Attended Kutztown State University, 1980-81.

Career

Pegasus Players, Sheppton, PA, puppeteer, 1979-83; Walt Disney World, Orlando, FL, animator, 1983; St. Benedict's Preparatory School, Newark, NJ, art teacher, 1986—; Parsons School of Design, New York City, instructor, 1986—. Author and illustrator of children's books. *Member:* Society of Children's Book Writers and Illustrators.

Awards, Honors

Children's Choice, International Reading Association and Children's Book Council (IRA-CBC), 1997, for *Newt.*

Writings

FOR CHILDREN; ALL SELF-ILLUSTRATED

Rolling, Bradbury Press (New York City), 1986.
Claude and Sun, Bradbury Press, 1987.
Mr. Floop's Lunch, Orchard Books, 1990.
While the Shepherd Slept, Orchard Books, 1991.
Elmer Blunt's Open House, Orchard Books, 1992.
The Last Christmas Present, Orchard Books, 1993.
Mouse TV, Orchard Books, 1994.
Gertie and Gumbo, Orchard Books, 1995.
Newt, HarperCollins, 1996.
The Pillow War, Orchard Books, 1997.
The Robobots, DK Publishing, 1998.
Jazzbo and Friends, Hyperion, 1999.

ILLUSTRATOR

Pat Upton, *Who Does This Job?,* Bell Books (Honesdale, PA), 1991.
Lee Bennett Hopkins, selector, *It's About Time: Poems,* Simon & Schuster, 1993.
Dayle Ann Dodds, *Ghost and Pete,* Random House, 1995.
Susan Hightower, *Twelve Snails to One Lizard: A Tale of Mischief and Measurement,* Simon & Schuster, 1997.
Heather Lowenberg, *Little Slugger,* Random House, 1997.

Sidelights

Author and illustrator Matt Novak has created a number of picture books for preschoolers and primary graders centering on a great variety of phenomena guaranteed to capture the attention of a child. Alligators, salamanders, loud thunderclaps, and television are just some of the subjects featured in his books. Novak has also provided pictures for books by other writers, including Susan Hightower's *Twelve Snails to One Lizard* and Heather Lowenberg's *Little Slugger.*

Novak's first self-illustrated book, *Rolling,* is a story about thunder. The author's illustrations take center stage in this work, which, as a reviewer in *Publishers Weekly* noted, "consists of two long sentences stretched out over twenty-seven pages." In the book, wrote *School Library Journal* contributor Virginia Opocensky, "Thunder, the mysterious, overpowering sound that frightens nearly every child at one time or another, is depicted by Novak as a visible cloud-like force." The illustrator's "lines are deft and true," asserted Denise M. Wilms of *Booklist,* "displaying a fine sense of form; gentle pastel washes keep the mood light despite the windy bluster."

Claude and Sun depicts an entirely different weather phenomenon as its main character, Claude, follows his best friend, the sun, through the course of the day. Some reviewers suggested that "Claude" is actually Claude Monet, the celebrated French painter who is credited as a central figure in what came to be known as the Impressionist movement. "The books's theme itself," wrote Karen K. Radtke in *School Library Journal,* "expresses the basic tenet of Impressionistic art—that light reflecting off an object creates what our eyes see." Radtke noted references to other artists such as Georges Seurat, Vincent Van Gogh, and Auguste Renoir, and held that "within this very simple storyline is a multifaceted art lesson."

Another of Novak's self-illustrated tales, *While the Shepherd Slept,* is an amusing comedy of errors. During the daytime, the shepherd sleeps while his flock sneaks off to perform in a stage show called *Baa-Baa Broadway.* The wayward sheep come back just as the shepherd wakes up, and he praises them for their trustworthiness: "You are all so good," he says. "You never wander." But the joke is on the sheep: at night while they're asleep, the shepherd himself sneaks off to perform in his own vaudeville review. A critic in *Publishers Weekly* called the book a "gentle, droll tale of secret lives ... a sheer delight." This "simple, funny book," suggested Carolyn

Vang Schuler in *School Library Journal,* "will surely bring applause" with its clever scenes.

Elmer Blunt's Open House features very little text, making it, in the opinion of some reviewers, a good book for preschoolers to "read" by themselves and thus gain the feeling that they are truly reading. "As in *While the Shepherd Slept,*" wrote Liza Bliss in *School Library Journal,* "Novak explores the question of what really happens when you're not looking." In this story, Elmer Blunt hurriedly leaves for work, leaving the door wide open. During the day, all manner of animals and a burglar enter his home, so that when Elmer comes back at night he exclaims, "I really made a mess this morning!" Bliss concluded that *Elmer Blunt's Open House* is "a book that's sure to add a lot of fun to family reading." "Bursting with action and uninterrupted by narrative," Opocensky observed in *Five Owls,* "the illustrations beg for one-on-one sharing with a preschooler. This one is lots of fun." A commentator in *Publishers Weekly* maintained: "Since Novak's ... gleeful, high-spirited art tells the story so adeptly, this is a great one for preschoolers to 'read.'"

The Last Christmas Present tells the story of a conscientious elf named Irvin who, after Santa accidentally leaves one present behind, goes out of his way—far out of his way—to make sure that it gets to the child who is supposed to receive it. *School Library Journal* contributor Jane Marino noted that "the simple text and captions

are perfect for beginning readers, who can share with parents or enjoy the fun all by themselves." A *Kirkus Reviews* critic observed that the "unexplored territory" through which Irvin must go to take the present to its rightful owner is "a satisfyingly risky area with chasms, wolves, sharks, and similar amusements."

The family of mice in *Mouse TV* has only one television set, and since there are ten of them, each with different tastes, this leads to conflict of an amusing kind. On successive pages, Novak portrays various family members' favorite programs, such as the game show *Get the Cheese* and the science program *It's a Frog's Life.* But when the TV goes on the blink, the mice are surprised to discover that they have plenty of other entertaining ways to spend their time: playing games, reading, and engaging in other healthy activities. "Nobody will miss the unapologetic dig at the [television] medium," wrote Stephanie Zvirin in *Booklist.* "Here's the perfect picture book for pint-size couch potatoes," she added. "The cleverest aspect of the message," maintained *School Library Journal* contributor Steven Engelfried, "is that TV-watching is never condemned or criticized.... Instead, Novak gently, and quite successfully, shows that there are countless ways to enjoy oneself as an active participant rather than as a passive viewer." Roger Sutton of the *Bulletin of the Center for Children's Books* commented that "the jokes are hip (in a way that kids and adults can share) and the drawing"—which Sutton

When Elmer Blunt hurries off to work and forgets to close his door, several animals and a burglar trespass and wreak havoc in his absence. *(From* Elmer Blunt's Open House, *written and illustrated by Matt Novak.)*

Novak's rhyming bedtime story follows siblings Millie and Fred, whose pillow fight escalates into a grand battle. (From The Pillow War, *written and illustrated by Novak.)*

compared to Maurice Sendak's illustrations in *A Hole Is to Dig*—"is clean and confident."

Gertie Goomba, the heroine of *Gertie and Gumbo,* spends a lot of time alone, because she lives "in the swampy South with her papa and five big alligators." A baby alligator named Gumbo becomes her best friend, and helps Gertie's dad with his alligator-wrestling act, which he stages for tourists in order to earn a living. A reviewer in *Publishers Weekly,* describing the author's "lighthearted" illustrations, noted that Novak depicts Gumbo in appropriately alligator-like activities such as "devouring inedible objects" and "popping out of the toilet," but also in such uncharacteristic undertakings as

learning to dance. "Gumbo's body language and toothy grins are splendid," concluded Zvirin in *Booklist.*

Another amphibious-type creature takes a leading role in *Newt,* three short adventures featuring a high-spirited salamander. "The bright and lively artwork and straightforward text," wrote Gale W. Sherman in *School Library Journal,* "make this reassuring easy reader a winner." Among Newt's comical experiences is his attempt to turn a fuzzy bug into something it is not: "Newt hitched the bug to a wagon of rocks," Novak tells the reader. "'Pull!' Newt shouted. The bug only looked at him with its twenty sad eyes." Nonetheless, wrote Roger Sutton in the *Bulletin of the Children's Books,* "Newt learns that his bug is pettably soft and makes a nice buzzing sound, and that that is enough." Sutton applauded the lessons handled with a light touch and called for further adventures with Newt.

In *The Pillow War,* siblings Millie and Fred get into a disagreement over who should be allowed to sleep with their dog, Sam; a pillow fight ensues. As the story continues, the fight escalates: "They fought down the stairs / onto the street, / where their neighbors joined in / with pillows and sheets." Zvirin of *Booklist* observed that "the rhyme is catchy, and the pictures are a riot of color and pattern," particularly "one special feast-for-the-eyes double-page spread that begs kids to pick their favorite characters out of the crowd." To reviewer Julie Cummins, this type of detailed crowd scene illustration called to mind the "Where's Waldo?" cartoon series. "It's a madcap escapade that becomes a nightcap story," Cummins wrote in *School Library Journal.* A reviewer in *Publishers Weekly* pointed out a quality many young readers would enjoy: "preschoolers can search out the [main characters] in each bustling spread and follow the amusing antics of a menagerie of animals caught up in the frenzy."

Among the works Novak has illustrated for others is Lee Bennett Hopkins's poetry collection, *It's About Time,* for which a critic in *Publishers Weekly* wrote: "Novak's soft pastel pencil drawings do much to bring unity to the divergent writing styles represented" in Hopkins's selections. Regarding Novak's work on *Twelve Snails to One Lizard* by Susan Hightower, a *Publishers Weekly* commentator maintained that "Novak's ... winsome earth-toned acrylics once again amuse, with lizards who juggle and hula, a beaver wearing a tool belt, and a pair of picnicking mice who cavort on several spreads."

Works Cited

Bliss, Liza, review of *Elmer Blunt's Open House, School Library Journal,* October, 1992, p. 94.

Cummins, Julie, review of *The Pillow War, School Library Journal,* March, 1998, p. 185.

Review of *Elmer Blunt's Open House, Publishers Weekly,* July 13, 1992, p. 54.

Engelfried, Stephen, review of *Mouse TV, School Library Journal,* October, 1994, pp. 95-96.

Review of *Gertie and Gumbo, Publishers Weekly,* August 7, 1995, p. 460.

Review of *It's About Time, Publishers Weekly,* May 31, 1993, p. 54.

Review of *The Last Christmas Present, Kirkus Reviews,* September 1, 1993, p. 1149.

Marino, Jane, review of *The Last Christmas Present, School Library Journal,* October, 1993, p. 46.

Opocensky, Virginia, review of *Elmer Blunt's Open House, Five Owls,* September-October, 1992, p. 12.

Opocensky, Virginia, review of *Rolling, School Library Journal,* September, 1986, pp. 125-26.

Review of *The Pillow War, Publishers Weekly,* February 9, 1998, p. 94.

Radtke, Karen, review of *Claude and Sun, School Library Journal,* May, 1987, p. 91.

Review of *Rolling, Publishers Weekly,* June 27, 1986, p. 87.

Schuler, Carolyn Vang, review of *While the Shepherd Slept, School Library Journal,* July, 1991, p. 62.

Sherman, Gale W., review of *Newt, School Library Journal,* July, 1996, p. 70.

Sutton, Roger, review of *Mouse TV, Bulletin of the Center for Children's Books,* October, 1994, p. 60.

Sutton, Roger, review of *Newt, Bulletin of the Center for Children's Books,* February, 1996, p. 198.

Review of *Twelve Snails to One Lizard, Publishers Weekly,* March 24, 1997, p. 82.

Review of *While the Shepherd Slept, Publishers Weekly,* January 4, 1991, p. 71.

Wilms, Denise M., review of *Rolling, Booklist,* August, 1986, p. 1692.

Zvirin, Stephanie, review of *Mouse TV, Booklist,* September 1, 1994, p. 53.

Zvirin, Stephanie, review of *Gertie and Gumbo, Booklist,* September 1, 1995, p. 89.

Zvirin, Stephanie, review of *The Pillow War, Booklist,* February 15, 1998, p. 1020.

For More Information See

PERIODICALS

Booklist, April 15, 1987, p. 1293.

Horn Book, May-June, 1991, p. 319.

Kirkus Reviews, August 15, 1992, p. 1066.

New York Times Book Review, February 26, 1995, p. 21.

Publishers Weekly, September 20, 1993, p. 37; July 4, 1994, p. 60; January 22, 1996.

School Library Journal, March, 1990, p. 199; October, 1995, p. 110; May, 1997, p. 100.*

—Sketch by Judson Knight

O–P

OUGHTON, (William) Taylor 1925-

Personal

Surname is pronounced *Aw*-ton; born March 25, 1925, in Glenside, PA; son of Robert B. (a manufacturer of worsted woolen materials for men's suits) and Elizabeth G. (a homemaker and community volunteer; maiden name, Rowe) Oughton; married Elizabeth Kaufmann (a registered nurse), September 6, 1947; children: Elizabeth, Robyn, William Taylor, Jr., Robert II. *Education:* Attended Ursinus College, Bucknell University, and Philadelphia Museum School of Industrial Arts (now Philadelphia College of Art). *Politics:* None. *Religion:* "Ex-Presbyterian, ex-Quaker."

Addresses

Home and office—P.O. Box 355, Jamison, PA 18929.

Career

Illustrator; worked for a studio in New York City and as a partner in a small advertising studio. Hussian School of Art, teacher of illustration, 1963; Bucks County Community College, teacher of illustration classes, 1964-71. Abington Music Theater, set designer, 1950-62. *Exhibitions:* Work exhibited in galleries throughout Pennsylvania as part of public and private collections; represented by Michelyn Galleries in New Britain and New Hope, PA, and by Artists' Gallery in Lambertville, NJ. *Military service:* U.S. Marine Corps, 1943-46; served in Okinawa and China; became acting platoon sergeant. *Member:* Open Space Committee of Warwick Township, local cooperative artists group, Warwick Township Historical Commission (past member).

Awards, Honors

Awards from New York Society of Illustrators, 1985, and Philadelphia and New Jersey advertising clubs; awards from poster, print, and stamp competitions, including Pennsylvania's Working Together for Wildlife print competition, 1992, New Jersey's pheasant/quail stamp competition, 1993, and New Jersey's poster competition for Wings 'n' Water Festival, 1995.

Illustrator

The Lonesome Sorrel, Winston, 1952.

Taylor Oughton

Trail North to Danger, Winston, 1952.

Cowboy Charlie, Viking, 1953.

Pride of Possession, Lippincott, 1960.

Countryman, Lippincott, 1965.

Frances Priddy, *Sam's Country: A Small Town in the Midwest,* McGraw, 1969.

Darrell A. Rolerson, *A Boy and a Deer,* Dodd, 1970.

The Dog Who Came to Stay, Lippincott, c. 1970.

Helen La Penta, *Pinky, the Cat That Overcame,* Criterion Books (New York City), 1971.

Hal Borland, *Penny, the Story of a Free-Soul Basset Hound,* Lippincott, 1972.

Lynn Hall, *Flash, Dog of Old Egypt,* Garrard (Champaign, IL), 1973.

Lynn Hall, *Bob, Watchdog of the River,* Garrard, 1974.

Justin F. Denzel, *Snowfoot, White Reindeer of the Arctic,* Garrard, 1976.

Dorothy Brenner Francis, *The Flint Hills Foal,* Abingdon (Nashville, TN), 1976.

Era Zistel, *Hi Fella,* Lippincott, 1977.

Great African-American Athletes, Ingram, 1996.

Great African-Americans Coloring Book, Ingram, 1996.

Elizabeth Ring, *Loon at Northwood Lake,* Soundprints (Norwalk, CT), 1997.

Contributor of nature illustrations to several editions of *The Boy Scout Handbook.* Contributor of illustrations to magazines, including *Reader's Digest, Saturday Evening Post, Holiday, Sports Afield, Field and Stream,* and *Cosmopolitan.*

Work in Progress

Illustrating a book on mallard ducks, for Soundprints/ Smithsonian.

Sidelights

Taylor Oughton told *SATA:* "I always liked to draw. That and English were my only two 'A' subjects. After World War II, while stationed in China, I drew a lot and sold or traded the work for meals. I felt it might be a way to earn a living, and I was right.

"Karl Sherman, a drawing teacher of the first rank, had us draw two chairs: one right side up, the other upside down. The upside down drawing was better. Why? We'd seen thousands of chairs and *believed* we knew what a chair looked like. We had possibly never seen one

Oughton's paintings grace Elizabeth Ring's tale of a loon and his mate who diligently protect their family from predators during the course of a summer. (From Loon at Northwood Lake.*)*

upside down, and so we paid more attention to it. Paying attention is the price of admission to a shared life.

"Later Sherman spotted an error I was making. I'd drawn and erased and redrawn an ear five or six times. He asked if he could draw on my paper, and I welcomed it. He drew the mouth! He explained that the drawing of the ear was okay, the problem was its relationship to the mouth. The arts are about relationships. The arts are a human response to what is out there and within. By putting things in their right place, we can see what the world is about, all over, and through time. A very small difference can create change that matters.

"I have spent most of my working life as an illustrator, painting to match or embellish the words of others, to feel what they write as advertising copy, editorial stories, or ideas about something. I present it in paint, and the *use* of art becomes something separate from the process of doing it for its own sake. Book illustration was and is a safety valve—a blending of arts where neither is out to *sell* the other, to *use* the other in any way. The author uses words to respond to events in the world and to share feelings. My response as an illustrator is through my own feelings.

"Appropriate action in painting (or in any of the arts) comes from the clear seeing and hearing that prompts distinct feeling. One can make a better drawing of anything by looking at the subject, rather than at the drawing in progress. Work created in this way has a relationship to anyone who sees it and is willing to pay attention to it. The more that *purpose* enters the picture (in terms of trying to sell an idea or behavior, or to 'make' someone have a certain feeling), the less successful the illustration will be. Such purpose can *prevent* the drawing from carrying the feeling, questioning, and awareness of author and illustrator to the reader. I have found this to be equally true in my life. When my behavior does not respond to what is out there in the world and within my feelings, it does not work.

"I have had interesting responses from readers in northern New England, the northern Midwest, and the Northwest, who think I must have visited a particular lake in each of those places. They all say that Northwood Lake looks very much like each of their lakes. I had never been near any of those lakes, but the comments tell me two things. There are lakes in the northern reaches of the United States that resemble each other. My illustrations contain the *elements* of these lakes in their relationships to one another, in such a way that readers recall feelings and emotions and memories, which in turn remind them of their relationships to places and the times of the world in which we live. That wasn't my purpose. I had seen other, similar lakes and had my own feelings about the natural world and the places I had seen. The illustrations were my response to these things and to author Elizabeth Ring's words about them. I remember a distinct feeling that the illustrations grew right out of the words as I read them."

PAUSEWANG, Gudrun 1928-

Personal

Born March 3, 1928, in Wichstadtl, Germany; children: one son.

Addresses

Home—Brueder-Grimm-Weg 11, 36110 Schlitz, Germany.

Career

Author, 1959—. Has also worked twelve years as a teacher in Germany and South America.

Awards, Honors

Recipient of several awards, including the Deutschen Jugendliteraturpreis (German Literature Award for Children's Books) and the Gustav-Heinemann-Friedenspreis.

Writings

YOUNG ADULT FICTION; IN ENGLISH TRANSLATION; ORIGINALLY PUBLISHED IN GERMAN BY RAVENSBURGER

The Last Children of Schevenborn (originally published as *Die letzten Kinder von Schewenborn,* 1985), translated by Norman M. Watt, Western Producer Prairie Books (Saskatoon, Canada), 1988, published as *The Last Children,* MacRae, 1989.

Gudrun Pausewang

Fall-Out (originally published as *Die Wolke,* 1987), translated by Patricia Crampton, edited with introduction, notes, and vocabulary by Susan Tebbutt, Manchester University Press, 1992, Viking, 1994.

The Final Journey (originally published as *Eine Reise im August,* 1992), translated by Patricia Crampton, Viking, 1996.

IN GERMAN; PUBLISHED BY RAVENSBURGER

Und dann kommt Emilio, 1974.

Kunibert und Killewamba, 1976.

Der Streik der Dienstmaedchen, 1979.

Rosenkawiesen: Alternatives Leben von 50 Jahren, 1980.

Die Not der Familie Caldera, 1981.

Die Prinzessin springt ins Heu, 1982.

Auf einem langen Weg, 1982.

Wer hat Angst vor Raeuber Grapsch, 1983.

Ich habe Hunger, Ich habe Durst, 1984.

Etwas laesst sich doch bewirken, 1984.

Friedens: Geschichten (stories; includes *Frieden kommt nicht von allein*), 1985.

Ein wilder Winter fuer Raeuber Grapsch, 1986.

Ein Eigenheim fuer Raeuber Grapsch, 1987.

Die Kinder in der Erde, illustrated by Annengert Fuchshuber, 1988.

Kreuz und quer uebers Meer, 1988.

Fern von der Rosinkawiese, 1989.

Geliebte Rosinkawiese, 1990.

Das Tor zum Garten der Zambranos, 1991.

Es ist doch alles gruen, 1991.

Das grosse Buch vom Raeuber Grapsch, 1992.

Der Schlund, 1993.

Der Weihnachtsmann im Kittchen, 1995.

Die Verraeterin, 1995.

Adi: Jugend eines Diktators, 1997.

Ich geb' dir noch eine Chance, Gott!, illustrated by Uschi Schneider, 1997.

Warum eigentlich nicht (previously published as *Ich habe einen Freund in Leningrad*), 1998.

Hinterm Haus der Wassermann, 1998.

1996-1997 Germanistikstudium, 1998.

Also author of more than thirty books in German, published by various companies.

Sidelights

Gudrun Pausewang is a German author of books for children, young adults, and adults. Three of these have been translated into English, all of which feature grim stories involving catastrophes such as the Holocaust or a nuclear accident. As someone who grew up in Nazi Germany, Pausewang knows what it is like to live through terrible times. The oldest of six sisters, she was born in Wichstadtl in Ostboehmen, Germany. After her father was killed on the Russian front in 1943, her mother was forced to raise half a dozen children alone. Somehow the family managed, and Pausewang became an educator. Pausewang taught in Germany for five years after the war, then left her homeland in 1956 to live in Chile, and then Venezuela, for seven years. During this time, she also visited North America. In 1963, she returned to Germany and taught in Mainz-

Kastel for four years. She then went back to South America, this time living in Columbia, where her son was born. When her son was two years old, Pausewang returned with him to Germany.

During her years of teaching and traveling, Pausewang began to write stories for both adults and children. In her books, the German author champions for world peace, global understanding, and social justice. These themes can all be found in her three best-known works, the novels *The Last Children of Schevenborn, Fall-Out,* and *The Final Journey.* The first two of these involve the dangers of nuclear technology. *The Last Children of Schevenborn,* an award-winning best-seller in Europe, is about the survivors of a nuclear attack told from the point of view of a boy named Roland. Having lived through World War II, the author is familiar with all the terrifying aspects of war, and she describes the horrors young Roland experiences in graphic detail. The boy witnesses the decay of his community and way of life as his friends and family die around him, and he himself suffers from radiation sickness. Pausewang offers no happy conclusions for her readers; instead, the book is a stern warning for humanity. "*Schevenborn* is a terrible, frightening, haunting story, all too convincing," declared *Canadian Materials* contributor Joan McGrath, while *Books for Keeps* critic David Bennett called the story a "bleak but gripping read."

Fall-Out is also a warning against the dangers of the nuclear world, but in this case, a power plant accident is the source of the tragedy. The novel opens with an accident at a reactor near young Janna's home. Janna is alone with her brother Uli, and the two siblings try to escape on their own. Pausewang adds tragedy upon tragedy as Uli is killed by a car, then Janna learns that the rest of her family has died in the power plant accident, and Janna becomes sick from radiation poisoning. The author contrasts people's typical reactions to these events by having Janna stay at the homes of two different aunts. One aunt encourages Janna to cover her head, which has become bald because of the radiation, and pretend that everything is fine; the other aunt and her family become activists who try to force people to recognize the dangers they face. By the end of the story, Janna has taken it upon herself to be a spokesperson for her fellow victims, who call themselves the Hibakusha after those who died at Hiroshima.

Pausewang clearly favors the side of the activists, rather than those who try to hide from the facts. Although many reviewers noted the grimness of the story, many agree, as Jane Inglis noted in *School Librarian,* that it "allows considerable discussion of the issues." The novel, as Roger Sutton pointed out in *Bulletin of the Center for Children's Books,* ends with "no real hope, false or otherwise." Calling the book a "realistic psychological novel" in a *Voice for Youth Advocates* review, Francine Canfield praised the "crisp and assertive language [which] explores the unspoken horror of the unknown long-term effects of exposure to radiation without overwhelming the plot." *Booklist* reviewer Janice Del Negro also noted the author's ability to create a swift-moving plot, claiming "the novel is a grim, unflinching, but fast-paced disaster tale with a strong message that does not overwhelm either the story or the characters."

Pausewang next tackled the heavy subject of the Holocaust with her novel *The Final Journey,* which takes place on a train bound for a concentration camp during World War II. Again, the author shows no mercy to her audience, as young Alice is shut up in a train cattle-car with her grandfather and a boy she has befriended. Her grandfather dies during the journey, and her friend is killed during an escape attempt. Pausewang describes with unrelenting honesty the sickening conditions in the car as corpses begin to pile up. *Horn Book* contributor Roger Sutton called the book "unsubtle, even crude," while also holding that, for this story, such an approach actually helps get the message across. "Relentless is certainly an understatement for this horrific, claustrophobic story," wrote Sutton, "but you have to put the word honest in there as well."

Pausewang offers no happy endings in these three books, her most popular and acclaimed works. Her brutal frankness in portraying ugly events makes for disturbing reading, but her messages are ones readers need to hear.

Works Cited

Bennett, David, review of *The Children of Schevenborn, Books for Keeps,* January, 1991, p. 9.

Canfield, Francine, review of *Fall-Out, Voice of Youth Advocates,* October, 1995, pp. 222-23.

Del Negro, Janice, review of *Fall-Out, Booklist,* September 15, 1995, p. 154.

Inglis, Jane, review of *Fall-Out, School Librarian,* August, 1995, pp. 118-19.

McGrath, Joan, review of *The Children of Schevenborn, Canadian Materials,* January, 1989, p. 19.

Sutton, Roger, review of *Fall-Out, Bulletin of the Center for Children's Books,* September, 1995, p. 23.

Sutton, Roger, review of *The Final Journey, Horn Book,* January-February, 1997, p. 66.

For More Information See

PERIODICALS

Publishers Weekly, May 29, 1995, p. 86.

*   *   *

PEARCE, Margaret (Jacquelyn Webb)

Personal

Surname legally changed from Brown to Pearce; born in Melbourne, Australia; daughter of William Charles (an inventor) and Olive Elizabeth (a Cornelli lace machine embroiderer; maiden name, Webb) Brown; married William McDonald, April 14, 1952 (divorced July 7, 1977); children: two sons, two daughters. *Education:* Monash University, B.A., 1979, and further study. *Politics:* "Leftish." *Religion:* United Church of England. *Hobbies and other interests:* Walking, swimming, reading, sketching.

Addresses

Home—P.O. Box 253, Belgrane 3160, Victoria, Australia. *Agent*—Dorothy Lumley, Dorian Literary Agency, Upper Thornehill, 24 Church Rd., St. Mary Church, Torquay, Devon TQ1 4QY, England.

Career

Writer.

Writings

FOR CHILDREN

The Circus Runaways, Puffin (Harmondsworth, England), 1978.

Altar of Shulaani: An Exciting Science Fiction Adventure, Penguin (Ringwood, Australia), 1981.

Wanted! A Horse, Ashton Scholastic (Gosford, Australia), 1983.

The Misfit, Kangaroo Press (Kenthurst, Australia), 1984.

One Day in the Life of a Maidservant (series), Macmillan (Melbourne, Australia), 1987.

The Castle Hill Uprising (series), Macmillan, 1987.

Marmaduke, Martin Educational (Cammeray, Australia), 1988.

Weekend of Herman John (series), Macmillan, 1989.

When Doggo Went Purple, Collins (Sydney, Australia), 1989.

The Secret in the Compost Bin, Omnibus (Norwood, Australia), 1990.

Margaret Pearce, with grandchild.

The Convertible Couch, Random House (Milsons Point, Australia), 1991.

Caught in Willaburra, Millennium Books (Newtown, Australia), 1992.

The Old Man in the Park, Random House, 1992.

Bolton Road Spy Catchers, Millennium Books, 1992.

Rilla and the School Play, Scholastic, 1997.

Birthday Surprise, Thomas Nelson (Melbourne, Australia), 1998.

The Edge of Forever, Literary Mouse Press (Kalamunda, Australia), 1999.

Party Poopers, Macmillan Education (Victoria, Australia), in press.

FOR YOUNG ADULTS

The Look of Love, Penguin, 1988.

Bobby and Frank (novelization of "Home and Away" television show), Collins, 1989.

Three's a Crowd, Transworld (Neutral Bay, Australia), 1991.

The Togetherness Routine, Longman Cheshire, 1991.

Weekend Territory, Longman Cheshire, 1993.

The Secret of the Third Seal, Longman Cheshire, 1995.

FOR ADULTS; ROMANCE NOVELS; AS JACQUELINE WEBB

The Lonely Heart, Robert Hale (London, England), 1990.

Roses Are for Romance, Robert Hale, 1991.

Shadows over Taralon, Robert Hale, 1992.

OTHER

Work represented in anthologies.

Sidelights

Margaret Pearce told *SATA:* "My father died when I was young. He ended up in the public service as a postal worker after his excursion in World War I, but he was more preoccupied with his inventions than with his regular income. My mother remained a widow and raised my brother and me alone. I moved into reading and books at about age seven, and I didn't move out of it. I seemed to spend most of my childhood sick, so I didn't spend that much time at any of the schools I was supposed to attend.

"My father's mother had been an actress and manager, who adapted stories for her stage productions. I started writing under the pseudonym of her name. As that side of the family was very supportive about my writing, I changed my name by deed poll to her name, Pearce, after my divorce and before I graduated from university.

"On my mother's side, my grandfather was a saddle maker until saddles went out of fashion, then he worked at a brewery for the rest of his life. All his forebears were weavers (dating back to the time they skipped the south of France for England after the revocation of the Treaty of Nantes) until they hit Australia in the 1850s and ended up mining for gold at Ballarat. My grandmother came from Cornwall and descended from a long line of miners. My mother carried on the family craft tradition by being apprenticed as a Cornelli machinist (this type of work is all done by computerized sewing machines nowadays).

"I used to read obsessively. It only had to have print on it to be readable. I read through friends' and relatives' bookshelves, and through begged and borrowed books and school and church libraries. There was no supervision or direction of my reading, so I read everything. If I was reading, it meant I was out of mischief, and my mother, who never found time to read, never checked what I read.

"I must have started writing and illustrating stories to amuse younger cousins at about age eleven. I remember them being awful stories; my cousins must have been very tolerant. I wanted to be an artist, but my mother steered me into doing a commercial course. I evolved into doing secretarial work, put a few years in public service, and ended up as a copywriter in an advertising agency before marrying and having four children. Then I moved into temporary office work for years before, through, and after my divorce, until I stopped working to start studying.

"After my degree, I got halfway through a diploma of education before dropping out. I like kids, but I am sure that I am not teacher material. I applied for and got a grant to write, and I have been writing consistently ever since. I also taught writing part-time for two years.

"My writing routine is similar to early toilet training. I sit in front of my blank screen every morning until I produce something. When my mind actually functions, my characters move along effortlessly, and I find writing very contenting. When I get writer's block, it is as if I have got something seriously wrong with me, like spinal paralysis, and my whole existence comes to a dead stop.

"I find it very comfortable to write for the upper primary/lower secondary level, first for my children and now for my grandchildren. I also like experimenting with different levels, and I enjoy reading and writing fantasy and science fiction."

For More Information See

PERIODICALS

Magpies, March, 1991, p. 29; November, 1991, p. 30.

*   *   *

POTTER, Margaret (Newman) 1926-1998
(Anne Betteridge, Anne Melville)

OBITUARY NOTICE—See index for *SATA* sketch: Born June 21, 1926, in London, England; died August 26, 1998. Upon graduation from secondary school, Potter received a scholarship to St. Hugh's College, Oxford, where she honed her research and writing skills. Potter taught in Egypt and England from 1947 to 1950 and, after marrying publisher R. Jeremy Potter, edited *The*

King's Messenger, a children's magazine, from 1950 to 1955. Thereafter, writing under several names, she penned more than fifty books ranging from romance and historical novels to family sagas. A prolific author, Potter published books nearly every year from the 1960s through the 1980s. In addition to her many novels for adults, she wrote a variety of books for children, including *The Touch-and-Go Year, The Story of the Stolen Necklace, Trouble on Sunday, Tony's Special Place,* and *Tilly and the Princess.* Potter wrote romance novels under the pseudonym Anne Betteridge, and penned her well-known tales of the Lorimer family, including *The Lorimer Line, Lorimers in Love* and *The Last of the Lorimers,* under the name Anne Melville. In addition to her books, Potter contributed many short stories to magazines. She continued to write until the time of her death. Potter's last book, *Debutante Daughters,* is to be published in 1999 under the name Anne Melville.

OBITUARIES AND OTHER SOURCES:

PERIODICALS

Times (London), September 11, 1998.

* * *

PRINGLE, Laurence (Patrick) 1935-
(Sean Edmund, Laurence P. Pringle)

Personal

Born November 26, 1935, in Rochester, NY; son of Laurence Erin Pringle (a real estate agent) and Marleah (a homemaker; maiden name, Rosehill) Pringle; married Judith Malanowicz (a librarian), June 23, 1962 (divorced, 1970); married Alison Newhouse (a freelance editor), July 14, 1971 (divorced, c. 1974); married Susan Klein (a teacher), March 13, 1983; children: (first marriage) Heidi, Jeffrey, Sean; (third marriage) Jesse, Rebecca. *Education:* Cornell University, B.S., 1958; University of Massachusetts, M.S., 1960; Syracuse University, doctoral studies, 1960-62. *Hobbies and other interests:* Photography, films, sports, surf fishing.

Addresses

Home—P. O. Box 252, West Nyack, NY 10994.

Career

Freelance writer and photographer; also a wildlife biologist and educator. Lima Central School, high school science teacher, Lima, NY, 1961-62; American Museum of Natural History, *Nature and Science* (children's magazine), New York City, associate editor, 1963-65, senior editor, 1965-67, executive editor, 1967-70; New School for Social Research, faculty member, 1976-78; Kean college of New Jersey, Union, writer in residence, 1985-86; *Highlights for Children* Writers Workshop, faculty member, 1985—.

Awards, Honors

New Jersey Institute of Technology Award, 1970, for *The Only Earth We Have;* honor book designation, New York Academy of Sciences, for *Natural Fire,* 1980; Distinguished Alumnus Award, University of Massachusetts Department of Forestry and Wildlife Management, 1981; John Burroughs List of Nature Books for Young Readers, 1991, for *Batman: Exploring the World of Bats,* 1993, *Jackal Woman: Exploring the World of Jackals,* and 1997, for *An Extraordinary Life: The Story of a Monarch Butterfly;* A Book Can Develop Empathy Award, New York State Humane Association, 1991, for *Batman: Exploring the World of Bats;* Orbis Pictus Award for Outstanding Nonfiction for Children (honor book), National Council of Teachers of English, 1996, for *Dolphin Man: Exploring the World of Dolphins,* and 1998, for *An Extraordinary Life: The Story of a Monarch Butterfly.* Pringle also received a Special Conservation Award, National Wildlife Federation, 1978, the Eva L. Gordon Award, American Nature Society, 1983, and the Nonfiction Award, *Washington Post*/Children's Book Council, 1999, for his body of work.

Laurence Pringle

Writings

FOR YOUNG PEOPLE; NONFICTION

Dinosaurs and Their World, Harcourt, 1968.

The Only Earth We Have, Macmillan, 1969.

(Editor under name Laurence P. Pringle) *Discovering the Outdoors: A Nature and Science Guide to Investigating Life in Fields, Forests, and Ponds,* Natural History Press, 1969.

(Editor) *Discovering Nature Indoors: A Nature and Science Guide to Investigations with Small Animals,* Natural History Press, 1970.

(And photographer) *From Field to Forest: How Plants and Animals Change the Land,* World, 1970.

(And photographer) *In a Beaver Valley: How Beavers Change the Land,* World, 1970.

Cockroaches: Here, There, Everywhere, illustrated by James and Ruth McCrea, Crowell, 1970.

Ecology: Science of Survival, Macmillan, 1971.

One Earth, Many People: The Challenge of Human Population, Macmillan, 1971.

From Pond to Prairie: The Changing World of a Pond and Its Life, illustrated by Karl W. Stuecklen, Macmillan, 1972.

Pests and People: The Search for Sensible Pest Control, Macmillan, 1972.

This Is a River: Exploring an Ecosystem, Macmillan, 1972.

Estuaries: Where Rivers Meet the Sea, Macmillan, 1973.

Follow a Fisher, illustrated by Tony Chen, Crowell, 1973.

Into the Woods: Exploring the Forest Ecosystem, Macmillan, 1973.

Twist, Wiggle, and Squirm: A Book about Earthworms, illustrated by Peter Parnall, Crowell, 1973.

Recycling Resources, Macmillan, 1974.

Chains, Webs, and Pyramids: The Flow of Energy in Nature, illustrated by Jan Adkins, Crowell, 1975.

City and Suburb: Exploring an Ecosystem, Macmillan, 1975.

Energy: Power for People, Macmillan, 1975.

Water Plants, illustrated by Kazue Mizumura, Crowell, 1975.

Listen to the Crows, illustrated by Ted Lewin, Crowell, 1976.

The Minnow Family: Chubs, Dace, Minnows, and Shiners, illustrated by Dot and Sy Barlowe, Morrow, 1976.

Our Hungry Earth: The World Food Crisis, Macmillan, 1976.

Animals and Their Niches: How Species Share Resources, illustrated by Leslie Morrill, Morrow, 1977.

The Controversial Coyote: Predation, Politics, and Ecology, Harcourt, 1977.

Death Is Natural, Four Winds, 1977.

The Gentle Desert: Exploring an Ecosystem, Macmillan, 1977.

The Hidden World: Life under a Rock, illustrated by Erick Ingraham, Macmillan, 1977.

Dinosaurs and People: Fossils, Facts, and Fantasies, Harcourt, 1978.

The Economic Growth Debate: Are There Limits to Growth?, Watts, 1978.

Wild Foods: A Beginner's Guide to Identifying, Harvesting, and Cooking Safe and Tasty Plants from the Outdoors, illustrated by Paul Breeden, Four Winds, 1978.

Natural Fire: Its Ecology in Forests, Morrow, 1979.

Nuclear Power: From Physics to Politics, Macmillan, 1979.

Lives at Stake: The Science and Politics of Environmental Health, Macmillan, 1980.

Frost Hollows and Other Microclimates, Morrow, 1981.

What Shall We Do with the Land?: Choices for America, Crowell, 1981.

Vampire Bats, Morrow, 1982.

Water: The Next Great Resource Battle, Macmillan, 1982.

Being a Plant, illustrated by Robin Brickman, Crowell, 1983.

"The Earth Is Flat"—and Other Great Mistakes, illustrated by Steve Miller, Morrow, 1983.

Feral: Tame Animals Gone Wild, Macmillan, 1983.

Radiation: Waves and Particles/Benefits and Risks, Enslow (Hillside, NJ), 1983.

Wolfman: Exploring the World of Wolves, Scribner, 1983.

Animals at Play, Harcourt, 1985.

Nuclear War: From Hiroshima to Nuclear Winter, Enslow, 1985.

Here Come the Killer Bees, Morrow, 1986, revised edition published as *Killer Bees,* 1990.

Throwing Things Away: From Middens to Resource Recovery, Crowell, 1986.

Home: How Animals Find Comfort and Safety, Scribner, 1987.

Restoring Our Earth, Enslow, 1987.

Rain of Troubles: The Science and Politics of Acid Rain, Macmillan, 1988.

The Animal Rights Controversy, Harcourt, 1989.

Bearman: Exploring the World of Black Bears, photographs by Lynn Rogers, Scribner, 1989.

Nuclear Energy: Troubled Past, Uncertain Future, Macmillan, 1989.

Living in a Risky World, Morrow, 1989.

The Golden Book of Insects and Spiders, illustrated by James Spence, Western Publishing, 1990.

Global Warming: Assessing the Greenhouse Threat, Arcade, 1990.

Saving Our Wildlife, Enslow, 1990.

Batman: Exploring the World of Bats, photographs by Merlin D. Tuttle, Scribner, 1991.

Living Treasure: Saving Earth's Threatened Biodiversity, illustrated by Irene Brady, Morrow, 1991.

Antarctica: The Last Unspoiled Continent, Simon & Schuster, 1992.

The Golden Book of Volcanoes, Earthquakes, and Powerful Storms, illustrated by Tom LaPadula, Western Publishing, 1992.

Oil Spills: Damage, Recovery, and Prevention, Morrow, 1993.

Chemical and Biological Warfare: The Cruelest Weapons, Enslow, 1993.

Jackal Woman: Exploring the World of Jackals, photographs by Patricia D. Moehlman, Macmillan, 1993.

Scorpion Man: Exploring the World of Scorpions, photographs by Gary A. Polis, Scribner, 1994.

Fire in the Forest: A Cycle of Growth and Renewal, illustrated by Bob Marstall, Simon & Schuster, 1995.

Dinosaurs!: Strange and Wonderful, illustrated by Carol Heyer, Boyds Mills Press (Honesdale, PA), 1995.

Coral Reefs: Earth's Undersea Treasures, Simon & Schuster, 1995.

Vanishing Ozone: Protecting Earth from Ultraviolet Radiation, Morrow, 1995.

Dolphin Man: Exploring the World of Dolphins, Atheneum, 1995.

Taking Care of the Earth: Kids in Action, illustrated by Bobbie Moore, Boyds Mills Press, 1996.

Smoking: A Risky Business, Morrow, 1996.

An Extraordinary Life: The Story of a Monarch Butterfly, illustrated by Bob Marstall, Orchard Books, 1997.

Elephant Woman: Cynthia Moss Explores the World of Elephants, photographs by Cynthia Moss, Atheneum, 1997.

Nature!: Wild and Wonderful (autobiography), photographs by Tim Holmstrom, Richard C. Owen (Katonah, NY), 1997.

Everyone Has a Bellybutton: Your Life Before You Were Born, illustrated by Clare Wood, Boyds Mills Press, 1997.

Drinking: A Risky Business, Morrow, 1997.

Animal Monsters: The Truth about Scary Creatures, Marshall Cavendish, 1997.

One Room School, illustrated by Barbara Garrison, Boyds Mills Press, 1998.

Bats: Strange and Wonderful!, Boyds Mills, in press.

FICTION; PICTURE BOOKS

Jesse Builds a Road, illustrated by Leslie Holt Morrill, Macmillan, 1989.

Octopus Hug, illustrated by Kate Salley Palmer, Boyds Mills, 1993.

Naming the Cat, illustrated by Katherine Potter, Walker, 1997.

OTHER NONFICTION

(And photographer) *Wild River* (adult nonfiction) Lippincott (Philadelphia), 1972.

(With editors of Time-Life Books) *Rivers and Lakes* (adult nonfiction) Time-Life (New York City), 1985.

OTHER

Contributor to *Audubon, Ranger Rick's Nature Magazine* (sometimes under the pseudonym Sean Edmund), *Highlights for Children,* and *Smithsonian;* also contributor of essays to professional magazines on children's literature and education and to books including *Celebrating Children's Books: Essays on Children's Literature in Honor of Zena Sutherland,* edited by Betsy Hearne and Marilyn Kaye, Lothrop, 1974; *The Voice of the Narrator in Children's Literature,* edited by Charlotte Otten and Gary Schmidt, Greenwood, 1989; *Nonfiction for Young Adults: From Delight to Wisdom,* edited by Betty Carter and Richard Abrahamson, Oryx, 1990; *Vital Connections: Children, Science, and Books,* edited by Wendy Saul and Sybille Jagusch, Heinemann, 1991. Contributor of forward to *Macmillan Children's Guide to Endangered Animals* by Roger Few, Simon & Schuster, 1993.

Work in Progress

A Dragon in the Sky, for Orchard; *Environmental Movement,* for Morrow; *Gambling,* for Morrow.

Sidelights

A prolific author of nonfiction, fiction, and picture books, as well as a photographer, Laurence Pringle is considered one of the most distinguished writers of informational books for readers from the early primary grades through high school. A former wildlife biologist who has created more than eighty books for children and young adults, he is recognized for writing authoritative, well-researched works that inform his audience about the natural sciences and the environment in a manner considered both accurate and interesting. Pringle is noted for transforming complex material on scientific and ecological subjects into lucid, balanced overviews of sophisticated topics, some of which are not often treated in books for children. Several of the author's titles are regarded as definitive references that are among the best literature available on their subjects. Characteristically, Pringle's works provide information on nature and the environment while emphasizing the dangers that threaten the earth and its resources. Several of these books are about the world's rivers, forests, oceans, and deserts as well as about man-made hazards such as nuclear energy, nuclear war, global warming, oil spills, pollution, acid rain, and radiation. Pringle also writes about what we can do to protect our environment, such as recycling, fighting world hunger, and saving the earth's biodiversity. In addition, he has addressed such subjects as mammals, insects, birds, and fish as well as related topics, including the animal rights movement and what happens to tame animals released in the wild; he is also the author of a collection of biographies of prominent

When Jesse and Becky's mother goes out for the night, their dad becomes the leader of an evening of games. (Cover illustration by Kate Salley Palmer.)

naturalists who have worked with such animals as wolves, scorpions, bats, dolphins, and elephants.

Pringle takes a holistic approach to his subjects, employing direct, factual outlines that include histories, habits, and current findings as well as suggestions for further observation. While some of his books are straightforward accounts of his subjects, others—particularly those that explore controversial issues—take a more questioning approach. In these works, the author is credited for presenting strong cases backed with examples and statistics. Even though Pringle is sympathetic to a certain view, he presents arguments from opposing sides in a way that is considered both objective and dispassionate. As a literary stylist, Pringle is commended for the clarity and fluidity of his texts, which are praised for their lack of both condescension and scientific jargon. He is also credited for the quality of his photographs, which most often represent wildlife and natural settings. Although some critics of certain titles have claimed that Pringle's methods are too simplistic, most reviewers laud the author for the freshness of his approach and acknowledge his books as fascinating and valuable resources for both students and teachers. Writing in *Children and Books,* May Hill Arbuthnot, Dianne L. Monson, and Zena Sutherland noted that Pringle combines "the ability to explain logical relationships and the succinct marshalling of facts that clarify such relationships, especially when they are intricate.... The breadth of Pringle's interests is indicated by the fact that, although he trained as a wildlife biologist, his books often consider the total environment, sociological factors, and legal or critical implications of biological problems." A critic in *Kirkus Reviews* added, "Whatever the issue, Pringle can be counted on to draw the lines, identify the parties, make the connections among interest, action, and effect—and demonstrate an approach that young readers can profitably apply to other issues." Writing in *Children's Books and Their Creators,* Susan M. Maguire commented, "Pringle strives to correct popular but incorrect theories about everything from dinosaurs to killer bees. A firm believer in challenging authority, he encourages young readers always to keep an open mind and never stop exploring new alternatives for old scenarios. His books can be counted on to provide clear, accurate, thoughtful perspectives on complex topics."

Born in Rochester, New York, Pringle grew up in Mendon, a rural town just south of his birthplace; in his essay in *Something about the Author Autobiography Series (SAAS),* the author stated, "I was a country boy." His father, Laurence Erin Pringle, was born in Brooklyn and, after moving upstate, worked on the assembly line at Eastman Kodak for twenty-one years; however, his son wrote in *SAAS,* "his heart was in the country." Pringle's mother Marleah learned to cook fish and game, while Larry and his older brother Gary explored the woods and pasture that comprised the abundant land around their home. Pringle was educated in a one-room schoolhouse, where a single teacher covered the first through eighth grades; in 1998, he wrote a book based on his experience, *One Room School.* In 1945, the schoolhouse closed, and Pringle was sent to a central school in Honeoye Falls, a village of approximately two thousand. This school, the author recalled in *SAAS,* "had a library ... that fed my hunger for books. As I edged toward adolescence, books became increasingly important. Whether fiction or nonfiction, they allowed me to escape from an often unhappy reality." The son of parents who had difficulty expressing love, Pringle felt, as he wrote in *SAAS,* "neglected, unappreciated, lonely. I found comfort outdoors, and spent many hours roaming the Hopper Hills, exploring its forests, springs, and ponds." One day, Pringle found a book at home that, he wrote in *SAAS,* "seemed to awaken a deeper interest in the natural world. One May day I noticed some little birds flitting among the half-formed leaves of an elm. Their colors were so striking: I wondered what they were. We didn't have many books, but did have one introductory guide to birds, and in it were the species of warblers I had seen. I was hooked."

Pringle began to focus on birds, attracting and identifying them and finding their nests; later, he began building birdhouses and subscribing to *Audubon* magazine, which, he says, "may have triggered my interest in wildlife photography." When he was twelve, Pringle received a camera—a Kodak Baby Brownie; he was later given a Kodak Hawkeye and, he wrote, "did the best I could photographing bird nests and wildflowers." About the same time, Pringle received his first rifle, a .22, "a routine step in that place and time, when virtually all boys (and a good many girls) were encouraged to become hunters," he noted in *SAAS.* After he shot his first squirrel, Pringle experienced mixed feelings, "including regret as I watched life fade from his eyes." However, successful hunting earned respect and, as the author acknowledged in *SAAS,* "I was hungry to succeed at something." Pringle began hunting, trapping, and fishing, sometimes with his father and brother. At fifteen, he began keeping a nature journal; in reviewing his notes, Pringle noted in *SAAS,* "I was already moving beyond the basic 'what species is that?' level of interest to 'why' and 'how' questions about nature." In 1951, Pringle and his family, which also included sisters Marleah Anne and Linda Mary, moved to Rush, New York, where his father, now a real estate agent, could be closer to his customers. "At our new home," Pringle wrote in *SAAS,* "I put hundreds of hours into habitat improvement on our five acres of land, actually digging a small pond with an earthen dam, building birdhouses and bird feeders, transplanting shrubs and wildflowers." As a teen, Pringle enjoyed reading and baseball as well as activities connected with nature. In 1952, he submitted an article to the "True Experiences and Camping Trips" section of *Open Road* magazine, a periodical similar to *Boys' Life.* The article described Pringle's observations of crow behavior; later, the author—who was paid five dollars by *Open Road* for his contribution—wrote in *SAAS,* "I learned that my explanation was dead wrong."

After graduating from high school, Pringle worked for a year in the kitchen of the county hospital while continuing to hunt, trap, study birds, and follow base-

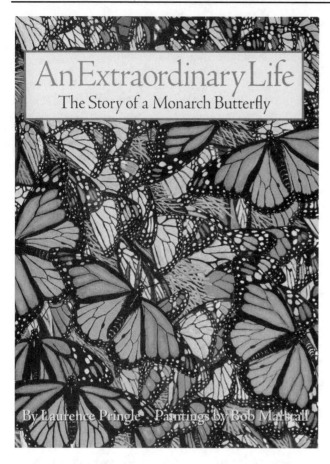

Pringle's narrative recounts the life cycle of a female monarch butterfly, including her migration flight from New England to Mexico and back again. (Cover illustration by Bob Marstall.)

ball. In 1954, he began life as a freshman at Cornell University, majoring in wildlife conservation. Of his college experience, Pringle wrote in *SAAS,* "Many successes in my life—and a few disasters—have come as total surprises, as something I never dreamed of. Cornell was certainly an extraordinary surprise, one that has opened doors to so many adventures of mind, body, and spirit." At Cornell, Pringle's interest in nature was nurtured by his classes and by vacations with friends. For example, he spent winter holidays in the Adirondack Mountains following the trails of fishers—fox-sized members of the weasel family—and other wildlife; in 1973, he published *Follow a Fisher,* a work that shows how following a fisher's tracks leads to information about its hunting, eating, mating, and mothering habits. While in college, Pringle took two courses on writing nonfiction for magazines and won a campus photography contest with a nature photo he had taken; shortly after graduation, Pringle had an article published in *The Conservationist,* the environmental magazine of New York State. The author wrote in *SAAS,* "Having a byline with an article and credit lines with photographs felt so good; I began to aim for national outdoor magazines." In 1958, he began a master's degree program at the University of Massachusetts at Amherst. His research on cottontails earned Pringle a degree although he contin-

ued to pursue his interest in mammalian predators. While trapping, tagging, and releasing bobcats, he captured several coyotes, among the first to be caught and identified in Massachusetts. In 1977, the author published *The Controversial Coyote: Predation, Politics, and Ecology,* a work that attempts to separate fact from fiction regarding coyotes and other predators. Pringle went to Syracuse University to earn his Ph.D. in wildlife biology; however, after having several more of his nonfiction articles and photographs published, Pringle, as he wrote in *SAAS,* "had reached a turning point and made a choice I have never regretted—by early 1961 I had given up on the doctorate and was enrolled in journalism."

Shortly after entering the School of Journalism at Syracuse, Pringle contracted hepatitis. After recovering at home, he began teaching science at Lima Central School in Lima, New York. Pringle wrote in *SAAS,* "I was the entire science department of this small school, teaching physics, biology, general science, plus a half-year of science for the seventh and eighth grades." In 1962, Pringle married librarian Judith Malanowicz; the couple later had three children, Heidi, Jeffrey, and Sean. In 1992, Pringle took an education class at Syracuse as well as a course in article marketing taught by an editor at the magazine *Better Homes and Gardens;* Pringle noted in *SAAS* that each "of three articles I began in his class was published." In 1963, Pringle was looking for a job; he found one opening, an editorial position with the fledgling magazine *Nature & Science,* a periodical for children published by the American Museum of Natural History. Shortly after writing an article for editor Roy A. Gallant, Pringle was hired as associate editor. He wrote in *SAAS,* "If I had found no openings, I might have given up on the dream of working for a magazine and become a science teacher. Or, if I had found a job with a magazine for adults, I might have never written for young readers." In his essay in *Fourth Book of Junior Authors and Illustrators,* Pringle revealed, "Most of what I know about writing, especially writing for children, was learned during the seven years that *Nature & Science* existed"; he added, "At *Nature & Science,* we took great care that both text and illustrations were clear and accurate, and I apply the same standards to my books." Pringle became a senior editor and then executive editor of *Nature & Science* before the magazine's demise in 1970. Roy Gallant, himself a popular author of science books for children, suggested to Pringle that he begin writing works for the young.

In 1968, he published his first book, *Dinosaurs and Their World.* A basic treatment of selected dinosaurs, their evolution, and how paleontologists learn about them, *Dinosaurs and Their World* was praised by a reviewer in *Science Books:* "There are in print a great many dinosaur books for children, but this is one of the best because it is a well-researched and carefully written narrative.... Irrespective of how many dinosaur books elementary and public libraries own, they need this one." Writing in *SAAS,* Pringle noted that this book "in both hardcover and paperback editions sold more than 70,000 copies and stayed in print long after some of my later titles had expired." Pringle followed *Dinosaurs and Their World* with *The Only Earth We Have,* a work that outlines the dangers to the earth from pollution, solid wastes, pesticides, and the disruption of animal and plant communities. A critic in *Kirkus Reviews* noted, "In summary form, what every conservationist would like every child to absorb . . . . [T]his is as good a way to get young or older people to react as any we have." In 1971, Pringle explored the issue of human population growth in *One Earth, Many People,* a work which a critic in *Kirkus Reviews* claimed "should be required reading for the generation that stands to inherit the earth and its problems." A reviewer in *Science Books* added, "Rarely does a book present so completely in so little space the basic components of population dynamics."

During the remainder of the 1970s, Pringle continued to publish well-received titles on the earth and its animals. By 1974, he had received a divorce from his first wife, married and divorced his second, and had become a freelance writer. *Listen to the Crows,* the first of several of the author's works to be named a Notable Book by the American Library Association, was published in 1976. Through his explanation of the various forms of crow communication, Pringle demonstrates that the oft-

maligned crow is one of the most intelligent of birds. A critic in *Kirkus Reviews* commented, "Trust Laurence Pringle to avoid the lockstep animal biography formulas. His appreciation for the common but redoubtable crow avoids generalities and focuses on the amazing versatility of the bird's voice box . . . ." Pringle soon published another of his most highly regarded books, *Death Is Natural.* This work, which explains how death in the plant and animal worlds is a necessary part of nature's recycling process, was called "[a] remarkable book for children as well as some adults!" by R. Gregory Belcher of *Appraisal: Science Books for Young People.* Pringle received a special conservation award from the National Wildlife Federation in 1978; in the words of the Federation, the author was honored for being "the nation's leading writer of books on biological and environmental issues for young people."

In 1979, Pringle published two titles that are considered among his most controversial, *Natural Fire: Its Ecology in Forests* and *Nuclear Power: From Physics to Politics.* In *Natural Fire,* the author explains that since forest fires are a natural force in the environment, we may be wrong to prevent fires and to put them out when they begin. Writing in *Horn Book,* Harry C. Stubbs comment-

In **One Room School,** *set in rural New York in 1945, Pringle reminisces about the last year of the one-room schoolhouse of his childhood. (Illustrated by Barbara Garrison.)*

Everyone wanted to pet the cat, so I opened the door of the carrier a bit. Kids reached in. Suddenly the cat bolted out and began to race around the room. He was scared. Everybody, including Miss Boniello, yelled in excitement. The cat dashed from under a desk and leaped away from all the noise . . . right out the window.

Pringle's upbeat story originated from his family's experience searching for a fitting name for the stray cat they adopted. (From Naming the Cat, *illustrated by Katherine Potter.)*

ed, "The book will create a certain amount of fuss," averring that less knowledgeable environmentalists would object. The critic concluded that Pringle "makes a very good case, and the book deserves to be read carefully and thoughtfully." R. Gregory Belcher of *Appraisal* noted that *Natural Fire* is a "provocative introduction" and concluded, "No doubt some of the less informed will argue against the use of this book in schools. They will be wrong." In *Nuclear Power,* Pringle presents an overview of the controversy surrounding his subject; although the author admits to an antinuclear bias, he presents cases both for and against nuclear power in what David G. Hoag of *Appraisal* called "unemotional language." The critic concluded, "If one feels that a children's science book may or should intermix science with politics, then this book ranks high." Writing in *School Library Journal,* Robert Unsworth commented that the author is "clear-headed, crisp, and always informative . . . . Pringle seems to have a sixth sense when it comes to knowing when enough information is enough."

In the early 1980s, Pringle wrote books about such subjects as vampire bats, water, plants, radiation, and scientific misconceptions. In 1983, he married teacher Susan Klein; the couple have two children, Jesse and Rebecca. The decade also saw Pringle continue his exploration of controversial issues; for example, he wrote two books on nuclear power, *Nuclear War: From Hiroshima to Nuclear Winter* and *Nuclear Energy:*

Troubled Past, Uncertain Future, as well as a work on the composition and effects of acid rain, *Rain of Troubles: The Science and Politics of Acid Rain,* and a book on the animal rights issue, *The Animal Rights Controversy.* Reviewers consistently praised the author's objective overviews: for example, in his review of *Nuclear Energy* in *School Library Journal,* Alan Newman claimed that Pringle "gives an exceptionally knowledgeable and thoughtful treatment of a difficult subject" and called the work a "savvy, well-written book on a subject often confused by hysteria and misinformation." Pringle also created books that espoused the preservation of the earth, such as *What Shall We Do with the Land?* and *Restoring Our Earth.* In her review of the former title in *Booklist,* Denise M. Wilms commented that Pringle's "environmentalist bent is quietly apparent throughout" and that his thought-provoking work is "a first-rate starting point for background on a topic that will be increasingly in the news." Julia Rholes of *School Library Journal* concluded that the land use questions are important and that "this thoughtful, well-written book should be a must" wherever "the rights of society as a whole versus individual rights" is seriously discussed. During the 1980s, Pringle also began writing biographies of prominent scientists who work with animals, a series that provides information about both the figures being profiled and the animals they study. In her review of *Batman: Exploring the World of Bats,* the story of mammalogist photographer Merlin Tuttle, Karey Wehner of *School Library Journal* noted that the book "offers a unique perspective on these gentle mammals"; a reviewer in *Chicago Sunday Tribune* commented that Tuttle's "eloquent advocacy will convert most readers." In a review of *Scorpion Man: Exploring the World of Scorpions,* a volume that describes the work of biologist Gary Polis, Lauren Peterson predicted, "Young people with a natural curiosity about animals ... will be captivated." Pringle outlines the life and work of Cynthia Moss, a scientist without formal training, in *Elephant Woman: Cynthia Moss Explores the World of Elephants;* writing in *School Library Journal,* Susan Oliver said, "Cynthia Moss will fascinate young readers.... Elephants are extraordinary animals, Cynthia Moss is a great role model, and Pringle has brought them together in an exciting presentation"; a critic in *Kirkus Reviews* added, "This is an inspirational book for those interested in animal-related vocations ...."

In the 1990s, Pringle created some works that outline not only the damage being done to the earth but also the recuperative and preventative measures being taken on its behalf. For example, in *Living Treasure: Saving Earth's Threatened Biodiversity,* he discusses how millions of species of life are being destroyed as well as how the damage can be stopped. Writing in *Children's Literature Association Quarterly,* Mary Harris Veeder noted that Pringle has a "well-deserved reputation for taking on subjects others might consider impossible for younger audiences, such as global warming" and that the author "has an ear for the specific details that will impress, that are memorable"; Veeder concluded that, as Pringle explains it, biological diversity "means new foods, new medicines, and new knowledge about how all the parts of an ecosystem fit together. And because he can move beyond the notion of the rain forest as a pretty place, ... his readers can begin to understand exactly why the destruction of the rain forest makes no sense." With *Dinosaurs! Strange and Wonderful,* Pringle published the first of his informational picture books for preschoolers and early primary graders. An introduction to the popular creatures that explains basic facts about them as well as recent discoveries of paleontologists, the book "lives up to its subtitle," according to Sally Erhard of *Appraisal,* who added that Pringle's text "is full of just the right amount of information about dinosaurs for the preschool level." Writing in the same issue, Sharon Rizzo concluded, "This marvelous book is a great purchase for any young reader with an interest in dinosaurs." Among the most highly praised of Pringle's books in this genre is *An Extraordinary Life: The Story of a Monarch Butterfly.* Recounting the life cycle of a female monarch—including her migration flight from New England to Mexico—the Orbis Pictus award-winning book was called "superb" and "well-researched" by a critic in *Kirkus Reviews,* who also noted that *An Extraordinary Life* "finds extraordinary science in the everyday life of a butterfly." Susan S. Verner of *Bulletin of the Center for Children's Books* commented, "Pringle's passion for his subject enlivens what might have been just another dry science tome, and his prose is sprinkled with exciting infobits ...."

During the 1990s, Pringle also began writing books on substances, such as tobacco and alcohol, that directly affect people. For example, in *Smoking: A Risky Business,* the author provides, in the words of Mary B. McCarthy of *Voice of Youth Advocates,* a "fascinating history of tobacco and smoking." Calling the work a "strong addition to any collection," McCarthy noted, "Too often, young adult health books nag, harass, and condescend to their intelligent would-be readers. By adopting a journalistic approach, Pringle makes this topic interesting as both a health and political intrigue issue which forces readers to think about their government, health, and personal choices."

Pringle is also the author of two books with autobiographical relevance: *Nature! Wild and Wonderful,* in which he describes his own life in a book intended for readers in the early primary grades, and *One Room School,* an informational picture book about the last year of a one-room schoolhouse in 1945. In a review of *Nature!,* Marlene Gawron of *School Library Journal* commented that Pringle's autobiography "will entertain and inspire young readers," while Evelyn Butrico, writing about *One Room School* in another issue of the same periodical, concluded that it was "a gentle story" for younger children or a "good curriculum aid" for those studying "American history, the history of schools, or life in another era."

In addition to his nonfiction titles, Pringle is the creator of several works of fiction, picture books for younger children. His first book in this genre, *Jesse Builds a Road,* is a picture book inspired by his son of the same name in which a small boy playing with his trucks and bulldozers imagines that he is the driver of the real machines. Writing in *School Library Journal,* Judith Gloyer noted that the "weaving in and out of the imagination and reality is engaging," and readers will be loath to be "pulled back to reality." Pringle's next picture book, *Octopus Hug,* uses the names of his two youngest children, Jesse and Becky, as the names of his characters, who are depicted by illustrator Kate Salley Palmer as African Americans. When the children's mother goes out for the evening, their dad becomes the leader of an evening of games; he becomes a tree for climbing and a mechanical horse and gives the children a huge octopus hug. A critic in *Publishers Weekly* commented, "The imaginative antics that tumble across these pages could constitute a manual for bored babysitters." Another of Pringle's stories, *Naming the Cat,* is based on a family's experience of trying to name the stray cat that has entered their lives; several close calls make it apparent that the cat should be dubbed Lucky. A critic in *Kirkus Reviews* called *Naming the Cat* "a warmly appealing tale" that "lends itself to discussion of such questions as . . . 'Do cats always land on their feet?'." Writing in *Bulletin of the Center for Children's Books,* Janice M. Del Negro called *Naming the Cat* a "light but engaging tale" that is "certain to have listeners bursting to tell the stories of how they named their own family pets."

In evaluating his oeuvre, Pringle wrote in *SAAS:* "My approach to writing a book is like that of a teacher planning to present a subject to students—not 'how many facts, dates, and definitions can I jam into their heads' but 'what are the key ideas and how can I spark some enthusiasm about them.' As my knowledge of ecology has grown, so has my appreciation of diversity, complexity, and the interdependence of living and nonliving things. My books tend to encourage readers to feel a kinship with other living things, and a sense of membership in the earth ecosystem. I have also become an advocate of scientific thinking, or perhaps I should say just clear thinking. Challenging authority and accepted truths is a basic part of the scientific process. It has influenced my choice of book subjects, as I have questioned popular but incorrect notions about forest fires, dinosaurs, vampire bats, wolves, coyotes, and killer bees. These books give readers the truth, to the extent we know it, and also demonstrate that the explorations of science aim at a better understanding of the world. As long as we keep exploring, that understanding can change. I also encourage a skeptical attitude toward the fruits of technology and various vested interests that come into play with such issues as nuclear power, environmental health, biocides, or acid rain. My books on such subjects are never neutral; sometimes I am tempted to lean heavily toward one side of an issue. The temptation to do so is strong when one side mainly represents short-term economic interests and the other mainly represents concern about public health, maintenance of natural diversity and beauty, and the quality of life for both present and future generations. Temptation is also fueled by the knowledge that students are often subjected to the biased publications and films (free to schools), and advertisements of powerful economic interests, and are ill-prepared to detect the distortions and omissions of these materials. My books about controversial issues are not balanced—in the sense of equal space and weight applied to all sides—but are balanced by presenting arguments from the opposing interests, and a reading list that includes a diversity of views for those who want to explore the subject further."

In his essay "Science Done Here" in *Celebrating Children's Books: Essays on Children's Literature in Honor of Zena Sutherland,* Pringle noted, "The doing of science depends on such special human qualities as curiosity, passion, creativity, and veracity. Partly because of these characteristics, science has been called the greatest hope of the human race. Children's books have a vital role to play. They can make science and the universe more accessible to young people. They can stand for and appeal to the finest characteristics and highest aspirations of the human species." In 1987, while a faculty member of the *Highlights for Children* Writers Workshop at the Chautauqua Institution, Pringle spoke about those who write for children in an address he later quoted in *SAAS:* "[P]erhaps in each of our personal histories there are experiences that have left us with a special regard for children. Perhaps we believe, more strongly than most, that what happens to kids is awfully important. Perhaps we feel that it is too late to influence most adults, but that everything that touches a child's life, including magazine articles and books, can

make a difference in the future of that child, and in the future of the world."

Works Cited

Arbuthnot, May Hill, and Dianne L. Monson and Zena Sutherland, *Children and Books,* 6th edition, Scott, Foresman, 1981, pp. 456-57.

Review of *Batman, Chicago Sunday Tribune,* April 14, 1991, p. 6.

Belcher, R. Gregory, review of *Death Is Natural, Appraisal: Science Books for Young People,* winter, 1978, pp. 39-40.

Belcher, review of *Natural Fire, Appraisal: Science Books for Young People,* winter, 1981, p. 52.

Butrico, Evelyn, review of *One Room School, School Library Journal,* April, 1998, pp. 123-24.

Del Negro, Janice M., review of *Naming the Cat, Bulletin of the Center for Children's Books,* October, 1997, p. 65.

Review of *Dinosaurs and Their World, Science Books,* September, 1968, p. 114.

Review of *Elephant Woman, Kirkus Reviews,* November 1, 1997, p. 1648.

Erhard, Sally, review of *Dinosaurs! Strange and Wonderful, Appraisal,* winter, 1995, p. 55.

Review of *An Extraordinary Life, Kirkus Reviews,* February 15, 1997, p. 304.

Gawron, Marlene, review of *Nature! Wild and Wonderful, School Library Journal,* September, 1997, p. 199.

Gloyer, Judith, review of *Jesse Builds a Road, School Library Journal,* February, 1990, p. 78.

Hoag, David G., review of *Nuclear Power, Appraisal: Science Books for Young People,* fall, 1980, p. 54.

Review of *Listen to the Crows, Kirkus Reviews,* October 1, 1976, p. 1099.

Maguire, Susan M., entry in *Children's Books and Their Creators,* edited by Anita Silvey, Houghton Mifflin, 1995, p. 539.

McCarthy, Mary B., review of *Smoking, Voice of Youth Advocates,* April, 1997, p. 60.

Review of *Naming the Cat, Kirkus Reviews,* July 1, 1997, p. 1035.

Newman, Alan, review of *Nuclear Energy, School Library Journal,* April, 1989, pp. 124-25.

Review of *Octopus Hug, Publishers Weekly,* October 4, 1993, p. 79.

Oliver, Susan, review of *Elephant Woman, School Library Journal,* December, 1997, pp. 145-46.

Review of *One Earth, Many People, Kirkus Reviews,* April 15, 1971, p. 448.

Review of *One Earth, Many People, Science Books,* September, 1971, p. 144.

Review of *The Only Earth We Have, Kirkus Reviews,* September 15, 1969, p. 1017.

Peterson, Lauren, review of *Scorpion Man, Booklist,* January 15, 1995, p. 922.

Pringle, Laurence, essay in *Fourth Book of Junior Authors and Illustrators,* edited by Doris De Montreville and Elizabeth D. Crawford, Wilson, 1978, pp. 291-92.

Pringle, "Science Done Here," *Celebrating Children's Books: Essays on Children's Literature in Honor of*

Zena Sutherland, edited by Betsy Hearne and Marilyn Kaye, Lothrop, Lee & Shepard, 1981, pp. 108-15.

Pringle, essay in *Something about the Author Autobiography Series,* Volume 6, Gale, 1988, pp. 219-236.

Rholes, Julia, review of *What Shall We Do with the Land?: Choices for America, School Library Journal,* December, 1981, p. 72.

Rizzo, Sharon, review of *Dinosaurs! Strange and Wonderful, Appraisal,* winter, 1995, pp. 55-56.

Stubbs, Harry C., review of *Natural Fire, Horn Book,* December, 1979, p. 688.

Unsworth, Robert, review of *Nuclear Power, School Library Journal,* April, 1980, pp. 127-28.

Veeder, Mary Harris, "Children's Books on Rain Forests: Beyond the Macaw Mystique," *Children's Literature Association Quarterly,* winter, 1994-95, pp. 165-69.

Verner, Susan S., review of *An Extraordinary Life, Bulletin of the Center for Children's Books,* May, 1997, pp. 333-34.

Wehner, Karey, review of *Batman, School Library Journal,* July, 1991, p. 85.

Review of *What Shall We Do with the Land?, Kirkus Reviews,* November 1, 1981, p. 1350.

Wilms, Denise M., review of *What Shall We Do with the Land?, Booklist,* October 1, 1981, p. 239.

For More Information See

BOOKS

Children's Literature Review, Volume 4, Gale, 1984, pp. 172-86.

Nonfiction for Young Adults: From Delight to Wisdom, Oryx Press, 1990, pp. 71-80.

The Voice of the Narrator in Children's Literature, Greenwood Press, 1989, pp. 371-372, 377-382.

PERIODICALS

Appraisal, winter, 1996, pp. 48-49.

Booklist, September 15, 1993, p. 148; January 1, 1996, p. 812; December 1, 1996, p. 660.

Conservationist, March-April, 1990, p. 52; November-December, 1990, p. 50.

Horn Book, March-April, 1990, p. 222; November-December, 1995, p. 757; May-June, 1997, p. 344; January-February, 1998, p. 95.

Publishers Weekly, October 4, 1993, p. 79; January 2, 1995, p. 77.

School Library Journal, November, 1991, p. 132; March, 1995, pp. 217-18.

Scientific American, December, 1991, p. 150; December, 1993, p. 135.

Tribune Books (Chicago), January 12, 1992, p. 6.

Washington Post Book World, December 6, 1992, p. 18.

Wilson Library Bulletin, January, 1991, p. 109.

—*Sketch by Gerard J. Senick*

*   *   *

PRINGLE, Laurence P.
See PRINGLE, Laurence (Patrick)

R

REIM, Melanie (K.) 1956-

Personal

Born February 10, 1956, in New York. *Education:* State University of New York College at Buffalo, B.S., 1977; Syracuse University, M.F.A., 1984.

Addresses

Home—214 Riverside Dr., New York, NY 10025.

Career

Babel Communications (art and design studio), New York City, principal, 1981-98; Fashion Institute of Technology, New York City, adjunct professor of illustration, 1996—. Printmaker; Altos De Chavon Cultural Center Foundation, visiting faculty. *Member:* Society of Children's Book Writers and Illustrators.

Awards, Honors

Second-place award for illustrated nonfiction, New York Book Show, 1998, for *I Was Born a Slave.*

Illustrator

Jennifer Fleischner, *I Was Born a Slave: The Story of Harriet Jacobs,* Millbrook Press (Brookfield, CT), 1997.

Work in Progress

Vanishing Ark: An Alphabet of Endangered Species; research on rainforests.

Sidelights

Melanie K. Reim told *SATA:* "My career has spanned illustration, design and art direction for magazines, museums, advertising campaigns, special events, on-location reportage and most recently, writing and

Melanie Reims's stylized illustrations decorate Jennifer Fleischner's biographical account of author Harriet Jacobs, who suffered abuse as a slave, escaped, and spent years in hiding before being united with her children. (From I Was Born a Slave: The Story of Harriet Jacobs.*)*

illustrating children's books. I am an adjunct faculty member in the illustration department at the Fashion Institute of Technology in New York City and visiting faculty member at Altos De Chavon Cultural Center Foundation in the Dominican Republic.

"My work incorporates my commitment to drawing, painting, and printmaking, as well as my love for storytelling, folklore, history, myth, and my concern for the environment. With my sketchbook a constant companion, my drawings from my travels to museums, parks, concerts, parades, and exotic trips turn into an endless sea of influences and imagery."

For More Information See

PERIODICALS

School Library Journal, January, 1998, p. 123.

*   *   *

ROBINET, Harriette Gillem 1931-

Personal

Surname is pronounced "ro-bi-*nay*"; born July 14, 1931, in Washington, D.C.; daughter of Richard Avitus (a teacher) and Martha (a teacher; maiden name, Gray) Gillem; married McLouis Joseph Robinet (a health physicist), August 9, 1960; children: Stephen, Philip, Rita, Jonathan, Marsha, Linda. *Education:* College of New Rochelle, B.S., 1953; Catholic University of America, M.S., 1957, Ph.D., 1963. *Politics:* Democrat. *Religion:* Roman Catholic. *Hobbies and other interests:* Pets, bird watching, growing orchids and other plants, knitting, crocheting, sketching.

Addresses

Home and office—214 South Elmwood, Oak Park, IL 60302.

Career

Children's Hospital, Washington, D.C., bacteriologist, 1953-54; Walter Reed Army Medical Center, Washington, D.C., medical bacteriologist, 1954-57, research bacteriologist, 1958-60; Xavier University, New Orleans, LA, instructor in biology, 1957-58; U.S. Army, Quartermaster Corps, civilian food bacteriologist, 1960-62. Freelance writer, 1962—. *Member:* Society of Children's Book Writers and Illustrators, Mystery Writers of America, Sisters in Crime.

Writings

Jay and the Marigold, illustrated by Trudy Scott, Children's Press, 1976.
Ride the Red Cycle, illustrated by David Brown, Houghton Mifflin, 1980.
Children of the Fire, Maxwell Macmillan International, 1991.
Mississippi Chariot, Atheneum, 1994.
If You Please, President Lincoln, Atheneum, 1995.
Washington City Is Burning, Atheneum, 1996.
The Twins, the Pirates, and the Battle of New Orleans, Atheneum, 1997.
Forty Acres and Maybe a Mule, Atheneum, 1998.

Contributor to magazines.

Sidelights

Harriette Gillem Robinet grew up in Washington, D.C., and lived her childhood summers in Arlington, Virginia, near the home of Confederate general Robert E. Lee, where her ancestors had been slaves. In 1960, she and her husband moved to suburban Chicago, Illinois, where she began writing, and the birth of a disabled son proved to be an influential experience. Thus, the main character of *Jay and the Marigold* suffers from cerebral palsy, as was the case with Robinet's own child. Much of her other writing has been influenced, she once told *SATA*, by meeting other handicapped children and adults, who "have shared some of their anger, dreams, and victories." The focus of Robinet's later work, however, has shifted to American historical events, such as the Chicago fire, the Battle of 1812, and the emancipation of the slaves during and after the Civil War, events that she depicts through the lives of her fictional—and mostly African American—characters.

As in *Jay and the Marigold,* the protagonist of *Ride the Red Cycle* is disabled, in this case due to a viral infection received when he was two years old. Eleven-year-old Jerome faces a number of obstacles, of which race is a relatively minor one. Confined to a wheelchair, he cannot speak without slurring his words, but he is determined to participate in a Labor Day parade. "Among the countless recent books about handicapped children," wrote Karen M. Klockner in *Horn Book, Ride the Red Cycle* "stands out for its psychological acuity and compassion without sentimentality."

Harriette Gillem Robinet

The great Chicago fire of 1871 forms the backdrop for *Children of the Fire,* whose main character is named Hallelujah because she was born on an Easter morning. The child of runaway slaves, she is an orphan who grows through her experience in the vast conflagration that sweeps the city: "Selfish and callous at first," Zena Sutherland noted in the *Bulletin of the Center for Children's Books,* "Hallelujah gains sympathetic insight during the course of the fire and the start of the rebuilding." According to a reviewer in *Publishers Weekly,* "Hallelujah emerges as a likeable, spunky heroine who discovers her self-worth during the course of events."

Mississippi Chariot, as its name suggests, takes place further south. Set in rural Mississippi during the Great Depression, its title is taken from a code phrase—itself a reference to the spiritual "Swing Low, Sweet Chariot"—used by slaves to warn each other of impending danger. Twelve-year-old Abraham Lincoln "Shortning Bread" Jackson is trying to bring his father Rufus home from a chain gang, where he has been serving time for a crime he did not commit. Shortning Bread goes to great lengths to help his father, but ultimately the family has to face the fact that in the South in the 1930s, the deck is stacked against them. Despite the help of a white postmaster who helps free Rufus, the Jacksons are forced to head north to Chicago. A commentator in *Kirkus Reviews* concluded that "Robinet's ... character, Shortning, is ingenious and endearing."

Like several of her other books, *If You Please, President Lincoln* offers not merely a story, but an education in American history. The book involves an actual but little-known scheme to deport freed slaves, whom white workers feared would present dangerous competition for jobs, to Haiti in the Caribbean. The title refers to President Abraham Lincoln's Emancipation Proclamation of 1863, which freed the slaves—but only those in the Confederate states—thus doing little to help Robinet's protagonist, Moses, a slave in the pro-Union state of Maryland. Because he is a house servant, Moses is more sophisticated than many of the former "field hands" with whom he finds himself, and he has to overcome feelings of superiority. Like them, he is fooled by the promise of free land in Haiti, and when the former slaves find themselves deported to a virtual desert island, he has to rethink some of his attitudes toward the people around him. Moses becomes a leader among the group and helps them return to America, where he sets about to gain a college education. Of *If You Please, President Lincoln,* a reviewer in *Publishers Weekly* wrote, "Robinet combines desert-island drama with an insightful story of a mind gradually freeing itself." "Moses is a complex protagonist," Elizabeth Bush in the *Bulletin of the Center for Children's Books* observed, "whose struggle to control his own arrogance toward his less gifted and educated comrades lends insight into a legacy of slavery that threatened solidarity within new free black communities."

Virginia, the heroine of *Washington City Is Burning,* is also a house servant with conflicting loyalties. She

Twelve-year-old Pascal, a former slave with a withered arm and leg, attempts to establish a farm and get an education in the years following the Emancipation Proclamation. (Illustrated by Bessie Nickens.)

works for the family of James and Dolley Madison, and when Madison is elected President, she is proud of the fact that she will be a slave in the White House. She is, though, a slave nonetheless, and she cannot ignore the terrible conditions that confront many of her people. Like Hallelujah in *Children of the Fire,* Virginia is present at the scene of a great conflagration, the burning of Washington, D.C. by the British during the War of 1812. Again, critics noted the deft manner in which Robinet handled complex emotions and loyalties: a critic in *Kirkus Reviews,* who pronounced the book, "A fine, multilayered novel," cited the manner in which she portrayed "Dolley, who was brought up to believe slavery was wrong, yet keeps slaves out of political expediency." *Washington City Is Burning* is, in the words of Marie T. Wright in *School Library Journal,* "[a]n above-average choice for historical-fiction shelves."

The War of 1812 also provides the setting for *The Twins, the Pirates, and the Battle of New Orleans.* The twins, Pierre and Andrew, have not spent much time together, because their master has attempted to play one against the other—an example of one of the many ways in which slavery divided the African American community. When their father leaves them on some Gulf Coast swampland after escaping, they are forced to work together to find him, as well as the rest of their family. Challenges abound, as the boys must overcome not only war conditions, but pirates as well. A commentator in *Kirkus Reviews* called the book "[a]n exciting and unusual story about runaway slaves," and noted that, "[y]oung readers will relish the marvelous details of their diet (in which live snails play a large part), their adventurous expeditions across the swamps ... and many other fascinating features of their unconventional life."

Forty Acres and Maybe a Mule also combines a history lesson with a compelling narrative. This time, the story is set in the spring of 1865 and General Sherman has promised both blacks and whites the land that was abandoned after the Civil War. Along with some friends and his brother Gideon, a runaway slave who joined the Union army, twelve-year-old Pascal sets out for Georgia to find a Freedman's Bureau and claim a farm. The ragtag family begins to grow cotton, but encounters night riders, Republican operatives and eventual eviction from the farm due to the reversal of the act that declared blacks could own free land. Not to be deterred, Pascal and company set out to buy land on the Georgia Sea Islands. A reviewer in *Publishers Weekly* noted that "Robinet's resilient characters lend immediacy to the early events of Reconstruction." Of *Forty Acres and Maybe a Mule*, *School Library Journal* reviewer Kathleen Issacs said, "Once again, Robinet has humanized a little-known piece of American history."

Works Cited

Bush, Elizabeth, review of *If You Please, President Lincoln*, *Bulletin of the Center for Children's Books*, September, 1995, p. 27.

Review of *Children of the Fire, Publishers Weekly*, October 18, 1991, pp. 62-63.

Review of *Forty Acres and Maybe a Mule, Publishers Weekly*, November 2, 1998, p. 83.

Review of *If You Please, President Lincoln, Publishers Weekly*, June 26, 1995, p. 107.

Issacs, Kathleen, review of *Forty Acres and Maybe a Mule, School Library Journal*, November, 1998, p. 128.

Klockner, Karen M., review of *Ride the Red Cycle, Horn Book*, June, 1980, p. 303.

Review of *Mississippi Chariot, Kirkus Reviews*, November 15, 1994, p. 1541.

Sutherland, Zena, review of *Children of the Fire, Bulletin of the Center for Children's Books*, September, 1991, p. 20.

Review of *The Twins, the Pirates, and the Battle of New Orleans, Kirkus Reviews*, October 1, 1997, p. 1536.

Review of *Washington City Is Burning, Kirkus Reviews*, July 15, 1996, p. 1055.

Wright, Marie T., review of *Washington City Is Burning, School Library Journal*, November, 1996, p. 110.

For More Information See

PERIODICALS

Booklist, October 15, 1991, p. 441; November 15, 1994, p. 591; August, 1995, p. 1947; November 1, 1996, p. 501.
Bulletin of the Center for Children's Books, November, 1980, p. 63.
Children's Book Review Service, November, 1996, p. 35.
Kirkus Reviews, November 1, 1998, p. 1603.
School Library Journal, December, 1994, pp. 112-13; June, 1995, p. 132; December, 1997, p. 130.
Voice of Youth Advocates, October, 1995, p. 223.

—*Sketch by Judson Knight*

*   *   *

ROY, Gabrielle 1909-1983

Personal

Born March 22, 1909, in St. Boniface, Manitoba, Canada; died of cardiac arrest, July 13, 1983, in Quebec City, Quebec, Canada; daughter of Leon (a colonization agent) and Melina (Landry) Roy; married Marcel Carbotte (a physician), August 30, 1947. *Education:* Educated in Canada; attended Winnipeg Normal School, 1927-29. *Religion:* Roman Catholic.

Career

Writer. Teacher in a Canadian prairie village school, 1928-29, and in St. Boniface, Manitoba, 1929-37; worked as freelance journalist for *Le Bulletin des agriculteurs, Le Jour,* and *Le Canada. Member:* Royal Society of Canada (fellow).

Awards, Honors

Medaille of l'Academie Francaise, 1947; Prix *Femina* (France), 1947, for *Bonheur d'occasion;* received Canadian Governor General's Award for the following: *Bonheur d'occasion, Rue Deschambault,* and *Ces Enfants de ma vie;* Prix Ludger-Duvernay, 1955; Companion of the Order of Canada, 1967; Canadian Council of the Arts Award, 1968; Prix David, 1971; Knight of the Order of Mark Twain.

Writings

NOVELS

Bonheur d'occasion, Societe des Editions Pascal (Montreal), 1945, translation by Hannah Josephson published as *The Tin Flute* (Literary Guild selection), Reynal, 1947.
La Petite Poule d'eau, Beauchemin (Montreal), 1950, translation by Harry L. Binsse published as *Where Nests the Water Hen: A Novel,* Harcourt, 1951, revised French language edition, Beauchemin, 1970.
Alexandre Chenevert, Caissier, Beauchemin, 1954, translation by Binsse published as *The Cashier,* Harcourt, 1955.

Rue Deschambault, Beauchemin, 1955, translation by Binsse published as *Street of Riches,* Harcourt, 1957, reprinted, University of Nebraska Press, 1993.

La Montagne secrete, Beauchemin, 1961, translation by Binsse published as *The Hidden Mountain,* Harcourt, 1962.

La Route d'Altamont, Editions HMH (Montreal), 1966, translation by Joyce Marshall published as *The Road Past Altamont,* Harcourt, 1966.

(With others) *Canada . . .* (includes *La Petite Poule d'eau*), Editions du Burin (St. Cloud, France), 1967.

La Riviere sans repos, Beauchemin, 1970, translation by Marshall published as *Windflower,* McClelland & Stewart, 1970.

Cet ete qui chantait, Editions Francaises, 1972, translation by Marshall published as *Enchanted Summer,* McClelland & Stewart, 1976.

Un Jardin au bout du monde, Beauchemin, 1975, translation by Alan Brown published as *Garden in the Wind,* McClelland & Stewart, 1977.

Ces Enfants de ma vie, Stanke, 1977, translation by Brown published as *Children of My Heart,* McClelland & Stewart, 1979.

Fragiles Lumieres de la terre: Ecrits divers 1942-1970, Quinze, 1978.

My Cow Bossie, McClelland & Stewart, 1988.

Contributor to anthologies, including *Great Short Stories of the World,* Reader's Digest, 1972, and *The Penguin Book of Canadian Short Stories,* Penguin, 1980.

Adaptations

Bonheur d'Occasion was made into a feature film, 1983.

Sidelights

Gabrielle Roy, who grew up in rural Manitoba, used Montreal, St. Boniface, and the wilds of northern Canada as settings for her novels. *Saturday Night* critic George Woodcock believed that the complex mixture of cultures in rural Manitoba explains why Roy is "a Canadian writer of truly multi-cultural background and experience." Hugo McPherson, writing in *Canadian Literature,* commented: "Roy's experience has taught her that life offers an endless series of storms and mischances."

After her father's death in 1927, Roy attended the Winnipeg Normal Institute rather than a university for financial reasons. Following graduation, she taught at the Institute Collegial Provencher in St. Boniface until 1937. In that same year, she sailed to London, England, where she studied acting for six months at the Guildhall School of Music and Drama. She decided, however, that she preferred to write, and she began submitting articles on Europe and Canada to newspapers in St. Boniface and Paris, France, while continuing to travel throughout Europe. After returning to Canada in 1939, Roy settled in Montreal.

Roy filled her novels with people who are underprivileged, people of many nationalities and ethnicities, and minority people who have difficulty coping in a predominantly white society. "She records their plight with a tolerance and compassion that rests not on patriotism, humanism or religiosity, but on a deep love of mankind," McPherson stated. "Gabrielle Roy *feels* rather than analyzes, and a sense of wonder and of mystery is always with her." Jeannette Urbas, writing in *Journal of Canadian Fiction,* presented a similar view: "Roy immerses us directly in the suffering of her characters: we feel, we think, we live with them. The appeal is directly to the heart."

Roy, who was frequently compared to Willa Cather, provided insight into her own life with the publication of *The Road Past Altamont* and *Street of Riches.* These short story collections tell the story of Christine, a writer from Manitoba, who has wanderlust in her heart. The stories in *The Road Past Altamont,* in particular, reveal the profound influence of Roy's surroundings on her writing and life. As Penelope Power described it in *Kliatt,* "landscape, travel and character are the three forces at work in Roy's family memories."

In addition to writing novels for adults, Roy also wrote children's books, including *My Cow Bossie.* A popular children's tale in its original French, *My Cow Bossie* was translated into English in 1988. It tells the tale of a young girl who receives a cow as a gift. Like many of Roy's books for adults, the work is set in Manitoba in the early 1900s and is reminiscent of the writings of Laura Ingalls Wilder. Anne Louise Mahoney, writing for *Canadian Children's Literature,* commented that Roy "successfully weaves this appealing story with believable characters, unaffected dialogue, and honest emotions."

Canadian Forum critic Paul Socken stated that the link between all of Roy's writings is "people's lifelong struggle to understand the integrity of their own lives, to see their lives as a whole, and their need to create bridges of concern and understanding between themselves and others. . . . It is this very tension, and the success that she has demonstrated in dramatizing it, that makes Gabrielle Roy unique among Canadian writers."

Works Cited

Mahoney, Anne Louise, review of *My Cow Bossie,* *Canadian Children's Literature,* No. 62, 1994, p. 60.

McPherson, Hugh, *Canadian Literature,* summer, 1959, pp. 46-57.

Power, Penelope, review of *The Road Past Altamont,* *Kliatt,* May, 1994, p. 28.

Socken, Paul, *Canadian Forum,* February, 1978.

Urbas, Jeannette, *Journal of Canadian Fiction,* spring, 1972, pp. 69-73.

Woodcock, George, *Saturday Night,* November, 1977.

For More Information See

BOOKS

Babby, Ellen Reisman, *The Play of Language and Spectacle: A Structural Reading of Selected Texts by Gabrielle Roy,* ECW Press, 1985.

Contemporary Literary Criticism, Gale, Volume 10, 1979, Volume 14, 1980.

Dictionary of Literary Biography, Volume 68: Canadian Writers, 1920-1959, First Series, Gale, 1988.

Grosskurth, Phyllis, *Gabrielle Roy,* Forum House, 1972.

Hesse, Marta Gudrun, *Gabrielle Roy,* Twayne, 1984.

Hind-Smith, Joan, *The Lives of Margaret Laurence, Gabrielle Roy, Frederick Philip Grove,* Clarke, Irwin, 1975, pp. 62-126.

Lewis, Paula Gilbert, *The Literary Vision of Gabrielle Roy: An Analysis of Her Works,* Summa Publications, 1984.

Mitcham, Allison, *The Literary Achievement of Gabrielle Roy,* York Press, 1983.

PERIODICALS

Canadian Children's Literature, Nos. 35-36, 1984, pp. 27-37.

Canadian Literature, autumn, 1969, pp. 6-13; spring, 1981, pp. 161-71; summer, 1984, pp. 183-84.

Los Angeles Times Book Review, February 6, 1994, p. 12.

New York Times Book Review, January 30, 1994, p. 28.

Obituaries

PERIODICALS

Chicago Tribune, July 16, 1983.

London Times, July 18, 1983.

New York Times, July 15, 1983.

Washington Post, July 15, 1983.*

S–T

SACHAR, Louis 1954-

Personal

Surname pronounced *Sack*-er; born March 20, 1954, in East Meadow, NY; son of Robert J. (a salesman) and Ruth (a real estate broker; maiden name, Raybin) Sachar; married Carla Askew (a teacher), May 26, 1985; children: Sherre. *Education:* University of California, Berkeley, B.A., 1976; University of California, San Francisco, J.D., 1980.

Louis Sachar

Addresses

Home—Austin, TX. *Agent*—Ellen Levine Literary Agency, 432 Park Ave. S., Suite 1205, New York, NY 10016.

Career

Writer, 1977—. Beldoch Industries, Norwalk, CT, shipping manager, 1976-77; lawyer, 1981-89. *Member:* Authors Guild, Society of Children's Book Writers and Illustrators.

Awards, Honors

Ethical Culture School Book Award, 1978, and Children's Choice, International Reading Association and Children's Book Council, 1979, both for *Sideways Stories from Wayside School;* Parents' Choice Award, Parents' Choice Foundation, 1987, Young Reader's Choice Award, Pacific Northwest Library Association, and Texas Bluebonnet Award, Texas Library Association, both 1990, and Charlie May Simon Book Award, Arkansas Elementary School Council, Georgia Children's Book Award, University of Georgia College of Education, Indian Paintbrush Book Award (Wyoming), Golden Sower Award, Iowa Children's Choice Award, Land of Enchantment Children's Book Award, New Mexico Library Association, Mark Twain Award, Missouri Association of School Librarians, Milner Award, Friends of the Atlanta-Fulton Public Library (Georgia), Nevada Young Reader's Award, and West Virginia Book Award, Wise Library, West Virginia University, all for *There's a Boy in the Girls' Bathroom;* Parents' Choice Award, 1989, Garden State Children's Book Award, New Jersey Library Association, 1992, and Arizona Young Reader's Chapter Book Award, 1993, all for *Wayside School Is Falling Down;* nominee, Golden Archer Award, 1996-97, Garden State Children's Book Award, 1998, Indiana Young Hoosier's Book Award, Massachusetts Children's Book Award, and Young Reader's Choice Award, all for *Wayside School Gets a Little Stranger;* National Book Award, 1998, Best Books, *School Library Journal,* 1998, Fanfare list, *Horn Book,* Books in the Middle: Outstanding Titles of 1998,

Voice of Youth Advocates, "Blue Ribbons 1998" selection, *Bulletin of the Center for Children's Books,* and Newbery Medal, all 1999, all for *Holes.*

Writings

Sideways Stories from Wayside School, illustrated by Dennis Hockerman, Follett, 1978, new edition illustrated by Julie Brinkloe, Avon, 1985, Morrow, 1998.

Johnny's in the Basement, Avon, 1981, Morrow, 1998.

Someday Angeline, illustrated by Barbara Samuels, Avon, 1983, Morrow, 1998.

There's a Boy in the Girls' Bathroom, Knopf, 1987.

Sixth Grade Secrets, Scholastic, 1987.

Sideways Arithmetic from Wayside School, Scholastic, 1989.

The Boy Who Lost His Face (young adult novel), Knopf, 1989.

Wayside School Is Falling Down, illustrated by Joel Schick, Lothrop, Lee & Shepard, 1989.

Dogs Don't Tell Jokes, Knopf, 1991.

Monkey Soup (picture book), illustrated by Cat Bowman Smith, Knopf, 1992.

Marvin Redpost: Kidnapped at Birth?, illustrated by Neal Hughes, Random House, 1992.

Marvin Redpost: Is He a Girl?, illustrated by Barbara Sullivan, Random House, 1993.

Marvin Redpost: Why Pick on Me?, illustrated by Sullivan, Random House, 1993.

More Sideways Arithmetic from Wayside School, Scholastic, 1994.

Marvin Redpost: Alone in His Teacher's House, illustrated by Barbara Sullivan, Random House, 1994.

Wayside School Gets a Little Stranger, illustrated by Joel Schick, Morrow, 1995.

Holes, Farrar, Straus and Giroux, 1998.

Marvin Redpost: A Flying Birthday Cake, Random House, 1999.

Marvin Redpost: Class President, Random House, 1999.

Marvin Redpost: Super Fast, Out of Control!, Random House, in press.

Sidelights

Celebrated author Louis Sachar, winner of a National Book Award and the 1999 Newbery Medal for his novel *Holes,* is also recognized for his ever-popular story *There's a Boy in the Girls' Bathroom,* his "Wayside School" series for middle-graders, and his "Marvin Redpost" chapter books for younger readers. Sachar's trademark is a humorous and realistic portrayal and exploration of relationships and feelings; his storylines characteristically chart the efforts of his various characters to discover and then assert their young identities. Sachar's male and female protagonists struggle and learn to cope with the world—with not a little help from the funny bone—just as Sachar himself had to finally decide his own true professional identity: lawyer or writer?

Born in East Meadow, New York, Sachar moved with his family at age nine to Orange County, California, at a time when orange groves were still plentiful there. He was a good student and specially excelled in math, but it was not until high school that he fell in love with reading. Sachar attended college at Antioch in Ohio his first year, but upon the death of his father he returned to California to be close to his mother. Going to school at Berkeley, he majored in economics, but also took creative writing courses and continued to indulge his voracious reading habits. At one point in his studies, enchanted with Russian literature, he decided to learn the language so he could read these novels in their original version. "After taking a year of Russian," he once told *Something about the Author* (*SATA*), "I realized it was still Greek to me. A week into the semester I dropped out of Russian V and tried to figure out what other class I should take instead."

At this point, serendipity intruded into Sachar's life. An elementary school girl was handing out leaflets at his campus in the hopes of recruiting teachers' aides. Such work would earn him three college credits, enough to make up for the dropped language class. Without really thinking about it, Sachar took one of the leaflets and signed on as a teacher's aide. "Prior to that time I had no interest whatsoever in kids," Sachar told *SATA*. "It turned out to be not only my favorite class, but also the most important class I took during my college career." His interaction with the school kids was heightened when he became the lunchtime supervisor, and was known affectionately as "Louis, the Yard Teacher."

At about this same time, Sachar was reading *In Our Town,* a series of very short, interrelated stories by Damon Runyon, which gave him the idea of doing the same sort of treatment for a fictionalized school called Wayside. "All the kids are named after the kids I knew at the school where I worked," Sachar told *SATA.* He even put himself in the book as the character Louis the Yard Teacher. "I probably had more fun writing that book than any of my others, because it was just a hobby then, and I never truly expected to be published."

After he graduated from college, Sachar continued working on his thirty short stories about Wayside School, and finally sent off the finished manuscript at the same time he was applying to law schools. "My first book was accepted for publication during my first week at University of California, beginning a six-year struggle over trying to decide between being an author or a lawyer," Sachar told *SATA.* The book was a mild success with young readers, making Sachar's deliberations more difficult. After graduating from law school and passing the bar, Sachar proceeded to both write and practice law part-time. He continued working in this manner through his next several books, until he was established enough as an author to write full time.

Sideways Stories from Wayside School tells the tale of an elementary school thirty stories high, each classroom stacked on top of the other. There is a broad cast of characters, from school clown to bully to the favorite teacher, Mrs. Jewls. Sachar provides vignettes from many points of view which add up to a zany take on school days. Less episodic is Sachar's second book, *Johnny's in the Basement,* the story of eleven-year-old

Johnny Laxatayl who owns a fantastic bottle-cap collection, his claim to fame. Johnny's punning last name is intentional, for the boy looks something like a dog; however, he "lacks a tail." After his eleventh birthday, Johnny's parents suddenly push responsibilities on him in the form of dancing lessons and their plan for him to sell his prized cap collection, for which he receives $86.33. Johnny and his new friend, Valerie, blow the money on meaningless junk, "a preadolescent way to show contempt for adults' exploitation," according to *School Library Journal* contributor Jack Forman. Joan McGrath, writing in *Emergency Librarian,* found the book "full of sly humor." *Publishers Weekly* called *Johnny's in the Basement* "another corker" and concluded that "all the many characters in the story are superbly realized, particularly Johnny's eldritch little sister."

Sachar's third novel, *Someday Angeline,* is told with "unaffected humor and linguistic art" which "invest the story of Angeline Persopolis with pure magic," according to a *Publishers Weekly* critic. Angeline is eight with an I.Q. that soars off the charts, but this genius aspect has made her an outsider at school. Her mother is dead and her teacher loves to embarrass the precocious child. But Angeline finds another loner, Gary Boone, known as Goon, as well as a friendly teacher, Miss Turbone (Mr. Bone to the pun-loving Sachar), who "gladden" her life and support her through tough times in a book that readers will not want to see end, according to a commentator in *Publishers Weekly. Booklist*'s Ilene Cooper noted that children will enjoy "the sense of fun ... and the feeling of hope that comes shining through." Gary "Goon" Boone makes another appearance in Sachar's *Dogs Don't Tell Jokes.*

Sachar's fourth book was the work of several years, both in writing and in placing it with a publisher. Despite the troubles Sachar had with it, *There's a Boy in the Girls' Bathroom* is still one of his most popular and best-known books. Sachar intended in this work to tell the story of the transformation of a fifth grade bully from both the point of view of the bully-ish outcast in question, Bradley Chalkers, and also from the point of view of the new kid, Jeff Fishkin, who befriends Bradley. Publishers wanted Sachar to stick with Bradley's point of view, so publication was delayed with rewrites. In the event, the wait and extra work were worth it. The recipient of over a dozen state awards, *There's a Boy in the Girls' Bathroom* charmed critics and readers alike. A *Kirkus Reviews* critic called the "fall and rise of Bradley Chalkers, class bully" a "humorous, immensely appealing story," and noted that Bradley's transformation, under the tutelage of his shaky new friend and the school counselor, "is beautiful to see." Writing in *School Library Journal,* David Gale called the novel "unusual, witty, and satisfying," and added that Sachar "ably captures both middle-grade angst and joy." Sam Leaton Sebesta dubbed Sachar's book "a triumph" in *The Reading Teacher.*

Sixth Grade Secrets follows in the same vein of preadolescent social problems when Laura starts a secret club known as Pig City, whose members must confess

Thirty humorous tales about Sachar's popular Wayside School focus on the string of substitutes brought in when favorite teacher Mrs. Jewls takes a maternity leave. (From Wayside School Gets a Little Stranger, *illustrated by Joel Schick.)*

secrets to each other to insure they keep the existence of the club between them. When a rival club, Monkey Town, springs up, suddenly secrets abound in a "witty, well-paced story" that "shows off [Sachar's] impeccable ear for classroom banter," according to a review in *Publishers Weekly. Booklist*'s Ilene Cooper praised Sachar's "plotting with twists" that will "hold readers' attentions." With *The Boy Who Lost His Face,* Sachar ventured more into junior high and young-adult territory, using more mature language, some of which his publishers ultimately convinced him to tone down. In this work, David, the protagonist, has a fling with the in-crowd, only to learn in the end that there are more rewarding friendships to be pursued.

Letters from fans of his first book of stories convinced Sachar to return to his tales from Wayside School with *Wayside School Is Falling Down* and *Sideways Arithmetic from Wayside School.* Lee Galda, writing in *The Reading Teacher,* maintained that "humorous is the best way" to describe the former title, a "zany novel [which] will be cheered" by its audience. Once again, Sachar's humorous take on school life and his use of short chapters make for a perfect book to share in oral reading. Reviewing *Wayside School Is Falling Down,* Carolyn Phelan of *Booklist* remarked that "Sachar's humor is right on target for middle-grade readers," with episodes from the school cafeteria to a lesson in gravity from Mrs. Jewls when she drops a computer out the window. Phelan concluded: "Children will recognize Sachar as a writer who knows their territory and entertains them well." Sachar drew on his own love for math with the brainteasers gathered in *Sideways Arithmetic from Wayside School,* and in *Wayside School Gets a Little Stranger,* he once again returned to the thirty-story school with thirty new self-contained tales that relate what happens during Mrs. Jewls absence on maternity leave. Deborah Stevenson, writing in the *Bulletin of the Center for Children's Books,* called the book "smart, funny, and widely appealing," while a *Kirkus Reviews* commentator noted that "Sachar proves once again that he is a master of all things childish."

Sachar has also written a series of stories for younger readers, the "Marvin Redpost" chapter books, featuring Marvin of course, whose problems include nose-picking, questions about his identity, and troubles with his teacher. In the first title in the series, *Marvin Redpost: Kidnapped at Birth?,* nine-year-old Marvin, the only redhead in his family, thinks he was stolen from his real parents at birth. Marvin's friends agree that his concerns are quite valid, prompting the boy to confront his parents with his suspicions and urge them to get a blood test to prove him wrong. *School Library Journal* contributor Kenneth E. Kowen noted that the book is written almost totally in dialogue, praising the work as "fast paced, easy to read, and full of humor." Kowen concluded that Sachar's story "deals with issues of friendship, school, and being different, all handled with the author's typical light touch." Nose-picking gets the Sachar treatment in *Marvin Redpost: Why Pick on Me?,* in which Marvin is unjustly accused of picking his nose and becomes a social outcast as a result. Stevenson had high praise for this beginning chapter book in *Bulletin of the Center for Children's Books,* noting that Sachar, "a consistently talented writer of books for grade-school readers," circumvented the usual cutesy pitfalls of writing easy-readers "to produce a *tour de force* of the genre, a trim tome of energy, hilarity, and wisdom." Marvin gets in trouble again when he is entrusted with the care of his vacationing teacher's dog, Waldo, in *Marvin Redpost: Alone in His Teacher's House.* Waldo refuses to eat and eventually dies, leaving Marvin to deal with his feelings of guilt. Sachar has written seven titles in this series that has captured the hearts of young readers.

A departure for Sachar is his 1998 novel, *Holes.* Sachar's humor and ear for dialogue are in evidence here as in his other books, but at 235 pages, *Holes* weighs in as a real YA novel. The story of Stanley Yelnats, whose name, a palindrome, can be spelled backward and forward, the award-winning *Holes* earned a featured review in *Bulletin of the Center for Children's Books,* as Roger Sutton concluded: "We haven't seen a book with this much plot, so suspensefully and expertly deployed, in too long a time." In the novel, Stanley is wrongly accused of stealing a pair of sneakers and is sent to Texas's Camp Green Lake for bad boys as punishment. There the harsh female warden assigns him the task—along with other boys held there—of digging five-feet-deep holes in the camp's dried-up lake bed. A *Publishers Weekly* critic, calling the book "a wry and loopy novel," asserted: "Just when it seems as though this is going to be a weird YA cross between *One Flew Over the Cuckoo's Nest* and *Cool Hand Luke,* the story takes off—along with Stanley" as he and his new buddy, Zero, manage to escape. What follows, the *Publishers Weekly* commentator added, is a "dazzling blend of social commentary, tall tale and magic realism," as Stanley goes about getting rid of the Yelnats curse that has plagued his family for three generations. *School Library Journal* contributor Alison Follos also praised Sachar's novel, maintaining: "A multitude of colorful characters coupled with the skillful braiding of ethnic folklore, American legend, and contemporary issues is a brilliant achievement. There is no question, kids will love *Holes.*"

Whether pushing the bounds of the YA format, entertaining with the goofy goings-on at Wayside School, or following Marvin through the rocky shoals of third grade, Sachar "has shown himself a writer of humor and heart," as Sutton characterized him in the *Bulletin of the Center for Children's Books.* His many fans can only be happy that the legal profession was spared one more suit, and that the world of books gained a creator of wide range and depth.

Works Cited

Cooper, Ilene, review of *Someday Angeline, Booklist,* September 1, 1983, p. 91.

Cooper, Ilene, review of *Sixth Grade Secrets, Booklist,* November 1, 1987, p. 484.

Follos, Alison, review of *Holes, School Library Journal,* September, 1998, p. 210.

Forman, Jack, review of *Johnny's in the Basement, School Library Journal,* December, 1981, p. 68.

Galda, Lee, review of *Wayside School Is Falling Down, The Reading Teacher,* May, 1990, p. 671.

Gale, David, review of *There's a Boy in the Girls' Bathroom, School Library Journal,* April, 1987, p. 103.

Review of *Holes, Publishers Weekly,* June 27, 1998, p. 78.

Review of *Johnny's in the Basement, Publishers Weekly,* August 12, 1983, p. 67.

Kowen, Kenneth E., review of *Marvin Redpost: Kidnapped at Birth?, School Library Journal,* March, 1993, p. 186.

McGrath, Joan, review of *Johnny's in the Basement, Emergency Librarian,* May-June, 1982, p. 30.

Phelan, Carolyn, review of *Wayside School Is Falling Down, Booklist,* May 1, 1989, p. 1553.

Sebesta, Sam Leaton, review of *There's a Boy in the Girls' Bathroom, The Reading Teacher,* October, 1988, p. 83.

Review of *Sixth Grade Secrets, Publishers Weekly,* August 28, 1987, p. 80.

Review of *Someday Angeline, Publishers Weekly,* August 12, 1983, p. 67.

Stevenson, Deborah, review of *Marvin Redpost: Why Pick on Me?, Bulletin of the Center for Children's Books,* February, 1993, pp. 167-68.

Stevenson, Deborah, review of *Wayside School Gets a Little Stranger, Bulletin of the Center for Children's Books,* March, 1995, p. 248.

Sutton, Roger, review of *Holes, Bulletin of the Center for Children's Books,* September-October, 1998, pp. 593-95.

Review of *There's a Boy in the Girl's Bathroom, Kirkus Reviews,* February 1, 1987, p. 224.

Review of *Wayside School Gets a Little Stranger, Kirkus Reviews,* April 15, 1995, p. 562.

For More Information See

BOOKS

Children's Literature Review, Volume 28, Gale, 1992.
Twentieth-Century Children's Writers, Fourth edition, St. James Press, 1995.

PERIODICALS

Booklist, April 15, 1992, p. 1539; December 1, 1992, p. 680; March 15, 1993, p. 1369; May 1, 1993, p. 1592; June 1, 1994, p. 1822; March 1, 1995, p. 1273.
Bulletin of the Center for Children's Books, October, 1987, p. 37; October, 1991, p. 47; October, 1992, pp. 52-53; June, 1994, p. 334.
New York Times Book Review, November 15, 1998, p. 52.
Publishers Weekly, January 6, 1992, p. 64; February 13, 1995, p. 78.
Riverbank Review, Fall, 1998, pp. 32-33.
School Library Journal, May, 1989, p. 111; October, 1989, p. 122; September, 1991, p. 259; June, 1992, p. 102; January, 1994, p. 74; August, 1994, p. 68; April, 1995, p. 136.
Voice of Youth Advocates, December, 1998, p. 360.

—*Sketch by J. Sydney Jones*

*   *   *

Nick Sharratt

SHARRATT, Nick 1962-

Personal

Born August 9, 1962, in London, England; son of Michael John (a brewer) and Jill Alexandra (Davison) Sharratt. *Education:* Saint Martin's School of Art (London, England), B.A. (with honors), 1984.

Addresses

Home—Gloucestershire, England; and c/o Candlewick, 2067 Massachusetts Ave., Cambridge, MA 02140.

Career

Children's book illustrator and author.

Awards, Honors

Under Fives Book Prize (3-5 nonfiction category), SHE/ W. H. Smith, 1995, for *Ketchup on Your Cornflakes?;* Sheffield Children's Book Award, 1997, for *A Cheese and Tomato Spider;* Gold Winner, Best First Book, *Parents Magazine,* for *Twinkle, Twinkle, Little Star;* Children's Book Award, special award for contributions to winning books, 1998.

Writings

FOR CHILDREN; SELF ILLUSTRATED

Monday Run-Day, Candlewick, 1992.

The Green Queen, Candlewick, 1992.
Look What I Found!, Candlewick, 1992.
I Look Like This, Candlewick, 1992.
Don't Put Your Finger in the Jelly, Nelly!, Andre Deutsch, 1993.
Mrs. Pirate, Candlewick, 1994.
Snazzy Aunties, Candlewick, 1994.
My Mum and Dad Make Me Laugh, Walker, 1994, published in the United States as *My Mom and Dad Make Me Laugh,* Candlewick, 1994.
Caveman Dave, Candlewick, 1994.
I Went to the Zoopermarket, Scholastic, 1995.
Rocket Countdown, Candlewick, 1995.
A Cheese and Tomato Spider, Andre Deutsch, 1996.
The Pointy-Hatted Princesses, Candlewick, 1996.
Stack-a-Plane (board book), Levinson, 1996.
The Animal Orchestra, Walker, Candlewick, 1997.
(With Stephen Tucker) *My Day,* Oxford University Press, 1997.
(With Stephen Tucker) *My Games,* Oxford University Press, 1997.
Come and Play!, Levinson, 1997.
Ketchup on Your Cornflakes?: A Wacky Mix-and-Match Book, Scholastic, 1997.
What Do I Look Like?, Walker, 1998.
(With Stephen Tucker) *The Time It Took Tom,* Scholastic, 1998.
The Best Pop-Up Magic Book ... Ever!, Orchard, 1998.
Dinosaurs' Day Out, Walker, Candlewick, 1998.

FOR CHILDREN; ILLUSTRATOR

Jill Bennett, compiler, *Noisy Poems,* Oxford University Press, 1987.

Louis Fidge, *Learning to Spell 4,* Parent and Child Programme, 1987.

Carol Watson, *If You Were a Hamster,* Dinosaur, 1988.

Jerome Fletcher, *A Gerbil in the Hoover,* Corgi, 1989.

Rosemary Stones, *Where Babies Come From,* Dinosaur, 1989.

Ruth Merrtens, *Adding and Subtracting,* Parent and Child Programme, 1989.

Gina Fost, *Robots Go Shopping,* Ginn, 1990.

Jill Bennett, compiler, *People Poems,* Oxford University Press, 1990.

Jill Bennett, compiler, *Machine Poems,* Oxford University Press, 1991.

Jacqueline Wilson, *The Story of Tracy Beaker,* Doubleday, 1991.

Jill Bennett, compiler, *Tasty Poems,* Oxford University Press, 1992.

Jacqueline Wilson, *The Suitcase Kid,* Doubleday, 1992.

Tat Small, *My First Sticker Diary,* Scholastic, 1993.

Jacqueline Wilson, *The Mum-Minder,* Doubleday, 1993.

Elizabeth Hawkins, *The Lollipop Witch,* Orchard, 1994.

Valerie Bierman, editor, *Snake on the Bus and Other Pet Stories,* Methuen, 1994.

Judy Hindley, *Crazy ABC,* Walker, 1994, Candlewick, 1996.

Judy Hindley, *Isn't It Time?,* Walker, 1994, Candlewick, 1996.

Judy Hindley, *Little and Big,* Walker, 1994.

Judy Hindley, *One by One,* Walker, 1994, Candlewick, 1996.

Vince Cross, compiler, *Sing a Song of Sixpence,* Oxford University Press, 1994.

Roy Apps, *How to Handle Your Mum,* Hippo, 1994.

Jeremy Strong, *My Dad's Got an Alligator,* Viking, 1994.

Jacqueline Wilson, *The Bed and Breakfast Star,* Doubleday, 1994.

Jacqueline Wilson, *Cliffhanger,* Yearling, 1995.

Jacqueline Wilson, *The Dinosaur's Packed Lunch,* Doubleday, 1995.

(With Sue Heap) Jacqueline Wilson, *Double Act,* Doubleday, 1995.

Roy Apps, *How to Handle Your Gran,* Hippo, 1995.

Jill Bennett, compiler, *Playtime Poems,* Oxford University Press, 1995.

Thomas Rockwell, *How to Eat Fried Worms,* Orchard, 1995.

Jeremy Strong, *The Indoor Pirates,* Dutton, 1995.

David Kitchen, *Never Play Leapfrog with a Unicorn,* Heinemann, 1995.

Gillian Cross, *The Crazy Shoe Shuffle,* Methuen Children's Books, 1995.

Jeremy Strong, *There's a Pharaoh in Our Bath!,* Dutton, 1995.

Roy Apps, *How to Handle Your Dad,* Hippo, 1996.

Jacqueline Wilson, *Bad Girls,* Doubleday, 1996.

Jacqueline Wilson, *Elsa, Star of the Shelter,* A. Whitman, 1996.

Elizabeth Lindsay, *Hello Nellie and the Dragon,* Hippo, 1996.

Jeremy Strong, *The Hundred-Mile-an-Hour Dog,* Viking, 1996.

Thomas Rockwell, *How to Get Fabulously Rich,* Orchard, 1997.

Jacqueline Wilson, *Girls in Love,* Doubleday, 1997.

Jeremy Strong, *My Granny's Great Escape,* Viking, 1997.

Gina Willner-Pardo, *Spider Storch, Teacher Torture,* A. Whitman, 1997.

Gina Willner-Pardo, *Spider Storch, Carpool Catastrophe,* A. Whitman, 1997.

Emma Laybourn, *Robopop,* Yearling, 1997.

Gaby Goldsack, *Flower Power,* Hippo, 1997.

Jacqueline Wilson, *The Monster Story-Teller,* Doubleday, 1997.

Jeremy Strong, *Giant Jim and the Hurricane,* Viking, 1997.

Jeremy Strong, *The Indoor Pirates on Treasure Island,* Puffin, 1998.

Jacqueline Wilson, *The Lottie Project,* Doubleday, 1998.

Gillian Clements, *Calligraphy Frenzy,* Hippo, 1998.

Briane Morese, *Horse in the House,* Mammoth, 1998.

Jill Bennett, compiler, *Seaside Poems,* Oxford University Press, 1998.

Jacqueline Wilson, *Girls Under Pressure,* Doubleday, 1998.

Pat Moon, *Little Dad,* Mammoth, 1998.

(With Sue Heap) Jacqueline Wilson, *Buried Alive!,* Doubleday, 1998.

Roy Apps, *How to Handle Your Brother/Sister,* Hippo, 1998.

Geraldine Taylor, Gillian Harker, *Twinkle, Twinkle, Little Star,* Ladybird, 1998.

Jacqueline Wilson (reteller) *Rapunzel,* Scholastic, 1998.

Sidelights

Nick Sharratt is an English author and illustrator of early reader books. His simple books sometimes teach numbers or counting or colors, but usually they are just plain fun for children learning to read. Sharratt illustrates his work in bold, bright colors to portray situations from the everyday to the adventurous. In *Look What I Found!,* for example, a little girl goes to the beach with her family and discovers fascinating objects along the shore, while in *Rocket Countdown* readers learn about numbers while getting ready for a moon trip. Sharratt uses humor in some of his books to keep young readers entertained. *Monday Run-Day* depicts funny scenes, such as dogs dressed in ties for Friday's tie day; and in *Snazzy Aunties* a little boy's aunts wear or carry bizarre accessories.

My Mum and Dad Make Me Laugh, published in the United States as *My Mom and Dad Make Me Laugh,* is about a boy who has very odd parents. Father always wears clothes with stripes, while Mother always wears outfits with spots. Simon, however, prefers clothes that are gray. When the family goes on a safari, Father likes the animals that have stripes, such as the zebra, and Mother likes spotted creatures, including the leopards. Simon's favorite, though, is the elephant, and this explains why he always dresses in gray. This witty little jaunt drew praise from reviewers who enjoyed Sharratt's narrative and illustrative techniques equally. *School Library Journal* contributor Marianne Saccardi, for one, lauded the "pleasant, rhythmic quality" of the author's writing, as well as the "cartoon-style crayon drawings perfectly suit[ed to] the child narrator's tone." Carolyn Phelan, writing in *Booklist,* especially liked the illustra-

When Simon, his mom, and his dad go on a safari, they find their idiosyncratic preferences in clothes carry over to their choice of favorite animals. (From My Mom and Dad Make Me Laugh, *written and illustrated by Sharratt.)*

tions, calling them "bold and sassy and full of spotty-stripy detail."

Graphic design comes into play even more in books such as *Ketchup on Your Cornflakes?* Here Sharratt uses a dutch door technique that lets children combine pictures in funny ways. Sharratt's text can be split up as well, so that equally inappropriate combinations can be made to evoke laughs: "Do you like ice cream in your bathtub?" or "Do you like toothpaste on your head?" "Useful as toy, game, and concept book, this seems likely to provoke endless giggles and riffs on the theme," declared Deborah Stevenson in the *Bulletin of the Center for Children's Books.* Sharratt uses the same dutch door technique in *A Cheese and Tomato Spider* to combine people, animals, and various kinds of food.

Sharratt told *SATA,* "I've been making pictures for as long as I can remember, and I was nine when I decided I was going to be an illustrator by profession. As a child I always wanted the same things for birthdays and Christmas: a bumper pack of felt-tip pens and lots of drawing paper, and I liked nothing better than to spend all day in my room, drawing, eating sweets, and listening to the radio. Nothing's changed—except that

nowadays I use other media besides felt tips. A complete workaholic, I find it very hard to have weekends off, and I invariably sneak ongoing projects into my suitcase when I'm supposed to be taking a holiday. That's what happens when you really love your work!"

Works Cited

Phelan, Carolyn, review of *My Mom and Dad Make Me Laugh, Booklist,* June 1, 1994, p. 1845.

Saccardi, Marianne, review of *My Mom and Dad Make Me Laugh, School Library Journal,* August, 1994, pp. 145-46.

Sharratt, Nick, *Ketchup on Your Cornflakes?: A Wacky Mix-and-Match Book,* Scholastic, 1997.

Stevenson, Deborah, review of *Ketchup on Your Cornflakes?: A Wacky Mix-and-Match Book, Bulletin of the Center for Children's Books,* June, 1997, pp. 373-74.

For More Information See

PERIODICALS

Appraisal, summer, 1996, p. 32.

Books for Keeps, July, 1996, p. 7; March, 1997, p. 19.

Bulletin of the Center for Children's Books, June, 1997, pp. 373-74.

Kirkus Reviews, May 1, 1997, p. 727.

Publishers Weekly, March 23, 1992, p. 71; May 23, 1994, p. 86; September, 1994, p. 199; September 25, 1995, p. 56.

School Library Journal, June, 1992, pp. 102-103; November, 1992, p. 78; December, 1992, p. 91.

* * *

SHINE, Andrea 1955-

Personal

Born October 5, 1955, in New York; married Emmett Shine, 1979 (separated, 1997); children: Emmett Jr., Amanda. *Education:* Attended St. Olaf College, 1973-74, and State University of New York at Stony Brook, 1975-77. *Hobbies and other interests:* "Photography; etymology; music; reading; spending time with my son and daughter; going to Puerto Rico; playing scrabble; taking walks on the beach with the family dog; collecting art books, shells, sea glass, vintage pitchers, starfish, and my children's drawings."

Addresses

Home—20 Maple Street, Southampton, NY 11968. *Electronic mail*— ashine@suffolk.lib.ny.us.

Andrea Shine

Career

Fine artist and illustrator, 1983—; professional portrait artist. New York State Arts-in-Education Board of Cooperative Educational Services, fine arts consultant; Southampton College Continuing Education, Long Island University, NY, fine arts instructor; Southampton Public Schools, NY, fine arts instructor (summer intercession); Southampton Public Schools, committee member on Special Education, 1993-98. Rogers Memorial Library, Southampton Village, NY, 1998—. *Exhibitions:* Shine's work has been on display at Salmagundi Club, 1987; Gallery East, 1990-91; Elaine Benson Gallery, 1991, 1995, 1996, and 1998; Southeastern Ohio Cultural Arts Center, 1992; Dag Hammerskjold Center, 1992; Goodman Gallery, 1992-93; Vanderbilt Museum, 1993; Water Mill Museum, 1993-94; Newark Museum, 1994; Arlene Bujese Gallery, 1994; and Clayton-Liberatore Art Gallery, 1997.

Awards, Honors

Best-In-Issue Award, *Highlights for Children,* May, 1995, August, 1996, October, 1997; National Parenting Publications (NAPPA) Honors Award, 1998; "Pick of the List," *American Bookseller,* 1998, Christopher Award, 1999, both for *The Summer My Father Was Ten.*

Illustrator

Catherine A. Welch, *Danger at the Breaker,* Carolrhoda, 1992.

Catherine Deverell, *Stradivari's Singing Violin,* Carolrhoda, 1992.

Lisa Griest, *Lost at the White House: A 1909 Easter Story,* Carolrhoda, 1994.

(Reteller) Virginia Haviland, *Favorite Fairy Tales Told in Scotland,* Beech Tree, 1995.

Harriett Diller, *Big Band Sound,* Boyds Mills, 1996.

Clara Clark, *Nellie Bishop,* Boyds Mills, 1996.

Jim Haskins and Kathleen Benson, *Count Your Way Through France,* 1996.

Harriett Diller, *The Faraway Drawer,* Boyds Mills, 1996.

Holly Littlefield, *Colors of Germany,* Carolrhoda, 1997.

Marnie Laird, *Water Rat,* Winslow, 1998.

Pat Brisson, *The Summer My Father Was Ten,* Boyds Mills, 1998.

Work in Progress

Once I Knew a Spider, by Jennifer Dewey, for Walker; *I Think of You,* a self-illustrated picture book; a juvenile fiction chapter book.

Sidelights

Andrea Shine told *SATA:* "My parents moved with me to Europe when I was six months old. My father had been born and raised in Latvia; my mother was born in Madagascar and lived on that island in the Indian Ocean until she was seventeen years old. My family moved often as I was growing up in Europe, and I was sent to many different types of schools in different countries.

The next day was Saturday. My father and the old man worked all day together. When they were finished, they had a patch of ground carefully raked and planted with tomato and pepper plants, teeny tiny onions, and seeds for marigolds and zinnias. Now when my father looked at the garden, he didn't get a hard knot in his stomach.

Summer came, and every morning my father and Mr. Bellavista checked their plants. My father carried water from his apartment during dry spells and learned to tell what was a weed and what wasn't.

Shine's evocative illustrations enhance Pat Brisson's moving tale of a young boy who destroys his elderly neighbor's garden, then remorsefully builds a relationship with the old man. (From The Summer My Father Was Ten.*)*

Fluency in multiple languages notwithstanding, I was a shy child and found social interactions with persons other than my sister intimidating. I felt different from others and preferred the quiet of drawing in my room. Although my parents presented a seamless facade of moneyed elegance, respectability, and social standing, the reality of our home was severe and alcoholic. Because of that I was very withdrawn and from an early age; by way of my art, I retreated into a safer fantasy world of my own creation.

"I have been drawing since I could hold a pencil, and from the beginning, portraiture—the captivating study of who people are—has been a major fascination for me. All through school and college I kept my focus on representational portrait work. Years of honing my drawing and draughtsmanship skills led to successive portrait commissions, rendered in dense intaglio layers of colored pencil. I began receiving invitations to exhibit work in fine art galleries.

"Seeking a change after a decade of colored-pencil work at the professional level, I switched to watercolor. I felt instantly at home, confident, and exhilarated. I love the visual joy of confluent liquid colors as I direct their flow across the clear page. I use a very heavy thick French paper, smooth as silk and infinitely forgiving. The kind

of children's story I am compelled to illustrate is one featuring a quiet, apart child, the sensitive, sentient being who innately perceives life through a deeper more complicated lens.

In 1992, Shine made her entrance into the world of children's literature by illustrating *Danger at the Breaker,* a picture book written by Catherine A. Welch. The story, set in a coal mining town in Pennsylvania, describes eight-year-old Andrew Pulaski's first working day as a breaker boy sorting rocks from coal. Andrew learns that a coal miner's difficult and dirty job also holds fear and danger when an explosion threatens his father's life. Kay Weisman, reviewing *Danger at the Breaker* for *Booklist,* maintained that "Shine's arresting, richly colored illustrations will draw readers deep inside the emotions of the characters." Writing for *School Library Journal,* Gale W. Sherman also noted the emotional qualities of Shine's watercolors, describing them as "dramatic" illustrations which "add depth and emotion to Welch's historical novel."

Critics frequently point out how Shine's images of children demonstrate a subtlety of emotions that enhance the text and serve as counterpoint to the author's story. In a review of Harriett Diller's *Big Band Sound, Booklist* critic Hazel Rochman claimed: "Shine's beautiful, light-filled landscapes and portraits in watercolor and gouache celebrate the pulsing energy and joy of the girl and her music." Arliss, the young child in this story, enjoys the big band sounds she hears while watching TV with her mother, and so she creates her own big band sound using things around the house. After an outing with her mother, Arliss returns home to find her handmade drums gone by way of the garbage. Undaunted, she builds new drums from her neighbor's trash. Shine's paintings "credibly communicate the aspiring young musician's changeable moods," declared a writer for *Publishers Weekly.*

In *The Summer My Father Was Ten,* a group of ten-year-old boys chase after their baseball that has accidently landed in a neighbor's garden. However, the temptation of throwing tomatoes and red peppers proves too much for the young boys, and soon they tear up the entire garden. The owner, a lonely old man, loses heart when he sees the destruction, and he plants no seeds the following spring. Seeing this, the guilty young leader of the group apologizes, and the two work together to cultivate a new garden, forming a relationship that lasts for many years. When the boy becomes a father, he tells his daughter this story every spring as they begin to till the soil for a garden of their own. "The daily gardening work ... [is] celebrated in the gorgeously detailed pictures that show how a garden transforms a vacant lot," declared *Booklist* reviewer Hazel Rochman. A *Kirkus Reviews* commentator noted that Shine's illustrations capture "nuances of color, expression, and body language" along with the "beauty and bounty of tiny, lovingly tended gardens."

"Children are very wise; they think deeply, which has nothing to do with education," Shine continued to *SATA.* "They know what is right and wrong, in the true, mystical rich sense of those words. All too often, they are disallowed a voice; and even their obedient learned silence and submission is misconstrued. Children are most fully alive; as adults, we become somnolent, myopic. My illustrations are emotionally dense, layered pictorial hieroglyphics honoring the immense soulful dignity of the children who pass through this world."

Works Cited

Review of *Big Band Sound, Publishers Weekly,* December 18, 1995, p. 54.

Rochman, Hazel, review of *Big Band Sound, Booklist,* January 1, 1996, p. 843.

Rochman, Hazel, review of *The Summer My Father Was Ten, Booklist,* February 1, 1998, p. 913.

Sherman, Gale W., review of *Danger at the Breaker, School Library Journal,* September, 1992, p. 213.

Review of *The Summer My Father Was Ten, Kirkus Reviews,* February 1, 1998, p. 193.

Weisman, Kay, review of *Danger at the Breaker, Booklist,* March 1, 1993, p. 1244.

For More Information See

PERIODICALS

Booklist, February 15, 1993, p. 1059.
School Library Journal, March, 1996, p. 173; August, 1996, p. 132; August, 1996, p. 138.

*   *   *

SIERRA, Judy 1945-

Personal

Surname originally Strup; name legally changed in 1985; born June 8, 1945, in Washington, D.C.; daughter of Joseph L. (a photographer) and Jean (a librarian; maiden name, Law) Strup; married Robert Walter Kaminski (a puppeteer and elementary schoolteacher); children: Christopher Robin Strup. *Education:* American University, B.A., 1968; California State University-San Jose (now San Jose State University), M.A., 1973; further graduate study at University of California-Los Angeles.

Addresses

Home—4913 Indian Wood Rd., No. 507, Culver City, CA 90230.

Career

Puppeteer and storyteller, 1976—. Part-time librarian at Los Angeles Public Library, 1986—; teacher of children's literature and storytelling at Extension of University of California-Los Angeles. *Member:* National Association for the Preservation and Perpetuation of Storytelling, American Folklore Society, California Folklore Society.

Awards, Honors

Performing artist in residence at Smithsonian Institution, 1984; Best Books, *Publishers Weekly,* 1996, Fanfare List, *Horn Book,* 1997, and Notable Books for Children, American Library Association, 1997, all for *Nursery Tales Around the World.*

Writings

The Elephant's Wrestling Match, illustrated by Brian Pinkney, Lodestar (New York City), 1992.
The House that Drac Built, illustrated by Will Hillenbrand, Harcourt Brace (San Diego, CA), 1995.
Good Night, Dinosaurs, illustrated by Victoria Chess, Clarion (New York City), 1996.
(Reteller) *Wiley and the Hairy Man,* illustrated by Brian Pinkney, Lodestar, 1996.
(Reteller) *The Mean Hyena: A Folktale from Malawi,* illustrated by Michael Bryant, Lodestar, 1997.
Counting Crocodiles, illustrated by Will Hillenbrand, Harcourt Brace, 1997.
Antarctic Antics: A Book of Penguin Poems, illustrated by Jose Aruego and Ariane Dewey, Harcourt Brace, 1998.

Tasty Baby Belly Buttons: A Japanese Folktale, illustrated by Meilo So, Alfred A. Knopf, 1998.

The Dancing Pig, illustrated by Jesse Sweetwater, Harcourt Brace, 1999.

STORY COLLECTIONS

(With Robert Kaminski) *Twice Upon a Time: Stories to Tell, Retell, Act Out, and Write About,* H. W. Wilson, 1989.

(With Robert Kaminski) *Multicultural Folktales: Stories to Tell Young Children,* Oryx Press (Phoenix, AZ), 1991.

(Compiler) *Cinderella,* illustrated by Joanne Caroselli, Oryx Press, 1992.

(Editor and annotator) *Quests and Spells: Fairy Tales from the European Oral Tradition,* Bob Kaminski Media Arts, 1994.

Mother Goose's Playhouse: Toddler Tales and Nursery Rhymes, with Patterns for Puppets and Feltboards, Bob Kaminski Media Arts (Ashland, OR), 1994.

(Selector and reteller) *Nursery Tales Around the World,* illustrated by Stefano Vitale, Clarion, 1996.

Multicultural Folktales for the Feltboard and Readers' Theater, Oryx Press, 1996.

OTHER

The Flannel Board Storytelling Book, H. W. Wilson (Bronx, NY), 1987.

Storytelling and Creative Dramatics, H. W. Wilson, 1989.

Fantastic Theater: Puppets and Plays for Young Performers and Young Audiences, H. W. Wilson, 1991.

(With Robert Kaminski) *Children's Traditional Games: Games from 137 Countries and Cultures,* Oryx Press, 1995.

Storytellers' Research Guide: Folktales, Myths, and Legends, Folkprint (Eugene, OR), 1996.

Celtic Baby Names: Traditional Names from Ireland, Scotland, Wales, Brittany, Cornwall, and the Isle of Man, Folkprint, 1997.

Editor of *Folklore and Mythology Journal,* 1988—.

Sidelights

Interested in storytelling and puppetry arts from childhood, Judy Sierra has built a career as a writer in two areas: she has published numerous books about storytelling and related subjects, working closely with her husband, Robert Kaminski; and since the publication of *The Elephant's Wrestling Match* in 1992, she has also emerged as a writer of stories, many of them adaptations of folk tales from other countries.

The original story of *The Elephant's Wrestling Match,* for instance, comes from the African nation of Cameroon. In the tale, the mighty elephant challenges all the other animals to a test of strength, and each fails: "The leopard, crocodile, and rhinoceros all respond," Linda Greengrass reported in *School Library Journal,* "only to be easily thwarted by the mighty beast. Each time, Monkey beats out the results on the drum." In a surprising twist, the small but clever bat turns out to be the winner. But that is not the primary purpose of the story, which concludes by explaining that, because of his

In Judy Sierra's **Good Night, Dinosaurs,** *a family of dinosaurs performs very human bedtime rituals. (Illustrated by Victoria Chess.)*

anger at Monkey for spreading the news of his defeat, Elephant smashes Monkey's drum; for this reason, "you don't see monkeys playing the talking drum." A reviewer in *Publishers Weekly* noted that "Sierra's staccato retelling of this lively African tale crackles with energy," and Greengrass added that "listeners can almost hear the beating of the drum." Betsy Hearne of the *Bulletin of the Center for Children's Books* maintained: "The drama is simple enough for toddlers to follow but sturdy enough to hold other kids' attention as well."

In *The House That Drac Built,* Sierra took on literary and folk symbols more familiar to American children, inserting the character of Dracula into the nursery rhyme "The House That Jack Built." Thus as Nancy Vasilakas in *Horn Book* recounted, "Young audiences are introduced to the bat that lived in the house that Drac built, then to the cat that bit the bat, the werewolf that chased the cat that bit the bat, and so on through 'fearsome' manticore, coffin, mummy, zombie, and fiend of Bloodygore." Ghoulish as all this sounds, the story has a humorous twist, as a group of trick-or-treaters enters the house and puts everything right, re-wrapping the mummy and attending to the bitten bat. Noting its appeal at Halloween, *School Library Journal* contributor Beth Irish called the book "a definite hit for holiday story programs."

Whereas *The House That Drac Built* may not exactly be bedtime reading, *Good Night, Dinosaurs* certainly is. The book depicts a family of dinosaurs getting ready for

Using her counting skills, a wily monkey outwits a crowd of crocodiles to obtain bananas from a neighboring island.(*From* Counting Crocodiles, *written by Sierra and illustrated by Will Hillenbrand.*)

bed, brushing their teeth and then listening to lullabies and stories from their parents. "Young dinosaur fanciers will be charmed and undoubtedly claim this as their favorite go-to-sleep book," concluded Ann A. Flowers in *Horn Book.* Beth Tegart, writing in *School Library Journal,* dubbed *Good Night, Dinosaurs* "a pleasant read at bedtime for dinosaur fans as well as those who need a chuckle at the end of the day."

With *Wiley and the Hairy Man,* Sierra retold another folk tale, this one from the American South. Frightened by the Hairy Man, Wiley enlists the help of his mother to trick the monster three times, and thus forces him to leave them alone. "Through the use of dialogue without dialect and a lissome narration," commented Maria B. Salvadore in *Horn Book,* "Sierra captures the cadence of the oral language of Alabama." Like *The Elephant's Wrestling Match, The Mean Hyena* comes originally from Africa, in this case the country of Malawi, whose Nyanja people tell how the turtle got his revenge on the

title character after the hyena played a cruel trick on him. *School Library Journal* contributor Marilyn Iarusso called *The Mean Hyena* "a must for all folk-tale collections."

Counting Crocodiles takes place in a tropical location, although its setting is perhaps even more fanciful than that of Sierra's earlier tales. An unfortunate monkey finds herself on an island with nothing to eat but lemons, and longs to make her way to a nearby island with banana trees. There is only one problem: the Sillabobble Sea, which separates the two pieces of land, is filled with crocodiles. But the monkey, like many another small but clever creature in Sierra's stories, devises an ingenious plan to trick the crocodiles and obtain not only a bunch of bananas, but a sapling from which she can acquire fruit in the future. "The whimsical rhyme ... and the lively alliteration ('crusty croc, feasting fearlessly on fishes') add to the appeal," wrote Kathleen Squires in *Booklist.* A reviewer in *Publishers Weekly* praised

Sierra's collaboration with illustrator Will Hillenbrand: "Working with traditional materials, author and artist arrive at an altogether fresh presentation."

Works Cited

Review of *Counting Crocodiles, Publishers Weekly,* June 30, 1997, p. 75.

Review of *The Elephant's Wrestling Match, Publishers Weekly,* July 13, 1992, p. 55.

Flowers, Ann A., review of *Good Night, Dinosaurs, Horn Book,* July-August, 1996, pp. 474-75.

Greengrass, Linda, review of *The Elephant's Wrestling Match, School Library Journal,* September, 1992, p. 211.

Hearne, Betsy, review of *The Elephant's Wrestling Match, Bulletin of the Center for Children's Books,* February, 1993, pp. 190-91.

Iarusso, Marilyn, review of *The Mean Hyena, School Library Journal,* October, 1997, pp. 123-24.

Irish, Beth, review of *The House That Drac Built, School Library Journal,* September, 1995, p. 186.

Salvadore, Maria B., review of *Wiley and the Hairy Man, Horn Book,* May-June, 1996, p. 344.

Squires, Kathleen, review of *Counting Crocodiles, Booklist,* September 1, 1997, p. 135.

Tegart, Beth, review of *Good Night, Dinosaurs, School Library Journal,* April, 1996, p. 118.

Vasilakas, Nancy, review of *The House That Drac Built, Horn Book,* November-December, 1995, pp. 730-31.

For More Information See

PERIODICALS

Booklist, August, 1992, p. 2019; September 15, 1995, p. 173; March 1, 1997, p. 1177; April 1, 1997, p. 1306; September 1, 1997, pp. 120-21.

Children's Book Watch, November, 1992, p. 6; May, 1996, p. 3.

Horn Book, May-June, 1996, pp. 343-44.

Kirkus Reviews, July 15, 1992, p. 930; August 1, 1997, p. 1228.

Parenting, September, 1996, p. 209; December, 1996, p. 252.

Publishers Weekly, November 4, 1996, p. 48.

School Library Journal, April, 1997, p. 51; June, 1997, p. 39.

Science-Fiction Chronicle, June, 1995, p. 36.*

—Sketch by Judson Knight

Autobiography Feature

Robert Silverberg

1935-

Sometimes it feels like a marriage to me, and not a good one: unendingly troubled but eternal, unbreakable. Science fiction, for better or for worse, an inescapable lifetime union! Marked by constant restlessness, periods of compulsive infidelity, anguished re-evaluation, several trial separations, even a divorce—and yet, and yet, here I am still in the yoke after more than thirty years. I suppose there's no escape. I suppose I don't really want to escape, despite everything. When I was fifteen or sixteen I dreamed of becoming a famous science-fiction writer, and the dream came true, right up to and including the fulfillment of my juiciest adolescent fantasies. What, Mr. Silverberg, the fulfillment of all of your adolescent fantasies leaves you somehow still restless and troubled? Then you must be the sort of man who is inherently restless and troubled, no matter what the external circumstances of his life. Ah, I think we have it.

I was always the youngest in any group, owlishly precocious, a nastily bright little boy who was reading at three, writing little stories at six, spouting learned stuff about European dynasties and the sexual habits of plants at seven or eight, publishing illegible mimeographed magazines at thirteen, and selling novels at eighteen. I was too unruly and too clever to remain in the same class at school with my contemporaries, so I grew up two years younger than all my friends, thinking of myself as small and weak and incomplete. Eventually the passage of time saw to it that I caught up. The small boy became a man of more than medium height; the precocious child is now fiftyish and graying, an elder statesman in the microcosm of science fiction; I have had a career that others openly envy. The wounds I received from being fourteen years old in a universe of sixteen-year-olds are well sheathed in scar tissue. I have survived my own precocity. The trick now will be to deal with growing old.

I am an only child, born midway through the Great Depression. (There would have been a sibling, I think, when I was about seven, but it miscarried. I often wonder what pattern my life would have taken if I hadn't grown up alone, pampered, self-indulgent.) My ancestors were Jews from Eastern Europe, and my grandparents, three of whom survived well into my adulthood, were reared in rural Polish or Russian villages. My father was born in London in 1901 and came to the United States a few years later. My mother was born in Brooklyn, New York, and so was I.

I have no fond recollections of my childhood. I was puny, sickly, plagued with allergies and freckles. I was too clever by at least half, which made for troubles with my playmates. My parents were remote figures, my father an accountant who spent his days and many evenings adding up endless columns of figures, my mother a schoolteacher. I was raised mainly by our housekeeper and by my loving and amiable maternal grandmother. It was a painful time, lonely and embittering; I did make friends but, growing up in isolation and learning none of the social graces, I usually managed to alienate them quickly. On the other hand, there were compensations: intelligence is prized in Jewish households, and my parents saw to it that mine was permitted to develop freely. I was taken to museums, given all the books I wanted, allowed money for my hobbies. I took refuge from loneliness in these things; I collected stamps and coins, harpooned hapless butterflies and grasshoppers, raided the neighbors' gardens for specimens of leaves and flowers, stayed up late secretly reading, hammered out crude stories on an ancient typewriter—all with my father's strong encouragement and frequent participation. What did it matter to me that I was a troubled misfit in the classroom? I could come home, zip quickly through the too-easy homework, and escape into my other worlds.

Children troubled by the real world turn readily to the distant and the alien. The lure of the exotic seized me early. Those were the World War II years, and real travel was impossible, but in 1943 I discovered *The National Geographic* and off I went to Zanzibar and Surinam and the Great Barrier Reef in my imagination, decades before I ever reached those places in actuality. Then, an hour from home by subway, there was the American Museum of Natural History: mummies and arrowheads, mastodons and glyptodons, brontosaurs and tyrannosaurs. Sunday after Sunday my father and I made the pilgrimage, and I reveled in the wonders of prehistory, soberly lecturing him on matters Mesozoic. From dinosaurs and other such fantastic fossils to science fiction was only a short journey: to me the romantic, exotic distant past and the romantic, exotic distant future are aspects of the same thing, a time that is not *this* time.

First came Buck Rogers and *Planet Comics,* when I was seven or eight. Then Jules Verne when I was nine—I must have taken that voyage with Captain Nemo a hundred times—and H.G. Wells when I was ten, most notably *The*

Robert Silverberg with his wife Karen in their garden, 1998.

Time Machine (which promised to show me all the incredible eons I would never live to know) but also *Moreau* and *War of the Worlds* and the myriad short stories. There was Twain's *Connecticut Yankee,* which I also read repeatedly. (How early my obsession with time travel emerged!) And then, an eighth-grader in 1948, I learned about science-fiction magazines from a classmate.

The magazines' sleazy covers and gaudy titles repelled me at first. I was quiet, dignified, snobbish, not at all the sort of boy who was likely to read publications with names like *Thrilling Wonder Stories* and *Famous Fantastic Mysteries* and *Startling Stories,* especially since their covers were bright with paintings of hideous monsters and scantily clad damsels. (Sex was very frightening to me just then, there at the hour of puberty, and I had sworn never to have anything to do with women when I grew up. My life is littered with broken oaths.) But I did buy *Weird Tales* because the first issue I saw had a story about the Norse gods; I had gone through whole libraries of Norse mythology in early boyhood and the doings of Odin & Co. had powerful appeal for me. (They still do.) I bought *Amazing Stories,* then the most moronic representative of the genre, because it happened to publish an uncharacteristically respectable-looking issue about then. I bought John Campbell's sedate little *Astounding Science Fiction,* though many of the stories were opaque and unrewarding to my thirteen-year-old mind. Within a few months I had such an unquenchable thirst for science fiction that I was buying the other magazines too, however flashy their covers; for I had found that behind the covers all the magazines were pretty much the same, and all were wonderful.

And then the books, great meaty anthologies drawn from the s-f magazines of earlier years: *Adventures in Time and Space, The Best of Science Fiction, A Treasury of Science Fiction.* My father was more than a little baffled by my increasing obsession with all this trash, when previously I had occupied myself with decent books on botany and geology and astronomy, but he saw to it that I had whatever I wanted to read. One collection in particular had enormous impact on me: Donald A. Wollheim's *Portable Novels of Science.* It contained Wells' amusing *First Men in the Moon;* John Taine's *Before the Dawn,* which fed my always passionate interest in dinosaurs; H. P. Lovecraft's *Shadow Out of Time,* which gave me that peep into unattainable futures that was science fiction's greatest ecstasy for me; and above all Olaf Stapledon's *Odd John,* which spoke personally to me, as I suppose it must to any child who is too bright for his own good. I was up almost till dawn reading that book, and those four short novels marked me as, possibly, no other stories ever have.

I was still talking then of some sort of career in the sciences—botany, perhaps, paleontology, astronomy. But certain flaws in my intelligence were becoming apparent. I had a superb memory and a quick wit, but I lacked depth, originality, and consistency; my mind was like a hummingbird, darting erratically at great speed. I wanted to encompass too much and mastered nothing. Though I always got high marks in any subject that caught my interest, I was noticing that some of my classmates were better than I at grasping fundamental principles and drawing new conclusions from them. I doubt that I would have been of much value as a scientist. But already I was writing, and writing with precocious skill—for school

Robert, six months old, with his parents, Helen and Michael Silverberg.

newspapers and magazines, for my own abominable little magazine, and, without success, for the s-f magazines. The magazines sent my stories back, of course—usually with printed rejection slips but sometimes—when the editors realized they were dealing with a bright child of fourteen and not with a demented adult—with gentle letters suggesting ways I might improve my style or my sense of plot. I dreamed of the day when they'd send back a check instead. I spoke openly of a career as a science-fiction writer. Why a writer? Because my skills plainly were verbal ones: I suspected that writing was something I could do really well, perhaps the *only* thing I could do really well. Why science fiction? Because I loved to read it, though I had been through Cervantes and Shakespeare and that crowd too. And because writing science fiction would allow me to give free play to those fantasies of space and time and dinosaurs and supermen that were so gratifying to me. And because it seemed *possible* to be a minor Wells or Verne, whereas I knew I couldn't get into that larger arena with Cervantes and Shakespeare and the other writers who wrote out of deep knowledge of and engagement with the real here-and-now world, a world from which I felt wholly alienated. Finally, I had stumbled into the world of science-fiction fandom, an underground world of grubby little clubs and amateur magazines and tiny "conventions" in rented halls, a world much more congenial to me than the real one in which one had to contend with bullies and athletes and sex. I knew that my name on the contents page of *Astounding* or *Startling* would win me vast prestige in the world of s-f fans, prestige that I could hardly hope to gain in any way among my classmates.

So, then, my stories went forth, awkward miniature imitations of my favorite moments out of Lovecraft or Stapledon or Taine or Wells, and I read textbooks on the narrative art and learned a good deal, and I began also to read the stories in the s-f magazines with a close analytical eye, measuring the ratio of dialog to exposition, the length of paragraphs, and other technical matters that, I suppose, few fifteen-year-olds study as carefully as I did. Nothing got published, or even came close, but my skills were growing.

I was growing in other ways, too. When I was about fourteen I went off for the first time to summer camp, where I lived among boys (and girls) of my own age and no longer had to contend with being the youngest and puniest in my peer group. I had always been known as "Robert," but at camp they called me "Bob," and it seemed to me "Bob" was some entirely new person, healthy and outgoing and normal, whereas "Robert" was that spindly misfit, that maladjusted, isolated little boy. To this day I wince when some stranger presumes on my public persona and addresses me by the formal "Robert" with which I sign my stories—it sends me rocketing backwards in time to the horrors of being ten again.

This new Bob was able to cope. He grew to a reasonable height, halting just a bit short of six feet; he became a passable athlete; he learned how to manage conversations and sustain friendships. For a few years I led a split life, introverted and lonely at home, open and lighthearted and confident during the summer; and by the time I was about seventeen some integration of the two lives had begun. I had finished high school (where I had become editor of the school newspaper) and had declined to go immediately into college. Instead I spent a few months reading and writing, and then a few months working in a furniture warehouse among rough, tough illiterates who found my cultivated manner a charming novelty rather than a threatening intrusion, and then I went off to the summer camp, not as a camper but as an employee. In the autumn I entered Columbia University with old slates wiped clean: no longer morbidly too young, free now of local associations with the maladjustments of my childhood, I was able to pack past problems away and begin anew in the "Bob" persona.

I lived away from home in a little apartment of my own. I discovered previously unknown skills for drinking and carousing. I discovered that women were not really very frightening after all. I plunged myself into new worlds of the mind: Aquinas and Plato, Bartok and Schoenberg, Kafka, Joyce, Mann, Faulkner, Sartre. I continued to read s-f, but dispassionately, with the eye of one who was soon to be a professional; I was less interested in visions of ultimate tomorrows and more in seeing how other pros carried off their tricks. One of my stories was published—for a fee of $5, I think—by a little magazine called *Different,* primarily a haven for amateur poets. Another magazine asked me to do an article about s-f fandom; I did a competent professional job and earned $30. That was in September, 1953. I sent a short story, "Gorgon Planet," off to a magazine called *Nebula* published in Scotland, and in January, 1954 I got a check for $12.60.

Those early sales could be brushed aside as inconsequential—weak little pieces accepted by obscure magazines. But in that same January of 1954 I sold a novel to a well-known American publisher. That was something else. I was not yet nineteen years old, and I was a professional writer. I had crossed the threshold.

That novel! Its genesis went back almost three years. For the high-school paper that I edited I reviewed, in 1951, an s-f novel for boys published by Thomas Y. Crowell, an old-line New York firm. It was a clumsy, naive book, and my review demolished it so effectively that in the summer of 1953 the Crowell people invited me to examine and criticize, prior to publication, a new manuscript by the same author. I demolished that too, with such thoroughness that the book was never published. This time the Crowell editor asked me to the office and said, in effect, "If you know so much about science fiction, why don't you try a novel for us yourself?" It was an irresistible challenge.

The book I conceived in September, 1953, concerned the trip of four young space cadets to Alpha Centauri on a sort of training cruise. No plot, not much action. The cadets are chosen, leave for space, stop on Mars and Pluto, reach Alpha Centauri, become vaguely entangled in a revolution there, become disentangled, and go home. Some novel.

I wrote two or three chapters every weekend that autumn, working swiftly despite the pressures of college life. When eight chapters were ready I submitted them and received an encouraging note urging me to finish. The book was done by mid-November, 145 pages of typescript. Six weeks later came a stunning telephone call: they were sending me a contract. Of course, some changes would be necessary. In fact what was necessary was a complete rethinking of the story, though they were too kind to tell me that right away.

So I revised and revised, and draft after draft met with polite requests for more work. Six months later, the Crowell people decided to call for an outside reader's opinion; and the reader's report, which reached me at the end of October, made the job I had done on that unpublished book the year before look like praise. What was wrong, I was told, was that I really didn't know how to write. I had no idea of characterization or plotting, my technique was faulty, virtually everything except my typing was badly done. If possible, the reader said, I should enroll in a writing course at New York University.

A year earlier I might have been crushed. But by the fall of 1954 I'd sold a couple of short stories, I had written five or six more that seemed quite publishable to me (ultimately, I sold them all), and I felt that my technical grasp was firm, however faulty the execution of my first novel might be. After three hours of agonizing reappraisal I phoned my editor and proposed a total structural transformation of the book. By this time she must have come to doubt her original faith in my promise and talent, but she told me to go ahead. I knew it was my last chance. I compressed my opening nine chapters into two pages, put in six weekends of desperate work on the new version, and was rewarded on January 2, 1955—a year almost to the hour since I had been told a contract would be offered me—when I received a telegram: CONGRATULATIONS ON A WONDERFUL REVISION JOB ALL SET TO GO.

Revolt on Alpha C was published in August, 1955, to generally indifferent reviews. ("Inept and unreal . . . a series of old-hat adventures," said the *New York Times.* Too harsh a verdict, I think: the book is innocent and a little foolish, but not contemptible.) It remained in print in its Crowell edition for seventeen years, and a paperback edition published in 1959 still seems to enjoy a healthy life decades later. This strange persistence of a very young

Silverberg as a camp counselor, West Copake, New York, 1953. "In another few months I'd be a writer—but at the time the photo was taken, I was beginning to think that day would never come."

author's very unimportant first novel doesn't delude me into thinking I must have created a classic unrecognized in its own day, nor does it have much to do with my latter-day prominence in science fiction. That *Revolt on Alpha C* has stayed in print for thirty years is simply an odd fluke of publishing, but one that I find charming as well as profitable.

I was launched. On the strength of my first few sales I acquired an agent and sent him my backlog of unsold short stories. Then, assuming stories bearing his imprimatur would sell far more readily than unsolicited manuscripts by an unknown writer, I waited for the checks to flow in.

The flow was a bit sluggish, though. Two very short stories sold to minor magazines in June of 1954 and February of 1955 for a total of $40.50; in May 1955 came $49.50 for a rather more elaborate piece. But several quite ambitious stories which I thought worthy of the leading magazines of the time failed to sell at all. I drew a sinister conclusion from this. It was much harder—impossible, even—to get anything published that seemed to have an individual flavor. Science fiction editors were cautious, conservative folk who might allow a few pet writers to experiment with self-expression but who generally would buy only such stories as fitted their audience's expectations and their own publishing formulas. If I wanted to earn my living writing s-f, therefore—and to write anything else somehow seemed beside the point to me—it would be wiser to use my rapidly developing technical skills to turn out formula fiction at high speed, rather than to lavish passion and commitment on more individual stories that nobody wanted to publish. Thus began my lifelong struggle with the paradox of a career in science fiction. Once upon a time (and mainly in England) there had been a market for the sort of books by Wells, Stapledon, and Lovecraft that had so dazzled me when I was thirteen. But in the United States nearly all s-f was published in magazines, or occasionally in paperback books, marketed as light commercial entertainment. Ingenuity of concept was valued, yes, but nothing in the way of originality of style, richness of character development, or boldness of plot. Ray Bradbury was the field's token litterateur; everybody else was required to follow pulp-magazine formulas.

In the summer of 1955, just as that somber insight was crystallizing in me, the s-f writer Randall Garrett moved to New York and coincidentally rented a room in the hotel near Columbia University where I was living. He was eight years older than I, and had had some two dozen stories published. Alone in a strange city, down on his luck, he struck up a curious friendship with me. We were markedly different in personal habits, in rhythm of life, in philosophy, in background, but somehow these differences were a source of vitality rather than disharmony in the collaborative partnership that swiftly evolved. He was an established professional writer, but his discipline had collapsed and he was writing very little; I was unknown but ambitious. He had a scientific education; mine was literary. Garrett was an efficient storyteller, but his prose was mechanical; I had trouble constructing internally consistent plots, but I wrote smoothly and with some grace. Garrett's stories rarely delved into character; I was already concerned, as much as I could be at the age of twenty, with emotional and psychological depth. We began to work together.

Until then I had submitted all my stories by mail or else through my agent. Garrett took me to editorial offices. Editors, he said, bought more readily from writers they had met than from strangers, and lo! it was so. I sold five stories in August of 1955, three in September, three in October, six in November, nine in December. Many of these were collaborations with Garrett, but quite a few were stories I did solo, capitalizing on contacts I had made with his help. Suddenly I was something more than a beginner, here in my final year of college. I was actually earning a living, and quite a good living, by writing. The partnership with Garrett, which lasted until early 1957, accelerated the progress of my career by several years, I think.

Unfortunately there were negative aspects. Once, naively, I had assumed that if I merely wrote the best stories that were in me, editors would recognize their merits and seek my work. Now I was coming to see that there was a quicker road to success: to live in New York, to visit editors regularly, to manufacture fiction to fit their issue-by-issue needs. I developed a deadly facility. If an editor needed a 7,500-word story in three days to balance an issue about to go to press, he needed only to phone me, and I would concoct it. Occasionally I took my time and tried to write the sort of science fiction I respected as a reader, but usually I had trouble placing such stories, which reinforced my growing cynicism. By the summer of 1956—by which time I had graduated from college and had married—I was the complete writing machine, turning out stories in all lengths at whatever quality the editor desired, from slam-bang adventure to cerebral pseudo-philosophy. No longer willing to agonize over the gulf between my literary ambitions and my actual productions, I wrote with astonishing speed, selling fifteen stories in June of 1956, twenty the following month, fourteen (including a three-part novel, done with Garrett) the month after that.

This hectic productivity was crowned at the World S-F Convention in September, 1956 when the readership voted me an award as the most promising new writer of the year. The basis for this could only have been my ubiquity, since most of what I had published was carefully carpentered but mediocre, and much was wholly opportunistic trash.

By this time I was self-contained, confident, quite sure of what I was doing and why. A few older writers tried to shake my cynicism and persuade me to aim higher than sure-thing potboilers, but it was clear that potboilers were what I wanted to write. No one could argue with my success at pounding out penny-a-word dreadfuls. I was only a boy, yet already my annual income was beyond that of anyone in s-f except a few long-enshrined demigods—Bradbury, Clarke, Heinlein.

Why potboilers? Because, I said, not without some justice, potboilers were fundamentally what editors in my chosen field wanted to publish. Only a privileged few were allowed somehow to reach beyond the basically trivial formulas of magazine fiction. What I dared not admit to anyone else was an underlying feeling that I had opted to write mechanical junk because I had no gift for writing anything better. My craftsmanship was improving steadily, yes, but possibly there was some fatal defect of the soul, some missing quality, that kept me from using it toward any worthwhile purpose. And so there was, but it was one that time could be expected to heal: I was still only twenty-one years old, a neophyte in the world. Out of what fund of experience was I supposed to create worthwhile fiction? I will leave art to the artists, I said quietly, and earn a decent living doing what I do best.

By the end of 1956 I had more than a million published words behind me. I lived in a large, handsome apartment on Manhattan's desirable Upper West Side. I was learning about fine wines and exotic foods and planning a trip to Europe. Editors sought me, for I was efficient and reliable. My fellow writers viewed me with alarm, seeing me as some sort of berserk robot that would fill every page of every magazine with its uncontrollable output, and they deplored my utter lack of literary ambition. But yet they accepted me as one of their number, and I formed strong friendships within the close-knit s-f community. And I wrote, and I sold, and I prospered. My goal was to win economic security—to get enough money into the bank so that I'd be insulated against the financial storms that had buffeted most writers of my acquaintance. After that, who knew? I might even think about doing second drafts.

So it went through 1957 and 1958. I grew a beard and acquired other, less superficial, stigmata of sophistication. I journeyed to London and Paris, to Arizona and California, treating myself at last to the travels I hadn't had in

boyhood. And I learned the lore of the investment world and made some cautious and quite successful stock-market forays, seeking there the financial independence that I hoped would free me from the karmic wheel of high-volume hackery.

Not everything I wrote was touched by corruption. I still loved science fiction—the true stuff, not the pulp-magazine subvariety—for its soaring visionary expansiveness, for its mind-liberating power, and however dollar-oriented I became I still yearned to make some valuable contribution of my own. I felt guilty that the stuff I was churning out was the sort of thing I had roundly scorned in my fan-magazine critical essays of eight years before. I recall in particular one Sunday afternoon in 1957 when I talked shop at a party with three or four writers whose work I respected highly, and went home in an abyss of self-contempt, thinking that these men, my friends, were striving always to publish only their best while I was content to do my worst. Whenever I felt that sting I put aside hackwork and tried to write something more honest.

Scattered through my vast output of the late 1950s, then, are some quite respectable stories. Not masterpieces—I was still very young, and much more callow than most people suspected—but decently done jobs. Occasionally even now they find their way into anthologies. They were my comfort in those guilt-ridden days.

Particularly the novels. I genuinely hoped to achieve in books what was beyond me in the magazines. There were only a few publishers of s-f novels in those days, but I quickly found a niche with the least of them, a paperback house known as Ace Books. This small company published scores of novels a year in a rather squalid format, and was constantly searching for new writers to meet its hunger for copy. Its editor, the shrewd and experienced Donald A. Wollheim, worked miracles on a tiny budget, producing an extremely broad list ranging from juvenile action stories to superb novels by Isaac Asimov, Philip K. Dick, Clifford Simak, and other luminaries. Wollheim saw potential in me, perhaps as a mass producer of action fiction and perhaps as something more than that. I wrote ten novels for him, I think, between 1956 and 1963.

My Ace novels would be fruitful material for somebody's thesis. The first, *The Thirteenth Immortal,* was melodramatic and a little absurd, yet sincerely conceived; its myriad faults are those of its author's youth, not his cynical approach toward his trade. The second, *Master of Life and Death* (1957) was something of a tour de force, a maze of plot and sub-plot handled, I think, with some dexterity. *Invaders from Earth* (1958), the third, attempts a sophisticated depiction of psychological and political realities. *Stepsons of Terra* (1958) was an intricate, intense time-paradox novel. On the evidence of these four books, three of which are still in print, I would seem an earnest and ambitious young writer striving constantly to improve. But the later novels I wrote for Ace were slapdash adventure stories: I had learned that there was little money and less prestige in being published by Ace, and without those rewards I was content to do the minimum acceptable job. (A few of my other Ace books were better than that, but they were aimed at better markets and went to Wollheim only after others had rejected them.) I know that Wollheim was disappointed in the trend my work for him had taken; but at a flat rate of $1000 for a full-length novel I felt no motivation to work harder.

During the high-volume years I wrote a good deal that wasn't s-f: crime stories, a few westerns, profiles of movie stars, and other ephemeral odds and ends. Some of this work came to me on assignment from my agent, and some I sought because my rate of productivity was so high that the s-f field couldn't absorb all the wordage I was capable of turning out. Nevertheless I had the conviction, which I suspect remains with me, that to write s-f was my One True Task, and any other kind of writing was mere hackery done to pay the bills. Whatever my private feelings about the quality of most of my s-f at that time, I somehow still saw it as a loftier endeavor than my westerns and crime stories, which I published under pseudonyms: so much anonymous junk.

Late in 1958 the s-f world collapsed. Upheavals in distribution patterns put most of the magazines out of business. My kind of mass production became obsolete. To sustain what had become a comfortable standard of living I had to leave the cozy, incestuous s-f family and move into the general New York publishing scene.

The transition was quick and relatively painless. I was facile, I was confident, and my friends had friends. I hired out to any editor who undertook to pay on time. Though I continued to do a little s-f in 1959 and 1960, my records for those years show all sorts of strange titles: "Cures for Sleepless Nights," "Horror Rides the Freeway," "I Was a Tangier Smuggler," "Hot Rod Challenge," and so many others that it strains my own credulity. I recall writing one piece before lunch and one after lunch, day in, day out; my annual output climbed well above a million words in 1959 and went even higher in 1960 and 1961.

These were years of wandering in the wilderness. I lost my identity as a writer. In the past when people asked me what I did I told them I wrote science fiction; now, working anonymously in twenty different subliterate markets, I had no ready reply, so I went on saying I was a science-fiction writer. In truth I did have the occasional story in *Galaxy* or *Astounding,* and an Ace book now and then, to make the claim legitimate. Mainly, though, I was a manufacturer of utilitarian prose churned out by the yard. The work was stupefyingly boring, and, as the money piled up, I invested it shrewdly and talked of retiring by the time I was thirty, spending my days traveling, reading, studying. Already I was doing a good bit of that. In the winters my wife and I fell into the habit of going to the West Indies, where we became skin-divers and explored coral reefs. In the summers we made other journeys—Canada, Italy, the American Northwest. I worked only four or five hours a day, five days a week, which left ample time for my private interests—contemporary literature and music, art, ancient history. There was an almost total schism between my conscienceless, commercialized working-hours self and the civilized and fastidious man who replaced him in early afternoon. I was still only about twenty-five years old.

Unexpectedly the seeds of a new writing career began to sprout. In 1959 I had written a little science-fiction novel for children, *Lost Race of Mars,* for the house of Holt, Rinehart & Winston. The following year, after my Italian trip, I suggested to my Holt editor that I write a book for young readers on the excavation of the ruins of Pompeii. Holt considered the idea for quite a while but ultimately

At the World Science Fiction Convention, New York City, 1956: Silverberg (center) with writer Algis Budrys (left) and Charles Harris (right), sci-fi reader. "I had been married about a week and had graduated from Columbia a couple of months earlier, and at the convention I was given a Hugo Award as the most promising new author of the year."

declined it. Henry Morrison, who then handled my work at the large literary agency that represented me, told me he thought the project would fare better if I wrote not about one ancient site but several—say, Chichen Itza and Angkor and Babylon as well as Pompeii—and he even offered me a title for the expanded book: *Lost Cities and Vanished Civilizations*. On the basis of a brief outline, he sold it to a Philadelphia house of which I knew nothing, Chilton Books. When it was published in 1962, it was chosen by a major book club and received several awards.

And so I began to emerge from that wilderness of anonymous potboilerei. Now suddenly I was a writer of book-length nonfiction books on archaeology, on the American space program, on the life of Sir Winston Churchill, and ever so much more. I displayed gifts for quick, comprehensive research and orderly, uncluttered exposition that encouraged publishers to solicit my work. Once again I found myself launched.

As rapidly as I dared, I severed my connections with my sleazy magazine outlets and ascended into this new, astoundingly respectable and rewarding career. Chilton took another general archaeology book, *Empires in the Dust*. Holt accepted a biography of the great Assyriologist, Sir Austen Henry Layard. The New York Graphic Society commissioned a book on American Indians, and Putnam, one on the history of medicine.

The rhythm of my life changed dramatically. I still wrote in the mornings and early afternoons—wrote at almost the same incredible velocity as when I had been doing tales of Tangier smugglers—but now I spent the after-hours time taking notes in libraries and museums, and I began to assemble a vast private reference library at home. Though my early nonfiction books had been hasty compilations out of other popularizations, I swiftly became more conscientious; I went to primary sources and visited the sites of my subjects whenever I could. The results were visible. Within a year or two I was considered one of the most skilled popularizers of the sciences in the United States, with publishers eagerly standing in line as my changing interests took me from books on Antarctica and ancient Egypt to investigations of scientific hoaxes and living fossils. For the first time since becoming a professional writer nearly a decade earlier, I had won my own respect; but I had had to leave science fiction to do it.

I maintained a tenuous link with s-f, largely a social one, since, then as now, my closest friends were science-fictionists. I attended parties and conventions, and kept up with what was being published. But of actual s-f writing I was doing very little. There seemed no commercial reason to get back into it, even though it had recovered considerably from its 1958 swoon; I had more work than I could handle in my lucrative new field. Only the old shame remained to tweak me: I had served s-f badly, and I wanted to atone. When Frederik Pohl became editor of *Galaxy,* he suggested that I do short stories for him and offered me absolute creative freedom: I could write what I pleased, and, within reason, he undertook to buy it. With such a deal I could hardly blame the shortcomings of editors for the quality of what I wrote: I was my own master. In the

Silverberg, about 1966, photographed by Clifford D. Simak in his Minneapolis Tribune *office. "My Brooks-Brothers-and-bow-tie period."*

summer of 1962 I offered Pohl a short story, "To See the Invisible Man," inspired by Borges: a mature, complex story unlike anything I had done before. He published it and took, over the next couple of years, half a dozen more of similarly ambitious nature. Bit by bit I found myself drawn back into s-f, this time not as a producer of yard goods but as a serious, dedicated artist who was willing to turn away from more profitable work to indulge in s-f out of love.

At that time the science-fiction world was undergoing radical changes. The old pulp-magazine rigidities were dissolving. New writers were everywhere: Brian Aldiss, J. G. Ballard, Roger Zelazny, Samuel R. Delany, Michael Moorcock, and a dozen others. In the bad old days nearly everyone had written in an interchangeable manner, un-questioningly adopting standardized conventions of style and construction. Now editors were beginning to think—wrongly, as it turned out—that the readers were capable of accepting something richer. The requirement for neat plots and positive "upbeat" resolutions was abandoned. Stylistic experimentation was encouraged. I had been only too willing, in 1957 and thereabouts, to conform to the prevailing modes, for it seemed quixotic to try to do otherwise. Now an army of new writers and some brave new editors had boldly overthrown the traditional rules, and, a trifle belatedly, I joined the revolution.

But the nonfiction books remained my chief preoccupation. For one thing, to go back to mass production of s-f would be to defeat the purpose of returning; for another, I had nonfiction contracts two or three years into the future, and there was no question of a full-scale resumption of s-f. The nonfiction was becoming ever more ambitious, too; in the summer of 1963 I spent months working on one project alone, which I had never done before. (It was a book on the Great Wall of China—no mere cut-and-paste job, but an elaborate and unique synthesis of all available knowledge about the Wall.) Then, too, s-f had become more permissive but there still wasn't much money in it, and I was continuing to pursue my goal of economic independence, which mandated my centering my career in other fields.

One gigantic item of overhead had entered my life. Early in 1962 I had purchased an imposing house—a mansion, in fact—in a lovely, almost rural enclave in the northwest corner of New York City. I had always lived in apartments; now I had my own lawn and garden, my own giant oak trees, my own wild raccoons wandering about at night (in New York!). There was room for all my books and all I was likely to acquire for years to come. The third floor of the house, a separate four-room suite, became my working area, and we filled the rest of the place with books and paintings and objets d'art. It was a magnificent house, beautiful and stately. But the upkeep, taxes and cleaning and heat and all, ran to many thousands of dollars a year; though I still intended to retire from full-time high-volume writing as soon as possible, I was aware that by buying the house I had postponed that retirement by at least five years.

Driven by vanity, I suppose, or by intellectual pride, or merely by the feeling that it was time for my reach to begin exceeding my grasp, I tackled bigger and bigger projects. The Great Wall book was the first of these; then early in 1966 I embarked on a far more arduous task, a book called *The Golden Dream,* a study of the obsessive quest for the mythical land of El Dorado. After living under an

The author (right) with Philip K. Dick (far left), "the late, great science fiction writer," at the 1968 World Science Fiction Convention, Oakland, California.

impossible, brutal schedule for years, pouring out thousands of words a week, I knew more than a little about the psychology of obsession, and the book, 120,000 words long, was surely the finest thing I had ever done. It was published in an appropriately handsome edition by Bobbs-Merrill, was treated with respect by reviewers, and dropped into oblivion as fast as any of my hackwork. The book earned me no income beyond the small initial advance in the United States, was never published at all in Great Britain, and achieved only one translation, in France. I was disappointed but not discouraged; it would have been nice to grow rich on the book, but that was secondary to the joy and challenge of having written it. When I was nineteen I found it so dismaying to have difficulty selling my most seriously conceived stories that I took refuge in soulless wordmongering; but, no longer nineteen, I was learning to love my work for its own sake, regardless of its fate in the marketplace. Growing up a little, that is.

S cience fiction maintained its hold on me. In 1965 I built close associations with the two major s-f houses of the day, Doubleday and Ballantine. (Though I considered myself a very part-time s-f writer, I was still prolific enough to require two regular publishers.) To Ballantine I gave *To Open the Sky,* a pseudo-novel constructed from five novelettes I had written for Fred Pohl's *Galaxy.* To Doubleday I offered *The Time Hoppers,* an expansion of one of those ambitious short stories that I had had so much trouble placing in 1954. They were both good middle-of-the-road books, several notches above any s-f I had published until that time. Then came a bolder step: in January of 1966 I offered Ballantine a novel called *Thorns,* telling them, "What I have in mind is a psychological s-f novel, somewhat adventurous in style and approach and characterization." Betty Ballantine agreed to the gamble.

I spent the next few months writing the El Dorado book, and in June I fell mysteriously ill. All energy went

from me and I lost close to twenty pounds—though I was slender to begin with—in a few weeks. The symptoms answered well to leukemia and other dire things, but all I had, I discovered, was a metabolic upset, a sudden hyperactivity of the thyroid gland. This apparently can be caused by the stress of prolonged overwork, and I think the forced marches of El Dorado had much to do with it. I took it as a warning: I was past thirty and it was time to think realistically about slowing down.

Though greatly weakened, I wrote steadily—but at a reduced pace—through the infernally hot summer of 1966, while at the same time planning *Thorns* and doing preliminary research for another major nonfiction work, a study of the prehistoric Mound Builder cultures of the central United States. I was still gaunt and haggard when I attended the annual s-f convention at Cleveland at the beginning of September, but drug therapy for my thyroid condition was beginning to take hold, and just after the convention I felt strong enough to begin *Thorns.* The title describes the book: rough, prickly, sharp. I worked quickly, often managing twenty pages or more a day, yet making no concessions to the conventions of standard s-f. The prose was oblique and elliptical (and sometimes shamefully opaque in a way I'd love retroactively to fix); the action was fragmented in the telling; the characters were angular, troubled souls. I don't think anyone was expecting me to write a book like that. My fellow writers looked on me with a sort of respect for my productivity and professionalism, but they had long since given up hope that I would do anything more than a craftsman-like job of yarn-spinning and dollar-fetching.

I regained my health by the end of the year and eventually made a full and permanent recovery. Bit by bit I withdrew from my lunatic work schedule now: having written an unthinkable million and a half words for publication in 1965, I barely exceeded a million—still an absurd number—in 1966, and have never been anywhere near that insane level of productivity since. I worked less feverishly, content to quit early if I had had a good morning at the typewriter, and took more frequent holidays; and I began alternating s-f and nonfiction books to provide myself with periodic changes of rhythm.

For a man who was cutting back on his work schedule, though, 1967 was an extraordinary year. I wrote a novel for Doubleday, *To Live Again,* which surpassed anything I had done in complexity of plot and development of social situation. For Doubleday, also, I expanded an ambitious 1966 novella, "Hawksbill Station," to novel length. I did my vast Mound Builder book, which was as much a study of the myth-making process as it was an exploration of American Indian culture. (When it appeared in 1968, as *Mound Builders of Ancient America: the Archaeology of a Myth,* many reviewers, even those in the archaeological journals, assumed I was myself an archaeologist, and I received flattering if embarrassing invitations to lecture, to teach, and to write reviews. The book was greeted enthusiastically by professional archaeologists and has become a standard reference item.) There were three other big projects in this year of supposedly reduced output: the novels *The Masks of Time* and *The Man in the Maze,* and another Goliath of a nonfiction work, *The Longest Voyage,* an account of the first six circumnavigations of the world.

I was, in truth, riding an incredible wave of creative energy. Perhaps it was an overcompensation for my period of fatigue and illness in 1966, perhaps just the sense of liberation and excitement that came from knowing I was at last writing only what I wanted to write in the way I wanted to write it. In any event I look back in wonder and awe at a year that produced four significant novels, two 150,000-word works of history, several short stories, and—I have as much trouble believing this as you—no less than seven nonfiction books for young readers, each in the 60,000-word range. No wonder my peers regarded me as some sort of robot. I have no idea how I managed it all, working five hours a day five days a week, with time off for holidays in Israel and the West Indies and a week at Montreal's Expo '67.

Thorns was published in August of 1967. Many of my colleagues read it and it shook their image of my work. At least a dozen friends told me, with the frankness of true friendship, that the book had amazed them: not that they thought I was incapable of writing it, but rather that I would be willing to take the trouble. It seemed such a radical break from my formularized s-f of the 1950s that they thought of it as the work of some entirely new Robert Silverberg. I was pleased, of course, but also a little pained to realize how totally I had been judged all those years by the basest of what I had written between 1955 and 1958. *Thorns* was not all that much of a breakthrough for me; it represented only a plausible outgrowth of what I had begun to attempt in 1962's "To See the Invisible Man," and in the work that had followed it over a period of four years.

Those who had lamented my early decision to limit myself to hackwork rejoiced now that I was writing in my true voice at last. But those who had found pleasure in my old straightforward action stories were appalled by the dark, disturbing *Thorns*. One of my dearest friends, an old-line writer conservative in his tastes, explicitly accused me of a calculated sellout to the "new wave" of science fiction—of writing a deliberately harsh and freaky book to curry favor with the influential leaders of the revolution within s-f. That charge was particularly painful to me. Having blithely sold out as a young man so many times to any editor with the right price in his hand, I was stunned to find myself accused of selling out again, this time to the opposite camp, now that I finally had written something that grew from my own creative needs instead of the market's demands. By opting now to write a more personal, a less blatantly commercial, kind of s-f, I was (though I didn't realize it yet) setting myself up for a descent into confusion and creative paralysis.

Thorns was nominated for both of s-f's major awards, the Hugo given by the fans and the Nebula given by the writers. The novella version of "Hawksbill Station" also was on both ballots that year. It was the first time anything of mine had reached the final ballot in awards voting. (Ultimately I was destined to be nominated for more awards than any writer in the history of s-f.) But I won no trophies that year. (Ultimately I was destined to lose more awards than any writer in the history of s-f.) Naively I thought that all I had to do was write as well as I knew I could, and the awards and acclaim would follow automatically. And so they did, to a considerable extent; but there were many ugly surprises ahead.

The first of them had nothing to do with literary matters. I awakened at half past three one frigid morning in February of 1968 to the glare of an unaccustomed light in the house. Burglars have broken in, I thought, but no: the glare I saw was fire.

So out into the miserable night we went and watched the house burn. Papers stored in the attic, I think, had ignited. My wife and I carried our four cats and a flock of kittens to safety in the basement, and I seized the manuscript of my current book and a few ancient artifacts and cached them in the garage; then the firemen refused to let us return to the building, and we took refuge in the house across the way. By dawn it was over. The roof was gone; the attic had been gutted; my third-floor office was a wreck; and the lower floors of the house, though unburned, were awash in water rapidly turning to ice. A priest from a nearby Catholic college appeared and, unbidden, took several carloads of our houseplants to safety in his cabin, lest they freeze in the unprotected house. Then he returned and offered consolation, for I was in a bad way. No Catholic I, but I had felt the hand of some supernatural being pressing against me that night, punishing me for real and imagined sins, leveling me for overweening pride as though I had tried to be Agamemnon.

Winning the Nebula Award for the short story "Passengers," 1970.

Friends rallied round. My wife performed prodigies, arranging to have our belongings taken to storage (surprisingly, most of our books and virtually all the works of art had survived, though the structure itself was a ruin) and negotiating with contractors. I wasn't much good for anything for days—stupefied, God-haunted, broken. We moved to a small, inadequate rented house about a mile away as the immense job of reconstruction began. I bought a new typewriter, reassembled some reference books, and, after a few dreadful weeks, began once more to write.

In nine months the house was ready to be reoccupied, and by the spring of 1969 the last of the rebuilding was done and the place was more beautiful than ever. But I was never the same again. Until the night of the fire I had never, except perhaps at the onset of my illness in 1966, been touched by the real anguish of life. I hadn't known divorce or the death of loved ones or poverty or unemployment, I had never experienced the challenges and terrors of parenthood, had never been mugged or assaulted or molested, had not been in military service, had never been seriously ill. The only emotional scars I bore were those of a moderately unhappy childhood, and almost everyone has those. But now I had literally passed through the flames. The fire and certain other upheavals some months earlier had marked an end to my apparent immunity to life's pain, and had drained from me, evidently forever, much of the bizarre energy that had allowed me to write a dozen or more significant books in a single year. Until 1967 I had cockily written everything in one draft, rolling white paper into the machine and merrily typing away, turning out twenty or thirty pages of final copy every day and making only minor corrections afterward by hand. When I resumed work after the fire I tried to go on that way, but I found the going slow, found myself fumbling for words and losing the thread of narrative, found it necessary in mid-page to halt and start over, pausing often to regain my strength. It has been slower and slower ever since, and I have only rarely, and not for a long time now, felt that dynamic sense of clear vision that enabled me to write even the most taxing of my books in wild joyous spurts. I wasted thousands of sheets of paper over the next three years before I came to see, at last, that I had become as other mortals and would have to do two or three or even ten drafts of every page before I could hope to type final copy.

I hated the place where we settled after the fire. It was cramped, dirty, confused, ugly. But whatever its inconveniences and whatever my mood, I had to get back to work, for the rebuilding job was calling for thousands of dollars beyond the insurance payment. With most of my reference library in storage, nonfiction became impossible, and I was forced back into full-time s-f. One of the first things I wrote, in the early days of the aftermath, was a curiously lyrical novella, "Nightwings," to which I added a pair of sequels some months later to constitute a novel. Later in the year came a novel for young readers, *Across a Billion Years,* and somehow also, despite my despair and fatigue, a bawdy comic novel of time travel, *Up the Line.* The fire had shattered me emotionally and for a time physically, but it had pushed me, I realized, into a deeper, more profound expression of feelings. It had been a monstrous tempering of my artistic skills.

In September of 1968 I went to California for the s-f convention—my third visit to that state. I was struck once again by its beauty and strangeness. November saw me back in my restored house, working on the biggest of all my nonfiction books, an immense exploration of the Zionist movement in America. The publishers invested a huge sum of money in it, and told me the book would reach the best-seller list; but, as usual, nothing came of it but good reviews: the publishers perversely refused to advertise or promote, and sales were poor. I was destined never to win wide attention for my long nonfiction books.

My s-f, though, was gathering acclaim. *Masks of Time* failed by only a few votes to win a Nebula, as did the novella "Nightwings." But "Nightwings" did take a Hugo at the St. Louis convention in 1969. In the spring of that year I wrote a novel, *Downward to the Earth,* in part inspired by a journey to Africa and in part by my own growing sense of cosmic consciousness: I had never been a religious man, had never belonged to any organized church, but something had been set ticking in me by the fire, a sense of connections and compensating forces, and *Downward to the Earth* reflected it. For Ballantine, later in the year, I wrote my strangest, most individual book, *Son of Man,* a dream-fantasy of the far future, with overtones of Stapledon and Lindsay's *Voyage to Arcturus* and a dollop of psychedelia that was altogether my own contribution. Also I produced—slowly, with much difficulty—*Tower of Glass,* another highly ambitious book. My publisher for that was Scribner, then experimenting with s-f. I imagined that the publisher of Hemingway and Fitzgerald and Wolfe could move me toward the audience I had come to hope to reach: literate adults whose imaginations might be kindled by the imagery of science fiction. Double disillusionment there; Scribner treated my books as casually as all my previous publishers had, dumping them forth in small editions without benefit of promotion, and that audience of literate adults, though I had not yet come to realize it, may not exist. I was deceiving myself into thinking that s-f, which in the United States is regarded by publishers as adventure fiction for adolescents, could be approached with the same intensity of purpose that, say, Conrad or Faulkner or Malraux approached their material. I had moved too far, from cheerful young hack to keenly ambitious serious novelist, without seeing the folly of what I was trying to do.

The paradox of this stage of my career manifested itself ever more forcefully in 1970: I felt continued growth of my art, my power, my vision, and simultaneously it became more difficult to work. I tired more easily, I let myself be distracted by trifles, and when I did write I was lucky to get nine or ten pages written in a day. Still an immense output, but not what I had grown accustomed to pulling from myself in the vanished days of indefatigability. Nevertheless it was an active year that any writer would envy. I did *The World Inside,* a novel composed of loosely related short stories set within a single great residential tower; I think it and *Tower of Glass* are closer to pure s-f, the exhaustive investigation of an extrapolative idea, than anything else I have written. I did *A Time of Changes,* more emotional than most of my work and heavily pro-psychedelic. I did *The Second Trip,* a rough and brutal novel of double identity, and I wrote the last of my major nonfiction books, *The Realm of Prester John,* which I regard as a genuine contribution to scholarship. (Doubleday published it and no one bought it.)

By now it was clear that the s-f world had forgiven me for the literary sins of my youth. The critics had been reevaluating me, allowing me a place near the head of the class but invariably invoking my seamy early work before getting around to remarking on my startling transformation; now they took each new book on its own terms, as the work of a leader in the field, without expressing quite so much surprise that the former author of so much junk (more than a decade earlier!) was apparently capable of non-junk. My short story "Passengers" won a Nebula in 1970. *Up the Line* and one of the *Nightwings* series were on the ballot also, unsuccessfully. In the summer I was American Guest of Honor at the World Science Fiction Convention in Germany, somewhat to my surprise: I had begun to think that I might someday be chosen for this greatest of s-f honors, but I had assumed it was a decade or more in the future. I was a triple Hugo nominee that year also, but came away, alas, with a bunch of second and third place finishes.

My new working habits were entrenching themselves: revise, revise, revise. Projects that might have taken me two weeks in 1965 took three months in 1970. No longer did I sign contracts stretching two or three years ahead, for I knew I would be unable to meet such vast obligations. I phased out nonfiction entirely; I had had a good run in that career, but the burden of research now was more than I cared to carry, and the failure of my big books to have much commercial success had eventually had a depressing effect. Now that I was in my full stride in s-f, working at the top of my form and apparently enjoying public favor, I wanted to devote as much of my dwindling literary

energies as I could to the field I had always regarded as my special province.

Strangely, it was becoming hard for me to take the stuff of s-f seriously any more—all those starships and androids and galactic empires. Perhaps it was just fatigue, but I had come to believe that the chances that mankind would reach and colonize the planets of other stars were very slight indeed, and the stories set on such worlds now seemed idle fantasy to me. So too with many of the other great s-f themes: one by one they became unreal, though they continued to have powerful metaphorical and symbolic value for me. I discovered that much of what I was writing in 1971 was either barely s-f at all (*The Book of Skulls*) or was a kind of parody of s-f ("Good News from the Vatican," "Caliban," and other short stories) or employed a genuine s-f theme within an otherwise "straight" mainstream novel (*Dying Inside*). This inspired flickers of new guilt in me. I no longer had to apologize for shortcomings of literary quality; but was this new Silverberg really serving the needs of the hard-core s-f audience? Was he providing the kind of sincerely felt fiction about the future that the readers presumably were looking for, or was he doing fancy dancing for his own amusement and that of a jaded elite?

The pattern of awards in the field reinforced these doubts. I was getting nominated by twos and threes every year now for Hugos and Nebulas. In 1972 the Science Fiction Writers of America favored me with two Nebulas, an unusual honor, for my novel *A Time of Changes* and my short story "Good News from the Vatican"—but the writers have relatively sophisticated tastes, and I was faring far less well with the Hugos, awarded by a broader cross-section of the s-f readership. Though nominated almost every year, my books and stories invariably finished well behind more conservative, "safer" works. At the outset of my career I had sadly concluded that I needed to write junk to survive, because junk was what the readers wanted. The great literary transformation of s-f in the mid-1960s had seduced me into thinking that it was permissible now to work to the limits of my skill, treating the material of s-f with the full range of modern literary techniques. Publishers had encouraged me in this with a torrent of contracts. But the somber truth was beginning to emerge. The s-f revolution of 1964-71 had been a fluke, an anomaly; the bulk of the readers wanted the good old simple bang-bang adventure stuff. That was showing up in the Hugo voting results, and—belatedly—it was showing up in the paperback sales figures. I had been right the first time, it seemed. The science-fiction world was no place to try to be James Joyce.

In 1971 I at last achieved the partial retirement of which I had been dreaming for so many years. In late spring I simply stopped writing, not to resume until autumn. I had never, not since college days, gone more than four weeks away from my typewriter; now I took five months off, and felt no withdrawal symptoms at all. I read, swam, loafed; now and then I would work on anthology editing for an hour or so in the morning, for such editing was becoming increasingly important to me, but essentially I was idle all summer. A more complete break with the old Silverberg could not have been imagined.

In the garden of his new home in California, "The peak of my psychedelic period," 1972.

Further transformations of my life, unexpected ones, lay in wait. My wife and I were native New Yorkers. We loved the city's vitality, its complexity, the variety of experience it offered, and we had money enough to insulate ourselves from its inconveniences and perils. Our rebuilt house was more than a dwelling to us, it was a system of life, an exoskeleton. We assumed we would live in it the rest of our lives. But New York was in decline, and its deterioration was driving away our friends. Two by two they trooped away, some to distant suburbs, many to California; and by the autumn of 1971 we found ourselves isolated and lonely in a dangerous, dirty, expensive city that suddenly was too much for us. We were held fast by pride and pleasure in our house, yes; but timidly we began to talk about joining the exodus. Actually the city was not really all that bad, I must admit. But a restlessness had grown in us, particularly in me. It still seemed unthinkable to leave; we toyed with the notion of moving to California the way lifelong Catholics might toy with the idea of conversion to Buddhism, enjoying the novelty and daring of such an outlandish idea but never taking it seriously. In October of 1971 we flew to San Francisco for a reunion with many of our transplanted Eastern friends; we said we were considering moving, and they urged us to come. It was impossible to give up our house, we said. But before the end of the year we were out west again, and to our amazement we found ourselves placing a bid on a Bay Area house, a strange and beautiful one, an architectural landmark in a park-like setting. As if in a dream we put our cherished New York mansion up for sale and headed for California. It all happened so swiftly, in retrospect—less than six months from the moment the temptation first struck to the day we arrived, with tons of books and furniture, in golden California, in the new El Dorado.

California, then. A life at mid-point, a life in crisis. I wrote less and less: mornings only, and only between November and April, the rainy season in northern California. At first, getting used to my brave new world, I did nothing but short stories. The year 1972 saw me produce just 115,000 publishable words, or about what I would have done in an average month a decade earlier. In 1973, with great pain and difficulty, I managed a novella, "Born with the Dead," perhaps the best thing I have ever written. It won another Nebula, my fourth. That fall I wrote two short stories, "In the House of Double Minds" and "Schwartz Between the Galaxies." They took a terrible toll on me, weeks and weeks of ghastly revision, and one morning I came to a startling resolution: I would never write another short story. From now on, only novels, and all that winter of 1973-74 I struggled monstrously with a book called *The Stochastic Man*.

Something was happening. I was approaching forty; I was living in a strange land; my marriage of nearly twenty years was falling apart. And then in the autumn of 1974 I discovered that my books, all those marvelous novels of which I was so proud, were out of print. *Downward to the Earth* and *Thorns* and *Tower of Glass* and all the rest, almost every one of them an awards nominee, had failed to hold their own with the paperback audience; they were gone and the paperback publishers, many of them my close friends, would not reissue them. Junk was triumphant in the

bookshops. Cheerful escapist adventure, of the kind I had been so happy to churn out in 1956, was what was selling. But for me there was no going back. Returning to hackwork was inconceivable. Plunging onward, writing complex and demanding books at enormous emotional cost for a readership that didn't seem to exist, was equally impossible for me. I was in despair. Sales figures aren't everything, not even to a professional writer; but they are something, and not a small something. The publishers who refused to support my backlist books were still willing, and more than willing, to give me contracts for new ones, yes. But publishers, though they are often foolish, aren't *always* foolish. If my backlist books were deemed to be over the heads of the audience—too complex, too intense, too depressing to meet the escapist needs of the readership— then sooner or later there would be no contracts for new books either, and I would lose my franchise and my livelihood. Publishers admired my reliability and my professionalism, and I suppose saw me as an ornament to their lists; but their refusal to sustain the best of my earlier work (because the mass of the readers wouldn't) was a mortal blow. For months I pondered the problem of the out-of-print books. I pleaded with my publishers for reissues. "Maybe next year," they said, without much enthusiasm. Late in 1974 I set to work on my one remaining contract, a book called *Shadrach In the Furnace*. For the first few weeks I could manage no more than a paragraph or two a day. Then came a liberating revelation. My investments had made me financially independent. Very well, then: I would walk away from the struggle. After twenty years as a professional writer I would simply retire. There was no room for me in the s-f world, now that the counter-revolution was in full swing and the "literary" writers had been routed. I felt no particular impulse to write anything else. I was exhausted, burned out, done for. Like Coriolanus, I banished *them*. In a final burst of energy I finished *Shadrach* and early in 1975 I astounded everyone with a public and furious announcement that I was retiring forever.

The reactions were interesting. Predictably, the adventure-story fans responded with a "good riddance." Others, my loyal audience (and I really had one, I learned) bitterly reproached me for abandoning them, as though I had no right to stop writing. My friends, aware of how tired I was, approved of my decision but most of them knowingly told me I'd be back at work in six months, and that I *ought* to be. Only the closest and most loving ones seemed to believe that I meant it when I said I would never write again.

Beyond any doubt I was sincere. I had always been interested in botany, and since coming to California's benign climate I had become a passionate gardener. That was all I wanted to do; and for four years that was all I did. Here in my retirement publishers offered me contracts— seeing it as a challenge, perhaps, to lure me back to work— and with great delight I turned them down—even one carrying a $50,000 advance, vastly more than anyone had paid me during my career. "Sorry," I said. "I'm not a writer any more." There was immense vindictive pleasure in that for me. I pottered with my cacti and my fuchsias and my aloes; I read almost no s-f and paid no attention to publishing gossip; I woke each morning refreshed and eager to design the day for myself, and writing was never a

A relaxed moment at a science fiction convention, Los Angeles, 1976.

part of it. The years went by. I knew I would never write again, and it was tremendously exhilarating knowledge. When a friend did try to pressure me in 1977 into doing a short story for a special project of his, I made a game try and couldn't get two sentences into it. It was really over for me. As a boy I had yearned to write great science fiction books, and I had, and to my deep bewilderment it had not worked out anything as I had expected; but all that was behind me now. I had had my career. Now I had my garden.

I spent four years healing. Along the way, the paperback houses began to reissue some of my better books; but I stayed retired, and went on loving it. And then one sunny afternoon in the spring of 1978 I phoned my agent and told him I had decided to write another novel after all.

It was not, I explained, the end of my retirement. My wife and I had separated a year and a half earlier, and now she wanted to buy the house she had been renting. Very well: I would write a novel, put it up for auction with a lofty minimum bid, and use the proceeds to buy her her house. One book, one house, and then back to my gardening. That was very clear to me.

The science-fiction field had changed, not for the better, during my absence. In the aftermath of the Tolkien phenomenon, a new kind of novel dominated the lists, more fantasy than science fiction, a thing of wizards and elves and gentle princes and dark villains, often sprawling over three volumes. This stuff seemed to be crowding the old sort of s-f into a corner. The new readership, largely young and predominantly female, seemed to have an insatiable appetite for it. In designing the novel with which I would

return, I had no stomach for concocting pseudo-Tolkien, but I knew I had to avoid anything dark, depressing, or technically demanding. All in an instant I had my book, title and all: *Lord Valentine's Castle,* the story of a disinherited prince. Though science-fictional in form (the alien world of Majipoor, various life-forms, far future) the tone would be the one of the currently fashionable fantasies, though I could not help but tell the story in my own true voice.

There was little surprise at my return. Evidently everyone but me had known all along that I would eventually start writing again. We auctioned *Lord Valentine's Castle* to Harper & Row for what was then the largest sum ever paid for hardcover rights to a science-fiction novel—$127,500—and on November 1, 1978, I sat down with no little trepidation to begin the book. Somewhat to my amazement I did ten pages the first day, ten the second, and sailed along smoothly in that fashion for three months more until I was done with the first draft. Another two months for revisions; the book was turned in in April, 1979; and, as I had sworn, back I went into retirement. There I stayed for almost a year. But then I was lured into work again. Old friends had taken over the editorship of the slick new magazine *Omni.* They offered me a huge fee for a short story—as much as I had been getting for novels ten years before. I suppose it was an offer I couldn't refuse. I spent a tense week trying to regain the difficult skills of short-story writing after a seven-year layoff, discovered I still had the knack, did the story. And another. And another. And by easy stages, lubricated all the way by robust pay-scales, I tricked myself back into a full-time writing career.

The *Omni* stories were the first step. Then I began publishing fiction in *Playboy* as well. Though I had sworn I would never do a sequel to *Lord Valentine's Castle,* I wrote a few short stories set on the same planet, and toyed with the idea of assembling them into a book, *Majipoor Chronicles.* When my agent of twenty-seven years gave me what I considered bad advice about that project, I broke with him—a step as major as a divorce, in my mind—and signed on with the amiable and shrewd Kirby McCauley, whom I had come to know and like in the past few years. I left Harper & Row, also, dissatisfied with the promotional effort for *Castle,* and by so doing inadvertently set in motion a series of bizarre contractual twists that required me to publish my next book through a company I barely knew, Arbor House. It was an amazingly serendipitous bit of confusion, for in coming to Arbor House I stumbled into the publishing relationship I had been looking for all my life, with Arbor's difficult, volatile, cantankerous, brilliant top man, Donald I. Fine. Somehow this controversial publisher and I hit it off marvelously well at first contact and I knew I had found my home.

It has been an interesting time. After Arbor published *Majipoor Chronicles,* I talked Don Fine into allowing me to experiment with escaping s-f at last by doing a stark and gigantic historical novel, *Lord of Darkness.* He agreed, but only if I would also promise to write the much-clamored-for sequel to *Lord Valentine's Castle.* (In the course of writing and rewriting the enormous *Lord of Darkness* I came to retire my old manual typewriter in favor of a word processor, another momentous and valuable change.) *Lord of Darkness,* though it was well received critically, failed to find its audience: bookstores, seeing my name on it, automatically put it in the s-f section. I began to understand that for me there can be no escape from science fiction, no matter what I choose to write.

The Valentine sequel, *Valentine Pontifex,* was more successful; now to a whole new readership I was the author of the famous Majipoor trilogy. I went on to do one more book for Arbor House, yet another historical, *Gilgamesh the King,* but by the time it appeared Don Fine had left Arbor to start his own new company, and I followed him there with my next book, *Tom O'Bedlam.* There I intend to remain.

So here I stand in the mid-1980s with a congenial agent, a devoted publisher, a splendid word processor. My career thrives as never before, and I feel a sense of creative renewal, with new projects thrusting themselves on me all the time. Yet my struggle with science fiction continues. The audience is less demanding than ever—it clamors madly for books that offer simple rewards and easy gratification. All those harsh and intense books that cost me such effort in the 1960s and 1970s have come back into print again—"by the author of the Majipoor Trilogy" on the covers—and they have once again failed to find sufficient readers to keep them in print. They are, I think, splendid books; I remain intensely proud of them; but it seems a hopeless case to try to get the science-fiction audience to appreciate them. Nor do I find it in me to attempt to write new books in the mode of those: that would seem a futile, foredoomed endeavor. But I have no contempt for the work I do in this phase of my career. Since returning from retirement I have tried, and I think succeeded, to find ways of writing commercially successful novels without forfeiting an integrity won in the hardest possible manner; for my escape from the hack writing of my youth was no simple thing. Though I wish the science-fiction audience had a longer reach and a deeper grasp, I suspect that I will continue to go on working in that field despite the problems. I still respond to science fiction as I did when I was a boy, for its capacity to open the gates of the universe, to show me the roots of time. I read very little of it today, but I do go on writing it in my fashion, pursuing an ideal vision in a roundabout way, generally falling short, but coming closer, coming closer now and then, close enough to lead me to continue. For it seems I have no choice but to continue.

And a Postscript (Autumn of 1998)

"No choice but to continue," I said, back there in 1985. And that is the case, thirteen years later: I have continued to write science-fiction and fantasy. Still living in California, too, at the same address, and still working at the battered old metal desk that I have used since 1956. But how much else has changed for me in those thirteen years!

I have a different agent now, a different publisher, a different wife, a different computer, even different cats. The dark Mephistophelian beard of those 1980s photographs is now bright white. The long curling dark hair of the 1972 "psychedelic" photograph is much shorter now, and very much more sparse. The out-of-print books that had returned to print and then vanished again in the closing paragraph of my 1985 essay have all returned yet again and disappeared once more, and once more I am negotiating to have them reprinted. And I have written thirteen years'

worth of new books. And, finally: after all this time I still find myself caught between my decades-old desire to write complex and probing science fiction and the science-fiction audience's predominant wish for easy, light entertainment, despite the eternal irreconcilability of those two facts.

Things change, yes, but somehow the essences remain the same.

The cats, for instance. I find the company of cats necessary. I've had them about me my whole adult life. They make ideal writers' pets: quiet, slinky, beautiful, self-contained. I pamper my cats excessively and they generally live to fine old ages. The trouble is, though, that old age for a cat is fifteen or sixteen years, and I'm always devastated when they die. (My all-time favorite cat lived to be almost nineteen; her nearly-as-beloved predecessor lasted nearly as long.) The cycle has come around again: the cats of the 1980s finally went their way, one in 1993 and the other in 1998, and I am equipped now with successors to see me into the new century. The newest one, perhaps, will still be here when I'm gone. (I suspect that cats miss their people far less than people miss their cats.)

It used to be that one expected one's marriage to last longer than one's cats. Our culture is different now; one clings to one's pets, I gather, but spouses are discarded for the most trivial of reasons. I am of the pre-war vintage, though, raised amidst the turmoil of the Depression and then the war, and we are more retentive in our ways. Unhappy in my obviously collapsing first marriage but unwilling to take the climactic and to me gigantic step of divorce, I remained in a condition of stasis much too long. But eventually the situation became too unstable to sustain. We separated, finally, after twenty years, and I spent the next nine as a single man.

Then, while on a speaking tour in Texas in the spring of 1981, I met a bright, petite, articulate woman from New York who happened to be living just then in Houston and had decided to see what one of her favorite science-fiction authors actually looked like; we exchanged a few pleasant quips, I invited her to have lunch with me, we agreed to stay in touch by mail, and eventually (to her great surprise, I think, and mine as well) she (and her cat) came to live with me in California when her Texas marriage fell apart. Her name is Karen. We were married in February, 1987. She had had a background in journalism, and was a long-time reader of science fiction who had some thought of writing the stuff.

"This is how you construct a story, any kind of story," I told her, "and this is how you use a specifically science-fictional story situation to generate your plot," and I gave her two or three other handy writing tips, and over the past ten years she has had eight novels and about fifty short stories published under her maiden name, Karen Haber. (It seemed to both of us that her writing as Karen Silverberg would only cause confusion in the field where one Silverberg was already so well known.) We edit each other's manuscripts; we go to each other for suggestions when a story idea refuses to gell. Over the years I had heard rumors of the existence of such things as happy marriages; it's a pleasant novelty actually to be a member of one.

A writer's relationship with his agent is much like a marriage in many important ways. My first agent, like my first wife, had many fine qualities, but there were serious things wrong with both relationships, and in both cases I overstayed them by at least a decade. As my earlier essay tells, I went on in 1981 to a second agent, Kirby McCauley, for whom I still feel considerable personal affection. But Kirby's working methods and mine turned out to be incompatible, and we came to a friendly parting of the ways six years later. Since then I have been represented by the formidable Ralph Vicinanza, who is (as it should be between writers and agents) not only my agent but one of my closest friends. We have known each other since the mid-1970s, when he was in charge of foreign-rights sales for my first agent and impressed me again and again with his ability to do long-range planning and to bring those plans to fruition.

His shift to the McCauley agency in 1978 to hold the same post there was an important factor in my going to that agency a few years later; and when he left Kirby in the summer of 1987 to set up his own agency, handling domestic rights as well as overseas ones, I jumped at the chance to go with him. I was his first client, actually. Ralph's agency has grown enormously in the past decade, and by now he holds a dominant position in the science-fiction and fantasy field. We remain as close as ever, despite his greatly expanded responsibilities. We stay in constant contact, seeking each other's advice on personal as well as professional matters; we anticipate each other's thoughts, we finish each other's sentences. In the areas of our lives where we are different from each other, and there are some big ones, we are as different as day and night, but where we are similar we think with one mind. I could not have hoped for a better agent.

My publishers have changed, too. I would have preferred, as John Updike has done, to have remained with a single publisher all my life, but such things are hard to manage in today's immensely transformed publishing world. In my original autobiographical essay I spoke of having "stumbled into the publishing relationship I had been looking for all my life" with the "difficult, volatile, cantankerous, brilliant" Donald I. Fine. And I would gladly have remained with Don forever, except that the small company that he founded in 1984 soon became enmeshed in financial problems, and Don, in an attempt to solve them, entered into a complicated co-publishing arrangement with Warner Books that introduced a degree of chaos into my own career which I found myself unable to abide.

In time I felt compelled to leave Don for Warner, and Warner for Bantam Books, then under the guidance of another old friend of mine, Lou Aronica. I agreed to write five novels in as many years for Lou. The year was 1988. Lou was young, and had never worked anywhere but at Bantam; I fully expected him to stay there forever, and I intended to remain there with him.

But publishing is not like that any more; to my consternation Lou abruptly moved on to another house in 1993, leaving me in the hands of people at Bantam with whom I felt no rapport, and within a couple of years I had taken myself elsewhere too. My current publishing house is HarperCollins, where I am in the hands of a couple of long-time friends, John Silbersack and John Douglas. Will I still be there by the time this postscript appears? Will they? Will HarperCollins still exist as an independent publishing house at all? Things change too fast in publishing these days for me to make any predictions about such things. *Someone* will be publishing my books five years from now,

of that I'm sure. For all I know, I'll still be with HarperCollins. But there are no certainties nowadays.

I had to change computers, too. For someone as conservative as I am, that was a real ordeal. I had been one of the first science-fiction writers to use a computer, back in the dark ages before CP/M, let alone MS-DOS. It was a truly fine machine for its era, but the price I paid for my innovative stance back then was to find myself left alone, after a time, on a technological island, using a splendidly versatile computer and word-processing program both of which had the grave drawback of being totally non-compatible with anything used by anyone else.

One autumn day in 1991, while I was in the midst of writing a long and complex story with a serious deadline attached to it, my computer suddenly decided not to speak to its printer any more, and there was no one left on the planet who understood how to restore the link between those two pieces of obsolete equipment. By heroic measures that constitute an epic in themselves, my unfinished story was rescued from digital form; I keyed it into a newly purchased MS-DOS-based computer, employing a DOS variant of my word-processing program, and have used that machine ever since. Of course, it's pretty much obsolete too, now—the triumphant arrival of Windows swept MS-DOS into the wastebins of computer antiquity—but, in my doggedly conservative way, I still use it for my daily work, because my beloved old word-processing program can't be installed through Windows. (I have a Windows-based computer too, modem and all, but I use it only for e-mail and the Internet.)

My writing output has diminished gradually, here in the fifth decade of my career. Still, I remain a fairly prolific writer, though of course I have never returned to the tremendous, virtually unthinkable productivity of the fifteen years beginning in 1956. I hew pretty closely today to the pattern I set for myself in 1971, which is keyed to the California seasons: usually I begin work in October or November, when our rainy season begins, and carry on through to April or May. This leaves the six dry, sunny months of the California summer for gardening, swimming, travel, or whatever else I please.

Nevertheless, given my habit of intense concentration on my work and ferocious daily application to the task, a working year of five or six months is ordinarily enough to produce a novel and two or three shorter pieces. And thus it has gone over these thirteen years. 1985 saw *Tom O'Bedlam,* a character-driven novel set in the relatively near future—a book that I thought never received the attention it was due. A year later I tried something completely different in *Star of Gypsies,* which I intended as a rich, rollicking space story narrated by a Rabelaisian gypsy king very much unlike the author who created him. That book, too, failed to cause much of a stir, which I ascribe not to any deficiency on its part but to the confusions in my career that the collapse of the Donald Fine publishing company was beginning to cause.

I emerged from that debacle to enter a relationship with Warner Books, a company run by good-natured and well-intentioned people who didn't seem to know much about publishing science fiction. By the time I discovered that, though, I had expended an enormous effort in the creation of what was meant as a vast and visionary epic trilogy set in the unimaginably distant future. I intended the books as a way of showing my love for the sort of fiction that escorts readers through a wholly imaginary world realized with such richness of detail that it would remain part of their mental landscapes forever. But the first two novels in the trilogy—*At Winter's End,* published in 1988, and *The New Springtime,* which appeared in 1990—sold so poorly that the publisher made only a token offer for the rights to the third book, which would have been called *The Summer of Homecoming.* I did not have the heart to undertake so long and punishing a task for so little in the way of financial recompense, particularly at a time when the cost of my too-long-postponed 1986 divorce from my first wife was hitting me hard, and so I refused the offer and the third book has never been written. Which I greatly regret, because it was to have been the summation of the entire grand vision. But I see no way now that I can ever finish the trilogy, since it would be necessary to find someone to republish the first two books before bringing out the third, and I see no likely chance of that.

Four books in a row had failed commercially, although I had found each, in its very different way, personally rewarding to write. And I had, at least, been well paid during this difficult time, since each book carried a healthy guarantee in advance of publication. I would rather see my publishers make money on my books than lose it, but I always see to it that they, not I, carry the economic risk of

publication. There's no other way for a writer to guard against the usual gloomy fate of most publishing deals, which always begin with high hopes, warm feelings, and glowing promises, and generally end with catastrophic bungling on the publisher's part and disappointment for the writer.

So I banked my big Warner checks and went trundling on to the next publisher, who was Lou Aronica of Bantam Books: a man for whom I felt great personal affinity and one whose innovative publishing ideas had shot him to a lofty executive post at a preternaturally early age. We had had a brief publishing flirtation in 1981, which was thwarted by the odd contractual fluke that swept me off to Arbor House; but now Aronica lost no chance to tie me up for years, offering me not only a five-novel contract to write any sort of books I pleased, but also a lucrative three-book deal for collaboration with, of all people, Isaac Asimov.

Isaac had been, of course, one of my boyhood heroes when I was discovering science fiction, and later, after I launched my own professional career, we had become good friends. He was fifteen years my senior, but our lives had had much in common: two bright Jewish boys from Brooklyn, bratty and precocious when young, both educated at Columbia, prolific careers in science fiction afterward, troubled first marriages and expensive divorces followed by happy second marriages.

In the library of his home, 1982.

In 1988, when our collaborative deal surfaced, Isaac's health was beginning to weaken. He felt certain he had just a few years to live, and there were some big books on science he wanted to write, but his publisher—Doubleday—wanted him to write s-f. Since Doubleday now was affiliated with Bantam Books, Lou Aronica arranged a compromise: I would transform three famous novellas of Isaac's into novels under his close direction for Doubleday and Bantam, thus leaving Isaac himself free to write the nonfiction he yearned to do.

The arrangement was that we would plan the expansions of the stories together, but that I would write the first drafts myself, and that meant I needed to absorb and replicate Isaac's own literary style. His prose always was simple, lucid, straightforward. My own tone, somewhat more baroque, had to be suppressed. His narrative method relied almost entirely on dialog and bare-bones exposition; he had little interest in evoking sensory images, particularly visual ones, whereas I have always strived toward rich descriptive impact. But I found it was surprisingly easy to drop into the low-key Asimovian mode of storytelling, especially since I had his original stories ("Nightfall," "The Ugly Little Boy," and "The Bicentennial Man") to use as templates.

"Nightfall" was the first one I did, and it was a strange experience for me to find myself working with a story I had revered since I was twelve years old, adding new sections before and after it and even, to some degree, rewriting the original classic novella itself. But my expansion met with Isaac's enthusiastic blessing. He made relatively few revisions in my text, and the following year I went on to "The Ugly Little Boy."

For this one I was virtually on my own, because Isaac now was seriously ill, and he had neither time nor energy to contribute much to the book, though he did read my draft and give it unqualified approval. I think it was the most successful of the three, greatly extending and illuminating the existing story-line and the character of the protagonist and adding to it a whole layer of background material set in Neanderthal times.

As for the third book, which ultimately appeared under the name of *The Positronic Man,* I believe my work was an important extension of Isaac's moving original story, but I will never know what he thought of it, because he had been hospitalized by the time I finished the book and was in no condition to read my draft. The book appeared soon after his death in 1992. (A few years later it was purchased for filming by Disney, with Robin Williams starring in the movie.)

Meanwhile, alternating with the three Asimov books, I was writing novels of my own for Bantam: *The Face of the Waters* in 1990, *Kingdoms of the Wall* in 1991, *Hot Sky at Midnight* in 1992. The first was a hearkening-back to one of my big themes of two decades before, an isolated and alienated man's complicated quest for submergence in some kind of vast communal entity. It did quite well, going into several printings, my most commercially successful book in some years. The second, diametrically opposed in its conclusions, sent the primitive people of an alien land on a disillusioning search for their gods. Its sales were not quite as good. The third book, a kind of techno-thriller with

a greenhouse-effect world as its setting, had, I thought, an excellent chance of reaching an audience that went far beyond the usual s-f readership, but the publisher wrapped the book in a vivid, sensationalistic genre-fiction jacket that doomed any such hope, and the book did poorly.

I was beginning to understand by now that the modern science-fiction reader, weaned on television series and movie sequels, did not greatly want stand-alone novels. Such singleton items as *Tom O'Bedlam* and *Face of the Waters* and *Hot Sky at Midnight,* whatever their qualities might be, stood little chance of gaining public attention when they had to compete with the latest *Dune* novel, or the newest *Rama* book, or the current sequel to *2001,* or whatever. The series book dominated the marketplace utterly. So I began to plot a return to Majipoor, the world of *Lord Valentine's Castle,* my best-selling book. Bantam owned the paperback rights to *Castle* and its two sequels, *Majipoor Chronicles* and *Valentine Pontifex.* I hatched the idea of kindling new interest in Majipoor by writing a very short novel, *Mountains of Majipoor,* to catch the attention of new readers; Bantam would, at the same time, reissue the original trilogy.

It was another mistake. Very short novels, even if they are connected with well-known series, don't usually sell well either. Today's readers want fat books. *Mountains* did very poorly indeed and provided no help whatever for a reissue of the trilogy.

With two books left on my main five-book Bantam contract, I was in commercial trouble. And about this time, Lou Aronica left Bantam Books, and I was bereft of his invaluable counsel and support. I wrote the fourth Bantam book, *Starborne,* without much hope that the new administration at Bantam would get behind it. And then, even before *Starborne's* inevitable failure in the marketplace, I bailed out once more, buying back the fifth book in the Bantam contract and taking myself over to HarperCollins, the successor to Harper & Row, which was the company

Silverberg with the beard of his mature years,
1993.

for whom I had written *Lord Valentine's Castle* sixteen years before.

The plan was to write new Majipoor novels for them—full-length ones, big books in the modern mode that would appeal not to the science-fiction audience but to the far larger one that doted on fantasy. Through an intricate contractual maneuver I was able to bring the paperback rights of the previous Majipoor novels along with me, so that HarperCollins would be able to reissue *Lord Valentine's Castle* and its companions in paperback format along with the new books, giving me renewed visibility in this era of multi-volume series.

And so it happened. They put out *Castle* and *Chronicles* and *Pontifex* in handsome new reprint editions using Jim Burns' elegant cover art from the decade before, and I wrote *Sorcerers of Majipoor* in 1996 and its sequel, *Lord Prestimion,* two years later, with possible further Majipoor books to follow.

The Majipoor concept is essentially inexhaustible—a world ten times the size of Earth, with 14,000 years of history since the arrival of the first human settlers and a lengthy prehistoric period besides—and I could easily use it as a source for books for the rest of my life. But that's not what I want to do, however eager the readers are for more and more and more. It's not my intention to let the Majipoor books eclipse everything else I've done.

And so the book that immediately followed *Sorcerers of Majipoor* was not its sequel, though I already had that in mind, but rather a wholly unrelated science-fiction novel, *The Alien Years.* In that book I take the grand old H. G. Wells *War of the Worlds* theme and give it a post-modern spin, telling a tale of Earth's conquest that ends not with Hollywood heroics but with an unexpectedly anticlimactic resolution, quite deliberately intended. Some readers evidently were baffled by my apparent failure to finish the book with a pyrotechnic display and were annoyed, but in general *The Alien Years* has had an enthusiastic reception both critically and commercially. It appeared in the summer of 1998, just as I was finishing *Lord Prestimion.* And in the month I write this I am in negotiations both for the third novel in the current Majipoor sequence and for a new stand-alone science-fiction novel that's unlikely to win wide sales but which will satisfy whatever's left of my urge to write the kind of science fiction that I would admire if I were simply a reader of the stuff, not a professional writer with one eye on the royalty charts.

Not that I'm indifferent to the sales figures even now, of course. But my finances are in good order and I'm under no pressing need these days to aim my work for the mass audience, something I was never consistently able to do very well anyway. There's enough income from my existing books, and from such peripheral projects as the best-selling fantasy anthology *Legends* (1998), a collection of eleven big new novellas by the likes of Stephen King, Robert Jordan, Ursula K. Le Guin, and Anne McCaffrey that I edited for Tor Books, to see me through any likely expenses, leaving me free to write just the books I feel like writing. (There has also been a surprising and welcome burst of Hollywood interest in my work in recent years: the short story "Amanda and the Alien" has already been filmed, movies of *The Book of Skulls, The Man in the Maze, The Positronic Man,* and the short stories "Passengers" and "Needle in a Timestack" are in various stages of

becoming reality, and a number of further deals for stories and books of mine are approaching fruition.)

What I wanted, long ago back there in my Brooklyn boyhood, was simply to write a few science-fiction stories that someone would want to publish. After what seemed at the time like an endless period of travail and frustration, but which I now can see in retrospect was an eyeblink moment that led to overnight success, I did indeed accomplish that. And went on from there to spend decade after decade—I am halfway through the fifth of them now—achieving goal after goal, not merely getting published but building a significant career, attaining fame and fortune, winning awards, even writing some stories that I felt were on a par with the great works of science fiction that had drawn me inexorably into this field in the first place half a century ago. If I were looking at my own career from the outside, no doubt I'd envy myself tremendously. Why not? A long life of enormous and seemingly effortless productivity, financial success, and critical acclaim—what more could I have wanted for myself?

Here on the inside it seems a little different. The productivity was enormous, yes, but since the early 1960s, when I put the cheerful churning-out of anonymous hackwork behind me, the sentence-by-sentence job of writing has been by no means effortless for me, however others looking at my great output might think, and some projects have been downright agonizing. This problem has intensified as I grow older and the normal and natural decline of physical energy and imaginative vitality has set in. (Shakespeare did all his work before he reached 50; Dickens died at 58, Hemingway at 61. I'm older than that now. Among my own more immediate colleagues, Robert Heinlein and Isaac Asimov and Ray Bradbury had all produced most of the work for which they are known by the age of 45 or so.) And there has also been the ongoing and insoluble problem of the conflict between my literary ambitions and the fact that science fiction is primarily a species of mass-audience entertainment, an issue that has consumed no little quantity of my ingenuity and from time to time sapped my willingness to write at all.

So my career, marked as it has been by triumph after triumph, has often seemed to me like nothing but a formidable struggle. On half a dozen occasions in my life I have felt that it was a struggle in which I was no longer willing to engage; at least twice I have given it up entirely, only to find myself returning, willy-nilly, to contend against the often maddening forces that keep drawing science fiction back to its pulp-magazine roots. It seems impossible for me to walk away from science fiction altogether, despite my dissatisfactions with the way it is published and my lack of any financial pressure to go on writing here in my sixties.

And so this postscript ends where my original essay does, a dissonant chord resolving itself into an acceptance of an inescapable destiny. I suspect that if I am lucky enough to be asked to provide yet another autobiographical report thirteen years hence, I will once again be found grumbling about the deficiencies of the readership and the deplorably low level of publishing integrity in these modern times—and talking also about my two or three most recent books.

Writings

FOR CHILDREN; FICTION

Revolt on Alpha C, Crowell, 1955.

Starman's Quest, Gnome Press, 1959.

Lost Race of Mars, Winston, 1960.

Regan's Planet, Pyramid Books, 1964, revised edition published as *World's Fair,* 1992, Follett, 1970.

Time of the Great Freeze, Holt, 1964.

The Mask of Akhnaten, Macmillan, 1965.

The Gate of Worlds, Holt, 1967.

The Calibrated Alligator and Other Science Fiction Stories, Holt, 1969.

Across a Billion Years, Dial, 1969.

Sunrise on Mercury and Other Science Fiction Stories, Thomas Nelson, 1975.

(Editor with Charles G. Waugh and Martin H. Greenberg) *The Science Fictional Dinosaur,* Avon, 1982.

NONFICTION

Treasures beneath the Sea, Whitman Publishing, 1960.

Fifteen Battles That Changed the World, Putnam, 1963.

Home of the Red Man: Indian North America before Columbus, New York Graphic Society, 1963.

Sunken History: The Story of Underwater Archaeology, Chilton, 1963.

The Great Doctors, Putnam, 1964.

The Man Who Found Nineveh: The Story of Austen Henry Layard, Holt, 1964.

Men Who Mastered the Atom, Putnam, 1965.

Niels Bohr: The Man Who Mapped the Atom, Macrae Smith, 1965.

The Old Ones: Indians of the American Southwest, New York Graphic Society, 1965.

Socrates, Putnam, 1965.

The World of Coral, Duell, 1965.

Forgotten by Time: A Book of Living Fossils, Crowell, 1966.

To the Rock of Darius: The Story of Henry Rawlinson, Holt, 1966.

The Adventures of Nat Palmer: Antarctic Explorer and Clipper Ship Pioneer, McGraw, 1967.

The Dawn of Medicine, Putnam, 1967.

The World of the Rain Forest, Meredith Press, 1967.

Four Men Who Changed the Universe, Putnam, 1968.

Ghost Towns of the American West, Crowell, 1968.

Stormy Voyager: The Story of Charles Wilkes, Lippincott, 1968.

The World of the Ocean Depths, Meredith Press, 1968.

Bruce of the Blue Nile, Holt, 1969.

Vanishing Giants: The Story of the Sequoias, Simon & Schuster, 1969.

Wonders of Ancient Chinese Science, Hawthorn, 1969.

Mammoths, Mastodons, and Man, McGraw, 1970.

The Seven Wonders of the Ancient World, Crowell-Collier, 1970.

(With Arthur C. Clarke) *Into Space: A Young Person's Guide to Space,* Harper, revised edition (Silverberg not associated with earlier edition), 1971.

John Muir: Prophet Among the Glaciers, Putnam, 1972.

The World Within the Tide Pool, Weybright & Talley, 1972.

FOR ADULTS; SCIENCE FICTION

Master of Life and Death (also see below), Ace Books, 1957.

The Thirteenth Immortal (bound with *This Fortress World* by J. E. Gunn), Ace Books, 1957.

Invaders from Earth (also see below; bound with *Across Time* by D. Grinnell), Ace Books, 1958, published separately, Avon, 1968, published as *We, the Marauders* (bound with *Giants in the Earth* by James Blish) under joint title *A Pair in Space,* Belmont, 1965.

Stepsons of Terra (bound with *A Man Called Destiny* by L. Wright), Ace Books, 1958, published separately, 1977.

The Planet Killers (bound with *We Claim These Stars!* by Poul Anderson), Ace Books, 1959.

Collision Course, Avalon, 1961.

Next Stop the Stars (story collection; bound with *The Seed of Earth* [novel] by Silverberg), Ace Books, 1962, each published separately, 1977.

Recalled to Life, Lancer Books, 1962.

The Silent Invaders (bound with *Battle on Venus* by William F. Temple), Ace Books, 1963, published separately, 1973.

Godling, Go Home! (story collection), Belmont, 1964.

Conquerors from the Darkness, Holt, 1965.

To Worlds Beyond: Stories of Science Fiction, Chilton, 1965.

Needle in a Timestack (story collection), Ballantine, 1966, revised edition, Ace Books, 1985.

Planet of Death, Holt, 1967.

Thorns, Ballantine, 1967.

Those Who Watch, New American Library, 1967.

The Time-Hoppers (also see below), Doubleday, 1967.

To Open the Sky (story collection), Ballantine, 1967.

Hawksbill Station, Doubleday, 1968 (published in England as *The Anvil of Time,* Sidgwick & Jackson, 1968).

The Masks of Time (also see below), Ballantine, 1968 (published in England as *Vornan-19,* Sidgwick & Jackson, 1970).

Dimension Thirteen (story collection), Ballantine, 1969.

The Man in the Maze (also see below), Avon, 1969.

Nightwings (also see below), Avon, 1969.

(Contributor) *Three for Tomorrow: Three Original Novellas of Science Fiction,* Meredith Press, 1969.

Three Survived, Holt, 1969.

To Live Again, Doubleday, 1969.

Up the Line, Ballantine, 1969, revised edition, 1978.

The Cube Root of Uncertainty (story collection), Macmillan, 1970.

Downward to the Earth (also see below), Doubleday, 1970.

Parsecs and Parables: Ten Science Fiction Stories, Doubleday, 1970.

A Robert Silverberg Omnibus (contains *Master of Life and Death, Invaders from Earth,* and *The Time-Hoppers*), Sidgwick & Jackson, 1970.

Tower of Glass, Scribner, 1970.

Moonferns and Starsongs (story collection), Ballantine, 1971.

Son of Man, Ballantine, 1971.

A Time of Changes, New American Library, 1971.

The World Inside, Doubleday, 1971.

The Book of Skulls, Scribner, 1972.

Dying Inside (also see below), Scribner, 1972.

The Reality Trip and Other Implausibilities (story collection), Ballantine, 1972.

The Second Trip, Doubleday, 1972.

(Contributor) *The Day the Sun Stood Still,* Thomas Nelson, 1972.

Earth's Other Shadow: Nine Science Fiction Stories, New American Library, 1973.

(Contributor) *An Exaltation of Stars: Transcendental Adventures in Science Fiction,* Simon & Schuster, 1973.

(Contributor) *No Mind of Man: Three Original Novellas of Science Fiction,* Hawthorn, 1973.

Unfamiliar Territory (story collection), Scribner, 1973.

Valley beyond Time (story collection), Dell, 1973.

Born with the Dead: Three Novellas about the Spirit of Man (also see below), Random House, 1974.

Sundance and Other Science Fiction Stories, Thomas Nelson, 1974.

The Feast of St. Dionysus: Five Science Fiction Stories, Scribner, 1975.

The Stochastic Man, Harper, 1975.

The Best of Robert Silverberg, Volume 1, Pocket Books, 1976, Volume 2, Gregg, 1978.

Capricorn Games (story collection), Random House, 1976.

Shadrach in the Furnace, Bobbs-Merrill, 1976.

The Shores of Tomorrow (story collection), Thomas Nelson, 1976.

The Songs of Summer and Other Stories, Gollancz, 1979.

Lord Valentine's Castle, Harper, 1980.

The Desert of Stolen Dreams, Underwood-Miller, 1981.

A Robert Silverberg Omnibus (contains *Downward to the Earth, The Man in the Maze,* and *Nightwings*), Harper, 1981.

Majipoor Chronicles, Arbor House, 1982.

World of a Thousand Colors (story collection), Arbor House, 1982.

Valentine Pontifex, Arbor House, 1983.

The Conglomeroid Cocktail Party (story collection), Arbor House, 1984.

Sailing to Byzantium, Underwood-Miller, 1985.

Tom O'Bedlam, Donald I. Fine, 1985.

Beyond the Safe Zone: Collected Short Fiction of Robert Silverberg, Donald I. Fine, 1986.

Star of Gypsies, Donald I. Fine, 1986.

(Editor) *Robert Silverberg's Worlds of Wonder,* Warner, 1987.

At Winter's End, Warner, 1988.

Born with the Dead (bound with *The Saliva Tree* by Brian W. Aldiss), Tor Books, 1988.

The Masks of Time, Born with the Dead, Dying Inside, Bantam, 1988.

To the Land of the Living, Gollancz, 1989.

(With Karen Haber) *The Mutant Season,* Foundation/Doubleday, 1989.

The New Springtime, Warner, 1990.

In Another Country: Vintage Season, Tor Books, 1990.

(With Isaac Asimov) *Nightfall,* Doubleday, 1990.

Time Gate II, Baen Books, 1990.

The Face of the Waters, Bantam, 1991.

The Queen of Springtime, Arrow Books, 1991.

(With Isaac Asimov) *Child of Time,* Gollancz, 1991.

The Collected Stories of Robert Silverberg, Bantam, 1992.

(With Isaac Asimov) *The Ugly Little Boy,* Doubleday, 1992.

(With Isaac Asimov) *The Positronic Man,* Doubleday, 1993.

Kingdoms of the Wall, Bantam, 1993.

Hot Sky at Midnight, Bantam, 1994.

The Mountains of Majipoor, Bantam, 1995.

Starborne, Bantam, 1996.

Sorcerers of Majipoor, HarperCollins, 1997.

Alien Years, HarperCollins, 1998.

Legends, Tor Books, 1998.

Lord Prestimion, HarperCollins, 1998.

NONFICTION

First American into Space, Monarch Books, 1961.

Lost Cities and Vanished Civilizations, Chilton, 1962.

Empires in the Dust: Ancient Civilizations Brought to Light, Chilton, 1963.

The Fabulous Rockefellers: A Compelling Personalized Account of One of America's First Families, Monarch Books, 1963.

Akhnaten: The Rebel Pharaoh, Chilton, 1964.

(Editor) *Great Adventures in Archaeology,* Dial, 1964.

Man before Adam: The Story of Man in Search of His Origins, Macrae Smith, 1964.

Scientists and Scoundrels: A Book of Hoaxes, Crowell, 1965.

The Great Wall of China, Chilton, 1965, published as *The Long Rampart: The Story of the Great Wall of China,* 1966.

Bridges, Macrae Smith, 1966.

Frontiers in Archaeology, Chilton, 1966.

The Auk, the Dodo, and the Oryx: Vanished and Vanishing Creatures, Crowell, 1967.

Light for the World: Edison and the Power Industry, Van Nostrand, 1967.

Men Against Time: Salvage Archaeology in the United States, Macmillan, 1967.

Mound Builders of Ancient America: The Archaeology of a Myth, New York Graphic Society, 1968.

The Challenge of Climate: Man and His Environment, Meredith Press, 1969.

The World of Space, Meredith Press, 1969.

If I Forget Thee, O Jerusalem: American Jews and the State of Israel, Morrow, 1970.

The Pueblo Revolt, Weybright & Talley, 1970.

Before the Sphinx: Early Egypt, Thomas Nelson, 1971.

Clocks for the Ages: How Scientists Date the Past, Macmillan, 1971.

To the Western Shore: Growth of the United States, 1776-1853, Doubleday, 1971.

The Longest Voyage: Circumnavigators in the Age of Discovery, Bobbs-Merrill, 1972.

The Realm of Prester John, Doubleday, 1972.

(Contributor) *Those Who Can,* New American Library, 1973.

Drug Themes in Science Fiction, National Institute on Drug Abuse, 1974.

(Contributor) *Hell's Cartographers: Some Personal Histories of Science Fiction Writers,* Harper, 1975.

(Editor with Byron Preiss) *The Ultimate Dinosaur: Past-Present-Future,* Bantam, 1992.

Reflections & Refractions: Thoughts on Science-Fiction, Science & Other Matters, Underwood, 1997.

UNDER PSEUDONYM WALKER CHAPMAN

The Loneliest Continent: The Story of Antarctic Discovery, New York Graphic Society, 1964.

(Editor) *Antarctic Conquest: The Great Explorers in Their Own Words,* Bobbs-Merrill, 1966.

Kublai Khan: Lord of Xanadu, Bobbs-Merrill, 1966.

The Golden Dream: Seekers of El Dorado, Bobbs-Merrill, 1967, published as *The Search for El Dorado,* 1967, reprinted under own name as *Golden Dream: Seekers of El Dorado,* Ohio University Press, 1996.

Also author of one hundred other novels, 1959-73, under pseudonyms Dan Eliot or Don Elliott.

OTHER

(With Randall Garrett, under joint pseudonym Robert Randall) *The Shrouded Planet,* Gnome Press, 1957, published under names Robert Silverberg and Randall Garrett, Donning, 1980.

(Under pseudonym Calvin M. Knox) *Lest We Forget Thee, Earth,* Ace Books, 1958.

(Under pseudonym David Osborne) *Aliens from Space,* Avalon, 1958.

(Under pseudonym Ivar Jorgenson) *Starhaven,* Avalon, 1958.

(Under pseudonym David Osborne) *Invisible Barriers,* Avalon, 1958.

(With Randall Garrett, under joint pseudonym Robert Randall) *The Dawning Light,* Gnome Press, 1959, published under names Robert Silverberg and Randall Garrett, Donning, 1981.

(Under pseudonym Calvin M. Knox) *The Plot against Earth,* Ace Books, 1959.

(Under pseudonym Walter Drummond) *Philosopher of Evil,* Regency Books, 1963.

(Under pseudonym Franklin Hamilton) *1066,* Dial, 1963.

(Under pseudonym Calvin M. Knox) *One of Our Asteroids Is Missing,* Ace Books, 1964.

(Under pseudonym Paul Hollander) *The Labors of Hercules,* Putnam, 1965.

(Under pseudonym Franklin Hamilton) *The Crusades,* Dial, 1965.

(Under pseudonym Lloyd Robinson) *The Hopefuls: Ten Presidential Candidates,* Doubleday, 1966.

(Under pseudonym Roy Cook) *Leaders of Labor,* Lippincott, 1966.

(Under pseudonym Lee Sebastian) *Rivers,* Holt, 1966.

(Under pseudonym Franklin Hamilton) *Challenge for a Throne: The War of the Roses,* Dial, 1967.

(Under pseudonym Lloyd Robinson) *The Stolen Election: Hayes versus Tilden,* Doubleday, 1968.

(Under pseudonym Paul Hollander) *Sam Houston,* Putnam, 1968.

(Under pseudonym Lee Sebastian) *The South Pole,* Holt, 1968.

Lord of Darkness (fiction), Arbor House, 1983.

Gilgamesh the King (fiction), Arbor House, 1984.

Contributor, sometimes under pseudonyms, to *Omni, Playboy, Amazing Stories Science Fiction, Fantastic Stories Science Fiction, Magazine of Science Fiction and Fantasy,* and other publications. Also editor of more than sixty science fiction anthologies.

SINGER, Muff 1942-

Personal

Born February 14, 1942, in Chicago, IL; daughter of Bernard L. (a business executive) and Goldryn M. (a homemaker) Singer; married Rick Tuttle (a city official), April 25, 1976; children: Sarah Tuttle-Singer. *Education:* University of Texas, B.A., 1964. *Politics:* Democrat. *Religion:* Jewish.

Addresses

Home and office—3635 Tilden Avenue, Los Angeles, CA 90034.

Career

Writer. Formerly a Peace Corps volunteer stationed in the Philippines, 1965-67; a teacher in Los Angeles; and the chief of staff for a leader of the California State Assembly, for ten years. Volunteer in several political campaigns, including the presidential campaign of Robert F. Kennedy.

Awards, Honors

Blue Bonnet Belle Award for outstanding student, University of Texas.

Writings

(With Aneta Corsaut and Robert Wagner) *The Mystery Readers' Quiz Book,* M. Evans (New York City), 1981.

(With Nancy Lamb) *Rhyme and Reason,* Price Stern Sloan, 1987.

How Many Hippos?, Time-Life for Children (Alexandria, VA), 1990.

The Great ABC Treasure Hunt, Time-Life for Children, 1990.

Animal Rhymes and Scramble Puzzles, Price Stern Sloan, 1990.

Muff Singer

Balderdash the Brilliant, illustrated by John Wallner, Time-Life for Children, 1991.

Hello, Piglet!, illustrated by Rosalyn Schanzer, Reader's Digest (Pleasantville, NY), 1993.

Little Lamb Lost, illustrated by Schanzer, Reader's Digest, 1993.

Puppy Says 1, 2, 3, illustrated by Schanzer, Reader's Digest, 1993.

What Does Kitty See?, illustrated by Schanzer, Reader's Digest, 1993.

Bunny's Hungry, illustrated by Schanzer, Reader's Digest, 1993.

Little Duck's Friends, illustrated by Schanzer, Reader's Digest, 1994.

(With Nancy Lamb) *The World's Greatest Toe Show,* illustrated by Blanche Sims, Troll Bridgewater (Mahwah, NJ), 1994.

(With Nancy Lamb) *The Vampires Went Thataway,* illustrated by Blanche Sims, Little Rainbow, 1995.

(With Sarah Tuttle-Singer) *Look Around with Little Fish,* Reader's Digest, 1995.

All Year Round with Little Frog, illustrated by Rosalyn Schanzer, Reader's Digest, 1995.

Busy Bee, Reader's Digest, 1995.

Butterfly's Surprise, Reader's Digest, 1995.

Cricket's Song, Reader's Digest, 1995.

Lucky Ladybug, Reader's Digest, 1995.

Bethlehem's Busy: What's Going On?, illustrated by Lynn Adams, Joshua Morris (Westport, CT), 1996.

Little Bunny's Busy Book, illustrated by Cathy Beylon, Reader's Digest, 1996.

Baby's First Nativity, illustrated by Peter Stevenson, Joshua Morris, 1997.

Happy the Hippo, illustrated by Tony Hutchings, Reader's Digest, 1997.

Little Lamb's Big Question, illustrated by Swan T. Hall, Reader's Digest, 1997.

God's Little Lamb: A Little Hugs Book, illustrated by Susan Tittall, Standard, 1997.

A Puppy to Love, illustrated by Amy Flynn, Reader's Digest, 1997.

Let's Play, Little Lamb!, Readers Digest, 1998.

Baby's First Prayers: Original Poems, illustrated by Peter Stevenson, Joshua Morris, 1998.

Little Bunny's Special Day, Readers Digest, 1998.

Anna's Rubber Duck, Reader's Digest, 1998.

God's Little Puppy, illustrated by Amy Flynn, Standard Publishing, 1998.

The Littlest Reindeer, Reader's Digest, 1998.

"TINY HUGS" BOOKS; CO-WRITTEN WITH RISA SHERWOOD GORDON; ILLUSTRATED BY CATHY BEYLON

Bedtime for Tiny Mouse, Reader's Digest, 1997.

Quiet as a Tiny Mouse, Reader's Digest, 1997.

Tiny Monkey Can, Too!, Reader's Digest, 1997.

Tiny Penguin's Flying Lesson, Reader's Digest, 1997.

Tiny Pig's Big Adventure, Reader's Digest, 1997.

OTHER

Contributor of articles to periodicals, including *Children's West Side Parenting Magazine.*

Sidelights

Muff Singer told *SATA:* "After graduating from the University of Texas in Austin where I was active in student government, I served as a Peace Corps Volunteer teacher from 1965 to 1967, teaching children grades one through six in Iwahig, a penal colony in the Philippines. The children of prisoners and government employees played and studied together in this model penal colony where prisoners lived in cottages with their families. Upon returning to the United States, I worked for the poverty program as a teacher in Los Angeles and volunteered in the presidential campaign of Senator Robert F. Kennedy, where I met my future husband, Rick Tuttle. We both campaigned for various candidates and causes during our 'courtship.' For ten years, I worked as the chief of staff to a California State Assembly leader.

"I believe the best ideas I've had for my books for children come from children. Their humor and vivid perceptions have the quality of truth—no matter how fantastic the circumstances.

"I live in a small house in West Los Angeles with my husband, Rick, our seventeen-year-old daughter, Sarah, who coauthored a book with me, and an assortment of roses and cats."

Muff Singer has published dozens of picture books for toddlers and preschoolers, some of which are marketed with accompanying stuffed animals to match the character featured in the story. She is also co-author of a first

Emily Anderson and her friends form the Canal Street Club and plan an unusual exhibit for the school fair in an attempt to beat a rival gang for the grand prize. (*From* The World's Greatest Toe Show, *written by Singer and Nancy Lamb and illustrated by Blanche Sims.*)

chapter book called *The World's Greatest Toe Show,* which critics lauded for its brilliantly tantalizing first line and steadily humorous follow-through. From the first page, which explains that the toe in the title belongs to Emily Anderson's father and is kept in a matchbox, "readers know they're in the zone of great, gross grade-school humor," maintained Mary Harris Veeder in *Booklist.* Emily and her friends form the Canal Street Club and intend to exhibit the toe at the school fair with the hope of earning the grand prize and showing up a rival gang comprised of prissy Bunny Bigalow and Violetta Epstein. After the fair, Emily's father requests that his toe be disposed of properly and a barbeque cremation is planned. The antics add up to eight easy-to-read chapters that, according to Veeder, "deliver big laughs."

Works Cited

Veeder, Mary Harris, review of *The World's Greatest Toe Show, Booklist,* August, 1994, p. 2044.

For More Information See

PERIODICALS

Publisher's Weekly, October 6, 1997, p. 57.
School Library Journal, September, 1994, pp. 187-88.

*　　*　　*

SPECK, Nancy 1959-

Personal

Born April 8, 1959, in Carlisle, PA; daughter of John (an elementary school principal) and Helen (a high school English teacher; maiden name, Meals) Remaly; married Brian Speck (a marketing executive), November 3, 1984; children: Marta, Rachel. *Education:* Millersville University, B.A., 1981. *Politics:* Republican. *Religion:* Reformed Baptist.

Addresses

Home and office—337 Juniper St., Carlisle, PA 17013. *Electronic mail*—BriSpeck @ aol.com.

Career

Social worker in foster care, 1981-85; recruiter of foster parents, 1984-85; medical social worker at a nursing home, 1985-87; writer and public speaker, 1994—. *Member:* Society of Children's Book Writers and Illustrators.

Writings

FOR YOUNG PEOPLE; "FAIRFIELD FRIENDS DEVOTIONAL ADVENTURE" SERIES; ALL ILLUSTRATED BY JOE NORDSTROM

The Lightning Escape and Other Stories, Bethany House (Minneapolis, MN), 1997.
Firecracker Power and Other Stories, Bethany House, 1997.
Blaze on Rocky Ridge and Other Stories, Bethany House, 1997.
Cave Hill Treasure and Other Stories, Bethany House, 1998.

OTHER

The Secret of the Hidden Room, Pacific Press Publishing Association (Nampa, ID), 1999.

Work represented in anthologies, including *Crazy to Be Alive in Such a Strange World,* M. Evans, 1977; and *Together: How We Belong,* Troll Communications (Mahwah, NJ), 1997. Contributor of stories and rhymes to magazines, including *Highlights for Children, Turtle, English Journal,* and *Primary Treasure.*

Work in Progress

"A picture book about Lue Gim Gong."

Nancy Speck

Sidelights

Nancy Speck told *SATA:* "Whether retracing the Oregon Trail, visiting a Florida orange grove, or thinking up stories in my Civil War-era house (which our family is restoring), I am always in some stage of writing for children.

"Always a history lover, I like to write historical nonfiction for children. After researching and visiting the Oregon Trail, I wrote an article describing life in a covered wagon. I have also researched and written about a little-known Chinese-American, Lue Gim Gong, who immigrated to America in 1872 and created a year-round, frost-resistant orange. I traveled to both Massachusetts and Florida to visit his home and orange groves. The result is a biography for middle-school and high-school students.

"However, I consider my fiction stories for children to be my most important area of writing. My college degree in social work and years of experience working with children in the foster care system have given me unique insight into the need for teaching children Christian morals and values at an early age. When I found a lack of age-appropriate material on the market to use with my own children, I decided to create my own stories, and the 'Fairfield Friends Devotional Adventure Series' was born. The first four books in the series, *Firecracker Power, The Lightning Escape, Blaze on Rocky Ridge,* and *Cave Hill Treasure,* are sold in Christian book stores across the United States and

Canada, as well as in the United Kingdom, Australia, South Africa, New Zealand, and the Philippines.

"I currently divide my time between writing and presenting programs to many groups, including schools. My slide-show presentation, 'From Brain to Book,' which follows the entire production of a story, has been enthusiastically received by students and teachers alike."

*   *   *

STEVENSON, Sucie 1956-

Personal

Born Susan Stevenson, in 1956, in Greenwich, CT; daughter of James (a journalist, playwright, novelist, *New Yorker* cartoonist, and children's book author) and Jane (an artist; maiden name, Walker) Stevenson.

Addresses

Agent—Liza Pulitzer-Voges, Kirchoff/Wohlberg, Inc., 866 United Nations Plaza, Suite 525, New York, NY 10017.

Career

Illustrator and author of children's books. Has also worked as a manual laborer, shellfisher, housepainter, mason's helper, theater technician, set painter, mural painter, and flower delivery truck driver.

Awards, Honors

Garden State Children's Book Award, 1990, for *Henry and Mudge in Puddle Trouble,* 1992, for *Henry and Mudge Get the Cold Shivers,* 1993, for *Henry and Mudge and the Happy Cat,* 1994, for *Henry and Mudge and the Bedtime Thumps,* 1995, for *Henry and Mudge and the Long Weekend,* 1996, for *Henry and Mudge and the Wild Wind,* and 1997, for *Henry and Mudge and the Careful Cousin,* all written by Cynthia Rylant and illustrated by Stevenson; *Parenting*'s Reading Magic Award, 1992, for *Henry and Mudge and the Long Weekend,* and 1994, for *Henry and Mudge and the Careful Cousin,* both written by Cynthia Rylant and illustrated by Stevenson; Parent's Choice Award, 1994, for *Baby-O,* written by Nancy White Carlstrom; Best Books, *School Library Journal,* 1994, and 100 Titles for Reading and Sharing, New York Public Library, 1994, both for *Henry and Mudge and the Careful Cousin,* written by Cynthia Rylant and illustrated by Stevenson.

Writings

SELF-ILLUSTRATED CHILDREN'S BOOKS

Do I Have to Take Violet?, Dodd, Mead, 1987.
I Forgot, Orchard Books, 1988.
Christmas Eve, Dodd, Mead, 1988.
Jessica the Blue Streak, Orchard Books, 1989.
(Reteller) *The Princess and the Pea,* Doubleday, 1992.
(Reteller) *The Twelve Dancing Princesses,* Yearling, 1995.

(Reteller) *The Emperor's New Clothes*, Delacorte, 1997.

*ILLUSTRATOR; "HENRY AND MUDGE" CHILDREN'S
BOOKS; ALL WRITTEN BY CYNTHIA RYLANT*

Henry and Mudge: The First Book of Their Adventures,
Bradbury Press, 1987.

*Henry and Mudge in Puddle Trouble: The Second Book of
Their Adventures*, Bradbury Press, 1987.

*Henry and Mudge in the Green Time: The Third Book of
Their Adventures*, Bradbury Press, 1987.

*Henry and Mudge under the Yellow Moon: The Fourth
Book of Their Adventures*, Bradbury Press, 1988.

*Henry and Mudge in the Sparkle Days: The Fifth Book of
Their Adventures*, Bradbury Press, 1988.

*Henry and Mudge and the Forever Sea: The Sixth Book of
Their Adventures*, Bradbury Press, 1989.

*Henry and Mudge Get the Cold Shivers: The Seventh Book
of Their Adventures*, Bradbury Press, 1989.

*Henry and Mudge and the Happy Cat: The Eighth Book of
Their Adventures*, Bradbury Press, 1990.

*Henry and Mudge and the Bedtime Thumps: The Ninth
Book of Their Adventures*, Bradbury Press, 1991.

*Henry and Mudge Take the Big Test: The Tenth Book of
Their Adventures*, Bradbury Press, 1991.

*Henry and Mudge and the Long Weekend: The Eleventh
Book of Their Adventures*, Bradbury Press, 1992.

*Henry and Mudge and the Wild Wind: The Twelfth Book of
Their Adventures*, Bradbury Press, 1993.

*Henry and Mudge and the Careful Cousin: The Thirteenth
Book of Their Adventures*, Bradbury Press, 1994.

*Henry and Mudge and the Best Day of All: The Fourteenth
Book of Their Adventures*, Bradbury Press, 1994.

*Henry and Mudge in the Family Trees: The Fifteenth Book
of Their Adventures*, Simon & Schuster, 1997.

*Henry and Mudge and the Sneaky Crackers: The Sixteenth
Book of Their Adventures*, Simon & Schuster, 1998.

*Henry and Mudge and the Starry Night: The Seventeenth
Book of Their Adventures*, Simon & Schuster, 1998.

*Henry and Mudge and Annie's Good Move: The Eighteenth
Book of Their Adventures*, Simon & Schuster, 1998.

*Henry and Mudge and Annie's Perfect Pet: The Nineteenth
Book of Their Adventures*, Simon & Schuster, 1999.

*Henry and Mudge and the Funny Lunch: The Twentieth
Book of Their Adventures*, Simon & Schuster, 1999.

*Henry and Mudge and the Tall Tree House: The Twenty-
first Book of Their Adventures*, Simon & Schuster,
1999.

*Henry and Mudge and Mrs. Hopper's House: The Twenty-
second Book of Their Adventures*, Simon & Schuster,
1999.

*Henry and Mudge and the Great Grandpas: The Twenty-
third Book of Their Adventures*, Simon & Schuster,
1999.

*Henry and Mudge and a Very Special Merry Christmas:
The Twenty-fourth Book of Their Adventures*, Simon &
Schuster, 1999.

*Henry and Mudge and the Snowman Plan: The Twenty-fifth
Book of Their Adventures*, Simon & Schuster, 1999.

*Henry and Mudge and the Wild Goose Chase: The Twenty-
sixth Book of Their Adventures*, Simon & Schuster,
1999.

*Henry and Mudge and the Big Sleepover: The Twenty-
seventh Book of Their Adventures*, Simon & Schuster,
1999.

*Henry and Mudge and the Tumbling Trip: The Twenty-
eighth Book of Their Adventures*, Simon & Schuster,
1999.

Some of the "Henry and Mudge" books have been
translated into Spanish.

ILLUSTRATOR; CHILDREN'S BOOKS

Cynthia Rylant, *Birthday Presents*, Orchard Books, 1987.
David A. Adler, *I Know I'm a Witch*, Holt, 1988.
Niki Yektai, *Crazy Clothes*, Bradbury Press, 1988.
Barbara Ann Porte, *Ruthann and Her Pig*, Orchard Books,
1989.
Frieda Wishinsky, *Oonga Boonga*, Little, Brown, 1990.
Elvira Woodruff, *Tubtime*, Holiday House, 1990.
Nancy White Carlstrom, *Baby-O*, Little, Brown, 1992.
Joyce Champion, *Emily and Alice*, Harcourt, 1993.
Joyce Champion, *Emily and Alice Again*, Gulliver Books
(San Diego, CA), 1995.
Mary Small, *A Pony Named Shawney*, Mondo (Greenvale,
NY), 1996.
Anne F. Rockwell, *Once Upon a Time This Morning*,
Greenwillow, 1997.

OTHER

Also contributor of articles to magazines, including *New
Yorker*.

Sidelights

The daughter of famous cartoonist, illustrator, and
author James Stevenson, Sucie Stevenson was not

***Sisters Elly and Violet squabble while getting ready for
Christmas, until they begin to cooperate in crafting a
gift for their parents.*** (*From* Christmas Eve, *written and
illustrated by Sucie Stevenson.*)

certain she would ever follow in her father's footsteps. Although she enjoyed drawing, she once recalled in a *Publishers Weekly* interview with Diane Roback, "I didn't have any faith that I was any good." So, instead of pursuing more creative endeavors, Stevenson tried a number of odd jobs, including shellfisher, mason's helper, and truck driver. Eventually, however, she determined to put her artistic skills to use. She found her first success publishing articles in the *New Yorker* magazine, and later tried her hand at illustrating children's books. Submitting two works for publication to a variety of publishers, she was told that she had talent as an illustrator, but not as a children's author. Nevertheless, Stevenson soon wrote several of her own picture books in addition to illustrating the texts of other children's writers.

Stevenson found an agent, then the gained the support of publisher Richard Jackson at Orchard Books. This led to her well-known collaboration with author Cynthia Rylant on the "Henry and Mudge" series, which now includes nearly thirty books. Stevenson's father, who was best known for his *New Yorker* cartoons, had an important influence on her artistry. "What I aim for is a really loose style—simple, cartoony. I try to make things look the way they feel to me instead of how they actually look," she said in *Publishers Weekly*. This style has served as the perfect complement to the Rylant books, winners of numerous awards.

Stevenson's first book as both author and illustrator, *Do I Have to Take Violet?*, addresses a scenario that is very familiar to most siblings: an older sister, in this case a bunny named Elly, is forced by her mother to take her little sister, Violet, on a bike ride. Elly teases Violet with stories of monsters, and Violet tries to trick her sister, but the two eventually decide to get along. *School Library Journal* contributor Luann Toth wrote that the tale is "nicely done and certainly enhanced by Stevenson's ... paintings." Elly and Violet appear again in *Christmas Eve,* squabbling while trying to prepare a holiday gift for their parents. Diane Roback, writing in *Publishers Weekly,* praised Stevenson for making the childish rivalry in both books "uncanny and real," and called *Christmas Eve* "funny and dear."

Stevenson created another endearing character in Arthur Peter Platypus, Jr., who stars in *I Forgot.* Arthur's problem is that he cannot seem to remember anything. For example, he wears the wrong hat when it rains and forgets to take his lunch box to school. Then, one day, while pondering his troubles, he realizes that he remembers important things, such as his address and his mother's birthday, which is that very day. He takes balloons, banners, and flowers to his mother as a gift, and Arthur is happy to conclude that at least he remembers the most important things in life. Stevenson adds interest to the story by having Arthur try various methods to improve his memory, and her colorful art "captures the little platypus' movements and moods," according to a *Booklist* critic. Comparing *I Forgot* to Robert Kraus's *Leo the Late Bloomer, School Library Journal* contributor Pamela Miller Ness called Steven-

Stevenson contributes colorful illustrations to **Baby-O,** *Nancy White Carlstrom's tale of a family selling their goods at a market in the West Indies.*

son's story "a little book with a big, comforting message."

After 1989's *Jessica the Blue Streak,* a frenetic tale in which a puppy wreaks havoc in a little girl's house, Stevenson changed gears somewhat to become a reteller of fairy tales such as *The Princess and the Pea* and *The Emperor's New Clothes.* In her versions, however, the main characters are animals. *The Princess and the Pea* features bunnies in the roles of Hans Christian Andersen's characters, and Stevenson takes further liberties by setting the tale on a tropical island instead of in Europe. A *Publishers Weekly* critic dubbed the book "accessible and entertaining," appreciating Stevenson's humor. Stevenson offers another humorous tale, this time with an all-dog cast, in her interpretation of *The Twelve Dancing Princesses.*

For someone who was initially hesitant to pursue a career writing and illustrating, Stevenson has done very well for herself. In her first decade alone, she produced over thirty children's picture books, the beginning of what will hopefully be a prolific career. "I like picture books," she told Roback in *Publishers Weekly*. "I like having an audience of very young children—putting very few words on a page and having the pictures tell the whole story."

Works Cited

Review of *I Forgot, Booklist,* February 15, 1988, p. 1003.

Ness, Pamela Miller, review of *I Forgot, School Library Journal,* March, 1988, p. 177.

Review of *The Princess and the Pea, Publishers Weekly,* August 3, 1992, p. 71.

Roback, Diane, "Flying Starts: New Faces of 1987," *Publishers Weekly,* December 25, 1987, p. 36.

Roback, Diane, review of *Christmas Eve, Publishers Weekly,* December 23, 1988, p. 81.

Toth, Luann, review of *Do I Have to Take Violet?, School Library Journal,* June-July, 1987, pp. 90-91.

For More Information See

PERIODICALS

Booklist, January 1, 1989, p. 797; March 1, 1989, p. 1197; July, 1993, pp. 1980-81; February 1, 1994, p. 1012; April 15, 1995, p. 1509; January 1, 1996, p. 850; April 1, 1997, p. 1339.

Bulletin of the Center for Children's Books, May, 1988, p. 189; February, 1989, p. 159.

Horn Book, November/December, 1987, p. 735; May/June, 1988, p. 347; July/August, 1988, pp. 487-88; November/December, 1989, p. 795; May/June, 1990, p. 356; September/October, 1990, p. 598; November/December, 1991, p. 759; July/August, 1992, p. 449; July/August, 1993, p. 485; March/April, 1994, pp. 195-96.

Horn Book Guide, July-December, 1995, p. 95.

Publishers Weekly, January 13, 1989, p. 88; July 28, 1989, p. 222; January 6, 1997, p. 72.

School Library Journal, March 20, 1987, p. 78; April, 1989, p. 91; July, 1989, p. 76; May, 1990, p. 93; December, 1990, p. 24; April, 1994, p. 112; May, 1995, p. 94; March, 1996, p. 193; October, 1997, p. 109.

*   *   *

STILLERMAN, Marci

Personal

Born in Chicago, IL; married Jack Stillerman (a dentist), 1961; children: three. *Education:* University of Chicago, B.A.; Northwestern University, M.A.; University of California, graduate study. *Religion:* Jewish. *Hobbies and other interests:* Travel.

Addresses

Home—10551 Wilshire Blvd., Los Angeles, CA 90024. *Electronic mail*—marciess@aol.com.

Career

Writer. *Member:* Society of Children's Book Writers and Illustrators, Institute of Children's Writers, California Writers Society, Community Writers Association.

Awards, Honors

Distinguished Achievement Award, educational journalism category, Educational Press Association of America, 1991.

Writings

Nine Spoons: A Chanukah Story, illustrated by Perren Gerber, Hachai Publications (Brooklyn, NY), 1998.

Contributor to periodicals, including *Jack and Jill* and *Skipping Stones.*

Work in Progress

The First Thirteen Years of a Catawamptious Life, an autobiography; a young adult novel; research on the educational and social adjustment of children of gay and lesbian parents.

Sidelights

Marci Stillerman told *SATA:* "I can't remember a time in my life when I didn't want and intend to become a writer. All through grammar school, high school, and college, I wrote poetry and short stories, entered writing contests (and won some), and had my work published in newspapers and children's magazines. In high school and college, I worked on school newspapers and yearbooks and, while attending the University of Chicago, earned tuition by selling romance stories to pulp magazines like *True Confessions.* After graduating, I married and took a hiatus from writing while raising three children and travelling the world over. I resumed writing when my husband and I moved to Los Angeles in 1986, and I have been writing since then, first exclusively for children's magazines. About three years ago, I began writing literary short stories.

"At present I am doing research on the children of gay and lesbian parents, who are now beginning to appear in increasing numbers in schoolrooms all over the country, especially in big cities. Their number is small but bound to increase, since so many of the homosexual community are adopting and/or conceiving children. Many children are already in the schools, having to cope with two mommies, two daddies, or single gay or lesbian

Marci Stillerman

parents. I have written a picture book about the child of such a family.

"Travel has been an important part of my life and is my secondary passion. My husband and I have travelled to every continent, including Antarctica, but least extensively in the United States, which we are saving for our old age. India and East and West Africa have been our favorite places, and we have visited there several times."

*   *   *

STIMPSON, Gerald
See MITCHELL, Adrian

*   *   *

STUTSON, Caroline 1940-

Personal

Born September 14, 1940; daughter of Malcolm (a purchasing agent) and Randolph (a librarian; maiden name, Hardy) MacLachlan; married Al Stutson (a wood carver), September 5, 1964; children: A. C., Christine. *Education:* Metro State College, certificate in early education, 1978; attended the College of William and Mary, 1958-60, and the University of Denver, 1960-62. *Hobbies and other interests:* Hiking, puppetry, gardening, reading, and stitchery.

Addresses

Home—20 E. Woodland Circle, Highlands Ranch, CO 80126. *Agent*—Kendra Marcus Bookshop Literary Agency, 67 Meadow View Rd., Orinda, CA 94563.

Career

Bemis Public Library, Littleton, CO, children's librarian, 1961-65. Also employed as a kindergarten teacher and a special reading teacher in Littleton. Works as a part-time storyteller and puppeteer for Highlands Ranch Library, Highlands Ranch, CO. *Member:* Society of Children's Book Writers and Illustrators, Colorado Author's League.

Awards, Honors

Teacher of Excellence, Colorado Association for Childhood Education, 1991.

Writings

FOR CHILDREN

By the Light of the Halloween Moon, illustrated by Kevin Hawkes, Lothrop, Lee & Shepard, 1993.
On the River ABC, illustrated by Anna-Maria Crum, Roberts Rinehart, 1993.
Mountain Meadow 1, 2, 3, illustrated by Crum, Roberts Rinehart, 1995.

Caroline Stutson

Prairie Primer A to Z, illustrated by Susan Condie Lamb, Dutton, 1996.
Cowpokes, illustrated by Daniel San Souci, Lothrop, Lee & Shepard, 1999.
Star Comes Home, illustrated by Rick Reason, The Benefactory, 1999.

Contributor of poetry to magazines, including *Children's Playmate, Highlights, On the Line,* and *Spider.*

Adaptations

By the Light of the Halloween Moon was adapted for video by Weston Woods Studios, Inc., 1997.

Work in Progress

Night Train, for DK Ink; a collection of humorous poems about cats and dogs; research on assistance dogs.

Sidelights

Caroline Stutson told *SATA:* "Looking back at one's life is an interesting process. If enough time has passed, you can see the pieces fitting neatly together. Yet, on a day to day basis, so much seems haphazard and iffy.

"One of the few things I know for sure about my life is that I've always loved books. Shortly before I was born, longer ago than I'll publicly admit, my mother worked as a librarian at the Brooklyn Public Library in New York. I was lucky to have lots of early links with literature, from my mother's reading out loud to me, to a

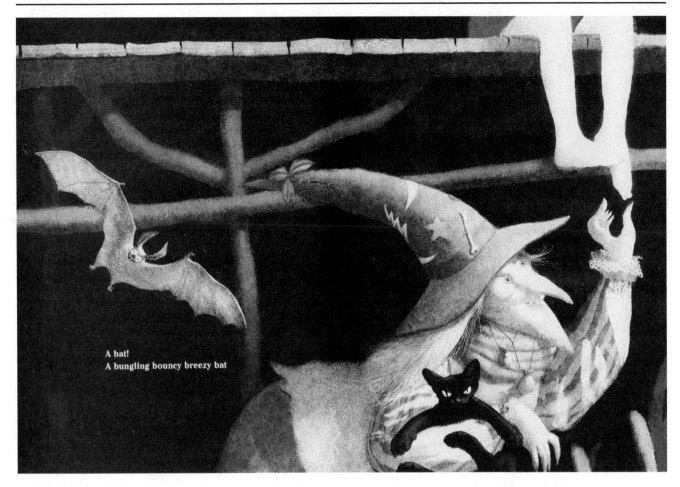

A bat!
A bungling bouncy breezy bat

In Stutson's Halloween poem, a little girl almost has her toe grabbed by a succession of eerie characters when she dangles her legs over a footbridge. (From By the Light of the Halloween Moon, *illustrated by Kevin Hawkes.)*

friend of hers who sent me copies of book reviews she wrote for a parenting magazine.

"In addition to listening to and reading books, I always enjoyed playing pretend. My best friend and I were careful to note where our adventure left off when it was time to go home. That way we knew where our chosen characters would begin the next day. Writing for children still lets me play pretend. All those 'what ifs' are great fun, and you get to create your own universe with a happy ending to boot.

"My writing began in kindergarten. I didn't know how to write words then, but every day after school I drew pictures and made up stories to go with the drawings. Later when we had writing assignments, I struggled with the spelling. I still struggle with spelling, but it doesn't stop me from writing any more. I just circle the troublesome words and look up how to spell them later.

"Today, things are so much better for the students I meet when I visit schools promoting my books. Some of their writing involves choice. They get to write about things that really matter to them, and they get to share their work with each other. They also get to respond to the literature they are reading. I can't help feeling a little envious.

"After I graduated from Massapequa High School on Long Island, New York, I went to William and Mary College in Virginia and two years later I transferred to the University of Denver. During those years I changed my mind a million times about what I wanted to do, finally majoring in theater arts—not a very practical decision for making a living.

"I've changed jobs quite a few times too. I've been a reading teacher, a kindergarten teacher, and a children's librarian, all of which connected me to books. Currently, I work part time doing puppet shows and story times at the Highlands Ranch Library in Douglas County, Colorado. In my office at home I have a huge trunk of puppets ready to pop out and be part of a new puppet show each week.

"A big part of my life has been spent being a mom. Our two children are grown now. Our daughter is a lawyer, our son, a police detective, and I am now a grandmother for the first time, having fun reading to my new grandson from my ever growing collection of books."

Stutson's fast-paced debut poem, *By the Light of the Halloween Moon,* holds a "toe" up for grabs. The toe belongs to a little girl who dangles her legs over a footbridge while playing a fiddle on Halloween night. A cat, a witch, a bat, a graveyard ghoul, a ghost, and a sprite all stream through this boisterous tale, and each character, more pleasurably gruesome than the one before, aims to grab the toe. A *Kirkus Reviews* critic called the poem a "catchy, lilting cumulative tale." Ilene Cooper declared in her review for *Booklist* that this "rousing" tale with "bouncy text" makes a "terrific choice for holiday story hours." Ann A. Flowers of *Horn Book* also praised *By the Light of the Halloween Moon,* describing the book as "rhythmically bouncy and appealing."

In *On the River ABC,* an ant floats down the river on a leaf. As he drifts, wildlife from A to Z pass before his makeshift vessel. Stutson ends her book with factual information about each of these animals that live in the western regions of the United States. *School Library Journal* contributor Kathy Piehl commented favorably on the lyrical quality of Stutson's writing, noting that the author "does not fall into the trap of singsong regularity." Piehl encourages teachers to use this picture book as a springboard for "children to create similar alphabet books based on trips in their own environment."

With *Prairie Primer A to Z,* Stutson once again presents a rhyming alphabet book, evoking the daily life of a Midwestern farm family in the early 1900s. Letters introduced help to explore life on a farm long ago: B is for "butter in the churn" and P is for "porridge in the pot." Unusual words such as "whirligig" and "velocipede" place the primer back in the era of homesteading. A critic for *Kirkus Reviews* suggested that the book may be too "old-fashioned" for today's "rough-and-ready preschool set," but Paula A. Kiely, writing in *School Library Journal,* called Stutson's book a "pleasant step back in time," pointing out that "young children will enjoy trying to pronounce" these forgotten words. Carolyn Phelan of *Booklist* suggested that the primer be used to introduce "today's young children to another time, another place."

Works Cited

Review of *By the Light of the Halloween Moon, Kirkus Reviews,* July 15, 1993, pp. 942-43.
Cooper, Ilene, review of *By the Light of the Halloween Moon, Booklist,* July, 1993, p. 1977.
Flowers, Ann A., review of *By the Light of the Halloween Moon, Horn Book,* November-December, 1993, p. 728.
Kiely, Paula A., review of *Prairie Primer A to Z, School Library Journal,* October, 1996, p. 107.
Phelan, Carolyn, review of *Prairie Primer A to Z, Booklist,* October 15, 1996, p. 437.
Piehl, Kathy, review of *On the River ABC, School Library Journal,* September, 1993, p. 220.
Review of *Prairie Primer A to Z, Kirkus Reviews,* September 15, 1996, p. 1408.

For More Information See

PERIODICALS

Children's Book Review Service, December, 1996, p. 41.
Library Talk, November, 1994, p. 37.

New York Times Book Review, May 11, 1997, p. 24.

* * *

SULLY, Tom 1959-

Personal

Born October 18, 1959, in Norfolk, VA; son of Thomas, Jr. (a banker) and Elizabeth (an artist; maiden name, Butler) Sully; married Susan Ryan (a writer), April 25, 1992. *Education:* Attended Antioch University, CA, 1977-79, San Francisco Art Institute, 1980-82, California Institute of the Arts, 1983-84, School of Visual Arts, 1990.

Addresses

Home—73 Moultrie St., Charleston, SC 29403.

Career

Illustrator, 1990—. The Institute for Art and Urban Resources, New York City, installer, 1979. Worked as a

Self-portrait of Tom Sully with his ancestor and namesake, noted 19th-century American portraitist Thomas Sully.

From **Tumbleweed Christmas,** *written by Alane Ferguson and illustrated by Sully.*

studio assistant to painter Donald Sultan, costume painter for the New York City Ballet and the American Ballet Theater, 1984-90. *Exhibitions:* Marty Whaley Adams Gallery, Charleston, SC, 1996; Loretta Goodwin Gallery, Birmingham, AL, 1997; City Gallery, Charleston, and Irene Morrah Ingold Fine Art, Greenville, SC, both 1998.

Illustrator

Susan Sully, *Fish & Soup: A Fish Tale,* Rizzoli International Publications (New York City), 1995.
Alane Ferguson, *Tumbleweed Christmas,* Simon & Schuster, 1996.

Contributor of illustrations to magazines and newspapers, including the *New Yorker, Atlantic Monthly, Time, Newsweek,* and *Washington Post.*

Work in Progress

Fine art and occasional illustration assignments.

Sidelights

Southern-born illustrator Tom Sully moved to New York City in 1984 to pursue an art career. While in New York, he made a name for himself with illustrations for such notable publications as the *New Yorker, Time,* and *Newsweek.* He also painted costumes for the New York City Ballet and the American Ballet Theater. Then, in 1996, he returned to the South and settled in Charleston, South Carolina, with his wife, writer Susan Sully.

Sully collaborated with his wife in 1995 to create *Fish & Soup: A Fish Tale.* In this silly story, a young boy feeds his goldfish, Glenda and George, a dose of Mephisto's Magic Grow Food, causing the fish to grow to human size. The overgrown fish decide to attend a costume ball, where they engage in some hilarious escapades.

Sully also provided the illustrations for Alane Ferguson's *Tumbleweed Christmas,* in which Scotty and his mother find themselves stranded in the desert when their car breaks down on their way to celebrate Christmas with Scotty's grandparents. However, the two are rescued by a mechanic named Jasper, and Scotty finds happiness in helping others while his own Christmas plans are on hold. *School Library Journal* contributor Jane Marino observed that "Sully's oil paintings have a stylized folk-art look to them, with figures slightly out of proportion and shadings of color that give texture to the art."

One of Sully's major projects is a series of paintings inspired by his return to the South, as he told *SATA:* "My work plays off the tensions between the sublime and the vernacular, the profound and the prosaic, the spiritual and the burlesque, which I find daily in the American South." Charleston was also the home of Sully's ancestor and namesake, the noted 19th-century American portraitist Thomas Sully. Of his elder's influence, Sully said: "I am always learning from my ancestor, especially regarding the empathy that he felt and expressed for his sitters, the freshness and sensuality of his brush and the immaculacy of his execution."

Sully also told *SATA:* "I've enjoyed illustrating children's books because of the opportunity they afford of telling a story largely through pictures. Though still available for a children's book project should the right one present itself, I am currently engaged in the production of fine art, including portrait commissions of children, who are a wonderful challenge as portrait subjects."

Works Cited

Marino, Jane, review of *Tumbleweed Christmas, School Library Journal,* October, 1996, p. 35.

For More Information See

PERIODICALS

Publishers Weekly, May 1, 1995, p. 58; September 30, 1996, p.90.

*   *   *

TABACK, Simms 1932-

Personal

Born February 13, 1932, in New York, NY; son of Leon (a house painter and contractor) and Thelma (a seamstress) Taback; married Gail Baugher Kuenstler (a writer), March 1, 1980; children: Lisa, Jason, Emily. *Education:* Cooper Union, B.F.A., 1953.

Addresses

Home—Willow, NY 12495.

Career

CBS Records, New York City, graphic designer, 1956-57; *New York Times,* New York City, designer, 1957-58; William Douglas McAdams, New York City, art director, 1958-60; freelance illustrator, 1960-63, 1970—; Ruffins/Taback Design Studio, New York City, partner, 1963-70. *Military service:* U.S. Army, private first class, 1953-55. *Member:* Illustrators Guild (president, 1976-78), New York Graphics Artists Guild (president, 1978-83), Society of Illustrators.

Awards, Honors

Best Illustrated Books designation, *New York Times,* 1965, for *Please Share That Peanut! A Preposterous Pageant in Fourteen Acts;* Children's Book of the Year selection, American Institute of Graphic Arts, 1970, for *There's Motion Everywhere,* 1979, for *Joseph Had a Little Overcoat,* and 1980, for *Laughing Together;* Notable Books, American Library Association (ALA), 1998, and Caldecott Honor Book, ALA, 1998, both for *There Was an Old Lady Who Swallowed a Fly.*

Writings

SELF-ILLUSTRATED

Joseph Had a Little Overcoat, Random House, 1978.

Simms Taback

(Adaptor) *There Was an Old Lady Who Swallowed a Fly,* Viking, 1997.

ILLUSTRATOR

Lewis Carroll, *Jabberwocky and Other Frabjous Nonsense,* Harlan Quist, 1964.

Sesyle Joslin, *Please Share That Peanut! A Preposterous Pageant in Fourteen Acts,* Harcourt, 1965.

Ann McGovern, *Too Much Noise,* Houghton, 1967.

John Travers Moore, *There's Motion Everywhere,* Houghton, 1970.

(With Reynold Ruffins) Harry Hartwick, *The Amazing Maze,* Dutton, 1970.

Janet Barkas, *Meatless Cooking, Celebrity Style,* Grove Press, 1975.

Mary Calhoun, *Euphonia and the Flood,* Parents Magazine Press, 1976.

Barbara K. Walker, compiler, *Laughing Together: Giggles and Grins from around the World,* Four Winds Press,

1977, as *Laughing Together: Giggles and Grins from around the Globe,* Free Spirit, 1992.

Harriet Ziefert, *Where Is My House?,* Grosset, 1982.

Harriet Ziefert, *Where Is My Dinner?,* Grosset, 1982.

Harriet Ziefert, *Where Is My Friend?,* Grosset, 1982.

Katy Hall and Lisa Eisenberg, *Fishy Riddles,* Dial, 1983.

Hariet Ziefert, *On Our Way,* four volumes (includes *On Our Way To the Forest, On Our Way to the Water, On Our Way to the Zoo, On Our Way to the Barn*), Harper, 1985.

Katy Hall and Lisa Eisenberg, *Buggy Riddles,* Dial, 1985.

Harriet Ziefert, *Jason's Bus Ride,* Viking, 1987.

Science Activity Book, Galison, 1987.

Harriet Ziefert, *Zoo Parade,* Harper, 1990.

Harriet Ziefert, *Noisy Barn!,* Harper, 1990.

Katy Hall and Lisa Eisenberg, *Snakey Riddles,* Dial, 1990.

Michele Urvater, *The Monday to Friday Cookbook,* Workman, 1991.

Gail MacColl, *The Book of Cards for Kids,* Workman, 1992.

In There Was an Old Lady Who Swallowed a Fly, *Simms Taback's self-illustrated, Caldecott Honor-book adaptation of the American folk song, readers peek into the old woman's stomach through increasingly larger holes in the pages.*

and if the princess, the cat, the clown,
the pirate, the pumpkin,

the astronaut, the bunny, and the
skeleton all run away, that leaves...

An escalating number of trick-or-treaters encounter two little witches in Harriet Ziefert's holiday counting book. (From
Two Little Witches: A Halloween Counting Story, *illustrated by Taback.*)

Katy Hall and Lisa Eisenberg, *Spacey Riddles,* Dial, 1992.

B. G. Hennessy, *Road Builders,* Viking, 1994.

Harriet Ziefert, *Where Is My Baby?,* Harper, 1994.

Nancy Antle, *Sam's Wild West Show,* Dial, 1995.

Michele Urvater, *Monday to Friday Pasta,* Workman, 1995.

Harriet Ziefert, *Who Said Moo?,* Harper, 1996.

Harriet Ziefert, *Two Little Witches: A Halloween Counting Story,* Candlewick Press, 1996.

Harriet Ziefert, reteller, *When I First Came to This Land,* Putnam, 1998.

Taback's works are included in the Kerlan Collection at the University of Minnesota.

Sidelights

A prolific illustrator of books for young children, Simms Taback is best known for his work with popular children's author Harriet Ziefert. Experienced in many media, Taback uses pen and ink and watercolor for most of his illustrations. In addition to works by Ziefert, he has illustrated a wide variety of picture books, beginning readers, riddle books, and others for authors that include Barbara Walker, Mary Calhoun, Katy Hall, Lisa Eisenberg, and B. G. Hennessy. Praising Taback's contribution to Hennessy's picture book *Road Builders, Booklist* contributor Hazel Rochman maintained that "Kids will pore over the detailed, brightly colored pen-and-ink drawings ... [that] show the precision and the power of

these marvelous machines." A *Publishers Weekly* reviewer of the same book commended Taback's use of "bold, attention-grabbing colors" in his "oversized, up-close-and-personal illustrations."

Born in New York City in 1932, Taback went to Music and Art High School (now LaQuardia) and planned originally to pursue a degree in engineering. However, his creative instincts won out, and Taback attended the Cooper Union, where he studied under Ray Baxter Dowden and Sid Delevanty and received his bachelors of fine arts degree in 1953. Beginning his career as a graphic artist with CBS Records, Taback later worked as a designer for the *New York Times* as well as for other Manhattan-based businesses before opening his own design studio in 1963. His first book illustration project, an adaptation of the nonsense verse of Lewis Carroll entitled *Jabberwocky and Other Frabjous Nonsense,* was published in 1964.

Taback's second illustration project, Sesyle Joslin's *Please Share That Peanut! A Preposterous Pageant in Fourteen Acts,* was named one of the *New York Times'* best illustrated books of 1965. After subsequently being paired with several authors to produce a variety of picture books—even, in one instance, a cookbook!—Taback linked up with author Harriet Ziefert on the beginning reader *Where Is My House?,* the first of many Ziefert texts featuring illustrations by Taback. In *On Our Way to the Forest,* one of a series of four readers,

Taback includes stickers of his animal characters and encourages readers to make their own pictures. *Two Little Witches: A Halloween Counting Story* finds a growing group of trick-or-treaters winding up at a house so scary that most run for home ... while one runs to fetch her broomstick. Praising Taback's addition of humorous details, *Booklist* contributor Susan Dove Lempke noted that "he keeps the design simple and clear to make the counting easy." In *School Library Journal*, Claudia Cooper commented that the illustrator's "large, primitive, watercolor-and-ink cartoons are especially delightful, both spooky ... and reassuringly familiar."

Riddle books are popular with children new to reading on their own, and Taback has illustrated several such works for authors Katy Hall and Lisa Eisenberg. *Snakey Riddles* offers scads of jokes and other wordplay featuring the slithery, scaly creatures, as well as Taback's "cleverly drawn, lively cartoon illustrations," which *School Library Journal* contributor Sharron McElmeel considered "the best thing about the book." *Fishy Riddles, Buggy Riddles,* and *Spacey Riddles* continue the fun, bringing "groans of enjoyment to primary-grade children and even bigger groans from adults who share them," according to McElmeel.

In addition to illustrating the works of others, Taback has adapted traditional tales with his own text, gracing each with his whimsical drawings. The first, *Joseph Had a Little Overcoat,* was cited as a notable children's book by the American Institute of Graphic Arts. Another book both written and illustrated by Taback, *There Was an Old Lady Who Swallowed a Fly,* is based on an American folk song. Teaching the valuable moral "never swallow a horse" to young readers, Taback also entertains his audience, including "details and humorous asides, from the names of different types of birds, to a recipe for spider soup," according to *School Library Journal* contributor Martha Topol. Taback's illustrations prove equally entertaining; Topol maintained that the old lady of the title, whose incredible appetite gets her into all sorts of trouble, "looks wacky enough to go so far as to swallow a horse" in this "eye-catching, energy-filled" work. Praising the book's collage-like format—Taback includes everything from the pages of nature guides to clips from the *Wall Street Journal* behind his humorous drawings—a *Publishers Weekly* contributor maintained

that "children of all ages will joyfully swallow this book whole." Cartoonist Gahan Wilson had enthusiastic praise for the book in his *New York Times Book Review* assessment, lauding the "widely varied gallery of flies" that appears on the book's back cover and applauding the concept for punching a hole through the page that allows the reader to see inside the gluttonous old lady, "a neat little gross-out in itself.... [that] converts the book into a marvelous toy and gives [readers] many wonderful chances to get inventive." Taback received Caldecott Honor Book recognition in 1998 for *There Was an Old Lady Who Swallowed a Fly.*

Works Cited

Cooper, Claudia, review of *Two Little Witches: A Halloween Counting Story, School Library Journal,* December, 1996, p. 110.

Lempke, Susan Dove, review of *Two Little Witches, Booklist,* September 1, 1996, p. 138.

McElmeel, Sharron, review of *Snakey Riddles, School Library Journal,* April, 1990, p. 108.

McElmeel, Sharron, review of *Spacey Riddles, School Library Journal,* June, 1992, p. 108.

Review of *Road Builders, Publishers Weekly,* June 20, 1994, p. 104.

Rochman, Hazel, review of *Road Builders, Booklist,* May 1, 1994, p. 1603.

Review of *There Was an Old Lady Who Swallowed a Fly, Publishers Weekly,* August 18, 1997, p. 91.

Topol, Martha, review of *There Was an Old Lady Who Swallowed a Fly, School Library Journal,* December, 1997, p. 101.

Wilson, Gahan, review of *There Was an Old Lady Who Swallowed a Fly, New York Times Book Review,* November 16, 1997, p. 56.

For More Information See

PERIODICALS

Booklist, February 1, 1992, p. 1042; July, 1995, p. 1885.

Publishers Weekly, June 21, 1993, p. 103; September 30, 1996, p. 85; May 4, 1998, p. 212.

School Library Journal, December, 1987, p. 96; May, 1988, p. 90; September, 1994, p. 208; August, 1995, p. 114.*

WEBB, Jacquelyn
See PEARCE, Margaret

* * *

WIRTHS, Claudine (Turner) G(ibson) 1926-
(C. W. Bowie, a pseudonym)

Personal

Born May 9, 1926, in Covington, GA; daughter of Count Dillon (a professor of geology) and Julia (Thompson) Gibson; married Theodore Wirths (a National Science Foundation executive), December 28, 1945; children: William, David. *Education:* University of Kentucky, A.B. (social work, English; cum laude), 1946, M.A. (clinical psychology), 1948; American University, M.Ed. (special education), 1980; additional graduate work at University of North Carolina and University of Maryland. *Politics:* Democrat/Independent. *Religion:* Episcopalian. *Hobbies and other interests:* "Hiking to find wildflowers, playing games, walking on stilts and reading."

Addresses

Home—P.O. Box 335, Braddock Heights, MD 21714. *Electronic Mail*—ClaudineW @ aol.com.

Career

Yale University, New Haven, CT, secretary and research assistant for departments of psychology and anthropology, 1946-47; North Carolina League for Crippled Children and Adults, Chapel Hill, program director, 1948-49; research psychologist with Savannah River Studies, Aiken, SC, for University of North Carolina, 1950-52; City Police Department, Aiken, police psychologist, 1952-56; Kirk School, Aiken, head teacher in special education, 1956-58; writer, 1958—; social science consultant in Rockville, MD, 1962-77; Green Acres

Claudine G. Wirths

School, Rockville, elementary school teacher, 1977-78; special education intern at Springfield, VA, high school, 1978-79; Gaithersburg High School, Gaithersburg, MD, special education teacher, 1979-81, coordinator of Learning Center, 1981-84; Frederick Community College, Frederick, MD, member of adjunct faculty, 1987-94. Member of U.S. Department of Defense advisory committee on women in the services, 1960-63, and Girl Guard Board of Salvation Army, 1961-62; board of directors of Montgomery County Health Association, 1967-71, and advisory board of Maryland Department of Natural Resources, 1975-78. *Member:* Phi Beta Kappa, Society of Children's Book Writers and Illustrators.

Awards, Honors

Conservation award, Maryland Environmental Trust, 1973; Award from Maryland-Delaware-D.C. Press Association, 1979, for feature story; Best Books for Young Adults, American Library Association (ALA), 1986, and Recommended Books for Reluctant Young Adult Readers, ALA, 1987, both for *I Hate School*.

Writings

FOR YOUNG ADULTS; WITH MARY BOWMAN-KRUHM

I Hate School: How to Hang In and When to Drop Out, illustrated by Patti Stren, Harper, 1987.
I Need A Job! Straight Talk about Working, Walch, 1988.
Where's My Other Sock? How to Get Organized and Drive Your Parents and Teachers Crazy, illustrated by Molly Coxe, Harper, 1989.
Are You My Type? Or Why Aren't You More Like Me? (with accompanying teacher's guide), illustrated by Ed Taber, Consulting Psychologists Press, 1992.
How to Get Up When Schoolwork Gets You Down, David Cook, 1993.
I Need to Get Organized, with accompanying audio tape, Walch, 1993.
Choosing Is Confusing: How to Make Good Choices, Not Bad Guesses, illustrated by Ed Taber, Consulting Psychologists Press, 1994.
I Need to Get Along with Other Types of People, Walch, 1995.
Upgrade—The High Tech Road to School Success, illustrated by Ed Taber, Consulting Psychologists Press, 1995.
Onramp to the Internet: A Writer's Guide to Getting Online, Children's Book Insider, 1996.
Choosing a Career in Law Enforcement, Rosen, 1997.
Coping with Confrontations and Encounters with the Police, Rosen, 1998.
(Under pseudonym C. W. Bowie, and with Bowman-Kruhm and Wendie Old) *Busy Toes* (picture book), illustrated by Fred Willingham, Whispering Coyote Press, 1998.
Coping with Discrimination and Prejudice, Rosen, 1998.

"TIME TO BE A TEEN" SERIES; WITH MARY BOWMAN-KRUHM

Your New School, illustrated by Patti Stren, Twenty-First Century Books, 1993.
Your Circle of Friends, illustrated by Patti Stren, Twenty-First Century Books, 1993.
Your Power with Words, illustrated by Patti Stren, Twenty-First Century Books, 1993.

"A DAY IN THE LIFE OF ..." SERIES; WITH MARY BOWMAN-KRUHM

A Day in the Life of a Firefighter, Rosen, 1997.
A Day in the Life of a Doctor, Rosen, 1997.
A Day in the Life of an Emergency Medical Technician, Rosen, 1997.
A Day in the Life of a Police Officer, Rosen, 1997.
A Day in the Life of a Coach, Rosen, 1997.

OTHER

(With Richard H. Williams) *Lives through the Years: A Study of Successful Aging*, Atherton Press, 1965.

Contributor of articles and short fiction to periodicals, including *Cat Fancy*, *Children's Book Insider*, *Guide*, *Humpty Dumpty*, *Law and Order*, *Journal of Clinical Psychology*, *Free Spirit*, *Vegetarian Times*, *Scholastic Scope*, and *Shadow Magazine*.

Sidelights

The author of several growing-up guides for young adults, Claudine G. Wirths has dedicated her adult years to working with middle-grade and high school students with learning disabilities. Among Wirths's books, many written with co-author Mary Bowman-Kruhm, are *How to Get Up When Homework Gets You Down* and *Choosing Is Confusing: How to Make Good Choices, Not Bad Guesses*, which was praised by *Booklist* contributor Stephanie Zvirin for its "common sense, ... nonstuffy style, and lots of relevant examples."

Born in Covington, Georgia, in 1926, Wirths was inspired to begin writing by one of her favorite children's book authors, Madge A. Bingham, who lived near her family's home on St. Simons Island. "When I expressed my great fondness for her books," Wirths once recalled, "[Ms. Bingham] urged me to write my own. My first work at age seven, 'The Tall Cat,' was not

Wirths's fanciful picture book, written under the pseudonym C. W. Bowie, pays tribute to the things that toes can do. (From Busy Toes, *illustrated by Fred Willingham.)*

published, but was highly satisfying to me, and I continued writing."

Submitting articles and short stories to various periodicals while embarking upon a career as a teacher and school psychologist, Wirths had scattered successes. "From my teens on there was the usual avalanche of rejection slips, but I kept on writing," she remembered. Her first major children's book, *I Hate School: How to Hang in and When to Drop Out,* wasn't published until she was over sixty years old, causing Wirths to remark that "success takes a little longer for some of us!"

Wirths became interested in young people with learning disabilities when she was introduced to the subject of dyslexia during graduate school in the late 1940s. "I was intrigued at the puzzle of how a bright child might fail to learn to read," she commented. When she became involved in police work in Aiken, South Carolina, she began to see the real problem: "Far too often, the child in trouble was learning disabled and a potential dropout. The frustration set up by the handicap of dyslexia turns school days into days of despair, and unless the child receives special help (and sometimes even when they do), school becomes a permanent nightmare for the child and their parents."

Wirths returned to graduate school in the late 1970s to study special education, and has since dedicated her time to writing, teaching, and lecturing on learning disabilities. Her books are co-authored by friend and colleague Dr. Mary Bowman-Kruhm, a reading specialist. "We share compassion for the student who has school problems and we hope to help them understand how they can best help themselves," Wirths explained. "Our books do not talk down to readers but they do use simple language and clear ideas."

Among the duo's works for young people are several books that help teens cope with the challenges and responsibilities of growing into adulthood, particularly as these relate to school and work. *I Hate School* provides solutions to homework difficulties and other school-related hassles in a question-and-answer format. Praising the authors for "approach[ing] their readers with the idea of making informed choices that put them in charge of their own lives, rather than just drifting along," *School Library Journal* contributor Joyce Adams Burner determined the book a "useful tool" for guidance counselors. A *Kirkus Reviews* critic also had praise for the volume. Calling the authors "teachers ... who have those proverbial eyes in the back of their heads [and] know what's going on," the critic commended Wirths and Bowman-Kruhm for a prose style that is compatible with readers having short attention spans, concluding

that *I Hate School* presents "a wonderful distillation of techniques successful students somehow discover on their own."

In *Where's My Other Sock? How to Get Organized and Drive Your Parents and Teachers Crazy,* Wirths and Bowman-Kruhm focus on middle-school readers. Dividing organizational skills into three primary areas, the authors suggest dividing big projects into smaller ones, taking charge, and finding one's own system. Their advice was characterized as "sensible if not profound" by *Bulletin of the Center for Children's Books* contributor Roger Sutton. Diane Pozar, commenting on *Where's My Other Sock?* in *School Library Journal,* maintained that "since the book is written in a light, entertaining manner, students should accept the tips," which have a practical application ranging from study habits to ways to organize one's bedroom to function more efficiently.

"Writing as a twosome has solved many of the problems that kept me from writing successfully in the past," Wirths noted of her partnership with Bowman-Kruhm. "I now keep to writing schedules, have a built-in editor, and best of all, have someone to talk to who is as passionately concerned about writing and about problems of the learning disabled as I am."

Works Cited

Burner, Joyce Adams, review of *I Hate School: How to Hang In and When to Drop Out, School Library Journal,* November, 1986, p. 110.

Review of *I Hate School: How to Hang In and When to Drop Out, Kirkus Reviews,* September 1, 1986, p. 1379.

Pozar, Diane, review of *Where's My Other Sock? How To Get Organized and Drive Your Parents and Teachers Crazy, School Library Journal,* December, 1989, p. 116.

Sutton, Roger, review of *Where's My Other Sock, Bulletin of the Center for Children's Books,* October, 1989, p. 48.

Zvirin, Stephanie, review of *Choosing Is Confusing: How to Make Good Choices, Not Bad Guesses, Booklist,* December 15, 1994.

For More Information See

PERIODICALS

Booklist, December 1, 1989, p. 749; May 1, 1994, p. 1601.

Bulletin of the Center for Children's Books, October, 1996, p. 40.

School Library Journal, March, 1997, p. 196; February, 1999, p. 113.

Autobiography Feature

Maia Wojciechowska

1927-

The Past's Truths

The past holds its own truths. They are private, not public truths. When you go back to your past alone, you take a chance at excavating forgotten pain while looking for remembered happiness. And you may, if you are lucky, understand the present better and even learn about your future. But going over your past publicly is somewhat like making a movie. You are its writer and its director and its star. But sooner or later you become its editor. From the patchwork of scenes you begin to discard, splice together sequences. The hardest decision is about what you leave out and what you retain, often at the risk of making yourself seem ridiculous. Is any of it true anymore? Is any of it false? The past, like the movies, holds its own truths.

I wrote the above in 1972 as a preface to *Till the Break of Day: Memories 1939-1942*. I can't quarrel with any of it, but I learned something fascinating since the publication of that book. The past's truths are not sharable. My two brothers remembered those years very differently, were affected by other events and other people. It was our communal past only as far as geography went, but emotionally we each had our own past and it must be, like fingerprints, inexplicably different for each of us.

My father died in 1954. He died a Pole, never wishing to become an American citizen, urging his children and everyone else born in Poland to keep their Polish citizenship, and saying sad, desperate things like: "As long as we remain Poles we will have to fight for the return of our country. If we relinquish that citizenship we won't any longer demand the return, to us, of a free Poland. We will forfeit every right! Even the right of exile! We must never surrender ourselves to another country for we are Poles, robbed of our land. But we must return to a free Poland, either by fighting to free it or demanding an investigation into why Poland was sold." The year before he died this most private of men spoke at public meetings about the necessity not to compromise this "freeing of Poland." He wrote urgent letters trying to appeal to the conscience of those who "sold" Poland, who could "redress that treason" which happened at Yalta and was confirmed in Teheran. Until the last day of his life he considered himself "on forced leave" from the Polish Air Force, ready at a moment's notice to be called back to his job as a soldier. "We must expect to shed blood again," he said to his sons who would argue that Poles had shed enough blood.

A year before his death I promised my father that if he became terminally ill I would drive him up to a mountaintop and leave him there to die. "I want my body to rest in Poland," he said. "The Polish earth is light for us, the foreign soil too heavy." I did not know how sick he became after a routine operation. I didn't know until it was too late. My brother Chris swears he was murdered on orders from Moscow and there was a mysterious nurse who came from Washington and stayed until he was dead and then disappeared as suddenly as she had appeared. I didn't even go to his funeral for I knew I would only have to bury him again, in Poland, and my mother wished him there, in California, where she could tend his grave. Poles are as good at tending their dead as they are at dying.

Returning to Poland

By the time I was thirty-four I was most eager to grow up. I felt emotionally arrested by the war. I was still, emotionally, twelve-going-on-sixteen, rebellions and angry, seesawing between total happiness and utmost despair, naive and trusting, yet cynical, the way only children can be cynical. I was given to totally idiotic, often shocking, declarations which were made to impress, badly, those who heard them. I was outrageous and didn't know how to be anything else, or didn't want to try to be anything else, such as a grown-up. I had not begun to write children's books, except for one picture book of no particular merit. I knew that it was high time to grow up and the only way I was going to do that would be to go back to Poland to bury that kid who was giving me too much trouble at thirty-four.

It was 1961 and I did not expect to cry so much. Everything there made me cry.

Those were the bad days, when the spirit flagged, when despair was heard howling throughout the land. I cried when a conductor accused me of not putting all my pennies in the box, accused me of cheating. I cried when I could not buy any paper to write on, because I was a writer although not an author. I cried when I managed to generate more garbage than a family of six. I cried when I talked to a doctor, a bone surgeon, and heard his story. He had been away from Poland for a year because he had devised some new technique of mending bones and had been invited to lecture in the West, in Belgium, France, Italy. When he came back to Poland, he was punished for having been away. He was given a desk and could not perform any operations. He got his pay but he saw no patients.

"Why and who is doing this to you?" I asked.

"The government. The bureaucrats. My hospital. And why? Because I got good at something and someone noticed. And that is not allowed. Everything must be kept on the level of mediocrity. If anyone shows talent it must be kept in the dark, it must not be used. They, the communists, dear lady, want us exterminated by mediocrity. That's how the communists kill. Not with guns, but by denying the possibility of greatness! Take that message back to your new country, to America. Stop arming yourselves with guns. Arm yourselves with excellence! Don't let shoddy movies be made, or once made, don't make them popular. You watch things on television that have no content, that say nothing new, show nothing of value and pretty soon you will become a communist. A communist is someone who, having no soul, supports anything that will kill the human spirit. Anything that diminishes godlike qualities in people is communism. That's why a good communist does not allow God anywhere around. That's why there are so very few communists in Poland and so very many in a country like yours, in America. I was there for a short time. They don't call themselves communists. They are materialists. Same thing."

Maia Wojciechowska with Aunt Walcia, Cracow, Poland, 1937.

I asked the doctor if we could have dinner because I wanted to argue with him about American values and how it's not the same to be a communist and a capitalist.

"I'm sorry," he said. "I must attend to my planned suicide tonight."

He walked away and I cried because I knew that he had lived too long in a place where reasons for living were made fewer each day.

I also cried in the theatre. Over the years I've seen a dozen productions of Chekhov's *The Seagull,* in maybe half-a-dozen languages. The production I saw in Poland was so superior to anything I had seen that it left me limp with gratitude. I cried because it was so splendid and because the peasants, who were bussed in from the countryside, laughed in all the wrong places.

One day, to make me laugh, a cousin took me to see what he did. He worked in the department of food supplies. He had a private office with a huge map of Warsaw. The map had multicolored pins on it. There were clusters of the same color all over the place, but each cluster was far away from the next. He explained his job. "I have to move different foods around so it will be very hard for people to find what they need." I did not understand.

He explained patiently, speaking slowly so that I would not miss the point: "What we have here, in communist Poland, is a government *against* the people. It's a government dedicating all its energies to making the citizens *continually* miserable. My job is to make sure people don't starve to death and yet hate themselves for being alive." He pointed to the cluster of blue pins. "Those pins are tomato paste cans. We have restrictions on everything. You cannot buy more than one of anything, but right here, in this part of Warsaw, you can find all the tomato paste you'd wish to look at. You have to go there to purchase tomato paste. Now right here," he pointed to the yellow cluster of pins, "I've placed our supply of onions for this week. Of course the paste and the onions will be moved around, but in clusters, in a few days. That's my job, moving foodstuff around. But right here there is nothing but onions, and here," he pointed to another cluster of pins, this time brown ones, "we've got potatoes." He smiled. "Now let's say that you want to make potato soup tonight. You will have to travel all over Warsaw for your ingredients. Here," he pointed to green pins way up north, "for salt, and here," he pointed south, "for pepper, and you already know where you go for potatoes, onions, and tomato paste. Of course you're in my office looking at the map. If you were out on the street trying to buy stuff for soup tonight, it would take you about six hours of scurrying around. How could a Polish housewife, after six hours spent in finding ingredients for soup, be expected to go to Mass? Or lead some protesters? Or gossip about us governmental bureaucrats? You see the government, through vermin like me, keeps the citizens busy. They have to scurry for necessities. The Moscow party thinkers studied rats and decided it was the best way of keeping people placid—make them scurry around like so many rats in a maze, just to stay alive."

I began to shake my head thinking how lucky I was not having to live in Poland, but his next words made me less happy.

"You, in your new country, are not so very much different from us. It's not the government that makes you

Uncle Stas, during Maia's only visit to Poland after World War II, Lodz, 1961.

scurry around. It's the advertisers; it's free enterprise, capitalism. You want new cars and new clothes, new ice boxes and sets, and they are all there, not hidden in clusters, not even rationed, but available all over. Of course they do cost money, so you have to scurry after money. We don't have unemployment. Everyone here has to work. In America they want to work. We don't want to work to keep this monster alive, but we have to. You don't have to, but you want to. Scurrying around for things that only money can buy, you have no time to pray or protest or wonder what happened to happiness in life. Someone in your country must have been studying rats as well."

I was being educated all the time in Poland. I went to the studios of the Polski Film and saw short films that were unbelievably great. "Why are they short?" I asked. "Because that's all the film they give us. Never enough for a feature." "But they are so great, can they be shown outside of Poland?" "No, they are too good. Poland exports only the mediocre, propaganda product. Nobody is going to see our good films. We have to knock off four awful films in order to be allowed to make one good one. And that is always a short one that nobody will see. But at least all of us working in film know what we can do if we were allowed. We're good!"

There was a whole new language in Poland in those days, having triple and quadruple meaning, a secret language which ridiculed the system, ridiculed life under the system, turned tears into laughter.

My second week in Poland I went to see Uncle Stas in Lodz. What was he doing in provincial Lodz? He was existing. He looked the same, almost, except older. He was still immaculately dressed, wore spats, carried a cane, had

his shoes brilliantly shined. He looked like prewar Uncle Stas. He told me that he could look like that in Lodz but wouldn't get away looking like that in Warsaw, so he stayed in Lodz because he valued the way he looked. He was obviously greatly admired and respected and had a coterie of friends gather around him for his ritual of tea drinking in a cafe. He had finally, after my grandmother died, married his mistress. And I finally found out from him what had happened to my beloved aunts, Walcia and Andzia.

It seemed that all through the war they managed, somehow, to survive in Warsaw. But after the uprising, when 99 percent of the city lay in ruins, the newly arrived communists ordered people to go to whatever relatives they might have outside of Warsaw. And my aunts were taken in by Uncle Stas in Lodz. He said that they were made "more strange" by the war. They still lived lives of "perfect cleanliness" but it must have been physically impossible. So their obsession with making everything sterile was now even more strongly wedged into their minds. He didn't say that they were madder than the hatter, but they must have been. He was very gentle telling me how it was impossible to lead the kind of life they led before the war. Even heating water was a luxury, and boiling it continuously to sterilize everything, as they wanted, was out of the question. And although he did not say it, I sensed that his wife and my beloved aunts must have waged a war as cruel as any.

Before the war my aunts, Andzia and Walcia, were allied with my grandmother against Uncle Stas's mistress, referring to her as "that harlot," if they referred to her at all. What was it like for my aunts, with their great sense of loyalty, to exist under the roof of the woman they had

Aunt Andzia, not long before her death.

Grandmother Stefania Rudakowska

thought despicable? And, more importantly, what was it like for Stas's wife? I didn't quite dare ask.

But my uncle sensed my curiosity and said: "Your aunts never talked to my wife. If they wished something they would communicate their needs to me and I would pass them on. My wife understood and forgave them, and your aunts kept their vows to my mother, your grandmother, never to speak to her. Anyway, life was not easy. They lived downstairs and we lived upstairs. They had one room with a small kitchen and the tragedy was, of course, that they never had enough hot, boiling water. But they managed and we saw them each day. But one day the door remained locked when I knocked, and Walcia said that Andzia was not feeling well. I asked if they needed anything and she said no. It went on like that for a week. Usually my wife would go to the market and try to get some food for all of us, and she too began to worry. At the end of the week I broke the door down."

He looked down as if terribly ashamed, and I held my breath knowing that something awful, tragic, had happened beyond the closed door.

"Walcia was combing Andzia's hair. She had your aunt Andzia dressed in a nightgown, seated on the chair, and Walcia was talking to her. There was this terrible smell in the room . . . Andzia had been dead for over a week by then."

I saw it all as if I were there, as if I, too, had combed her hair, not wishing her to leave yet, not wanting to be left alone in this world without her. They had always talked about it. Ever since I could remember anything at all, I remembered my aunts saying that they could never live one without the other. They had always planned to die together, and yet they would play those games of theirs—Andzia, the

angelic one, saying that she would die first because God was merciful. And Walcia, the strong, domineering one, saying that no such thing was going to happen. They would die together, at the same hour, the same moment. And as a small child I would listen to them, and I believed, without knowing, that they would die together. And now, knowing how it happened, I said my thanks to God. Andzia had to go first. It was only fair.

"The most cruel, the most ironic thing happened," Uncle Stas went on. "Walcia died the next day. She seemed perfectly healthy, except her mind was with her sister, refusing to accept her death. I had an autopsy performed and do you know what Walcia died of? Filth! Dirt!" He tried to find the piece of paper to show me the medical word. But in his agitation could not find it. "Can you imagine! It was Walcia, all along, all her life, who was such a nut about cleanliness. And she dies of filth!" He must have loved them, I decided then, because I had never seen him angry or shouting before. "I just don't know. Taking care of the dead body must have caused it. She had no immunity at all. She was the cleanest person in the world and they had water and the gas to boil it. Of course she did not die of filth! She died because she couldn't go on without Andzia. They were like twins."

I went alone to their grave. They were buried in one grave, actually in one coffin. "They would have wanted it that way," as Uncle Stas explained. He had already mentioned that it had cost him a pretty penny to get the grave digger to put them in the same box. I agreed. They would have wanted it that way. I brought some flowers and cleaned the grave of weeds. They had a very cheap, rusty little sign, just their names and dates of birth and death on a tin cross. I polished the cross as best I could. I was there for

Grandfather Rudakowski

a few hours, and in that short space of time I remembered all the thousands of hours we had spent together. And when I got off my knees to go home, I could not find my sunglasses. It was the strangest thing. I simply knew that they wanted something of mine with them and took the sunglasses. There was no other, no more logical explanation. They didn't ask, they took. And it was only right. I never gave anything to them that I could remember.

I came back from the cemetery determined to transport them to the family grave in Warsaw. I didn't care what it would take; this I had to do for them. My maternal grandmother had what always seemed to me the very best family grave site in all of Warsaw. It was located on the main avenue, just beyond the iron gate, the easiest of all graves to find.

My fondest memories had to do with All Souls' Day (Halloween in America) when the family gathered to pay their respects to their dead. The great cemetery would be transformed by millions of flickering candles, by an ocean of flowers. People bundled up would move by the light of those candles, in the shadows of those flowers, tending to the cleaning of their graves. Families had family graves, and the oldest seemed the best. Ours was one of the oldest and one of the biggest. The names of all the departed were etched into the marble, with plenty of marble left for new names and dates. Before the war everyone in the family knew there was enough space for twelve more coffins. Once the spaces were all filled, the crypt would be sealed forever. As it was, the big stone would be moved aside by a forklift whenever anyone was buried in that family grave.

Before going to Lodz to see Uncle Stas, I had visited the grave and the only new name on it was that of my grandmother, Stefania Rudakowska, 1866-1944. Andzia and Walcia always expected to be buried next to her, their sister. I always figured that I would end up there as well, and certainly my mother and father would be brought to rest there too. I was pretty sure that in spite of social and other differences not only Stas but his wife as well would end up there.

On my way back to Stas's apartment I decided to move my aunts immediately to Warsaw, to that marvelous family grave. When I told him, he looked very dubious.

"It will be very difficult," my uncle Stas said. "Maybe even impossible."

"Listen," I said, "in a bureaucracy such as this I know I'd need a permit. I am ready to grease some palms. I will transport them by train and I will travel with the coffin in the baggage car. I wish you'd come with me because I won't know how to arrange things on the other end, getting them in the family grave..."

"It will be impossible," Uncle Stas finally said, "because there is no more space left in our family grave."

"You're crazy," I said. "I was there only three days ago and Grandmother, your mother, is the only one who got buried there since the war. That would leave eleven spaces for eleven more coffins. Everybody knows that!"

"There is just one space left," he said.

"Come again?"

"Just one space left and I thought I could have it," he said.

It was my turn to get angry. I shouted at him that I would be bringing my mother and my father from America soon and tomorrow I was taking my aunts to that grave, and

that if he gave some spaces to his friends all he had to do was throw the stiffs out of there.

"You don't understand," he said after my anger was exhausted. "Things were very tough during the war. I was running the racetrack in Warsaw. My assignment from the underground was to financially ruin as many of the biggies in the Gestapo as I could..."

"How did we get into horses from the grave?" I asked, feeling that he was going to pull some con on me. After all, my uncle Stas was known before the war as the family con man.

"I was going to come to that, how that grave saved my life, but if you don't want to hear about it..."

"Sure," I said. He wouldn't lie to me, I decided. Not to his own niece. Not at his age.

We went out to his favorite cafe, and a small crowd gathered around us as he told me the story of the great race. He must have told it many times before, or was a better actor than I thought. He told it so well that I remember it as if it had been a movie. As a matter of fact it would make a great movie.

It seems that very shortly after the Germans invaded Poland in September of 1939, an order went out to reopen the racetrack and my uncle was put in some position at the top, having had connections there. (Actually the only connection I think he had was as a gambler. It was he, single-handedly, who lost a family fortune with his gambling. He rarely won. And my mother always said that it was he, her brother, who introduced my father to gambling. The two used to gamble together a lot.)

"By spring of 1940 I had gained the confidence of the top Gestapo men in Warsaw," my uncle was saying, and I began to concentrate on the story. "I had given them many tips on the right horses and they trusted me as their official handicapper. I began to figure out the way to totally ruin the top Gestapo dog in one single race." The crowd at the cafe drew nearer. "Everyone, from the jockeys to the grooms, and of course the top echelons of the Polish Underground, were in on the scam. Its secret name was NAG. I had promised the Gestapo man that if I ever found one single horse, preferably a long-shot that could make him rich, I'd let him know. I finally spotted the horse I wanted him to be ruined by, a filly with absolutely no chance of becoming a racing horse, not even if someone implanted wings on her back. She was brought to me by a peasant boy and offered to me for ten zlotys. 'She's as swift as the wind,' the kid said. That very day I went to see the Gestapo dog and told him there would be a filly, a 100-to-1 long-shot running next Saturday, and if he could manage to divest himself of a lot of his treasures he would bankrupt even the Swiss bankers with his winnings.

"The following day he sold both his cars for one-tenth their worth to a man who said he would get back his cars if he won. The man was one of ours. The Gestapo man let go of his great collection of paintings to a man who made him a loan and promised to give them back if he won the race. The man was also ours. He let go of his silver and his jewels to another of our men for a measly sum, but also with a promise that he could redeem the stuff. Altogether he was able to raise over a million zlotys for things worth one hundred times as much. But he was happy. After all he had a horse that could not lose, and he would have, after the race, one hundred million zlotys and would redeem all his

Father, Lt. Col. Zygmunt Wojciechowski, Washington, D.C., 1944.

treasures. He was a very happy man when he gave a party the night before the race. I was there, drinking champagne, eating caviar, and so were our men who had bought his things at low prices. Already those things were distributed where they could not be found, and the men themselves were ready to leave for parts unknown at the party's end. I, however, had decided to stick it out to the very end of the great race.

"You see it was all planned like a bank robbery, with a lot of bright people involved, with great precision in timing. We were so certain of our great success, of going down in history as the neatest con ever, that during the party I suggested our host call the Fuehrer himself and get him to place a bet on this sure thing that would have odds of 100-to-1. The Fuehrer told our host to put 100 zlotys on the horse. We raised our glasses and our host laughed after he had drunk the toast to the horse that would make him rich. He said that if something was to happen to that horse, he would be totally destroyed. I laughed right along with him."

Uncle Stas obviously enjoyed telling the story and took great pains that those who came to hear it heard it well. His voice was pretty loud in that cafe, and I caught myself thinking that maybe his great con was part of a con he was pulling on me.

"Everything had to go like clockwork for everyone to be safe after the race. This was to be the very last time Polish horses were racing for the Germans, that was the underground's decision. The ticket takers, the bet collectors, the barmen, and even the cleaning staff were to leave at the start of that race. The jockeys, of course, would have to take their chances but the Germans had great respect for them . . . and we knew they'd be safe—except, perhaps, for the jockey on that nag that would come in last. I myself had arranged for a plane to taxi up on the other side of the stands. The plane was as close to me as the starting gate, a mere hundred yards.

"She broke out well. She was wearing gold and a number eight. She was third and furthest from the rails when suddenly, before the first turn, I see her, the horse of history, our 100-to-1 nag, turn! She was making directly toward me, where I was standing, and I began to run toward the plane. She was a faster horse than I took her for. We reached the plane at the same time and the jockey jumped out of the saddle right at the plane's door. The filly was still running as we taxied off."

The small crowd broke into applause as the story came to the end.

"So what happened to eleven spaces in the family grave?" I asked him as he was waving to the waiter to refill his cup of tea.

He looked shocked, as if I had breached some rule of etiquette. I waited patiently.

"You did not guess how my life was saved?" he asked. "It was the owner of the plane, of course. I traded my escape for the ten spaces in the grave. You see," he lowered his head piously, "the pilot's family, all ten of them, were wiped out by a rare disease and he had no place to put them." His head remained lowered and after a while he began to snore. He was getting on in years and I felt sorry for him. But I still didn't believe him and when I got back to Warsaw I checked out the race story. It seemed to be true. A relative told me that Stas had something to do with it all, but didn't know exactly what.

"You might not remember," she told me, "but when you and your brother Zbyszek were small kids you always asked for money for your name-days and Christmas. For years nobody knew what you ever did with all that money but one day we found out that your uncle Stas was making bets with you kids. And he always won," she added.

"What happened to the family grave?" I wanted to know.

"During the war whenever Uncle Stas needed money, he'd sell a space in the family grave," she told me. "To tell you the truth, I think he had someone ferret horizontally from your family grave into others because it seems to me he sold about a hundred spaces during the war and you couldn't have had more than a dozen in yours."

Before leaving Poland I called Uncle Stas and told him that I was putting $100 in an envelope. It was to take care of the expense of removing all those strange stiffs from our grave and putting my aunts there. I reminded him that I'd be coming back with the bodies of my mother and father and I expected to find a lot of space there.

"I bet you," he said, "I'll die before my sister, your mother."

"How much?" I caught myself saying. And he answered, "A hundred dollars?"

Mexico, 1957: "The year I trained to be a bullfighter— with a brave cow who had been fought before."

A few years later my younger brother, Chris, went to Poland and found him in need of more care. He ordered the best wheelchair around and Uncle Stas travelled around Lodz in that as if it were his Cadillac. Chris wanted him to come to America, but Uncle Stas thought it was too late for him.

"If I were in my prime," he told Chris, "I would take on America."

"I'd like to see you in Las Vegas."

"You should have seen me in Monte Carlo."

Before he left Poland, my brother Chris made arrangements for a nurse and other amenities for my uncle, and the last two years of his life he lived in the manner he had been accustomed to, except more so. For over twenty years it was my other brother Zbyszek, who had been sending him, regularly, enough money to live on and keep up that front that was so important to him. After all, Uncle Stas was the only male member of our family who had always lived like a true aristocrat, having never had a job of any kind.

Retracing the Past in France

I did not get rid of that young Maia while in Poland, and a year later I went back to Europe to retrace my past in France to perhaps lose her there. In *Till the Break of Day* I had written about that colony of Poles in the town of Hyeres. I had one photograph of the four of us, my two brothers, Chris and Zbyszek, and my mother, in front of the hotel, and I used to stare at it and wonder. How come I looked so starved and they didn't? How come I looked so ugly and they didn't? How come the three of us kids looked so guilty? Or was it my imagination? And Mother, she looked so strong and stern, just the opposite of what she was. I wanted to remember more of it, revisit what I felt were the places where my most formative years were spent.

It was strange—in all those places there was only one ghost, that of my father. He had not been with us, not in Sables-d'Olonne, not in Bordeaux, not in Vichy, or Grenoble, or Hyeres, yet it was he, and he alone, I kept thinking of. I retraced nothing of my own past, found no clues to anything except the fact that I loved him dearly and he died without ever knowing how I had felt about him. I don't think I ever told him that I loved him.

Someone had once asked me what a growing kid needs most, and I had said: "A hero the kid can love, admire, forget his or her ego in front of, that's what a kid needs most."

My father had consistently been my hero. We had almost two years of "normal" life as a family and those two years were in Washington, D.C., where he was the Air Attaché at the Polish Embassy.

I didn't get to know him well. He was still shrouded, as always, in great mystery. What did he really think? About everything—the war, us being in America, the kind of life we led? What did he feel about being with us, around us, for so long this time? What did he want out of life, out of me? I don't know if those questions were so precise in my mind, or whether I was quite that curious then. Like all hero-worshippers that came before me, I was not about to demystify my hero. We played tennis together; I always lost to him. He would remind me that my mother wanted me to concentrate on my homework. (Didn't he care about my homework?) He thought my mother was right in

Maia on the Harley Davidson she rode through Europe, 1958.

wanting my lights out at eleven on weekdays. (Did he know that sometimes I was still reading when daylight came?) He took us for drives, to New York City one weekend (where I took pictures of the animals in the Museum of Natural History and lied in school that I had been to Africa for the weekend). And to Monticello where he spoke about the miracle of the American Declaration of Independence to us as if, suddenly, he wished to teach us something. It was so rare, his assuming the role of someone who wanted us to know something specific. He, my hero, my father, was just like mercury. I had once broken a thermometer and tried to get hold of the mercury and couldn't. So I knew he was like that.

I was not in love with my father during those years, fifteen to seventeen. I was in love with Lord Byron. In my wallet I carried his picture, one I took with my camera from an engraving in a book. We went to Fort Leavenworth, Kansas, for the fall of 1944, and I showed his picture to a girl who showed me the picture of her boyfriend.

"He looks strange, like a man or something," she said squinting, not understanding this was just a photograph of an engraving. "How old is he?"

I did some very fast calculation in my head.

"One hundred and fifty-six . . ."

It was the first time I heard anyone scream with a definite "EEEK" sound. The news of my having a boyfriend age 156 spread very fast. I couldn't even explain to anyone that he had died when he was only thirty-six, because whenever I tried to bring him up the kids would laugh too hard to care what I was trying to say.

But in Kansas, Lord Byron almost encountered some competition. He was tall and dark and handsome and had blue eyes. And he told me that his was the most important job on the football field. I used to go to every game and watch him intently but never could figure out what football was all about. He would mostly sit on the bench, or if

others were seated on the bench, he'd sit on the ground. And he had a bucket of water. Most of the time he held it, but sometimes he'd put it down and I would try to figure out if his putting down the bucket had anything to do with the screams of the crowd and the change in score. Sometimes it seemed like it did, sometimes it seemed like it didn't. At least five times each quarter this boy I was having a crush on would race to someone in the field, and that player would take a drink from the bucket, and then he would race back to the sidelines. I'd always break into wild applause and cheers of "yay!" whenever he'd race on the field and whenever he'd come back, but I was the only one applauding and yelling.

Years later, when I went to a Yale-Princeton game with my husband, Selden Rodman, I tried to explain to him what I knew about football and he thought I was crazy. By then they didn't have water boys on the fields. I still feel that boy was not really lying to me about his importance. He must have seen the game from his particular vantage point, and aren't we all just like him?

Back in America: Los Angeles and New York

Poland was taken away from us by a senile President Roosevelt and what I considered the two arch-villains of my time, Stalin and Churchill. After they met at Yalta, my father flew to London, certain that the Polish armed forces would mobilize and invade their homeland and free it from the new oppressors. After all, didn't we fight the war first; didn't we lose more men in uniform than any other country; didn't we, the Poles, suffer more; weren't we more determined to defeat the Germans and the Russians?

I was playing basketball at the Sacred Heart High School in Los Angeles when a weeping nun announced that President Roosevelt was dead. I applauded and shouted: "Thank God the bastard is dead!" and was immediately sent home and told not to show my face around for at least a week. What would happen to Poland now, I wondered.

What happened to Poland only Poles who were there know. The Russians looked around and picked the most Semitic-looking, Polish-speaking Jew as the chief of the secret police for Poland. His photograph along with his infamous deeds of cruelty and terror were in the papers everyday, reviving once again anti-Semitic feelings among the Poles, feelings killed by the Nazi persecution. Outside of Poland the communist propaganda machines used the Jews themselves to fan the flames of anti-Semitism. The Poles found themselves robbed of their dead. "Six million Jews were murdered in concentration camps," became a new fact and was accepted as the truth, while the factual truth was that three million Poles, who were not Jews, perished in those camps along with an equal number of Polish Jews. The communist rulers in Poland knew that as long as Poles appeared to be anti-Semitic nobody would give much of a damn about the country and what agony it was going through. And they succeeded. Until Solidarity in 1980 Poland was far away on the back burners of world consciousness. And with the advent of Solidarity, the world heard but did not understand what happened there. (And what happened was a total discreditation of communism by the workers, the very people communism was invented for. It was done by a worker called Lech Walesa, not by a philosopher or a politician.)

It became totally hopeless for my father to stay on in London, waiting for his president (there was, and still is, a Polish government-in-exile. It was, and still is, totally ignored) to give him and the rest of the Polish soldiers their marching orders. He returned to us in 1947, totally defeated in spirit. He had been away for more than two years and I could not bear to see him so sad. I fled to New York, to become a writer.

I had written a number of short stories, all on the theme of Poles in exile, and had given those stories to someone who knew Rupert Hughes, an American writer. One night Mr. Hughes called me up. It was after midnight. He was crying. He said he was that moved by my stories. I was on a New York-bound bus that same morning with thoughts of fame dancing in my head. Getting off the bus in Santa Fe, I was so taken by the place I missed that bus and a couple of others, while walking around promising myself to live there one day. (It took me almost twenty-five years to keep the promise. And when I went there to live, I only stayed ten years.) A few days later I managed to recover the manuscript and my suitcase from the terminal in New York City and went straight to what I considered the best publisher, Harper Brothers. I considered them the best because I liked the building they were in. It seemed to me to be as classy as my stories. I took the elevator to the

"editorial" floor and handed my manuscript to the receptionist with the words: "I shall be back tomorrow."

Unfortunately, I did not ask her to give it to someone to read. I imagined all that night, which I spent walking the New York streets, that someone was burning the midnight oil reading my words, crying perhaps, as Mr. Hughes had cried. I could not wait for the Harper offices to open the next day. I was there before the receptionist. When she finally assumed her chair I stood in front of her. I had come back for the contract but also I expected to make changes. Wordlessly she handed me back my manuscript. I took it to the nearest rest room, opened it. There was not even a rejection slip. Nothing. I was totally appalled and decided right there and then not to have anything to do with writing. I was finished with that career. I would resume my tennis career.

I spent the second night in New York City at the apartment of a friend of my mother's near Columbia University. I had exactly one dime to my name. Before I set off with it I used their phone to make an appointment to see a Mr. Elwood Cooke. I told him that I would be willing to teach tennis at his courts in Tudor City if he was willing to give me a job. He said to come and see him that very afternoon.

I walked all the way from Broadway and 111th Street to the Brooklyn Bridge. I considered it the most beautiful

Three generations: Maia with granddaughter Laina and mother, Madame Wojciechowska, Los Angeles, California, 1983.

bridge in the world. I threw my last dime into the East River from that bridge and then walked another sixty blocks to my appointment. I was free of worldly goods, I thought, free as a bird. I just wished I had wings because my feet hurt so much.

"You have the worst damn swing I've ever seen in my life," said Elwood Cooke as I demonstrated to him the swing taught to me by Henri Cochet and improved on by Rene Lacoste before the war. I told him that he didn't have to give me a job but he could not insult me. After all I was the Polish junior champion and had, back in 1936, in Cannes at the age of eleven taken the King of Sweden to 5-0, my favor. And would have beaten him at love but for my father who came by and ordered me to drop the set without offending the king. I did an artful job of losing.

"OK. You get $15 a week and a place to live."

I became a full-time tennis teacher and a part-time baby-sitter for his kid, Diana. I got a room in their apartment and started a long friendship with his wife, Sarah Palrey Cooke (later Danzig). The fifteen dollars didn't go far. Elwood was cheap in those days, Sarah was busy, and I had to feed myself. "I said a place to live, not room and board," my tough master would inform me whenever I asked for either a raise or some food.

There were all kinds of fringe benefits in spite of the fact that I did more rolling, brushing, and painting of the lines than I did teaching. I kept overhearing all sorts of marvelous things said about me. "She's either got the longest legs or the shortest shorts I've ever seen," was my favorite. I could go to Forest Hills and sit among the players and I met them all; they were Elwood's and Sarah's friends, of course. And my employers were champion players themselves.

When it rained I didn't work, instead I hustled pool. There was a terrific pool place on Forty-second and Third in those days. I would rush to it at the first sign of rain and bet whatever seemed decent that I could beat anyone in the place. I made all my shots behind my back in those days and used to upset the players with my constant chatter. They used to yell a lot at me to shut up but I made more money there than I did slaving away from five to midnight for Elwood Cooke.

But the best thing of all was meeting Selden Rodman. He was a poet, married, and lived right above the tennis courts. He could see me whenever he wanted to, but I could not see him because there was a tree growing by his windows that cast dark shadows. Was he watching me or wasn't he, I used to wonder. We fell in love, maybe at the same time. It must have been great love, for I used to run all the way from Sixty-seventh Street and Third to Forty-second and First at eleven each night just to get a glimpse of him buying the *New York Times*. We married in 1950. Had our daughter in 1951. Divorced in 1957. And remained friends ever since. (The nicest thing ever written about me can be found in the book of Newbery/Caldecott acceptance speeches. It was written by Selden.)

Before I got married to Selden I went to Monterey, California, to visit my family. My older brother was on his own by then, living in Los Angeles, working for NBC, about to get married. We had a picture taken together, the three of us, and we looked handsome indeed. I thought my father at peace. He had a good job teaching at the military language school. Chris for the first time seemed happy.

After all, he had the full attention of both of his parents now, he was alone with them, did not need to share anything. They looked like a normal family.

"American foreign policy," my father declared during that visit, "is run by imbeciles for idiots. They simply don't understand the nature of communism, which is not economic or social but spiritual. It is the destruction of the human spirit, that is what communism is!"

Whether he quit or was fired I don't know. All I know is that he had become a different sort of a fighter now. He wrote to everyone, appealing to the conscience of the world to reach out to Poland that was plunged into darkness behind the iron curtain. When my family came to visit us— Selden, our baby Oriana, and me—I was too busy being a housewife, a wife, and mother to wonder what had happened to his eyes. They were clouded now by despair as much as cataract. Later, when we visited my parents in California, he was a tragic figure. He spent his days in the garage doing carpentry, painting remembered buildings in Warsaw, writing letters on his typewriter. Once a year he would deliver telephone books. His solitude was interrupted only to play bridge, which he did the same way as he used to duel, and to argue Polish politics. There were now those who accepted the fate of Poland and were ready to return, or at least visit. There were factions urging "collaboration," "resumption of normal relationships." He went to Washington to denounce those new traitors in front of the Polish-American Congress. He wore his Polish uniform and spoke "for the dead soldiers who are not here to see Polish honor on the block of expediency." Polish-Americans did not understand him; there was not a trace of America in him. He spoke to them as a lover of Poland and they simply thought that he wanted them "to do something." I am sure he wanted them to die for Poland, just as he was willing to do. The most passionate of his speeches was interrupted by cries of "Enough!" by those who wanted to make accommodations now, not seek a new war. He went back to California totally defeated. He stopped to see me and Selden and tried to make us understand that he had witnessed "the second selling of Poland," but we did not understand his pain.

The autopsy report said nothing about my father having died of a broken heart caused by being away from the country without which he could not exist. All along, from the beginning when I was a small child, I knew he loved someone better than any of us. I remember once shouting at my mother: "Why aren't you unfaithful to him? He cheats on you all the time. With Poland!"

Becoming a Full-time Writer

My mother was a better wife than she was a mother, I felt, and I was going to concentrate on being a good mother since I didn't have all it took to be a good wife. I was far too independent. I used to take off and ski-bum when I grew restless, and I grew restless a lot. But how could an independent, restless woman be a good mother? Wasn't I happy when Oriana, age three, packed up a little bag and said she was running away from home? I told her to write once in a while and waved good-bye. She kept walking up the driveway dressed in a coat far too warm for the day, and I kept sneaking from one bush to another, watching her hesitant progress. I was letting go of my child, like a bird mother. That was good mothering. The kid didn't make it all the way to the road. She turned back and went into her room to unpack.

"I decided not to run away," she told me later.

"I think that was a terrific decision," I told her.

She was being brought up by me not to feel guilty, which I considered the greatest sin of parenting. Still by the time we got divorced, when she was seven, I thought it was Selden, not I, who would make a better parent. After all, I was still not out of my adolescence. I had gone to Europe on my Harley Davidson and trained to be a bullfighter in Mexico. I was still not grown up enough to be a full-time mother. What I would be good at, I thought, would be a weekend mother. But if Selden ever remarried, I would grow up in a hurry. The kid was ours, but she would become my responsibility, not his new wife's.

I went to Spain for six months in an attempt to grow up. I wrote a god-awful self-pitying novel and slept a lot, a coward's easy escape from life. I felt guilty as hell over that "wise" decision I had made, leaving Oriana with her father.

Becoming a full-time writer "for a living" was my way, I think, of growing up. That I began to write children's books was perhaps my way of not cutting myself away from childhood too drastically. After I developed a short story into the novel *Shadow of a Bull*, I resigned my job as a publicity director for a publishing firm and went to Los Angeles to tell my mother and brothers that I had decided to become a writer. So far I was out ten dollars, which I paid Oriana for the use of the title. I couldn't come up with one; she came up with a handful and our choice was *Shadow of a Bull*.

My family was not impressed. "You made a horrible mistake divorcing Selden," they all said to me. I went to see the children's librarian at the main branch of the L.A. Library. I heard that she was the "greatest living authority" on children's books. Not having read any but having written one, I was most anxious to know what she would think.

"I gave up my last job to become a children's book writer," I announced to this perfect stranger. "I would like your opinion about the book I just wrote." She looked relieved that I didn't have the manuscript with me.

"What is it about?" she asked.

"It's about a boy who is being forced to become a bullfighter."

"It's about bullfighting?" she asked in an incredulous voice.

"It has bullfighting for background."

"What I would advise you to do is to get your job back. No librarian will buy a book about bullfighting and children's books are bought by librarians."

I was totally defeated as I walked to her door to go out into the world deprived of my chosen profession.

"Of course," she said to my back before I had a chance to close her door, "I could be wrong. If it's very well written it won't matter that it's about bullfighting."

"It is!" I shouted and danced out of her office.

The first publisher who saw it, Atheneum, bought the book. To me it was not so much a children's book as a very artful conversion of a short story into a short novel. I had written it in two weeks, using the short story as an outline. They made me change the ending and the editor inserted a word, "companionable," on the last page which drastically

"The three of us," Maia with her two brothers, Chris (left) and Zbyszek, Los Angeles, California, 1984.

altered an already phony ending. By the time I learned that I won the Newbery Award, I hated the book. But during the award dinner in Detroit, I spotted the librarian from Los Angeles, rushed off the podium, and reminded her how we met. She didn't remember me. So much for fame and glory.

I spent a lot of time that year, 1965, autographing and taking out that damn word "companionable" from the last page. (Atheneum, threatened by me with a lawsuit, finally managed, in the sixth edition, to eliminate that word that was never mine, that I objected to in manuscript, in galleys, in page proofs, and in the first edition. The time it took me to erase it from every copy I ever came across I estimate was greater than the time it took me to write the book. Irony!)

By the time *Shadow* came out, I was living with Oriana: during the summer in a tower in New Jersey, and during the winter in Selden's guest house. I bought her a horse and, when she didn't like to ride her, I rode her and wrote a love book to the creature *(A Kingdom in a Horse)*. Later I would buy Oriana a Morgan and myself a pony and we would race each other, me hating each moment, she adoring it all.

My kid had grown up splendidly. I don't know exactly when I decided that she was far superior to her parents, as a human being, but I certainly knew it the day she wrote on my back, with a magic marker: "This is my mother in whom I am well pleased."

She had explained that in case the plane crashed (I was flying somewhere), when my body was found they would know that I was loved by a daughter. And she didn't paraphrase some writer! She paraphrased God, the Father!

I was having a marvelous time, with her, with my writing, with life, and out of the blue I learned I had cancer. Strange! I had wanted to die five years before and the cancer was five years old. I was sure that, at least in my case, the disease made a sort of suicidal sense. But not now, not for me. I almost died of curious and self-induced complications but recovered from a deathbed when I had to chase away some kids who broke into the house. But that's too long a story for here.

I always had to have a very valid reason for writing another book, since each book, I figured, would kill at least five trees. I use a lot of paper, writing and rewriting, and of course my books are printed on paper. If I thought that the bindings take glue and it takes horses to make glue, I don't think I would write at all.

I wrote *Hollywood Kid* because I wanted to know desperately how life would be for a boy if his mother were Marilyn Monroe. I wrote *A Single Light* to find out how good a writer I was. I said to myself, what if I took for my major character someone who did not speak, who could not hear, and who did not really think all that much? I'd be up against a brick wall or in the rapids without a paddle. But if I pulled it off, I'd know that I was a good writer. To get rid of some guilts about not marrying a man with three boys, I wrote *Hey, What's Wrong with This One?* and dedicated the book to the kids. By the time the book came out, they were not speaking to me.

That book was too easy so I challenged myself with the next. What if I'd write a monologue? As I was working on *Don't Play Dead before You Have To,* a book was published, a novel by Philip Roth, which also used that form. I didn't read *Portnoy's Complaint* until I finished mine and decided that he was better out of the starting gate but I won the race making it all the way to the finish line.

I was surprised to discover that many people, maybe even Lewis Carroll himself, confused *Alice in Wonderland* with *Through the Looking Glass,* which I thought a far better book. Walking through Harlem I saw a girl who looked as if she might be losing touch with reality and I wrote *Through the Broken Mirror with Alice.* When I handed the book to my editor, she said: "Blacks don't play chess." I said bullshit. I saw a whole slew of old black guys playing chess. "Black children don't understand chess." So I drove to Harlem and picked up a kid and asked him if black kids know about chess. He told me he played all the time. I put a dime in the pay phone and had him talk to my editor. He told her that most kids were like him and chess was not only for honkeys.

I felt like writing my personal requiem for bullfighting because in Spain a hungry young man without a sense of honor was a sensation. His name was El Cordobes and he was cheapening everything Manolete stood, and died, for. And that's how *Life and Death of a Brave Bull* came about. I finally had to rewrite the very first book I ever wrote. I did it from memory because it was about how I was growing up during the war and I called that one *Till the Break of Day.* There was also *Winter Tales from Poland,* a shoddy publishing job.

I was being difficult with editors. Too critical of the stuff that was coming out and finding favor with the critics as well as the readers, so I stopped writing. When I went back to it, after five years of not practicing my craft, it was because I could not find the truth about Hemingway's end. I found these words of his, written to his brother:

> Nothing is worth a damn but the truth as you know it, and create it in fiction.

And I wrote about a man like him and guessed at what might have happened to bring him to such a sad end. I wrote it as a novel for adults and its title is *The People in His Life.*

And then in 1984 I went back to a book I had written for kids ten years before when I thought I could publish my own stuff. *How God Got Christian into Trouble* didn't seem to have aged badly while lying in a drawer. I had liked it all along and made it shorter and simpler for younger kids. I think younger kids tend to be nicer nowadays. My own kid, Leonora (twelve going on ten), doesn't want to grow up and I don't blame her. After all, it took me a few dozen years to make the move myself.

Three Stages in Life

I figure that there are three stages in everyone's life. Childhood and youth which shape us, although we're far too dumb to know that. Adulthood, which is sort of like gathering chips and looking for a good poker game to get into. And old age, the wise age. Which can turn into Lent or Advent. It ought to be either a great wait for redemption or being a witness to it. But it's certainly that stage of life where things have to begin to make sense or else we've been doing nothing but wasting time.

My third stage of life began when Leonora came into my life one day in early 1973. I had married for the second time and knew the marriage to have been a dreadful mistake, not only because Richard Larkin was twenty years younger than I, but also because he was in some ways much too old for me. Our adopted daughter Leonora was just perfect. She was a baby and it would be years, I felt, before she would object to my loving her too much. She never left me for the first two years. I carried her first across my chest, then on my back. And at two I sent her off to school, just so she could be free of my hugs and kisses for a while each day.

She must have been born an entertainer, or at least must have decided to have an entertainer's soul before she was even one year old. If she doesn't sing, she dresses up; if she doesn't dress up, she dances; if she doesn't dance, she is performing a play she has created. She lives in a multiplicity of worlds she creates, and the only cruel world she inhabits is that of school. She has always been mocked, made fun of, and it keeps hurting more rather than less. It doesn't matter that I keep telling her that of course the kids will have to be mean, how could they help themselves? After all, she is the greatest, the sweetest, the most wonderful kid in the world. They're jealous and that's why they are mean. She is special and they are not.

"You don't understand," she tells me. "You never needed friends when you were a kid. But I do. I want friends."

We keep thinking that it will change. She is only ten, having already been eleven and twelve, and she wants to go back to two and stop there. Of course they are not all mean and nasty and cruel in her school. There are some very nice kids who stand out just like Leonora does. Their eyes, like hers, are kind and bright instead of dull and nasty. (I've just written a story about a very special kid and a bunch that aren't, inspired, of course, by Leonora's life.)

And Leonora, like Oriana, has Haiti. She had gone there several times and will go this year again, to get away from the familiar, from TV and the cruelty of kids and the necessity to conform. She will go to that special country where people instinctively know that it is important to laugh, on a daily basis, and not to take such things as politicians seriously.

It's hard to be writing for kids and know that the fullness of life doesn't happen until you're fifty. Maybe it's not like that with others, but I finally came of age at fifty. It happened the day I got kicked out of school in Socorro, New Mexico. I was on a Federal grant, the only time I ever took a penny of taxpayers' money and, for a good reason, I had to ask the principal what made him such an asshole and got kicked out of his school.

It was the most wonderful time of my life, a time of daily beatitudes for a whole month. Everything began to make sense, suddenly, beautifully. The past, the present, the future—mine and the world's—became splendidly, horrendously right! I had a whole month of perfect happiness. I don't know why it didn't last, but maybe it will happen again in heaven, this state of total integration. It was a marvelously spiritual experience, and I am sure I could never have had it before getting to that ripe age of fifty.

I had it all, in a different sense from Helen Gurley Brown. I had all that I ever wanted to have, which did not include money or power. I saw people change. Most especially my mother, after she was eighty and suddenly, beautifully, let go of so much junk that she treasured.

I saw her two weeks before she died and was astounded at the sudden peace that seemed to radiate from her. We talked, that last time, about death, and she told me how, all through her life she never feared it, and how now she was looking forward to it as if to a friend's visit. That last time when I saw her, she said that if she had anything to say about her departure from this life, she'd ask God to take her on a Friday in May, at 3:00 p.m. "But," she added smiling, "that would be too frivolous a request to pray for." She died on Friday, May 24th, at 3:00 p.m. as a companion was helping her to lie down for a rest. I, who envied her all my life, her grace, her beauty, and her relationship with her husband, give thanks to my Lord for having seen my mother work towards the salvation of her immortal soul even after her body betrayed her.

I saw my older daughter become a marvelous human being, her very own person, and a great artist. And I saw her marry a splendid young man who not only makes her happy but who seems to grow wise ahead of time. And I finally had talks with my brothers. And I am beginning to see the terrific adult that Leonora will become. And I helped some kids understand certain things, kids like Keesha, our Fresh Air friend. And most of all I lived long enough to become a grandmother.

It must be the best-kept secret in the world. Nobody had told me, nobody's telling anyone, what a sheer, splendid, uncontaminated joy it is to be a grandparent! It would be hard for a kid to understand that it's worth growing old simply for that. For grandparenthood. Laina is her name and happiness is her game. And it's no secret that we love each other.

A Writer as a Time Traveller

Sometimes it seems to me that I have lived across not merely oceans but centuries and have seen customs and people fundamentally altered. Deities have come and gone and idols of old have been replaced by the idolatry of a new age. But what has changed most of all, in a profoundly sad, perhaps irreparable way, are the children. They took the various follies of our century, it seems to me, squarely on the chin, and have been denied eternal truths in the process.

Children, as far as I still understand them, have but one job. Being children. It comes naturally. It comes with the territory. But it no longer seems to entail what it did when I was a child. Childhood must have been declared by someone very uncool, a waste of time, un-American even, counter to the Protestant work ethic. "Make them young consumers," I figure some guy who took early retirement from the military industrial complex said to our legislators, and educational bureaucrats listened and added another dictum about the young: "Don't make them wonder about anything."

They seem to own so much and know so much without pleasuring in their possessions or their knowledge. Their questions are fewer and far less interesting each year. And nothing of the old backbone shows below the sweat shirts and t-shirts, and that gutsiness that was the trademark of youth, with which the young always gave a goosing to those older, is no longer there to declare: "How dare you screw up our future, you creeps?" They don't rebel like they used to. Or offend like they used to. Perhaps we've all gone beyond shock into sheer amazement that all has been said and seen.

But did we have to pave the great generational divide with sexual awareness? Wasn't there a better way? Wouldn't it have been preferable to let it stay? After all, adults are not children, it's a different world out there. But no, it's all the same pasture now. The cows and bulls are gone but what remains is fertilizer just lying there. Not used to grow anything. Just something there to step into. For both young and old, the same b.s.

Travelling through time one develops a keen ear for the relationship between cause and effect and the clash that is the result of such encounter. If you didn't travel you wouldn't get much societal isolation. One develops a kind of roadside wisdom. Hasn't Cicero commented on this before? Or Augustine, didn't he know about that? And as you pass an inner city without a plant in sight, you still can see a jungle because nobody took the trouble to weed and trim, everything's gone to seed.

As you travel, your road signs are symbolic of what you see. Could it be that there is more to Nikes than meets the eye? If you want to create the greatest distance between the feet and the brain, what would you sell the young, shoes or hats? If kids are natural learners and you want to wean them away from that, wouldn't you make them learn about gays by second grade and how to use condoms by eighth grade? There won't be a chance at graduation time for someone to stand up and say: "Hey, we haven't learned a thing about God! And I don't mean religion, which must be like God's digestive track."

But I am getting far afield into political incorrectness while I wanted to ask just why the hell did we take it away from them, the only thing they could call their own? Were we jealous that we wasted ours? But childhood, like all of God's gifts, is not wasted. Ever. It makes us what we are. It's a recyclable commodity.

Lately I've been spending an hour a week with a therapist. Those sessions are rather weird for I keep trying to convince her that there are some old remedies for all the ills that beset us today. I keep wishing that she knew what I know, now at seventy-one, that there is nothing new under the sun. But she is too young to know that. It's still easy for her to imagine that newness is part and parcel of life. I am very cynical about the new and have become appreciative of why old wines do not mix with the new. I figure that before Freud and specialists in such things as eating disorders, before Weight Watchers and Alcoholics Anonymous, before the Primal Scream and assertiveness, there were the mortal sins (giving in to selfish desires and transitory enjoyments) which resulted in grave illnesses. And nobody got well without reaching for the gifts of the Holy Spirit which were ours for the asking.

I offer to her my knowledge that healing must take into account that we do have a warning system, that self-indulgence for centuries before ours always seemed to result in self-loathing. And the sure cure was forgiveness and a determination to resist temptation next time around.

"Shouldn't a bulimic know about gluttony? And that it's nothing new and that as Rome disintegrated there were vomitaria all over the place? And isn't it time to talk about the sin of vanity to an anorexic? And didn't I hear you say just the other day that you were pleased because someone got very angry? But there are far too many angry people who don't even know that anger is a cardinal sin! And how can you make anyone well without teaching them how wonderful it feels to forgive, and how much more wonderful it is to ask to be forgiven?"

When I try to bring to her attention that nothing I ever did that was good in my life I did on my own but with the help of the Holy Spirit which endows me with courage and perseverance, patience and wisdom, and all the other stuff that makes me happy to be alive, she thinks I am talking "religion" while I think I am talking common sense and giving her hints at what can turn any sinner into a saint and many a pervert into a martyr. But she has not learned, in her many courses, anything about self-denial and grace. Nobody told her about the Inner Resources which we all have and which not one of us need to buy, only cultivate.

Husband Selden Rodman with granddaughter Laina, 1995.

Maia's daughter Oriana Rodman McRae (right) and granddaughter Laina McRae.

Wondrous Children

There are certain wondrous children still among us, but there are fewer and fewer of them each year. Untouched by political correctness, attached to the eternal. One of them is my granddaughter. She is alone very often and uses her aloneness to do magical things that cannot be done with others. She becomes an artist, when alone. She reads when alone. She daydreams, when alone. She is totally, wholly a child, a state of being that is truly blessed. She looks very vulnerable, very beautiful, very mysterious, when she is alone. Alone she is truly a miracle.

When I was her age I was, I think, very much like her. We have our great differences as well as great similarities and, of course, we have the time traveling to consider. I've done so much more of it than she, and that is what makes us strangely alike and yet strangely different. She is embarrassed by me as I was embarrassed by my grandmother when I was her age. She told me the other day that she would be a rich person if she had a nickel for each time I embarrassed her. We both laughed over that. I am a fairly embarrassing adult. I talk too loudly and too much and with an accent yet, and after being elected to office (the local Council of Mahwah), I resigned in despair after three and a half years. I tend to have a morbid view of our collective future. I gave a talk to her classmates in her Catholic school last year and asked what they thought of the entertainer Madonna, and before they could answer I told them that

Madonna was a slut. That truly embarrassed Laina. I was embarrassed for her Catholic school, for keeping the news that Madonna is a slut from her and her classmates. After all, if a Catholic school does not proclaim Madonna a slut, who's going to do the job? (I must have figured I had to.)

Each birthday when I tried to hypnotize her birthday guests, or told them outrageous fortunes pretending to be a Gypsy, or tried to scare them silly with ghost stories, I embarrassed her. I tell her she should be secretly happy to have me around because there are fewer and fewer "weird people" around, and by the time she's my age maybe everybody will look as if they came from the same cookie cutter. But at her age she wishes me to be the same as others.

Last night I tried to remember if I could have grown rich if I had a zloty for every time my grandmother embarrassed me. Not unless I counted all the other relatives, the aunts and uncles and cousins, and added the domestics to the list of those who embarrassed me when I was a kid.

My grandmother died without my telling her how I felt about the open house she kept, where not a single hour went by with the kitchen being devoid of smells of cooking, the table empty of dishes. I never told her that it embarrassed me to look at her back as it rounded more and more each year, and how she became smaller and closer to earth at the same time that I was shooting straight up. What embarrassed me about her was the way she made sure the scarf was tight around my throat at the same time that it covered my cheeks. What embarrassed me about her was the way she could work a miracle and repair a doll I broke in anger. And the way she expected me to say something smarter than those first words I uttered at the age of four and a half when I finally decided to speak: "Why must the world be so cruel?" (I thought myself extremely clever.)

My therapist writes down what I tell her of my childhood, and she thinks that I am very unusual because I've overcome what appear to her to be a series of nightmarish and traumatic incidents. I never think of them as such. I think of them as adventures, during which I had to use my head, rather than my emotions, or I wouldn't have survived half of them. But she is devoted to people expressing emotions, and I think, to tell you the truth, that if she tried to tap the mind instead, she'd be out of business in short order. But then I could be wrong. That's one of the disadvantages of being a time traveller, nobody's guaranteeing you that you are right.

After I got elected nobody in my family allowed me to speak to them of the many toils and troubles I got into on the Council of the Township I tried to serve. But on a recent visit to California, I snuck a little piece of advice to my grandniece Amanda. When nobody was around I told her:

"The first person who asks you for your social security number, say that you don't have one, that you don't believe that the Founding Fathers would want you to have one. That way the government won't know you're alive, and with luck you won't know that the government is alive, either. And that comes from a duly elected public official, mind you."

I am looking forward to having a talk with my grandnephew Dimitri Papavassilou, who, I figure, could start a peaceful revolution and reclaim the United States from the cynicism of the people and put the country back in the lap of the people, where it is supposed to be. But he isn't quite ready to listen to me. So I figure I better write some books and prepare him for a future that is either going to be very bleak, very funny, or maybe nonexistent.

People who don't believe that a miracle is coming when things get the darkest don't know how life works for people who believe in the goodness of the Lord. Shortly after I queried a half-dozen publishers if they could find some use for me as a writer who wants to keep the kids in touch with eternal truths (life, death, happiness that doesn't depend on money, etc.) and having not heard from any of them, my kid brother, Chris, wrote to me proposing I do fourteen books for him for children. Of course I jumped at the chance, because we happen to share an awful lot in common, among them deep depression about where our kids are being led and by whom. So now he is my publisher and I am his writer and sometimes we treat each other like siblings and have fights, but not often. We are doing a series of stories, most of them with sports for background, but also some with careers as a focal point for DREAMS. We both feel that without having dreams kids tend to give up on life as only an exercise in tedium occasionally interrupted by surprises. A kid has got to know what it takes to make dreams come true. They are being told too many lies by too many people who make a living at being politically correct. And political correctness does not last. The simple truth is that each and everyone of us, rich or poor, black or white, American or not, we all have within us the potential to be winners. At anything we set our mind. And there is nobody in charge, actually, except us. That comes from the fact that God when creating us gave us free will. That was the only quarrel my mother had with God.

"Why did He do that? We'd be so much better off without it."

But I always told her that she was totally wrong.

"If we had no free will, it would all be very boring. And I could not write fiction."

I don't know if she changed her mind about "God's only mistake," as she called it, but I am sure by now she knows His reason why he made lives so interesting for us.

It's wonderful the freedom my brother is giving me in making up those stories in the series called "Dreams of . . . ." With each title I can explore the troubles kids can get into when they are pursuing a singular path, the hard work that it takes to achieve a goal and all the obstacles that stand in the way. And as I write these stories I keep thinking that the Founding Fathers when they promised us "pursuit of happiness" knew more about human nature than we had ever given them credit for. It certainly doesn't fit into the annals of history of any country to be so whimsical as to guarantee its people the right to go for it. What we hope to accomplish, at Pebble Beach Press, is the equivalent of a cheer for America's kids, a sort of literary Nike cry: "Just do it!" I think we've already done it with golf, football, soccer, and tennis. We're going to do it with other sports and careers as well. The only problem is that unless librarians support us, our children won't even know that we are taking on shoddiness, violence, and hopelessness and talking about greatness, character, and dreams as choices during that great adventure called "growing up."

If someone would ask me, "What would you change if you had a chance to change something?" I would say everything. Because I had it all. The width and the depth of it. And I would grab for something new.

October 1998

I didn't finish out my four-year term as Councilwoman. Six months before the end of my term, I resigned. It was too hard to continue pretending that I could change anything. Without a consensus there is no way to do that. And the six others on the Council seemed embarrassed by me. I'd ask, at least once a month, if anyone could tell me what was "the public good" we swore to serve. They wouldn't answer. I don't think they knew. And that's all I wished to serve. The president of the Council would gavel me down when I'd speak. I would often race from my seat to where the audience would be, but there was nobody there, to speak to the council as a member of the public. But often they would close the public meeting portion before I made it to the floor. So much for democracy.

We should have compulsory public service in this country. Everyone with a driver's license should have to give up a year, at minimal wage, to serve the public good. Elective government doesn't work because the egos of those elected interfere with common sense, which is not much different from the common good.

There were only three novels in the Dreams series. One on golf, one on football, and one on soccer. They didn't

The author with daughter Leonora, 1996.

sell. My brother, my publisher, of Pebble Beach Press didn't want to play by the rules. He didn't set a "pub date" with review copies going out a few months before publication. Without reviews to guide them, librarians did not order those books. But maybe the concept of having novels about how dreams, through hard work and devotion to them, could become a reality is not something they thought kids would want to read. Other writers, the ones who sell, might be realists. I remain a dreamer.

Maybe that's the difference, but also there is God in my life. I think it's my love of Him and my interest in Him that interferes with any interest publishers and agents might otherwise have in me. Or maybe it's no longer so important to make a living at my chosen craft. I make a living being a nanny, which also allows me to be among the most interesting human beings: babies and children.

I keep writing books but don't finish them, since ending something always seems to me to be the beginning of something else (for a writer it's publication). And publication does not seem to be in the cards for me. I always had multiple book contracts. Without one maybe I simply can't finish what I begin. I don't feel like a loser, though. I know I am politically incorrect, for I don't seem to want to hide how I feel. And I feel madly in love. With God and the world He created, and which, it seems to me,

disappoints Him so often nowadays. Fiction, in a way, had become nonfiction for me.

Summing Up

My mother used to say that we all better be careful what we are, because in old age it's all going to be terribly visible. I think I let myself be afflicted way too much with a social conscience. A lot depends on what you had to survive. I wouldn't have made any bets on anyone who, like I, had to survive Liberace, the Monkees, and Lawrence Welk, but we all did without losing our minds. However, those who had to survive Menudo and Milli Vanilli might not do so well. And how about those who are listening to Marilyn Manson, Snoop Doggy Dogg, what will the future hold for them? And it's not going to be easy to get over Madonna (the singer) as mother and Howie Mandel as a talk show host and John Tesh as a performer.

In a crazy world such as we have today (hundreds of thousands aborting while hundreds of thousands are praying for babies to have and to love, millions spent on dieting while millions starve, and New Age at the end of 2,000 years of Christianity, Dennis Rodman, Fran Drescher, the Spice Girls, etc., etc.), we need some words of wisdom to fend off the general suckiness. I suggest—for those who don't have a Bible handy— Pogo's dictum "I've seen the enemy and the enemy is us" and the anonymous "There is no free lunch."

There are consequences, though that is not being generally believed—and certainly not taught in kindergarten or even college. Consequences, socially and personally, can be pretty devastating. The watershed mark of my personal despair came with the publication of *I'm O.K., You're O.K.* I could not believe in either but I learned not to read anything on the best-seller list. I thought the right consequence for the great popularity of Judy Blume was for me to give up writing books for children. I'd have nothing to say to those kids who read such stuff, except maybe: "Beware of reading about plastic characters or you might become a soulless phoney."

If I were not so delighted and enriched by being a Catholic, I would have given up on Christianity the first time I saw a televangelist on TV. A lot of Christians today believe that because they were saved they don't need to protect the honor of God among the believers. He's so dishonored, so often by those who accept Christ as a teacher instead of the Son of God who, as a Man, was the most dangerous person ever to walk this earth. Dangerous to whom? The powerful, the rich, the hypocrites, the self-confident, the proud, the selfish, and the satisfied among them, which would include most politicians and most of those who are affluent and think they have it made. He certainly was partial to the poor, the sick, and most especially the children, and we don't treat any of those He loved most with either respect or even interest. I think in the next century we who believe ourselves to be Christians have to make a study of why He loved those we admire the least.

I live for the daily miracles now. Starting with daily Mass, I see and experience them all the time. There are small miracles, like God paying my bills when I don't have the money, to large ones like Princess Diana and Mother Teresa dying within days of each other. What fodder for thought that was! You can feed on that miracle for years. Just think, neither, I believe, smoked, and both are gone! And how very different they were! The way they looked! One was tall, one was short; one was beautiful to look at and the other only beautiful if you looked to how she lived and what she did.

What is this thing about our infatuation with the East? (I can see Mother Teresa's reasons, India is so very poor and has such cruel gods she certainly would have been attracted to it.) I think it started with that very phoney book, *Siddhartha,* and pretty soon we had all sorts of gurus the Beatles were listening to and then Deepak Chopra, the mega guru of today. Why would anyone settle on nonsense when the Truth was born among us, and we have a record of it being killed but rising from the dead?

We are all united by wondrous bonds and some pretty funny experiences, such as the bridges of Madison County and Barbra Streisand's wedding, the psychic network, and a new, communal malady: our intense dislike, or love, of people we don't even know (celebrities).

Were the times of my youth any better? You bet you! We still had a sense of sin and decency. Gluttony was not yet called bingeing, a part of an eating disorder, which results in throwing up the food you didn't want to eat in the first place, but did in spite of all those starving Haitians who would not have barfed any of it.

Getting old in America is a miserable chore. A lot of wisdom is dying out because nobody listens to the old who have had a lot of experience making mistakes and knowing what those were. The young would not have to repeat all that stuff if they just had faith in their parents or grandparents. But a lack of faith is what we've got, and that's very regrettable. Of course in my youth we had a lot of faith and were very disappointed, but life without trusting is very sad. At least we still have God, for those who know that the truth is somewhere out there, as the *X Files* would have it. Actually it's here. If only people were not so afraid of facing it. It doesn't make you blind, as some would have it. It makes you see. Very clearly. And makes you laugh. Very often. Life is good, even at seventy-one. And I certainly expect it to be much better. After death.

Writings

FOR CHILDREN; FICTION

(As Maia Rodman) *Market Day for Ti André,* illustrated by Wilson Bigaud, Viking, 1952.

Shadow of a Bull, illustrated by Alvin Smith, Atheneum, 1964.

A Kingdom in a Horse, Harper, 1965.

The Hollywood Kid, Harper, 1966.

A Single Light, Harper, 1968.

Tuned Out, Harper, 1968.

Hey, What's Wrong with This One?, illustrated by Joan Sandin, Harper, 1969.

Don't Play Dead before You Have To, Harper, 1970.

The Life and Death of a Brave Bull, illustrated by John Groth, Harcourt, 1972.

Through the Broken Mirror with Alice (includes parts of *Through the Looking Glass* by Lewis Carroll), Harcourt, 1972.

Winter Tales from Poland, illustrated by Laszlo Kubinyi, Doubleday, 1973.

How God Got Christian into Trouble, Westminster, 1984.

THE "DREAMS" SERIES, PUBLISHED BY PEBBLE BEACH PRESS

Dreams of Golf, 1993.

Dreams of the Superbowl, 1994.

Dreams of Soccer, 1994.

NONFICTION

Odyssey of Courage: The Story of Alvar Nunez Cabeza de Vaca, illustrated by Alvin Smith, Atheneum, 1965.

Till the Break of Day: Memories 1939-1942 (autobiography), Harcourt, 1972.

FOR ADULTS

(As Maia Rodman) *The Loved Look: International Hairstyling Guide* (nonfiction), American Hairdresser, 1960.

(Translator) *The Bridge to the Other Side,* by Monika Kotowska, Doubleday, 1970.

The Rotten Years (nonfiction), Doubleday, 1971.

(As Maia Rodman) *The People in His Life,* Stein and Day, 1980.

WOLFER, Dianne 1961-

Personal

Born October 28, 1961, in Melbourne, Australia; daughter of Donald (a manager) and Audrey (a teacher) Davidson; married Reinhard Wolfer (a systems manager), December 23, 1984 (died, 1995); children: Sophie. *Education:* Melbourne State College, Diploma of Teaching; Western Australian Institute of Technology (now Curtin University), Certificate of Fluency in Japanese. *Hobbies and other interests:* Travelling, reading, swimming, bush-walking, photography, yoga.

Addresses

Home—P.O. Box 421, Denmark 6333, WA Australia. *Electronic mail*—dianne @ denmarkwa.net.au.

Career

Teacher, Western Australian Education Department, 1984-87 and 1991-92, Japan International School and the American School in Japan, Tokyo, 1987-90. Has taught missionary children in remote western Nepal and intensive Japanese classes for airline employees. Guest speaker, 1993—; Society of Women Writers (Western Australian Branch), editor, *Papermates* magazine, 1996—; guest appearance on radio programs, 1998; runs writing classes and workshops. *Member:* Society of Women Writers (Western Australia branch), Fellowship of Australian Writers, Children's Book Council, Amnesty International, Australian Conservation Foundation.

Awards, Honors

Bronze Quill Award, Society of Women Writers, 1992, for "Gokiburi" (short story); Third Place, Dame Alexandra Hasluck Awards, Society of Women Writers, 1994, for "The Red Bucket" (short story); South-West Literary Award, South-West Development Authority, 1995, for *Christmas Lunch;* Furphy Award for best published novel, Fellowship of Australian Writers, 1995, and Third Place Award, Western Australia Young Readers Book Awards, 1996, both for *Dolphin Song;* Mary Grant Bruce Short Story Award, Fellowship of Australian Writers, 1997, for "Donkey Ears" (short story).

Dianne Wolfer

Cassie has qualms about moving when her father is transferred to the remote Nullarbor Plain in southern Australia.

Writings

FOR YOUNG ADULTS

Dolphin Song, Fremantle Arts Centre Press (Fremantle, Australia), 1995.
Border Line, Fremantle Arts Centre Press and International Specialized Book Services (Portland, OR), 1998.

OTHER

Author of one-act play *Christmas Lunch,* 1995. Work represented in anthologies, including *Going Down South,* 1992, and *Going Down South Two,* 1993. Contributor of short stories, poems, and articles to magazines, including *Lucky, Western Word, Nature and Health, Infant Times, Western Review, Let's Travel,* and *In Perspective.*

Work in Progress

Choices (tentative title), young adult novel; texts for picture books; stories for younger readers.

Sidelights

Dianne Wolfer told *SATA:* "I feel very lucky to be able to live in a beautiful area on the southwest coast of Western Australia. My home is surrounded by bushland, and it's a short drive to the dramatic beaches of the Southern Ocean. Parrots, wrens, and lorikeets feed outside my window, and if I'm up early I see kangaroos nibbling on my neighbor's lawn (our lively dog hasn't learned to ignore them yet!). In spring, the bush shows off its wildflowers and whales calve in the bays offshore.

"As you may have guessed, the environment and unique beauty of the corner of Australia in which I live play an important part in my writing. I am interested in the conflicts that occur when humans meet nature, so my books have environmental undercurrents and themes. Friendship and the bonds between characters are also of great importance to me as a writer.

"I love traveling and have lived in several countries (Thailand, Nepal, and Japan). My family and friends are scattered around the world, and I hope that, through my writing, I can foster an interest in other countries and cultures. I hope to write a story set in both outback Australia and urban Germany. This will be the story of Ella, one of the characters in *Border Line.*

"The things I like most about writing as a profession are that I can work my own hours and that I am able to go to schools and other communities to meet interesting people."

For More Information See

PERIODICALS

Australian Book Review, June, 1995, p. 62.

*   *   *

WOODRUFF, Joan Leslie 1953-

Personal

Born April 4, 1953, in Albuquerque, NM; daughter of Charles (a mechanic) and Lila Ray (a registered nurse; maiden name, Siler) Woodruff; married Paul Harold Ney, 1978 (divorced, 1995). *Education:* Loma Linda University, B.S., 1975; attended California State University, San Diego, 1976; California State University, San Bernardino, M.Ed., 1983. *Religion:* Buddhist. *Hobbies and other interests:* "Raising happy animals, caring for my ranch."

Addresses

Home—P.O. Box 687, Mountainair, NM 87036.

Career

San Bernardino Community Hospital, San Bernardino, CA, Director of Occupational Therapy Services at Hand

Joan Leslie Woodruff

Rehabilitation Clinic, 1975-77, director and administrator of clinic, 1976-87; Riverside American Indian Center, Riverside, CA, member of board of directors, 1987-91; Torrance County, NM Alcohol and Drug Abuse Planning Council, member of executive board and alcohol/drug dependency counselor, 1993-98. Administrator and clinical representative for Redlands Hospital, Redlands, CA, 1980, Martin Luther Memorial Hospital, Anaheim, CA, 1982, a hand surgeon in Fullerton, CA, 1983, and Hemet Valley Hospital, Hemet, CA, 1984. Volunteer substance abuse counselor; volunteer to help abused animals. *Member:* Occupational Therapy Association (certified and registered occupational therapist, 1975—; Specialist Adviser to Hand Rehabilitation Division, 1985-98).

Writings

Traditional Stories and Foods: An American Indian Remembers, Esoterica Press (Barstow, CA), 1990.
Neighbors (novel), Third Woman Press, (Berkeley, CA), 1993.
The Shiloh Renewal (novel), Black Heron Press (Seattle, WA), 1998.

Contributor to professional journals, magazines, and newspapers, including *Our Town, News from Native California,* and *Indian-Artifact.*

Work in Progress

When the Rainbow Set on the Vega, a fiction/suspense novel with a psychological landscape showing the effect of substance abuse on the family and community.

Sidelights

Joan Leslie Woodruff told *SATA:* "I am an American Indian woman, with some Anglo ancestry. My family is a mix of odd but wonderful people. I write because of them. My life has been full of stories and crises. The sad stuff is where the books come from. I try to add humor, but I want to show my readers that suffering can lead to growth and compassion."

*   *   *

WOOLF, Paula 1950-

Personal

Born September 12, 1950, in Fort Smith, AR; daughter of James C. (an aircraft maintenance supervisor) and Lorean (Giddeon) Woody; married Steven B. Woolf (a corporate finance officer), June 6, 1970; children: Jason, Kevin, Lindsay. *Education:* Columbia College, Columbia, MO, A.A., 1970; Bradley University, B.S. (summa cum laude), 1972; University of North Texas, M.Ed., 1988. *Religion:* Baptist.

Addresses

Home and office—15245 Highgrove Rd., Alpharetta, GA 30004.

Paula Woolf

Career

Teacher at public schools in East Peoria, IL, 1973, Dallas, TX, 1973-75, Garland, TX, 1976-78, Plano, TX, 1981-88, and Evans, GA, 1991-93; Fulton County Schools, Atlanta, GA, teacher of the gifted, 1997—. *Member:* Society of Children's Book Writers and Illustrators.

Writings

Old Ladies with Brooms Aren't Always Witches, Royal Fireworks Publishing (Unionville, NY), 1998.

Work in Progress

Two middle-grade novels, *Mother Served Pizza, Father Served Time* and *Diamond in the Rough;* a picture book, *Earl the Pearl.*

Sidelights

Paula Woolf told *SATA:* "Some of my fondest childhood memories center around books. I recall many a summer hour spent under a large shade tree devouring book after book. I remember the excitement of the trips to the library—a huge, old building in our small city that was both intimidating and inviting. I look back on the trips to the dime store to purchase a book with money I had earned selling lemonade or doing errands around the house.

"My children's literature class in college was undoubtedly my favorite. Imagine having an *assignment* to read dozens and dozens of classics—much more my cup of tea than memorizing formulas in chemistry or calculating square roots in algebra. I wondered if my dormitory suitemates thought I had 'lost it' as I lay on my bed at night, chuckling out loud to the antics of Winnie the Pooh or sniffling softly as I read the final pages of *Charlotte's Web.*

"My love affair with books continued as I entered my chosen career of teaching. Although books have been an integral part of my elementary classroom curriculum, for me the greatest thrill continues to be the weekly class visits to the library. I love just to stand back and watch the faces of the children as they pull books off the shelves and discuss their favorites with each other.

"I don't know when the idea first occurred to me that I could write a book of my own. I do know that, over the years, I have become disillusioned with some of the contemporary children's books I have read. While I think there is a place for all styles and genres of books, I seem to pick up more and more books that deal with themes that I consider too adult for the average elementary student. Some are depressing, some are troubling, some are hard to follow, and some are simply boring.

"I have no illusions of being another Beverly Cleary or E. B. White. However, I do feel my years of teaching have given me insight into what children enjoy. That is the primary goal of anything I write for children—to create an entertaining story with a satisfying ending. If a child reads the last page, sighs, and thinks to himself, 'Hmm, that was a good story,' then my book has accomplished its purpose."